D1085020

CONVERSATIONS IN SELF PSYCHOLOGY

Progress in Self Psychology
Volume 13

Progress in Self Psychology
Editor, Arnold Goldberg, M.D.

Progress in Self Psychology invites articles relevant to psychoanalytic self psychology to be submitted for publication. Send the original manuscript (double-spaced with references) and three copies to:

Arnold Goldberg, M.D.
122 South Michigan Avenue
Chicago, IL 60603-6107

If the article is accepted, a diskette will be required as well. All submissions are refereed. Papers will not be returned if unacceptable.

CONVERSATIONS IN SELF PSYCHOLOGY

Progress in Self Psychology
Volume 13

Arnold Goldberg
editor

THE ANALYTIC PRESS

1997   Hillsdale, NJ   London

©1997 by The Analytic Press
101 West Street
Hillsdale, NJ 07642

ISBN 0-88163-258-9
ISSN 0893-5483

Printed in the United States of America
10 9 8 7 6 5 4 3 2 1

This volume is dedicated to

MICHAEL F. BASCH, M.D.

May 5, 1929–January 24, 1996

Acknowledgment

We would like to thank Ms. Christine Susman, who provided secretarial and editorial assistance.

Contents

V APPLIED

Contributors

Sharone Abramowitz, M.D. is Director, Behavioral Health Training, Primary Care Medicine, Alameda County Medical Center and Member, Psychoanalytic Institute of Northern California.

Howard A. Bacal, M.D., F.R.C.P.(C) is Training and Supervising Analyst, Institute of Contemporary Psychoanalysis, Los Angeles and Training and Supervising Analyst, Southern California Psychoanalytic Institute, Los Angeles.

Doris Brothers, Ph.D. is Cofounder, Faculty, and Training and Supervising Analyst, The Training and Research Institute for Self Psychology, New York City and Member, Board of Advisors, Institute for the Advancement of Self Psychology, Toronto.

Amy Eldridge, Ph.D. is Faculty, Institute for Clinical Social Work and Adjunct Professor, Loyola University School of Social Work.

James L. Fosshage, Ph.D. is Cofounder, Board Director, and Faculty, National Institute for the Psychotherapies, New York City and Core Faculty member, Institute for the Psychoanalytic Study of Subjectivity, New York City.

George Hagman, M.S.W., is Faculty, Institute of the National Psychological Association for Psychoanalysis and Instructor, Training and Research Institute for Self Psychology.

Lisa Hirschman, Ed.D. is a Psychologist in private practice and the Consulting Psychologist to The Center for Women's Health at Scripps Clinic in San Diego, California.

Betsy Kassoff, Ph.D. is Department Chair, Feminist Psychology Program, New College of California and Faculty, Supervisor, and former Clinical Director, Operation Concern of California Pacific Medical Center.

Rosalind Kindler, M.F.A., M.C.A.P.C.T., R.D.T. is Faculty, Toronto Child Psychotherapy Program and Registered Drama Therapist, Toronto, Ontario.

Kenneth L. Koenig, M.D. is Training and Supervising Analyst, Institute of Contemporary Psychoanalysis, Los Angeles and in private practice in Santa Cruz, California.

Annette Lachmann, M.A. is Lecturer, The New School for Social Research and Adjunct Lecturer, John Jay College of Criminal Justice.

Frank M. Lachmann, Ph.D. is Core Faculty, Institute for the Psychoanalytic Study of Subjectivity and Training Analyst, Postgraduate Center for Mental Health.

Joseph Lichtenberg, M.D. is Faculty, Washington Psychoanalytic Institute and Clinical Professor, Department of Psychiatry, Georgetown University.

Marc L. Miller, Ph.D. is Senior Faculty, Training and Research Institute for Self Psychology and Faculty, Suffolk Institute for Psychotherapy and Psychoanalysis.

Arnold Wm. Rachman, Ph.D. is Training and Supervising Analyst, Postgraduate Center for Mental Health, New York City and Founder, The Sandor Ferenczi Institute, New York City.

Thomas Rosbrow, Ph.D. is Supervising and Personal Analyst and Core Faculty, Psychoanalytic Institute of Northern California and Supervisor, Mt. Zion/U.C.S.F. Medical Center.

Gordon Schulz, Psy.D. is Clinical Psychologist, Circuit Court of Cook County in Chicago and Member, Psychologists United for Quality, Teamsters Local 743.

David Shaddock, M.A. is Adjunct Faculty, John F. Kennedy University and Member, Self Psychology Association of the Bay Area.

R. Dennis Shelby, Ph.D. is Core Faculty, Institute for Clinical Social Work and Candidate, Institute for Psychoanalysis, Chicago.

Brenda Clorfene Solomon, M.D. is Training and Supervising Analyst, Chicago Institute for Psychoanalysis and Clinical Assistant Professor of Psychiatry, Abraham Lincoln School of Medicine, University of Illinois.

Ruth Stein, Ph.D. is Faculty, Israel Psychoanalytic Institute and School of Medicine, Tel Aviv University.

Marian Tolpin, M.D. is Training and Supervising Analyst, Institute for Psychoanalysis, Chicago and Clinical Professor of Psychiatry, Chicago Medical School.

Introduction

Joseph Lichtenberg

What is "progress" in self psychology and how do we bring it about? One strategy is to measure progress by expansion and illustration of the basic tenets Kohut bequeathed to us. Marian Tolpin lifts the concept of building compensatory structures out of Kohut's many suggestions about the paths to reach one's inner design. Through a case study of Anna Freud and her self-restorative relationship with Dorothy Burlingham, Tolpin describes how the brilliant daughter of an overwhelming father and neglectful mother progressed in her development despite a primary deficit in self-structure. Fosshage, in his discussion of Tolpin's paper, seeks progress in another direction. While accepting Tolpin's account of Anna Freud's development, he challenges the concepts of primary and compensatory structures and even that of deficit. For deficit, he substitutes problematic psychological schemas and, for compensatory structure building, he suggests the relentless search for different attachment experiences or success in other motivational systems. How might the reader take this disparity? I recommend that the reader enjoy it. Tolpin's paper has the great advantage of its aesthetic appeal through the coherence of the story it tells. Kohut meant to leave some of his concepts as loose nonlinear evocations, instruments for conceptual play. I believe that with his immersion in the realm of creativity Kohut understood that discovery is enhanced when "science" does not pull the strings too tight around a conceptual framework. He recognized that this had happened with ego psychology. Kohut did not win adherents to self psychology primarily because of concepts like narcissistic libido, bipolar self, and primary or compensatory self-structures, all of which have been or could be superseded. As was true of Freud, a major appeal of Kohut's *Analysis of the Self* came from the "telling of lives"—his rendering of the clinical experiences rang true to clinicians who had wrestled, usually with limited success, with similar problems in their patients and themselves. The sense of fit of clinical "truth" that came with the Studies in Hysteria, Dora, The Rat Man, The Wolfman, and with Kohut's cases, especially The Two Analyses of Mr. Z, as well as with Tolpin's tale of Anna Freud, derives from internal nonlinear emotional aesthetic coherence. Progress often occurs when narrative conviction transcends theory. The new discovery can then be tested in the clinical arena and, after a while, theory can catch up with the intuitive sensibility of creative minds.

In his paper on listening perspectives, Fosshage turns the argument around. In his discussion of Tolpin he argues for a more comprehensive, tightly reasoned theory than Kohut's conception of compensatory structures allows. In his presentation of the necessity and value of an other-centered listening, he argues that self psychology has tied effective listening during analysis too tightly to emphatic perception. Fosshage's argument invites readers to ask themselves: can you possibly decenter so much from your own reactions only to remain absorbed in the state of mind of your patients? Moreover, on reflection, would you want to? When we remember the initial opposition stirred by Kohut's emphasis on empathy in the 1970s—too mystical, too emotional—we can appreciate that an almost all-inclusive theory of empathy became the hallmark of self psychology. Kohut spent much time during lectures and in writing trying to explain and defend what he meant by empathy. Fosshage continues this trend. Progress can occur when established theoretical constructs are revisited and critiqued constructively.

Eldridge illustrates the case study method more as an instructional narrative in itself than to illustrate a theoretical proposal. She presents her experience with her patient's recreation of a highly emotional traumatic state through painful flashbacks. In this way, she revisits Freud's experiences with a reaction only now seen through the lens of self psychology. Freud, as a positivist observer, underplayed the emotional significance of co-creating the clinical experience and the therapist's affective attunement and conviction about the actuality of the past events. Eldridge, as a contemporary self psychologist, demonstrates the progress we have made in understanding the empathic matrix or intersubjective field in which therapeutic change occurs.

Another holdover from Kohut's original theory is the concept of archaic, as in "archaic grandiosity" and "archaic idealization." Kohut contrasted the archaic with the mature as the sequence by which transformations of self occur through optimal frustration and transmuting internalizations. Hagman uses archaic in a more descriptive manner buttressed by infant studies in order to set the stage for an investigation of mature selfobject experiences. Kohut had made his own set of criteria for a mature self—wisdom, humor, transience. Hagman notes the need to focus on relatedness and moves the discussion to friendship, love, sexuality, marriage, parenting, and creativity. In this extension of the psychological perspective to what Wolf has called life cycle issues, Hagman moves from those aspects of "self" transformations to self with others and to self-transcendence in creativity. Progress in this effort comes neither through a clinical narrative nor through a theoretical breakthrough, but from intuitive reasoning.

In one of his most sweeping insights, Kohut moved the focus for modern mankind from Guilty to Tragic. He thereby ushered in a shift from anxiety and guilt to shame and humiliation as principal scourges of our times. Stein's paper on shame in the analyst can be viewed as taking up both of these issues by her implicit implication that while an analyst could place anxiety and guilt as intrapsychic disturbances of the patient (or countertransference in the analyst), shame and humiliation tend to play out in an intersubjective field of mutual influence. A therapist working within a self psychological framework will be apt to experience shame from a number of sources—shared as a result of empathic sensitivity, triggered by concerns of the freed-up involvements of "optimal provisions," or what Stein calls excess, and through the monitoring of perceived empathic failures. Stein also adds to our appreciation of the role of shame that it functions as a signal to warn analysts to regulate possible breaches in enactments. Here progress is being made by isolating a significant affect and studying its effect on the clinical exchange—extending the contributions of Morrison, Broucek, and Schore.

Appropriate to the many routes for progress, Miller, in the final paper of the clinical section, employs intersubjective theory. Miller's choice of a broad field theory of diverse influences fits well with his approach. Miller considers a colleague's paper in which the colleague, by a period of self-analysis, helped to resolve an impasse with an overly compliant—actually avoidant—patient. The layering of complexity resembles mirrors behind mirrors behind mirrors: the theory of Stolorow et al. hovering over Miller who looks at his colleague's self-analysis, successes and failures with his patient while the colleague and Miller look at the patient, her struggles and stances, and then at the process that unfolds between colleague and patient as he, Miller, construes it. And Miller accomplishes more. He brings in the oft-stated criticism that self psychologists will opt for the "helpful" sustaining of the patient's self-cohesion when an even more helpful and needed exploration of underlying pathological beliefs and repetitions are allowed to slide by. I see Miller saying: yes, it does happen; yes, it happened over and over in this case, but it doesn't have to happen *within* a self-psychological (intersubjective) approach. Using the language of motivational systems, rather than Miller's, more consistent attention to indications of aversiveness by the patient, by the analyst, and especially by both will allow for reflective consideration of many enactments before they become entrenched in the fabric of the clinical experience.

The two papers on supervision take another slant by bringing in concepts from outside self psychology. Koenig describes his supervision with Joan Fleming, a well-known traditional analyst trained in the mode before self psychology. Rosbrow introduces the theories of Weiss and Sampson whose research and therapeutic proposals are cocontemporary with self psychology. As many self psychologists have found, control mastery theory offers many useful perspectives. These papers are fine contributions to our literature on supervision but go beyond "the what to do" by revealing the value to be found in comparing concepts developed outside of our main groupings with our own.

The group of papers on sexuality are particularly exciting and forward moving. Psychoanalysis began with theories of sexuality and, despite or because of it, has floundered badly in the treatment of the so-called "perversions," probably because of that pejorative label itself. In the papers by Shelby and Kassoff and discussion papers by Solomon and Abramowitz, the flashpoint is whether male and female homosexuals should be treated only or primarily by male and female homosexual therapists, respectively. Along with Brothers's case study of sado-masochistic fantasies in a traumatized young woman, these papers reveal the sensitivity of the authors to the plight of young people who have to suffer the searing shame of experiencing the impossibility of being empathically understood by people closest to them. Self psychology can help to restore the sense of empathic sensitivity to these patients' unsuccessful experiences of seeking selfobject vitalization, but certainly offers no guarantee of authentic responsivity since the therapist, regardless of theory, has to deal with his or her own deeply entrenched prejudices. These papers guide the way to self psychologists in opening their "selves" to the receptivity needed to work with deeply traumatized patients whose attachment and sensual and sexual needs often led them into desperate self-defeating pursuits.

The three papers in the therapy section raise the intriguing possibility that we have established a generally agreed upon way of working with the more or less "average expected" patient and are ready to progress further through amalgams of creative borrowings from other techniques. If a generally agreed upon mode of approach during treatment exists, these papers would indicate the language of the theory, whether intersubjective, selfobject matrix or motivational systems, can be combined with favorable effect on the process; when what is needed for special situations is beyond the conventional one-on-one talk therapy. Shaddock reports on the failure to help a very troubled adolescent boy through the use of a conventional empathic approach. He then turned to working with the boy's mother and stepfather in a "conjoint family therapy" using the guidance of intersubjective theory broadly. Helped by a mix of relating, understanding, and direct advice, the parents made changes that had a highly desirable ameliorative effect on the boy. Hirschman's modification of her usual approach took the form of what she calls "detailing," an active form of inquiry into what might have passed as trivial incidents in the lives of survivors of extreme abuse. Because of their past these patients are extremely inhibited in their inner world and thereby, without Hirschman's creative energetic help, unable to relate experiences either to themselves or their therapist. Hirschman's modification, an extension of self-delineation and mirroring, involves the sensitive building up from subtle affective cues. Kindler's modification allowed her to enter into the spooky fantasy world of confusion, chaos, and fear of a 10-year-old boy and bring him back into contact with a world of selfobject experiences of vitalization and soothing. With poetic sensitivity, Kindler utilized her training in drama therapy and the use of drawings to help him break out of his passivity and withdrawal. As with the modifications of Shaddock and Hirschman, Kindler illustrates that the techniques central to self psychology are elastic enough to reach very troubled patients in combination with imaginative utilization of the therapist's creative use of self.

Two of the final papers apply self psychological constructs to markedly aberrant behavior. Schulz examines prostitution based on a fictional character in the movie *Klute*. Annette and Frank Lachmann explore murder in the absence of personal connections based on a continuing study of all-too-real serial killers. Contrary to the pattern of abuse found in the childhood of other serial killers, the subjects of their current studies, Arthur Shawcross and Jeffrey Dahmer, were not subject to physical brutality. To explain different aspects of their subject's cruelty to animals and humans, including murder and cannibalism, the Lachmanns employ both motivational systems theory and Goldberg's schema for the development of perversion: a primary structural failure of the self, a vertical split, and killing with or without sexualization as a source of temporary stabilization of the self. Schulz also employs Goldberg's schema to explain the psychopathic and narcissistic vulnerability of the prostitute in *Klute*. In addition, he refers to intersubjectivity and returns to Kohut's original proposal of transmuting internalization— an explanation that for the most part is rarely referred to currently.

Rachman's informative study of Ferenczi makes progress by reaching backwards in time in order to demonstrate kernels of many of the central principles of self psychology in the final experimental stage of an earlier master clinician. Rachman's paper raises a question many others have asked about Kohut: why did he not reference or give credit to precursors of his ideas? Numerous authors have noted the obvious similarities of portions of self psychological theory to Winnicott and Rogers, as well as Ferenczi. Kohut's sense of his illness causing him to push rapidly forward has been cited as well as his possible and, at times, probably lack of familiarity with at least some of those cited (not Ferenczi, as Rachman demonstrated). I believe a possible answer lies in Kohut's theory itself. Some authors are driven to support their confidence through idealization; they *want* to seek precursors from Freud on to feel self-assurance from the protective shadow of great men or women (even when they contradict them). Other authors gain their confidence from the freedom to move forward on their own, unhampered with having to square their ideas with those of many others—they are what I would call self-mirrorers. They then look for further supporting mirroring from their contemporaries. Kohut was, I think, more inclined to be one who wanted to push forward unhampered while being reverent in his personal attitudes.

What does a survey of the contents of this volume of *Progress in Self Psychology* suggest? I believe the authors present a consistent indication of theoretical pluralism. Whether considering theory, clinical practice, or supervision, the method used would seem to be to pick and choose, mix and match. For analysts who trained in the 1950s and early 1960s, this pragmatic pluralism is a shocking development. We recognized the dominance of ego psychology as a given. Brilliant educators like Kohut presented ego psychology as the natural outgrowth and culmination of Freud's dual drive—tripartite structural conception of the mind. Ego psychology was regarded as the mainstream of psychoanalysis and the Education Committees of the Institutes of the American Psychoanalytic Association enforced a narrow adherence. Looking back, the belief we held of one mainstream was more illusion than fact. For example, where I was trained, Sullivan's theory of an interpersonal field infiltrated our thinking whatever orthodoxy we ascribed to. Interpersonal theory, Winnicott's holding environment, and Fairbairn's object seeking are subtle, generally unacknowledged influences in the writings of Loewald, Searles, and other outside-of-the-New-York-Psychoanalytic-Institute theoreticians. The fixed orthodoxy of neutrality and abstinence was preached vigorously but never followed exactly.

Eissler's description of parameters was a classicist's codification of the omnipresent deviations, and Stone's physicianly attitude was a direct attempt at correcting the abuses of a nonresponsive rigidity based on a terror of "contamination" and "gratification." For all the predominant theories of the time, ego psychology, object relations, and Kleinian and Lacanian theories, unity on a broad scale did exist. Psychoanalysis for all these theories was based on intrapsychic conflict involving structures of the mind. Each of these theories utilized a concept of sexual and aggressive drives and oedipal and preoedipal developmental phases in varied proportions of emphasis. Self psychology began under a similar banner with the intent to expand and explore the prevailing theory through the discovery of selfobject transferences and narcissistic configurations. Rapidly, two historical events occurred—the prevailing unified acceptance of ego psychology began to dissolve, and self psychology went in a direction of its own. Only now we must say self psychology went in *directions* of its own. Given our contemporary pluralism, do we still have a "banner" under which self psychologists can proceed without disagreement? We all believe in the power of empathic listening and sensitivity in both treatment and development. We subscribe to the significance of the creation and maintenance of the cohesion of the self; only some of us would say of the *structure* or organization of the self, and others of the *sense* of the self. We recognize the lifelong significance of the way in which the environment is experienced for the maintenance of self-cohesion but will ascribe varied significance to different features in the field—the subjectivity of one or another participant and the "field" itself. Overall, the papers in this volume attest to self psychology's having created a liveliness of discourse as well as an effective method of being with and treating those whose self-cohesion has been depleted or impaired.

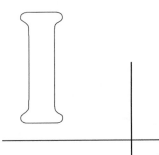

Clinical

Chapter 1

Compensatory Structures: Paths to the Restoration of the Self

Marian Tolpin

REVITALIZATION OF ONE SECTOR
OF THE SELF IN DEPTH

Compensatory structures, by definition, make up for primary deficits in the self by revitalizing just one of its sectors—mirrored ambitions, idealized goals, or twinship/alterego feelings with others like ourselves. [1] For their formation, compensatory structures, like primary structures, require self–selfobject bonds, for example, our mutual attachments with "important others" whose responsiveness makes us feel confirmed, strengthened, and expanded. Our subjective experience of these bonds, particularly after primary structures have been injured by faulty responsiveness (as I discuss later), goes a long way toward repairing the injuries and reestablishing a functional self.

Restorative experiences that are consistent enough are preserved as "inside" structures, for example, in the form of capacities for increased

---

[1] Before Kohut recognized twinship experiences and transferences that build up the self, he described the sector of ambitions and ideals as essential constituents of the "bipolar self" and its selfobjects—the self consisting of the pole of the "grandiose exhibitionistic self" and the "idealized parent imago." Time does not permit going into the objections to using Kohut's terms for these healthy, naive self-configurations. Suffice it to say his language has led to much misunderstanding and contributes to confusion of the healthy configurations with the pathological forms that emerge when the child's mirroring, idealized, and twinship selfobject experiences are consistently and/or traumatically faulty.

security, confidence, and the zest and initiative to pursue goals (see Tolpin, 1971). With further strengthening (in life bonds or via selfobject transferences) the augmented capacities form a continuum with our unique endowment, skills, and talents. The result is a revitalized sector. It can improve our psychological balance just enough to firm up a path that keeps us going: pursuing ambitions or reaching for goals that hold out some promise of fulfillment and give our lives meaning.

In my discussion I illustrate the "cure"[2] of an unmirrored self (i.e., a changed psychological balance) by revitalization of the twinship sector. My example is Anna Freud's twinship bond with Dorothy Burlingham. I shall also discuss a brief clinical vignette, described by Guntrip (1969), to make a crucial point: the first attempts to establish compensatory structure that eventually revitalizes the self have to be recognized for what they are. Guntrip's vignette shows a failed attempt at analysis because the compulsive search of an enfeebled self for an idealized source of strength was mistaken for a regression to infantile wishes and "archaic" (infantile, pregenital) "part objects." I shall come to the illustrations after outlining the three broad sectors of the self, their roots in mirroring, idealizing, and twinship (self–selfobject) bonds, and their affectively charged ideational contents that can make any one of them the chief motivating force in a restored self.

SELF SECTORS ESTABLISHED IN SELF–SELFOBJECT BONDS

The mirroring, idealizing, and twinship sectors of the self begin their lengthy development in universal "wired-in" tendencies of intact human beings: tendencies to need and want and actively seek out the whole variety of mutual attachments that provide the psychological ingredients we need for growth. Any one of the sectors of the self can be revitalized over the course of life, with two provisos: that there is an other (or others) in our lives who is responsive enough and that there remains in us the inner capacity for reactivated developmental momentum that enables us to make use of selfobject functions. The crucial point to bear in mind here is that self-development is an "open system": the task of maintaining and restoring the self is by no means limited to infancy and early childhood (most schools of analytic thought greatly restrict our view of life course development)—it is a life cycle task, and cure by compen-

---

[2] The definition of *cure* by compensatory structures is revitalization of even one sector in depth via a self–selfobject bond and a changed psychological balance. It is obvious that this definition does not include criteria for cure formulated by other analytic theories that define cure as libidinal progression, relinquishment of infantile wishes and objects, "object detachment," the achievement of genitality, heterosexuality, etc.

satory structures remains a potential possibility throughout life (see, for example, Guntrip's [1975] powerful description of the restorative effects of his analysis with Winnicott late in his life. The issues of restoration of the self by compensatory structures and transformations of narcissism [Kohut, 1966] warrant separate discussion).

IDEATIONAL CONTENTS AND AFFECTIVE MOTIVATIONAL FORCE

Broadly speaking, each sector of the self is a different psychological configuration, constituted by different developmental needs and expectations, each with its characteristic ideational content and its powerful, affectively charged motivational force. There is the sector of (1) the child-self that actively seeks out and expects an alive, bright-eyed, engaged (mirroring) parent to whom he/she says, "Look at me and admire and applaud me and what I can do; I'm great and what I do is great"; (2) one that seeks out and looks up to the admired (idealized) parent, expecting to be bolstered and "uplifted" and who says, "You're great, what you are and what you do is great; you belong to me, I belong to you, therefore, I'm great too"; and (3) the child-self that looks for and expects alikeness, belonging, and kindred spirit experiences—twinship/alterego experiences that are also self-expanding and self-enhancing—and who says, "We're just alike, we're in step with each other, we're both great when we're together." (For example, a very intelligent, attractive, appealing woman who knew nothing of the self psychology theory of twinship told her analyst that she only felt attractive and worth something when she "doubled" with the sister she admired, looked up to, and wanted to be like. At a time of severe crisis in his life, when he was attempting to emigrate to the United States and find an internship, Kohut thanked a close friend for his help and wrote, "[Your] . . . great efforts . . . have allowed me and you to grow together into a common we" (letter to Siegmund Levarie, August 23, 1938, in Cocks, 1994, p. 39. Kohut was expressing his gratitude to Levarie, who was attempting to help him with his plans to emigrate from Paris and find an internship in Chicago).

To repeat, self sectors consist of valid needs to be enjoyed, admired, and confirmed in our naive feeling that we are the center of our world; to be supported and strengthened and helped to recover from inevitable anxieties and inevitable injuries to our pride; and to have the self-enhancing experiences of being like others who are like ourselves. Each sector undergoes expectable changes in contents and transformations as the self grows up, ages, and declines. Optimally, for example, our wired-in tendency as children to pursue the idealized, "powerful" parent who lifts us up and restores our equilibrium and well-being is transformed, in continuing self–selfobject experiences, into capacities to reach out for sustaining adult bonds of love, friendship, and collegiality and capacities to strive toward idealized goals and live up to our own beliefs and values; then we experience our own efforts to reach goals and live up to values as a source of feeling uplifted and confident. And so it is with the other transformations: the mirroring sector—"admire me and tell me I'm great," "Look ma, no hands!"—undergoes expectable transformations into adults' self-esteem and ambitions (including the ambition to enjoy and sustain the next generation); the pursuit of these further enhances self-esteem and provides a cohesion-fostering sense of direction and purpose. The "doubling, we're just alike" sector is transformed into bonds of kinship, friendship, and alikeness that increase self-esteem by contributing to feeling expanded and enhanced.

COMPENSATORY STRUCTURES AND THE TWO-PART DEVELOPMENTAL SEQUENCE

The structures that compensate for serious deficits in the self and its sectors have their beginnings in a developmental sequence that we see very frequently—both in ourselves and in our patients. The sequence is part injurious to the self and its growth and part beneficial. The injurious part is deeply rooted in a self–selfobject bond with a parent who is consistently unable to respond to normal childhood needs because his or her capacities for mirroring acceptance, enthusiasm, and applause; supports, strengths, and guidance that the child can idealize; or the twinship experiences of being a kindred soul are seriously deficient. With an unresponsive, erratic, depressed, or negligent parent, the child experiences what the film maker François Truffaut called *The 400 Blows*— severe disappointments, fragmentation anxiety, depletion depression, and blows to self-esteem, often of traumatic proportions. When blows to cohesion, pride, and well-being are experienced over and over again, "primary structural deficits" in all sectors of the self are inevitable.

In spite of "400 blows" it is still possible to form self–selfobject ties that make up for the primary deficits; this is the next part of the developmental sequence. Even though their experience of themselves is seriously injured, initially healthy children and adolescents do not give up easily. "A self that had been threatened in one sector . . . manage[s] to survive by shifting its psychological point of gravity toward another one" (Kohut, 1977, p. 83). "Shifting the point of psychological gravity" and seeking out another who can respond to injuries and needs has great transformational potential. Drawing on their own resources—especially remaining initiative and hope—originally healthy children and adolescents attempt to turn toward the other parent (if there is one) or to another more available person, often a sibling, friend, a grandparent, other relative, or teacher. And now they look for the twofold responses they need to *recover from the blows and compensate for what was missing with the parent who could not respond.* (At the same time, partly, at least, they turn away psychologically from the most development-thwarting parent.) The responses they elicit can be the start of the formation of structures that may eventually, if bolstered enough, restore one of the sectors, even though it was injured and sustained primary structural deficits. And now for a poignant example of revitalization of one sector of an unmirrored self—an example from life (to a certain extent the restoration of the self that occurs in treatment but imitates life).

A LIFE-SAVING TWINSHIP—"THERE MUST BE SOMEONE TO CONFIRM ME"

My glimpse into Anna Freud's inner life and the "400 blows" from which she recovered via the twinship with Dorothy Burlingham is based on intensely personal letters, poetry, notes she kept on her dreams and free associations, and notes about her own struggles that she used for psychoanalytic papers. She left these private writings, along with the rest of her literary estate, when she died at the age of 86. (Excerpts of her personal writings can be found in Elizabeth Young-Bruehl's [1988] biography; letters to her friend Eva Rosenfeld are published in Heller [1992].) The writings reveal that as a child, adolescent, and young adult, she suffered intense feelings of shame and chronic feelings of worthlessness and was frequently depleted and depressed; that she became addicted to sexualized defensive measures, particularly beating fantasies, masturbation, and daydreams; and that she also attempted to protect her vulnerable self by relinquishing her own wishes and living through others. The defensive measures were compulsive attempts to fill in deficits in her vitality, initiative, and feelings of pride and self-worth. To say this differently, the mirroring and idealizing sectors of her self-organization were seriously injured in her childhood and adolescence. The consequence of the injuries was that she entered adulthood with primary structural deficits in both the sector of ambitions and idealized goals—her own goals and ambitions (apart from her father's) were insufficiently established and could not provide her with a feeling of aliveness and a reliable sense of her own worth and value or with the sustenance and sense of direction that comes from belief in ourselves and our own efforts and abilities to reach idealized goals.

THE UNMIRRORED ADOLESCENT SELF–ADDICTION
TO DEFENSIVE MEASURES

Anna Freud entered her adolescence still feeling like the insatiable child (her family reputation) who was unwanted and worthless. She had experienced significant rebuffs from both parents and from her pretty sister Sophie, whose looks her father enjoyed, and was left with the feeling she was unimportant to both parents as well as to her siblings. She did not feel recognized, confirmed, strengthened, or enjoyed by anyone except Josephine, her nursemaid. (It seems to me that in her view that Anna Freud had three mothers, Young-Bruehl greatly exaggerates the significance of Josephine's care of the unwanted child.) Suffering from extremely low self-esteem, manifested in intense shame and awkwardness about her body-mind-self, she avoided social life; suffering from the listlessness and fatigue she called "laziness," she was a lonely exile with the feeling that there was "no circle where I am at center" (the quotation is from her favorite poem by Rilke; see Young-Bruehl [1988, p. 128]).

Her personal writings reveal, over and over again, that Anna Freud's chief motive force, the "continuous and undisturbed thread of psychical activity" (Freud, 1909, p. 143), the "repetition compulsion" if you will, was no more or less than an originally normal developmental need: she desperately wanted to be told that she and what she did were good. She tenaciously hung on to the need for affirmation, and it persisted as a nucleus of health in spite of her feelings of the faulty responsiveness that led to her feeling unseen and unwanted, and never accepted, praised, or confirmed for who and what she was. In place of mirroring acceptance, her mother was rejecting and critical, and her father and his colleagues who befriended her accepted her idealization of them (she was always "looking way up to them"). She experienced constant pressure to be like them and what they wanted her to be. (In adolescence she attached herself to a number of older women—mostly women analysts or mates of analysts. She admired these women, and had a crush on some of them, but they were too glamorous or successful to be a genuine source of sustenance or mirroring for her. Her father found the men who showed interest in her wanting, and she dutifully agreed.) However, there was one source of recognition that was gratifying and enlivening; her age-mates, childhood girlfriends, and cousins admired her story-telling capacities and enjoyed and applauded the adventure stories she made up and told with zest. Friendships, then, a greatly underestimated source of admiration and enjoyment, gave enough support to her and her skills and talents for revitalization of the twinship sector when, much later, her true twin came into her life.

In the meantime, Anna Freud did what traumatized children and adolescents usually do if they have the chance. First, she turned away from her mother's criticisms and lack of pleasure in her and her body (her attempts to turn to her sister Sophie as an alternative and to form an alikeness bond with her were consistently rejected). At age 12 she became depressed and anorexic after being tricked by both parents into an appendectomy with no preparation (when her mother learned the date of the surgery, she did not tell Anna). "All I knew was that I was going in [to the hospital] for an examination," she told her friend Manna Friedmann when remembering the childhood trauma during her terminal illness (Young-Bruehl, 1988, p. 54). The betrayal, experienced as a massive blow, led her to turn to her father as she began a desperate campaign to get him interested in her. As is frequently the case, she blamed her mother for the treachery and looked to her idealized father for another chance for mirroring. His genuine acceptance and admiration of her could have begun to "make up" for her mother's rejection and betrayal and could have acted as a seed or nucleus for later revitalization of the mirroring sector—the most damaged sector of her self. However, the mirroring from him that she hoped for, to authenticate herself, was not forthcoming.

Freud was content to be idealized; and he accepted Anna's gross identification with him and psychoanalysis. The only one of the Freud children who evinced any interest in psychoanalysis (his son Oliver was to be his successor until his obsessional neurosis dashed his father's hopes for him), Anna found a way of getting close to him. If she could not have *his* enjoyment of her, the next best thing was for her to have something of his—the books he wrote; his letters to her answering her questions about psychoanalytic concepts; and his analysis of her dreams, symptoms, and depleted, ruminative states. (Later, she derived temporary benefits from the inadvertent mirroring the actual analysis with him provided.)

In short, from age 12 on, Anna attempted to restore herself by absorbing her father by way of psychoanalysis. This turn to him and his works was crucial for the beginnings of compensatory structures—for the development of the skills and talents she was later able to integrate via the twinship into what she would call her "real self." Freud almost literally let her sit at his feet at his Wednesday night psychoanalytic meetings. However, his letters to her are painful testimony to his inability to resonate with his daughter's mirroring needs, either during her childhood or adolescence (for example, see Sigmund Freud to Anna Freud, February 2, 1913, in Young-Bruehl, 1988, p. 59). In fact, his letters show that he openly rejected her needs for mirroring confirmation: he exerted strenuous pressure on her to be more like other girls (i.e., more like what he thought a girl should be), chided her for looking for reassurance, urged her to be self-sufficient, and openly expressed his disapproval of what she described as being "very tired" and doing "nothing all day long when I am not sick" (Young-Bruehl, 1988, pp. 57–58). Anna's frequent depleted (depressed) states were prompted by, and followed, her compulsive masturbation and beating fantasies which she confided to her father during an enforced separation when he admonished her to learn to enjoy herself as a girl.

Instead of eliciting mirroring and response to her naive idealizing needs, she lived more and more through defensive measures, particularly compulsive masturbation fantasies. These were sexualized efforts to preserve herself—addictive because the happy ending she made up was temporarily enlivening, repetitive because they could not make up for her injuries, which secondarily contributed to making her feel worse about herself. In her fantasy she reexperienced her injuries, shame, and humiliation over and over again, and, in her fantasy, she made up for the mirroring she missed. The first part of the fantasy involved a concretization of her injured self—a youth was tortured by the henchmen of a cruel knight. As he neared the point of death from the torture, the knight relented; he came to see the youth's great virtues, ordered the torture to stop and did everything in his power to heal the youth's injured body and nurse him back to life.

Solaced, recognized, and finally valued, only in the sadomasochistic fantasies with which she tried to save herself, Anna Freud was left with her exceptional endowment, largely unused (she was a very anxious, lackluster student and her abilities were not recognized), and with the defensive measures that covered over the serious primary structural deficits but could not either fill them in or make up for them. More and more, she made use of another defensive measure to save herself: she made up a vicarious form of mirroring. In the face of her father's continuing pressure and overt insistence that she give up her "insatiable wishes" and become self-sufficient, Anna attempted to vitalize her unmirrored feminine self by "giving over" her own mirroring needs, for recognition and fulfillment in love, to other young women. The limited experience of fulfillment she experienced came, then, only when she participated vicariously in a friends' love-life (see her letters to Eva Rosenfeld in Heller [1992]). The young governess she would describe later to illustrate "altruistic surrender" in *The Ego and the Mechanisms of Defense* (1946, pp. 133–139) is a barely disguised version of herself. Unmarried, childless, shabby, and inconspicuous (p. 134) the governess had the "insatiable wishes," like her own, that she was pressured to give up—childhood longings to keep up with her siblings, to be admired for her cleverness, for pretty clothes, for children, and for her father to admire her naked body. Like her proxy, the governess, Anna did not feel pretty enough to find the satisfactions girls and women could obtain, and she did not feel clever enough to be a boy who would be admired by her father.

THE YOUNG ADULT SELF—REACTIVATION OF THE NUCLEUS OF HEALTH

Anna Freud entered young adulthood lacking the independent initiative she needed to put her many gifts to work for herself. She obtained the inferior education to be a teacher that was available to her (Freud did not think his daughters needed a good education, unlike some of his friends who saw to it that their daughters obtained a medical education). The fact that she was considered a very good teacher did not allay her unsureness or her lack of an inner sense of direction that would be satisfying, nor did it decrease her inhibitions, including her unfulfillment in love. No wonder she jumped at the chance for a five-day-a-week analysis with her father that at first brought exhilaration and an unaccustomed sense that she "was standing up straighter" (Young-Bruehl, 1988). The analysis with her father provided Anna with a great deal of inadvertent mirroring from which she benefited. However Freud's theory of what ailed her left her inner life substantially unchanged. She accepted her father's theories about her (he saw her beating fantasies as disguised oedipal/erotic wishes and/or wishes for a penis, which led to a severe superego that demanded punishment), and, because she wanted so badly to please him she simply stopped telling him that what she really needed was confirmation. (I shall discuss this further.)

I have described the analysis elsewhere (Tolpin, 1992). Suffice it to say here that, in spite of her father's and her own best efforts to make her into something she could not be, Anna Freud never abandoned her inner insistence that, "I have to have something for myself." "There must be others who say that something [I have done] is good; there must be others who confirm me" (Young-Bruehl, 1988, p. 133). The nucleus of health remained, in spite of the traumatic disappointments and rejection she experienced (in this connection see Anna Freud's [1946] description of the governess's paralyzing disappointment that elicited the vicarious satisfaction solution [p. 137]). Furthermore, her inner insistence that she had to have affirmation remained the chief motivating force in her life, despite the fact that, at the very same time, she accepted her father's view that her continuing search for affection from others was a sign that she was a worthless, discontented, insatiable person (Young-Bruehl, 1988, p. 134).[3]

With Dorothy and the mutual (self-saving) twinship bond they forged, she belatedly formed her own "circle of health," a circle where she was finally at the center in the eyes of someone truly important to her. (The complex bond included Dorothy Burlingham's children. Analytic treatment was only one of the many "parenting" functions Anna Freud served for the Burlingham children.) The 50-year-long twinship that saved her went two ways: each was for the other the transformational selfobject neither ever had before. In their correspondence (while separated in 1939 because of the war) they "agreed that they were each other's twins, or twins for each other, in their ideal friendship" (Young-Bruehl, 1988, p. 139). Specifically, Anna felt that Dorothy, unlike any other important person in her life, truly wanted her, believed in her, found her precious and worth having (she came to trust that for Dorothy the relationship was "the most precious [one] she ever had" [Young-Bruehl, 1988, p. 138]; before Dorothy, since she was very little, it was "as if I were seeing myself through the eyes of the other and were worth just as little to myself as I was to [them]," [letter to Eva Rosenfeld, in Heller, 1992, p. 138]). With Anna's belief in her, Dorothy also came to believe in herself. She became even more of a twin to Anna (and Anna to her) in the course of their bond—like Anna, she was analyzed by Freud, became an analyst, was Anna's twin in "hands on work" and research with children during the London Blitz, and contributed to the psychoanalytic literature, on a more modest, but significant, scale. (Many of Burlingham's psychoanalytic interests and contributions began in her understanding of herself, her influence on her children, and her longings to have a twin. For particular interest in light of the twinship with Anna Freud, see Burlingham [1945], only one of many papers dealing with twins.)

In the beginning of the twinship tie, Anna was, as usual, unsure of herself and insecure. She doubted that Dorothy could really want her and was terribly fearful when she thought that Dorothy would once again turn to a relationship with a man. As always, in spite of the analysis, in spite of herself, she looked for reassurance. This time, the life-

---

[3] The important point is that inner resistance and cure by compensatory structure goes only so far as to strengthen one sector in depth. Structures formed in self–selfobject bonds do not fill in primary deficits or make up for all of them. Anna Freud retained her idealization of her father, even in the face of her own studies of children's basic "developmental needs." She emphasized that these needs must be recognized and responded to by parents. Nevertheless, she never questioned Freud's placing drive wishes, including an unconscious wish for punishment, in the center of disorders like hers.

saving reassurance she needed was there. Dorothy was unstinting in reassuring Anna that their tie was "the most precious relationship [she] ever had" (Burlingham to A. Freud, Dec. 1, 1939, in Young-Bruehl [1988, p. 138]). Finally, Anna believed it. At last, Anna felt she was precious to someone she cared for, that Dorothy wanted her the way she was, and at last she came out of herself—she was no longer the lonely "hermit" (letter to Lou Andreas Salome in Young-Bruehl [1988], p. 192), living in the sexualized fantasies of torture, rescue, and healing of her unmirrored self.

The insufficiently established structures to maintain and restore her own belief in herself were part of the twinship bond, but the belief in herself was also now partly "inside" as a motivating force. Indeed, an internal psychological point of gravity shifted: she turned away from all the unsuccessful attempts to engage with others who did not respond to her mirroring needs, from the idealizations that failed to provide her with her own sustaining goals. When her inner balance changed, the depletion, depression, and inhibition that interfered with her making use of her gifts (skills and talents) underwent a transformation: the twinship finally provided the necessary ingredients for authentic healing and growth. Thus, in 1934 Anna Freud wrote to Andreas-Salome: "Something in me got freed, so that I can start writing. . . . I am looking forward to it and now I have new ideas all the time which was not the case earlier . . . [the book *The Ego and the Mechanisms of Defense]* is really close to being I. . . . nearby is Dorothy and . . . everything is well" (in Young-Bruehl, 1988, p. 204).

In fact, all was good enough in the sector of the self that was so deprived of life-providing mirroring responses. Instead of seeing herself through the eyes of others and feeling worthless, she saw herself through Dorothy's eyes and her own. The affirmation and consolidation of the self that Anna Freud experienced in a twinship were the basis for the formation of a compensatory path: the unmirrored self was revitalized; the story-telling self valued by age-mates was enhanced and expanded and integrated into a continuum with her skills and talents. With all of these, she then lived a life that was meaningful and fulfilling for her—she was a productive "we-self" in pursuit of what finally came to be her own and Dorothy's shared goals.

The twinship sector of the self that was revitalized and enlarged in Anna Freud's case does not fulfill traditional psychoanalytic expectations of cure—it has taken a long time for the field to learn that many of the criteria for cure are artifacts of a theory that was not broad enough to encompass the self as a unit in its own right—a self that can recover from severe injuries and be revitalized when valid needs (like those of Anna Freud's) are not mistaken for insatiable infantile wishes that have to be suppressed and relinquished. An example follows of the failure to distinguish childhood wishes that have to be relinquished from needs that have to be responded to.

FAILURE TO SEE A CONSTRUCTIVE FORWARD MOVE

Guntrip (1969) concluded that a patient initially turned to him for help and then fled the analysis because his theory (a version of British object relations greatly influenced by Fairbairn and Winnicott) "missed the real point." He thought he was dealing with the patient's infantile wishes and, as a consequence, failed to see the patient's need for the analyst's support in a struggle to make a "constructive and forward-looking move" (p. 51) to save himself. The example Guntrip provides illustrates the kind of forward move and need for support that can prove to be the beginning of compensatory structures, provided the move is recognized as such.

A shy, schizoid professional man in his forties sought analysis because of an embarrassing symptom—"he was intensely preoccupied with breasts and felt compelled to look at every woman he passed." There were other "childish feelings [not specified] he intensely disliked admitting" (Guntrip, 1969, p. 34). The patient told Guntrip he believed that his preoccupation with breasts was somehow connected to his cold and unresponsive wife who was like his mother. He added that he always thought of his mother as "'buttoned up tight to the neck'" (p. 50).

Guntrip (1969) attributed the patient's distress over his symptom to a regression to infantile oral wishes for security at the breast (pp. 49, 50). With interpretations to this effect (not specified), the patient's preoccupation with breasts subsided. Guntrip took this to be a sign of analytic progress. Shortly, however, the presenting symptom was replaced by a "spate of fantasies" so compulsive and all-absorbing that they interfered with the patient's work. All were variations on the same theme: in the fantasies the patient retired to an isolated seacoast, built himself a strong house, and walled it off from the life going on outside. The series came to a climax Guntrip did not understand at the time: the patient built himself an impregnable castle on top of what Guntrip described as a breast-shaped mountain and walled it around with impassable defenses. "The authorities camped round about and tried to storm the citadel but were quite unable to break in" (Guntrip, 1969, p. 50). Sometimes he emerged in disguise to inspect the outside world, but no one could get in contact with him. "Finally [the patient] saw me coming up the mountain side, hurled great boulders at me and drove me off. . . . One or two weeks later the patient suddenly broke off the analysis, using a passing illness of his wife's as an excuse" (p. 50).

In his retrospective reassessment of his patient's failed attempt to get help, Guntrip (1969) came to profound conclusions. To put it simply, he said that the patient's looking at breasts was, indeed, oral; however, the theory that led him to see the voyeurism as a regression to an earlier state of drive and object relations was incomplete, and it misled him. Freud's idea of "instinctive drives" (oral, anal, incestuous) and wishes to return to earlier "erotic happiness . . . misses the real point" (p. 53). The "orality" involved in looking at breasts was an expression of the patient's active attempt to "stay born," to actively struggle to "stay in object-relationships" as a separate ego (p. 50) and go on living (p. 53). In other words, Guntrip said he failed to see that the patient was trying to make a "constructive and forward-looking" move (p. 51): a part of his personality (a tendril of the self) looked at breasts "to stay in object-relationships" (p. 50).

Commentary on the Case

Looked at in the light of the need for compensatory structures, Guntrip's patient *turned to* the analyst and looked for the selfobject functions that could save him from further fragmentation. The voyeuristic symptom was, at one and the same time, an unconscious emergency defensive measure and the clue to the attempt at a forward move: the failing self sexualized the need to remain attached and regain cohesion. That is to say, the need of the self for strengthening, cohesion-restoring structure was symbolically represented as the "good breast" or the self–selfobject experiences that were unconsciously sought as a source of needed strength and comfort. The defense of sexualization to hold the self together and the selfobject transferences that reactivate forward developmental moves remained for Kohut to describe. However, Guntrip's assessment of the failed attempt at treatment is critical: he realized that analytic theory misled him clinically with its focus on instinctual drives and on age and stage regressions and fixations. The patient's voyeurism and his retreat from the world of the living into his walled-off fortress was not encompassed by seeing the symptoms as a wish to return to warded off orality or, to go further, regress to the nirvana of the womb, as he had originally thought. Moreover, Guntrip's idea of the unseen "forward move" is also critical: it is one of a number of important ideas in the psychoanalytic literature that could not be fully utilized, while drive and object relations theories occupied the center of analytic attention. (The literature I am referring to, not yet anchored in an understanding of vital selfobject needs and repair of injuries, is mentioned by Anna Freud

[1965, p. 27] in her discussion of Edward Bibring's [1937] idea of "innate urges to complete development"; also see Miller [1985] for Kohut's discussion in supervision [shortly before his death] of the "leading edge of development" and the "maturational push," concepts that he had not made sufficiently explicit in his published work, and my recent paper [Tolpin, 1997].)

The patient's compulsive symptom, then, was the sexualized sign of a fragmenting self in an emergency state, desperate for psychological structure that would hold him together and strengthen him. Although symptoms and signs were not understood as a tendril of looking for what he needed, the patient initially complied with the analyst's theory and its implied criticism of his "childish needs";[4] he suppressed the symptom. Then he got worse. His spate of fantasies suggest that the mistaken interpretation (that he was looking for security at the breast) was experienced as a further assault on an already endangered self. His very survival as an independent self was threatened when Guntrip did not understand his need for structure, and he had no recourse but to fortify himself with his own [mental] devices and wall himself off from his unresponsive world.

Guntrip's clinical vignette highlights a critical issue for all therapies, whether analysis or psychotherapy, whether long-term and intensive, or short-term and brief: it is essential to understand needs for selfobject functions, no matter how fragmented or sexualized the expression of the need is. It is this understanding that guarantees that needs to revitalize the self will not be traumatically disregarded again in their transference reactivation. With the availability of empathic resonance to reactivated needs, "the interrupted maturational push . . . will begin to reassert itself spontaneously as it is reactivated in analysis in the form of selfobject transference" (Kohut, 1984, p. 78).

THE BROADENED REACH OF THE IDEA OF CURE BY COMPENSATORY STRUCTURES

Kohut thought that a second chance to strengthen and expand compensatory structure leads to the most frequent form of cure (a view that applies to therapists, as well as to their patients). No wonder, then, that he assigned the formation of compensatory structure a position of inestimable importance in normal self-development (in all phases of life), in

---

4 The compliance is understandable, it is one form the wish for help often takes—after all he turned to the analyst with the hope of being helped and, no doubt, tried to make use of the interpretations. Contrast this initial compliance with Kohut's (1977) Mr. Z, who initially fought the interpretations and finally submitted as he had done with his mother.

disorders of the self and their analytic cure. In fact, the developmental and clinical correlates of this view of a second chance at establishing a firm enough self are worth mentioning since they are the "stuff" of which the psychology of the self is made (see Kohut, 1984):

(1) Every self consists, to a considerable extent, of compensatory structures—this is inevitable given the fact that some disappointments and frustrations of basic needs are part and parcel of the human condition.[5] (2) These structures can be formed at every phase and stage of self-development—there is no reason for psychoanalysis to focus so exclusively on the earliest infantile stages. (3) Structures that compensate for primary deficits are largely responsible for establishing the self in original self-development and in the reestablishment of a strengthened self in treatment. (4) There is not one kind of healthy self; there are many kinds. (5) There is no single analytic or psychotherapeutic road to cure: there are many, depending on the specific make-up and health potential of a specific patient. (6) There is not an ideal goal to be reached; self psychology does not formulate a psychoanalytic utopia. Erikson (1950) observed that every school of psychoanalytic thought formulates a utopia; "mature genitality" is the utopia of drive and ego psychology. His ironic note suggests that each school of analytic thought idealizes its own vision of psychic reality.

These developmental and clinical correlates of compensatory structures express the broad reach of self psychology and its greater freedom from doctrinaire and moralistic notions of health and maturity. Kohut made the point that: "We do not formulate a norm for [analytic] cure derived from [Freudian, Kleinian, Mahlerian, Kohutian] theory. There are many good lives that cannot be defined by such norms. There are many good lives, and some great and most fulfilled, not lived by individuals who [for example] were heterosexual" (Kohut, 1984, p. 7).

CONCLUSION: THE CHANGED ACCENT ON NORMAL SELF-DEVELOPMENT

The concept of cure by compensatory structures calls for a theoretical shift that places our clinical accent on the normal development of the self and its constructive forward moves. Even though the shift simply calls for a change in emphasis, it is not easy to accomplish. With the exception of self psychology most schools of psychoanalytic thought

---

[5] Further, Kohut thought that a self characterized by predominance of compensatory structures constitutes the most frequent matrix of capacity for high achievement—despite high degrees of childhood trauma the most productive and creative persons have been able to acquire new structures by finding new routes toward inner completeness (Kohut, 1984, p. 44)

(knowingly or not) accent pathology by adhering to an ingrained (Freudian) tenet: transferences to the analyst are a new edition of the formative pathology, an artificial disease—the transference neurosis; the work of the treatment largely consists of curing the reactivated childhood pathology, especially pathology of earliest stages of life. Anything else has been regarded with suspicion and considered to be "just" staying on the surface, "just" doing psychotherapy, "just" strengthening defenses, avoiding core issues of sexuality and aggression, and so forth.

It should be obvious to therapists that, even if we wanted to, it is impossible to ignore primary structural deficits and their serious consequences. For example, the stunting of the sectors of the self, the tremendous intensification of thwarted needs, and the tenacity of self-protective measures are vitally necessary but further derail normal development. It is equally impossible to ignore the serious problems that primary deficits and defensive measures create when reactivated in transferences that mainly repeat the most traumatic and need-thwarting aspects of development. Nevertheless, two radically new ideas have to be integrated to make full use of the concept of compensatory structures as a path to restoration of the self: the idea that *cure takes place in transferences that revive still remaining healthy needs and expectations of responsiveness and the idea that these transferences are by no means limited to earliest stages of childhood—they include the needs of the self over the entire course of life.* In other words, the infantile wishes and objects that have received the strongest analytic accent are not the deepest layers of the psyche. Needs that were once normal remain in the depths of the unmirrored self, of the self that suffers from shame and lacks idealized goals, of the self that is chronically enfeebled and/or fragmenting. It is the reactivation of the deepest needs in self–selfobject transference that is potentially transforming when the transferences are understood and explained; it is these needs and the responses to them that can revitalize the self, albeit in only one of its sectors.

To conclude, I anticipate that we shall continue to explore treatment that accents remobilization of normal aspects of development and constructive forward moves. Such explorations are among the many forward moves ahead to further our understanding of the remobilization of normal development and the various ways that compensatory structures are established that restore the self.

REFERENCES

Bibring, E. (1937), On the theory of the therapeutic results of psycho-analysis. *Internat. J. Psycho-Anal.*, 18:170–189.

Burlingham, D. (1945), The fantasy of having a twin. *The Psychoanalytic Study of the Child*, 1:205–210. New York: International Universities Press.

Cocks, G. (1994), *The Curve of Life*. Chicago: University of Chicago Press.

Freud, A. (1946), *The Ego and the Mechanisms of Defense*. New York: International Universities Press.

—— (1965), *Normality and Pathology in Childhood*. New York: International Universities Press.

Freud, S. (1909), Analysis of a phobia in a five-year-old boy. *Standard Edition*, 10:5–149. London: Hogarth Press, 1955.

—— (1917), "A child is being beaten." *Standard Edition*, 17:179–204. London: Hogarth Press, 1955.

—— (1920), The psychogenesis of a case of homosexuality in a woman. *Standard Edition*, 18:147–172. London: Hogarth Press, 1955.

Guntrip, H. (1969), *Schizoid Phenomena, Object-Relations and the Self*. New York: International Universities Press.

—— (1975), My experience of analysis with Fairbairn and Winnicott. *Internat. Rev. Psycho-Anal.*, 2:145–146.

Heller, P. (1992), *Anna Freud's Letters to Eva Rosenfeld*. Madison, CT: International Universities Press.

Kohut, H. (1966), Forms and transformations of narcissism. *J. Amer. Psychoanal. Assn.*, 14:243–272.

—— (1977), *The Restoration of the Self*. New York: International Universities Press.

—— (1984), *How Does Analysis Cure?* ed. A. Goldberg & P. Stepansky. Chicago: University of Chicago Press.

Miller, J. (1985), How Kohut actually worked. *Progress in Self Psychology, Vol. 1*, ed. A. Goldberg. New York: Guilford, pp. 13–30.

Tolpin, M. (1971), On the beginnings of a cohesive self. *The Psychoanalytic Study of the Child*, 26:316–352. New Haven, CT: Yale University Press.

—— (1992), Self-esteem deficit, beating fantasies, and a life-saving twinship resolution: A study of Anna Freud. Unpublished paper delivered at American Psychoanalytic Association Seminar for Clinicians, New York & Chicago.

—— (1997), The forward edge of development: The changing accent of psychoanalysis. Unpublished paper delivered to New York Psychoanalytic Institute for Self Psychology, New York.

Young-Bruehl, E. (1988), *Anna Freud*. New York: Summit Books.

Chapter 2

"Compensatory" or "Primary": An Alternative View. Discussion of Marian Tolpin's "Compensatory Structures: Paths to the Restoration of the Self"

James L. Fosshage

Marian Tolpin, in characteristic fashion, has given us a clear and cogent discussion of Kohut's concept, compensatory structures, and their crucial role in the face of thwarted development in realizing the program of the nuclear self. Assessing that the universality of compensatory structures is insufficiently recognized, Tolpin delineates, in keeping with Kohut's (1984) formulations, how further consolidation of compensatory structures is a central pathway in development and psychoanalytic treatment to the "restoration of the self."

In my brief discussion I wish to raise some theoretical and developmental issues concerning the concept of compensatory structures and, then, to revisit the clinical example of Anna Freud.

On the basis of observing the transference, Kohut (1971, 1977, 1984) delineated three basic selfobject needs: the needs for mirroring, idealizing, and twinship. Subsequently, Stolorow, Brandchaft, and Atwood (1987) have described self-validating and self-delineating needs,

Presented at the Master Class of the 17th Annual Conference on the Psychology of the Self, October 20, 1994, Chicago, IL.

and Wolf (1980) and Lachmann (1986), the adversarial selfobject need. While additional selfobject needs may be identified, all selfobject needs are descriptions of thematic experience required for development and maintenance of the self. Selfobject experience builds and maintains, what we have called, self-structure.

In light of the variety of selfobject needs and experiences, what do we mean by "primary structure," "compensatory structure," and "primary deficit"? In his bipolar conceptualization of the self (in which alterego or twinship selfobject needs were placed under the rubric of mirroring), Kohut (1977) viewed the child as having essentially two chances, that is, through mirroring and idealizing selfobject experiences, of building a "functioning self." Each selfobject need has its own developmental trajectory with mirroring experience leading to ambitions, one pole of the self, and with idealizing selfobject experience leading to ideals, a second pole of the self. (When, in Kohut's later thinking, twinship became the third central selfobject need, an individual could be viewed as having three chances of building a self.) Thwarted experience in one selfobject arena results in a deficit in structure formation. As this occurs, the individual turns to the other arena of selfobject experience with a greater imperative to consolidate and maintain a functioning self. As the second pole of the personality, using Kohut's language, is established, it is called a compensatory structure because the structure carries the added imperative or "compensatory" weight of the previous failure to establish a functioning self.

Development of each pole of personality normally occurs simultaneously. Thus, it would be experience that establishes what is "primary," that is, first, in formation of structure or in deficit. While Kohut maintained that the primary deficit could occur in either pole, he typically observed it in the mirroring arena. He (Kohut, 1977) states: "Most frequently a weakness in the area of exhibitionism and ambitions is compensated for by the self-esteem provided by the pursuit of ideals; but the reverse may also occur" (p. 4). Kohut's clinical examples consistently locate the primary deficit as occurring in the mirroring arena (for example, in the cases of Mr. M [Kohut, 1977] and Mr. Z [Kohut, 1979]).

The conceptualization of compensatory structures suggests, as Tolpin made clear, that there are various pathways to a vitalized, functioning self. In viewing varying degrees of compensatory structures as universal, Kohut (1984) writes: "There is not one kind of healthy self—there are many kinds. And there is no single analytic road toward cure—there are many, depending on the specific health potential of a specific analysand" (p. 44). Kohut's enthusiasm for "many kinds" of a healthy self follows from, but is more expansive than, the implications of the concept of the bipolar self. The bipolar self suggests that there are only two primary avenues and, with the addition of twinship, there are three. The *content* of these primary avenues of self-formation, however, can vary considerably, creating many pathways.

Recognizing the possibility of multiple pathways to a healthy self leads us to a radical clinical departure. It suggests that the patient may not need to reexperience the original trauma associated with the primary deficit and to fill in the missing structure but, instead, may establish a viable self through further consolidation of the healthy or compensatory structures.

Kohut's notion, what Tolpin delineated so cogently today, that a thwarted individual will strive to find another developmental pathway, is strongly supported empirically. What is meant by an alternative developmental pathway, though, is crucially important. Does the pathway to the formation of compensatory structures involve a different selfobject need and a different sector of personality? *Or* does the individual shift to a different relational matrix to provide the missing selfobject experience, that is, within the area of the "primary deficit" I will return to this issue in a further assessment of Anna Freud.

Let us first take a closer look at the terminology. The term *structure*, as others have pointed out, tends to connote an overly rigid and static state that fails to capture the dynamic fluidity of psychological experience and process. In its place, terms like *regulatory* or *modulating capacities, organizing patterns,* and *motivational systems* all seem better in capturing both the flux as well as the consistency of human experience.

Self structure, in Kohut's (1977) terminology, that is first established is called "primary," except when it follows a deficit. While the new structure established following a deficit is still primary in that it is the first self structure, it is now called compensatory structure, robbing it, if you will, of its primary status. Does naming the structure compensatory connote that it is somehow lesser? Rather than referring to the establishment of a primary structure that compensates for past failures, it is called a compensatory structure. Does this terminology connote, accurately or inaccurately, that there is still something basic, something primary, missing in the person? Does calling the structure compensatory rather than primary contribute to the difficulty in overcoming the traditional clinical notion that the analysand must regress to the original trauma and area of primary deficit to assure a successful psychoanalysis? Can an individual achieve a functioning self through compensatory structures, as Kohut indicated, but, in contrast to Kohut, must the individual find and fill in the missing primary ingredients to establish a *more fully* vitalized sense of self? To avoid terminological conundrums and to reflect more accurately the complexity of psychological development, I suggest that we eschew the adjectives *primary* and *compensatory* with regard to structure and simply refer to psychological organizations, assessing whether or not a particular organization is self-enhancing or self-debilitating, vitalizing or devitalizing. We could more accurately describe the intensified need for selfobject responsiveness in the face of previous failures as carrying a compensatory imperative without describing the structure or organization as compensatory. The question remains, however, as to whether or not it is necessary to find the missing ingredients in order to establish a more fully thriving sense of self.

The term *primary structural deficit* has also led to much confusion. Deficient selfobject experience arrests self-development. Kohut (1984) meant an arrest in the developmental program of the nuclear self. As the innate program is actualized, self-structure is established. When initial development is arrested, primary structure, according to Kohut's theory, fails to be built, leaving a primary deficit. Experience that is deficient in meeting selfobject needs, however (and this is what was not adequately recognized), still forms psychological organization, typically of a self-debilitating variety. The focus on deficits in the formation of self-structure, that is, a positive cohesive sense of self in keeping with intrinsic design, resulted in the initial overlooking of the formation of negative structures or organizations, for example, negative self, other and self-with-other schemas. Recognizing clinically the tenacity of these negative images of self and other, the analysis of problematic schemas have subsequently become far more central in self psychology (e.g., Atwood and Stolorow, 1984; Stolorow at al., 1987; Lachmann and Beebe, 1992; Lichtenberg, 1989; Lichtenberg, Lachmann, and Fosshage, 1992; Brandchaft, 1994; Fosshage, 1990, 1992, 1994).

To speak of primary and compensatory structures and sectors of self related to selfobject lines of development, in addition to the problems just noted, requires identifying with precision the particular selfobject needs involved. While the identification and delineation of various selfobject needs and transferences are conceptually and clinically heuristic, are these selfobject needs and transferences so distinct and identifiable in life and in the analytic arena? Moreover, does the developmental pathway to "compensatory" structure formation involve a different selfobject need and a different sector of personality? Or does the individual turn to a different relational matrix to provide the missing selfobject experience, that is, within the area of "primary deficit"? Let us revisit the "case" of Anna Freud so beautifully described by Marian Tolpin.

Anna felt unrecognized and unaffirmed in her family, leaving her as a lonely exile "with the feeling there was 'no circle where I am at center.'" Her experience with her idealized father was marred by having to "look way up," which both precluded a self-enhancing experience and contributed to negative feelings about herself.

While, as Tolpin writes, "The mirroring and idealizing sectors of her self-organization were seriously injured," she states that the most damaged sector of her self was the mirroring sector. While in Anna's case her search for the necessary mirroring experience was central, it is often difficult to discern which "sector" is damaged more, because mirroring, twinship, and idealizing experiences and "sectors" are intricately interwoven. In every mirroring and idealizing experience there has to be a little of the other. Mirroring is not vitalizing unless it is provided by a person who is somewhat idealized. Idealizing is only self-enhancing when the idealized person is experienced as implicitly affirming, and a self-enhancing feeling of essential alikeness, a twinship experience, entails some background of affirming and admiring components.

The primary enlivening experience for Anna occurred with her friends, who especially admired and applauded her storytelling. The success in forming relationships with friends must have created a set of expectancies that opened the avenue for a similar self-restorative friendship experience with Dorothy Burlingham later in her life. While Tolpin refers to these friendships as twinship experiences (and the corresponding twinship sector of personality) in which there is a self-enhancing sense of an essential likeness, the mirroring component, that is, the admiration of her storytelling, appears to be the prominent feature in these relationships. Moreover, in Tolpin's description, Anna was forever seeking the needed mirroring experiences, the area of "primary deficit." Even when accepted into analysis by her father, she did not form a compensatory structure around an idealizing selfobject experience, but, instead, as Tolpin writes, "[she] never abandoned her inner insistence that, . . . 'There must be others who say that something [I have done] is good; there must be others who confirm me.'"

It was on the basis of these enlivening friendships that Anna was able to forge a healing relationship with Dorothy. Tolpin describes this as a twinship bond. While Anna most likely felt an essential likeness with Dorothy, Anna's feeling that Dorothy "truly wanted her, believed in her, found her precious and worth having" were clearly in the forefront of Anna's experience and were the longed-for mirroring ingredients. Anna, in my view, did not form compensatory structure in a different sector of her personality involving twinship selfobject experience. It appears, instead, that she was able to find the crucially needed mirroring experience in the relationship with her, if you will, "idealized twin." In fact, Tolpin notes these mirroring components within the twinship but retains the notion of a compensatory path: "The affirmation and consolidation of the self that Anna Freud experienced in a twinship were the basis for the formation of a compensatory path." Anna, from my vantage point, found the needed mirroring experience in another relational context and, therein, was able to self-right, not through establishing compensatory structures, but through finding vitalizing experience of the very sort that was absent within her family, that is, experience related to the "primary deficit."

Thematic devitalizing experiences leave in their wake not only deficits, but problematic organizing patterns. These patterns subsequently interfere with finding and constructing needed selfobject experience. It was Anna's successful childhood friendships that enabled her, later in life, to create with a responsive person the needed mirroring friendship.

A person who is in need of particular selfobject experiences will search for the missing ingredients in other contexts, often engaging other motivational systems. Anna, for example, turned to sexual fantasies (the sexual/sensual motivational system) to seek the needed mirroring attachment experience. Another common example is a person who, thwarted in gaining sufficient mirroring experience, turns to work (involving the exploratory/assertive motivational system) to create needed selfobject experience. While work may provide efficacy pleasure that (compensatorily) bolsters a sense of self, and probably more so for the healthier individual, the missing selfobject component that, if not defended against, remains in the foreground, or not far in the background, is the needed affirmation from others.

In conclusion, the notions of primary and compensatory structure, while importantly positing multiple pathways to self-restoration, mislead us, in my view, in suggesting that a person with a primary deficit in selfobject experience can establish a fully healthy functioning self involving a different sector of personality and selfobject need. Selfobject experiences based on different selfobject needs may reestablish a functioning self yet are insufficient for developing and maintaining a fully thriving self. In contrast, I propose that essential selfobject experiences are needed for development, and if they are not found in one arena, the individual will relentlessly seek these very ingredients in different relational contexts, on occasion engaging additional motivational systems. Within psychoanalytic treatment, the problematic organizing patterns, a point that cannot be overemphasized, must be illuminated and gradually transformed to enable the individual to construct and assimilate needed selfobject experiences. Thus, it is the use of different relational contexts and additional motivational arenas for gaining, not a different type of selfobject experience, but the developmentally necessary and previously missing selfobject experience that provides fundamentally the multiple pathways to the most vitalized, healthy sense of self.

REFERENCES

Atwood, G. & Stolorow, R. (1984), *Structures of Subjectivity*. Hillsdale, NJ: The Analytic Press.

Brandchaft, B. (1994), To free the spirit from its cell. In: *The Widening Scope of Self Psychology, Process in Self Psychology, Vol. 10,* ed. A. Goldberg. Hillsdale, NJ: The Analytic Press, pp. 209–230.

Fosshage, J. (1990), Clinical protocol. The analyst's reply. *Psychoanal. Inq.,* 4:461–477, 601–622.

——— (1992), Self psychology: The self and its vicissitudes within a relational matrix. In: *Relational Perspectives,* ed. N. Scolnick & S. Warshaw. Hillsdale, NJ: The Analytic Press, pp. 21–42.

——— (1994), Toward reconceptualizing transference: Theoretical and clinical considerations. *Internat. J. Psycho-Anal.,* 75:265–281.

Kohut, H. (1971), *The Analysis of the Self.* New York: International Universities Press.

——— (1977), *The Restoration of the Self.* New York: International Universities Press.

——— (1979), The two analyses of Mr. Z. *Internat. J. Psycho-Anal.,* 60:3–27.

——— (1984), *How Does Analysis Cure?* ed. A. Goldberg & P. Stepansky. Chicago: Universtiy of Chicago Press.

Lachmann, F. (1986), Interpretation of psychic conflict and adverserial relationships: A self-psychoanalytic perspective. *Psychoanal. Psychol.,* 3:341–355.

——— & Beebe, B. (1992), Representational and selfobject transferences: A developmental perspective. In: *New Therapeutic Visions, Progress in Self Psychology, Vol. 8,* ed. A. Goldberg. Hillsdale, NJ: The Analytic Press, pp. 3–15.

Lichtenberg, J. (1989), *Psychoanalysis and Motivation.* Hillsdale, NJ: The Analytic Press.

——— Lachmann, F. & Fosshage, J. (1992), *Self and Motivational Systems.* Hillsdale, NJ: The Analytic Press.

Stolorow, R., Brandchaft, B. & Atwood, G. (1987), *Psychoanalytic Treatment.* Hillsdale, NJ: The Analytic Press.

Wolf, E. (1980), On the developmental line of selfobject relations. In: *Advances in Self Psychology,* ed. A. Goldberg. New York: International Universities Press, pp. 117–132.

Chapter 3

Response
to Fosshage

Marian Tolpin

I appreciate Dr. James Fosshage's thoughtful and challenging discussion and want to briefly respond to his main criticism: that the idea of compensatory structure is misleading, possibly acting as an interference with the main analytic objective—the formation of "primary structure" and establishment of a fully healthy, fully vitalized self. However, before turning to this area of major disagreement, I want to emphasize that Fosshage and I are in essential agreement on many points that are basic to self psychology and to my argument, as well as his: "structure" is simply one of a number of possible metaphors, a shorthand, that denotes a whole array of capacities, organizing patterns, defenses, and motivational/direction-setting intrapsychic configurations; vitalizing mirroring experiences that enhance self-esteem development are integral to the idealizing dimension of self–selfobject experience, and an idealizing component is integral to mirroring and twinship experiences; "structural deficits" are not "empty spaces" or holes to be filled "in" (for some the structural metaphor is taken literally and reified as a concretized version of the self as an empty inner space); and deficits, persisting, intensified needs, and defensive measures that protect the self become *persisting modes and motivations* that shape "primary structures" and are part and parcel of the self organization.

THE MAJOR DISAGREEMENT: REVITALIZATION OF A SECTOR NOT QUITE ESTABLISHED

Fosshage sees my example of the mirroring affirmation Anna Freud experienced with a woman she felt was her twin as an illustration of the restoration of a *fully healthy, vitalized self* via the formation of "primary" structure. However, my claim is far more modest (the same is

29

true of Kohut's claim for Mr. Z's compensatory path): the example is intended to illustrate the firm enough establishment of *one functional sector of the self*—in fact, in this instance, a fairly narrow self sector consisting of the satisfactions afforded by devotion to the twinship and to psychoanalysis. Figuratively speaking, the *mutual* mirroring, affirming, self-enhancing twinship bond breathed new life into this sector and belatedly enabled Anna Freud to feel worthwhile enough to find fulfillment previously unavailable to her weakened, shame-ridden, "always looking up to the others" self.

The *contents* of the strengthened sector—the intense longings for her idealized father to recognize and affirm (mirror) *her*, and her intense devotion to his work (the substitute for him)—were established as part of herself, starting at age 12 and continuing on. That is, after the traumatic deception she blamed on her mother, the last straw for the unmirrored childhood self, she turned to "Papa" as an alternative source of the mirroring confirmation (a new relational context, as Fosshage puts it) that she failed to find from either her mother or her siblings. However, the affective coloring of these earlier established *contents* (her immersion in psychoanalysis) and their suffusion with a *subjective glow of worthwhileness* did not accompany the idealization of her father—he and his colleagues remained "way up" while her self-esteem remained way down. The infusion of these contents with the *subjective glow of worthwhileness*, dependent on the partnership established between the two women, made these contents usable, made them into a functional path for self-realization. Lacking the glow of worthwhileness, Anna Freud's analytic endeavors left her unfulfilled and unwanted for herself, of use to others and of no use to herself. (Anna Freud and Dorothy Burlingham lived out a shared commitment to psychoanalysis in many different aspects of their original work, together and in their respective contributions. It could be said that their contributions to the field were suffused with the increased self-investment that each of them experienced in connection with their bond.)

The main point I am making in connection with the twinship I used as an example is this: an alternative or compensatory pathway is established, in some instances at least, when aspects of earlier self-organizations are drawn on, while at the same time some of the most problematic features of these earlier organizations (in Anna Freud's case, extreme shame propensity, depression, and defensive use of fantasy and sexuality) are buffered and bypassed. Whether the self is reestablished via primary or secondary structures cannot be decisively established apart from the clinical evidence provided by individual analyses and the specific transferences that are established.

Finally, I want to at least mention a critical issue that can only be assessed clinically in connection with the selfobject transferences patients establish. The issue can be illustrated in connection with Anna Freud and Mr. Z (Kohut's first attempt to articulate the idea of firmly establishing a weakened self sector while bypassing the more "primary" one). In all likelihood, the mirroring Anna Freud experienced in a twinship bond was not comparable in either depth or intensity to the mirroring that the originally healthy child sought in the self—selfobject experiences in her family (with mother, father, and siblings), nor did it compare to the intensity of the fantasies she began to construct in an attempt to save and heal herself. I believe that the same issue can be seen in Mr. Z—the establishment of an idealizable father transference in the second analysis with Kohut was sufficient to effect a significant reorganization and consolidation of a path to greater self-cohesion and vitalization than previously. However, the intensity of his thwarted mirroring needs, stemming from the original experiences with his mother and father, was essentially bypassed as he turned away from the faceless (nonmirroring) mother to the revived image of the less intensely invested father. Mr. Z was able to work with more zest, and he made a solid enough marriage with a solid enough woman. However, Kohut's account of Mr. Z's cure via compensatory structure suggests that his relationship to his work and to his wife was solidifying rather than passionate and vitalizing!

The type of transference and the type of cure, by way of primary structures that fully revitalize the self or compensatory structures that revive the self just enough, depends largely on what the patient makes of the new edition of self—selfobject experience: in some instances, the selfobject transferences revive original (primary, if you will), in-depth strivings for the mode of selfobject experiences that were rebuffed. However, in many instances primary tendencies that were sufficiently weakened, along with defenses to protect the self from these, do not enter into viable transferences. In this case, the idea of compensatory structure is a radical theoretical and clinical departure that makes possible a solid enough form of cure.

Chapter 4

Listening/ Experiencing Perspectives and the Quest for a Facilitating Responsiveness

James L. Fosshage

Owing to the ongoing paradigmatic shift from positivistic to relativistic science and, now for many, to hermeneutics, we view the psychoanalytic encounter, today, as consisting of two participants, with their respective subjectivities and perspectives, interactively influencing each other in their experience of themselves and of the other. We now describe the analytic relationship as an intersubjective field (Stolorow, Brandchaft, and Atwood, 1987), a relational field (Greenberg and Mitchell, 1983; Mitchell, 1988), a mutual influence system (Sander, 1977, 1985; Beebe, Jaffe, and Lachmann, 1992), or, more recently, a dynamic, dyadic, intersubjective system (Stolorow, 1995).

To view the analytic relationship as a complex interactive system (Fosshage, 1995a) requires a far-reaching reconceptualization of the analyst's activities of listening and responding. No longer is the analyst seen as an objective listener, but as a subjectively organizing perceiver of events. No longer is the analyst seen as a removed nonparticipant, but as an interactively influencing participant. No longer is the analyst seen

This paper served as the center of focus for Panel III at the 18th Annual Conference on the Psychology of the Self, San Francisco, October 22, 1995. Morton Shane was the Chair; Howard Bacal and Paul Ornstein were the discussants.

as a mere observer of transference, but as a variable co-determiner of transference. No longer is the analyst seen as anonymous, but as a perceived and palpable presence. No longer is the analyst seen as striving to be abstinent, but as attempting to be facilitatively engaged and responsive. No longer is the analyst seen as solely an interpreter, but as a responsive person who interprets. No longer is the analyst seen as totally neutral, but as intricately involved in attempting to help the patient.

In an effort to contribute to this ongoing reconceptualization, I wish to: (1) delineate two listening/experiencing stances and their use in facilitating analytic work; (2) briefly address the expanded range of the analyst's responses and the striving for facilitating responsiveness; and (3) examine the distinction between "selfobject relatedness" and "intersubjective relatedness" and its relationship to the two listening perspectives, as a guideline for an analyst's responsiveness.

I will begin my discussion of listening perspectives and the quest for facilitating responsiveness with a clinical vignette. J was a highly articulate, good-looking man in his mid-forties who had recently suffered a mild heart attack. The heart attack precipitated his seeking psychoanalytic treatment, for it had brought into bold relief his dissatisfaction with himself and his life, specifically that he was not living at an emotionally deep level. He described how he often felt as if he were performing and not fully present. There were those rare moments of freedom, primarily on treks away from New York, when he felt more fully himself. He had never married, and the heart attack intensified his desires for an intimate relationship and a family. He had dated one woman on and off for the past 6 years but could not bring himself to marry her because the relationship seemed lifeless. He kept searching for the perfect woman with whom he could sustain a passionate engagement. Similarly, while successful in a variety of career pursuits, he often found himself, after the initial excitement of a new career endeavor, becoming bored in what felt like monotonous work. He envied those who were able to sustain a meaningful involvement in their work.

J's parents, coming from an aristocratic European background, worked tirelessly in the father's professional business in New York City. Apart from his father's frightening violent rages, primarily aimed toward J's older siblings, especially his brother, the atmosphere was formal and unemotional, even "deadly." The sterility of the home environment was sharply etched in a model scene (Lichtenberg, Lachmann, and Fosshage, 1992) where J, as a boy, set up a fix-it shop in the doorway to his bedroom and waited longingly for hours for someone in his family to stop by and use it. Even in his attempt to connect through work, which had premium value in his family, he failed to elicit the recognition and sense of importance he so desired.

The issue I wish to focus on is that J articulated with considerable urgency his search for lasting vitalizing involvement with a woman and his work. He often repeated this theme, conveying a sense that he was determined, yet totally stymied and frustrated, as to how to bring it about. I was aware of feeling moved by his impassioned expressions to feel more vitally alive and, on those occasions, found myself deeply engaged and speaking with a heightened intensity as well, spontaneously matching his affect level. In light of this, it took me initially by surprise when J first complained of my lack of emotion. He felt that I was too laid back, not passionate enough, and not really caring. As I reflected on the origins of J's experience, I thought that on occasion my moments of fatigue or laid back self-states could easily have contributed to his perception. I was also aware that, at certain times, J's routinized discussions and difficulty in being in touch with and expressive of affective experience had a deadening effect on me, a scenario that we gradually unraveled. I remained convinced, however, of my own intense emotional expressions to J that he seemed to miss and wondered about what the discrepancy in our subjective experiences meant.

While we were able to use, to a limited extent, the discrepancy in our subjective experiences (Wolf, 1988; Fosshage, 1994) to further explore the origins of J's experience, we noted, with far greater effectiveness, the discrepancy between *his* more frequent experience of me as emotionally "dead" with *his* occasional experience of me as passionate. We used this discrepancy in his experience of me to gradually identify his proneness to experience me as indifferent and "lifeless" based on a thematic experience with his parents. More specifically, it became clear that J wanted to impact me, wanted to feel that I cared. Yet his lacking just this sort of selfobject experience appeared to make it difficult for him to experience me in this manner and, on those occasions when he did, to be able to "hold onto" the experiences, for they seemed to drift into oblivion. Based on his lived experience and subsequent expectations of the affectless, noncaring other, he was, I believe, often unable to register expressions of my emotional involvement with him. And, in anticipating deadness, he often affectively shut down, which, in turn, contributed to a "deadening" of me. While we identified his experience of me as "emotionless" to be thematic by noting its frequent occurrence in other relationships, as well as its familial genesis, his contribution to his experience of me as lifeless could not be meaningfully addressed until he had an alternative experience of me. In order for us to create that needed alternative experience, I had to be sufficiently emotionally expressive so that J could feel that I was meaningfully engaged with him, that he could impact me, and that he mattered. To talk about this did not suffice; words without sufficient affective expression were too pale and neither registered nor mattered.

To provide the requisite affective responsiveness cannot be considered simply a matter of technique. It involved, as Kohut (1977) suggested, an empathic resonance with J's feelings and strivings. Out of this empathic resonance I spoke with more intense affect, and J was able more often to experience me as alive, caring and emotionally engaged with him. While my affective responsiveness perhaps communicated understanding of his plight, it, in my view, provided (using John Lindon's term, 1994) a specific needed responsiveness that enabled us to create together needed relational selfobject experience.[1]

Yet this new vitalizing experience was not sufficient, for J could not sustain a memory of these new experiences without establishing new memory categories (that is, new organizing patterns).[2] To facilitate the establishment of new categories of experience, we noted the contrast between these new experiences and his "older" thematic expectations. I also attempted to help J gain and maintain a perspective on his patterned view of the other as lifeless through closely tracking his experience, specifically what followed ongoing selfobject experience and what precipitated ruptures.[3] We discovered that the older and more firmly rooted view of the lifeless other, offering a cohesive sense of familiarity, easily reemerged and usurped psychic space, diminishing his hope for needed responsiveness. Another route to his feeling lifeless, we discovered, focused on J's protective retreat from experiencing and expressing his feelings for fear of the retaliatory "father," for fear that he would be hurtful (like father), and for fear that his feelings would not be responded to (dread of the repetition of the past, Ornstein, 1974).

With this illustration in mind, I offer a synopsis of what I believe were the facilitative treatment features. The analysis of the transference and the analyst's sufficient responsiveness to selfobject needs combined to create needed self-enhancing relational experiences. These needed

---

[1] I use the term *relational selfobject experience* to refer to vitalizing attachment experiences. Kohut's mirroring, idealizing, and twinship selfobject experiences all occur within the attachment arena. Lichtenberg et al. (1992) posit that selfobject experience can occur in any one of our proposed five motivational arenas. For example, cognitive mastery can be a vitalizing (selfobject) experience. See later discussion for further explication.

[2] The psychoanalytic concept of organizing patterns, originally borrowed from Piaget's work on cognitive schemas, gains further validation in its correspondence with procedural memories in cognitive psychology and with neural memory networks in neurophysiology.

[3] The "patterned view of the other" is frequently viewed as J's projection of his "lifelessness" onto the other, thereby overlooking his schemas of the other. Both his view of the other as lifeless and his own lifelessness had to be addressed in the analysis.

experiences, in turn, gradually led to expectations of responsivity and to the establishment of new and more vitalizing percepts of self, other, and self-with-other. More specifically, the analysis of the transference involved two central parts. First, we were able to identify and interpret through *empathic inquiry* the repetitive organizing pattern of the "lifeless" and deadened other. Through my "deadened" experience as the other, using the *other-centered listening stance* (to be delineated), we were able to observe (interpret) the impact of this organizing pattern on his relationships. Second, through empathic inquiry, we were able to create an analytic ambiance (Wolf, 1988) of safety, acknowledgment, and understanding that facilitated his expression of his determined search for the developmentally requisite mirroring selfobject experience. In response to these relational selfobject needs, I became, through affect resonance and role responsiveness (Sandler, 1976; Lichtenberg et al., 1992), more emotionally expressive and affirming to enable us to create together the needed selfobject experience. In other words, my interpretation (understanding and explaining) of the transference served both to expand awareness and to provide interactionally a needed mirroring response. Additional responsiveness to J's striving for needed mirroring selfobject experience, however, was required.[4] And now to our theoretical topic at hand.

THE ANALYST'S LISTENING/EXPERIENCING PERSPECTIVES

Freud (1911–1915) described that the analyst needs to listen to an analysand with an "evenly hovering attention," which, in Anna Freud's (1936) words, is "equidistant from id, ego and superego." The task was to hear "objectively" and "neutrally" the latent content embedded in an analysand's associations. Epistemologically framed within the positivistic science of the day, the analyst was viewed as an objective observer, able to decipher the true unconscious meanings of the analysand's articulations.

Relativistic science subsequently clarified that (1) an analyst's observations are shaped not only by the patient, but also by the analyst, and (2)

---

[4] Several reviewers of this paper suggested that the focus on needed responsiveness, rather than on interpretation, renders the process to be no longer psychoanalytic. The reviewers' comments, I believe, emanate from a combination of an intrapsychic emphasis (that is, insight) in understanding therapeutic action and an "objectivist" position in which interpretation is viewed neither as a particular type of responsiveness nor as an inherent ingredient of the analytic interaction. In contrast, I view that interpretation is one very important ingredient of a facilitating responsiveness.

there are two perspectives in the analytic arena, neither of which is "objective." In response to this shift, Kohut (1959), updating psychoanalytic epistemology, formulated and recommended the consistent use of what he called the empathic mode of observation. When using the empathic mode, the analyst's task is to hear and to understand the analysand's experience from within the analysand's perspective, recognizing that the analyst still shapes, more or less, what is heard. While all analysts variably use the empathic mode of perception, self psychologists, following Kohut, stipulate that we need to listen consistently from within the patient's perspective.

All psychoanalysts aim to understand the patient's subjective experience. The use of the empathic mode of perception is primary in that pursuit, yet questions emerge. How do analysts *experientially* listen? Are there other viable ways of gathering data in the psychoanalytic enterprise? And on the basis of what listening stance or stances do we inquire and explore?

I have previously proposed that analysts can shift experientially between two principal listening vantage points (Fosshage, 1995b).[5] An analyst can resonate with the patient's affect and experience from within the patient's vantage point, the *empathic mode of perception* (what I also call the subject-centered listening perspective)—self psychology's emphasis. An analyst can also experience the patient from the vantage point of the other person (in this case, the analyst) in a relationship with the patient, what I call the *other-centered listening perspective* (also referred to as "as-the-other" listening stance), frequently an emphasis in object relations and interpersonal approaches. While both listening/ experiencing modes are variably shaped by the analyst's subjectivity (including the analyst's theories), the other-centered mode, frequently being less near to the patient's immediate experience, potentially lends itself to more idiosyncratic shaping by the analyst. When an analyst inquires as to a patient's feeling about a transaction that occurred in the analysis, the analyst is attempting to hear the patient's perspective, the empathic or subject-centered mode. When we view patients, for example, as seductive, controlling, humorous, or sensitive (or Anna Ornstein's, 1984, description, at the same conference, of her patient's "feel-sorry-for-me posture"), we are listening and experiencing the patient as the other in a relationship with the patient, the other-centered perspective. When we listen, for example, to so-called extra-analytic

---

[5] Lichtenberg (1984) delineated three different listening stances: the outside observer, an interested companion, and a listener within. I believe that the first two stances entail the use of a combination of the two principal listening perspectives proposed here (see Fosshage, 1995b, p. 382).

situations, we make assessments not in an "objective" fashion, but through oscillating from the within and as-the-other perspectives with both the patient and the other person to decipher what is occurring.

I have proposed that in psychoanalysis the empathic and other-centered stances are the two principal methods of listening to our analysands' experiences and that important data are gathered through each listening stance. While it is primary and crucial to understand from within the patient's perspective, listening as the other in a relationship with the patient (keeping in mind our variable shaping of our experience) adds important data to understand how the patient tends to construct relationships. *While we cannot safely infer motivation on the basis of the effects on others, the effects on others can inform us about relational scenarios.* In oscillating between these two listening/experiencing perspectives, an analyst can learn more about the patient's self and self-with-other experience. With J, for example, I learned about his fear and experience of deadness in relationships through *empathic inquiry.* I learned through my experience *as the other* in a relationship with J about how J, through his aversiveness to affect, currently contributed to the deadness of the other that he readily experienced in his relationships. The data gathered through each listening/experiencing stance were used interpretively to provide a more comprehensive understanding of J and his relationships.

When self needs are in the foreground, the empathic mode in its singular focus on a patient's self-experience is facilitative of self-cohesion. When a patient shifts to self-with-other concerns, listening and experiencing as the other in a relationship with the patient—the other-centered perspective—can provide needed information about a patient's relational experience. This other-centered information involves how a patient contributes to his relational experience, not only through his organization of experience, but also through his impact on others. While a patient who primarily needs a mirroring experience can easily be thrown into self-disequilibrium by the intrusion of the analyst's remarks based on the other-centered perspective, to remain exclusively in the empathic mode of listening can result in depriving a patient of information needed to understand his relational experience.

THE ANALYST'S RESPONSES

Apart from exploratory questions, Freud designated interpretations to be the principal form of intervention, for the aim of interpretation is to bring about insight, the principal change agent within the classical model. In contrast, Ferenczi began a long lineage, developed in British object relations and here in the various relational approaches, of emphasizing the relational experience as being central to the therapeutic action in psychoanalysis (Friedman, 1978; Gill, 1994). From an interactive systems perspective, a patient's relational experience more comprehensively encompasses the complexity of the interaction within the analytic situation and includes, but is not limited to, the expansion of awareness or insight. Emphasis on a patient's relational experience that is co-created by patient and analyst, in turn, opens the door to recognizing the broad range of analysts' responses. Let us follow the development within self psychology.

True to his classical roots, Kohut viewed interpretation as the principal form of intervention. In the 1970s and 1980s Kohut and many self psychologists recommended that we interpret selfobject needs, not "gratify" them (see Goldberg, 1978). As a legacy of classical theory, this dichotomy between "gratifying" (i.e., responding to) or interpreting selfobject needs (i.e., to understand and explain the patient's selfobject needs) was created, and interpretation became, for a number of years, in self psychology the singular acceptable analytic intervention. Ironically, interpretation, in this formulation, still carried remnants of positivistic purity. Viewing interpretation as "objective" obfuscated that it was a response of the analyst (Gill, 1994; Namnum, 1976) that could "gratify" selfobject needs (Bacal, 1985; Terman, 1988; Fosshage, 1995a).

Yet Kohut, in concurrence with Ferenczi (1932), Alexander (1956), Fairbairn (1958), Winnicott (1965), Balint (1968), and Guntrip (1968) among the most notable, recognized that interpretation alone is insufficient. An analyst cannot be a computer, using Kohut's language (1977), but must be engaged at the deeper levels of his or her personality. An analyst must be sufficiently responsive (akin to Winnicott's, 1965, notions of a "good enough mother" and of a "facilitating environment") to enable the analysand to make use of the analyst for developmental and regulatory purposes. A patient, for example, may need his analyst to be sufficiently affirming to establish a positive sense of self. Kohut (1977) called this modulated responsiveness the "average expectable empathic responsiveness" (pp. 252–261) or, more simply, "empathic responsiveness." By empathic responsiveness, he was referring to an analyst's human warmth and emotional responsiveness emanating from a deep involvement in working analytically from an empathic perspective.

Kohut never deviated from the importance of interpretative work, yet, when considering therapeutic action, the center of gravity gradually shifted away from insight, the product of interpretation, to self-development occurring within the "self-selfobject" matrix of the analytic relationship. Kohut (1984), in his last book, suggested that change does not take place in the cognitive sphere per se, but occurs principally through the emergence of selfobject needs in the transference and the reparation through interpretation of the inevitable and optimally frustrating selfobject ruptures. While reparation of selfobject ruptures was the principal route to self-development, he also included (although mentioning it only once in his last book) ongoing selfobject experience within the analytic relationship as structure producing. To use Kohut's (1984) words, "[the analyst's] on the whole adequately maintained understanding leads to the patient's increasing realization that, contrary to his experiences in childhood, the sustaining echo of empathic resonance is indeed available in this world" (p. 78). In the following paragraph, Kohut responded to the anticipated "ill-disposed critic" of calling this process a "corrective emotional experience" with an unabashed acceptance, "So be it" (p. 78).

It is this internalization of the ongoing selfobject tie that Marian Tolpin (1983) and this repetitive "experience of the analyst-as-understanding" that Terman (1988) subsequently emphasized as structure building. And emerging out of infant research, Beebe and Lachmann (1994) conclude that the most salient avenue of structure building observed in the infant–caregiver dyad is that of ongoing regulations, that is, the characteristic patterns of regulatory interactions. Thus, from Kohut's emphasis on rupture, optimal frustration, and repair, our model of analytic change is shifting to an emphasis and focus on the patterns of regulatory interactions, of which rupture and repair is only one, and not necessarily the most important, that occurs in the analytic relationship. Examples of regulatory interactions (in this instance, regulatory for the patient) that, through their consistency, typically (depending on their meaning to a patient) facilitate analysis and a patient's development include (1) the implicit affirmation inherent in an analyst's concentrated listening and interest in a patient's experience, (2) the patient's self-empowering experience of impacting the analyst, (3) the calm and safe ambiance of an analytic relationship, (4) the mutual self-reflection, (5) the validation of a patient's experience, (6) the experience of the analyst-as-understanding, (7) the analyst's interpreting that expands awareness, (8) the patient's efficacy experience of change, and (9) the analyst's efforts to help the patient by offering a fundamental underpinning of emotional support.

While sustained empathic understanding and explanation was primary for Kohut's theory of therapeutic action, his reference to the ongoing selfobject experience within the analytic relationship as having curative value opened the door in our theory of technique to include a broad range of interventions (Bacal and Newman, 1990; Fosshage, 1991) that facilitate selfobject experience. For example, Kohut conceived of a developmental line of empathy in which the analyst's response needs to be attuned to the patient's varying and progressive capacity for experiencing empathy, from the need for physical touch to experience a holding environment, to the capacity to use words metaphorically to create the same environment. Thus, physical touch, judiciously used, might be required to provide the necessary empathic connection. In Kohut's (1981) last address, he described a now well-known case of offering his two fingers to be held by his deeply depressed patient to create the needed selfobject experience. While Kohut posits a line of development for empathy, the range of responses required for empathic contact at any given moment, in my judgement, can vary considerably for each individual, depending on stressors and variable self-states.

These theoretical shifts, namely, (1) extricating ourselves from classical theory and the notion of gratification as encumbering, (2) recognizing that analytic cure does not occur solely in the cognitive sphere (i.e., the meaning and power of insight is anchored within the analytic relationship), and (3) increasingly emphasizing the curative importance of needed relational selfobject experience, have gradually broadened the view of the analyst's activity beyond the bounds of exploration and interpretation. These shifts have enabled us to recognize the analyst's complex involvement in the analytic relationship. These movements within self psychology have reciprocally influenced and been influenced by developments within relational approaches to psychoanalysis at large (Greenberg and Mitchell, 1983; Mitchell, 1988; Skolnick and Warshaw, 1992; Fosshage, 1992, 1995a).

A new term was needed that would better capture and help us to conceptualize the broad range of the analyst's activity, specifically the analyst's responsiveness that facilitates self-development. In keeping with Kohut's terminology, Anna and Paul Ornstein (1984) use the term *empathic responsiveness,* which they describe as "when our listening position is taken up in the center of the patient's subjective world . . . and we make the effort to register, accept, understand, explain and communicate the meaning of his thoughts and feelings" (p. 7). In anchoring an analyst's responses solely within the empathic mode, "empathic responsiveness," however, does not highlight those facilitative interventions that are based on the other-centered listening stance. While one could argue that interventions using other-centered data must be anchored within an empathic grasp of the patient to be facilitative, clinically these interventions are emanating from a different listening vantage point, which, in my judgement, cannot be properly housed under the rubric of empathic responsiveness. Moreover, is the description of "understanding, explaining and communicating the meanings of the patient's thoughts and feelings" sufficiently inclusive to adequately explain all of an analyst's facilitative actions that occur in the analytic encounter (a topic that I will address in more detail)? And lastly, as pointed out by Brandchaft (1988), there has also been a tendency, beginning with Kohut, to conflate two usages of the term *empathy*, using it to refer to a listening mode and a particular type of intervention. These two usages have created considerable confusion as to what is meant by *empathy*. (In response to this need for a terminological distinction, Stolorow, 1993, has suggested, more recently, the terms *empathic inquiry* and *affective responsiveness* [similar to P. Tolpin's, 1988, optimal affective engagement] to demarcate an investigatory stance and a type of an analyst's response, respectively. While affective responsiveness specifies a certain kind of response, it is not meant to and cannot be a rubric that houses all interventions.)

To capture the broad range of analysts' responses, Howard Bacal (1985) has provided us with a more inclusive term, optimal responsiveness. As an over-arching rubric, *optimal responsiveness* has subsequently gained considerable currency within self psychology and served as the topic of focus in Morton Shane and Estelle Shane's presentation at the 1994 Self Psychology Conference.

In 1985 Bacal broadly defines optimal responsiveness "as the responsivity of the analyst that is therapeutically most relevant at any particular moment in the context of a particular patient and his illness" (p. 202). Bacal, like the Ornsteins, initially emphasized in his description of optimal responsiveness "the therapist's acts of communicating his understanding to his patient" (p. 202). Yet interpretation, for Bacal, is only one form of communicating understanding to a patient and not necessarily the most therapeutic. Expanding the interactive avenues for communicating understanding, Bacal notes that, frequently, a patient requires some noninterpretive action to feel understood. He (1988) has aptly described this as the patient saying to the analyst, "Be who I need you to be; don't just interpret it."

For example, I recall in a session over 20 years ago that I was making an interpretation and was priding myself over what I thought to be a particularly astute formulation. When I finished, my patient said, "Oh Jim, your words are so soft and comforting, just pour them over me." It was the affective tone of my words, not the content, that carried the day. Unless my patient was defending against, which I did not feel to be the case, the rather remarkable "insight" I thought I was presenting, we could say that I, inadvertently, was able to be in action what my patient needed—probably intuitively regulating my vocal tonality in keeping with her need for soothing and comfort.

When an analyst is who a patient needs him to be, is communication of understanding the basis of therapeutic action? Understanding involves the analyst's interest, acknowledgment, validation, and acceptance of the patient's experience and, on occasion, an explanation that expands awareness. While communication of understanding is central to the analytic process and therapeutic action, it falls short, in my view, in capturing the full range of what patients seek and developmentally need. For J, my more intense engagement and heightened affect may have conveyed my understanding to him about his need for others to be emotionally present. More importantly, however, my actions significantly contributed to a developmentally needed relational experience. While in such instances understanding of the patient may serve as the basis for an analyst's action, understanding is a background feature for both patient and analyst in the action itself. Similarly, when an anxious patient is in need of a calm, protective person, an analyst's calm and soothing attitude conveys more than understanding—in Lindon's (1994) terminology, the analyst's attitude "provides" the responsiveness needed for the patient to self-regulate.

In a similar vein, when an analyst provides an educative response, for example, helping the patient to deal with an eating problem, a sleep irregularity, or a work situation, the analyst's response to be facilitative must be based on an accurate understanding of the patient's immediate needs, capacities, and meanings but is far more than just a communication of understanding. In these instances the communication of understanding is more a background experience; the foreground experience is the direct help and responsiveness to the management of these issues (Frank, 1993; Lichtenberg et al., 1992, 1996).

Perhaps in response to such considerations, Bacal (1990) importantly both broadened and particularized his concept of optimal responsiveness as "the therapist's acts of communicating to his patient in ways that that particular patient experiences as usable for the cohesion, strengthening, and growth of his self" (p. 361). In other words, optimal responsiveness refers to the therapist's responses that facilitate a patient's selfobject experience and, therein, encompasses the Ornsteins' "empathic responsiveness," Paul Tolpin's (1988) "optimal affective engagement," Stolorow et al.'s (1987) "affective responsiveness," Lindon's (1994) "optimal provision," and the Shanes' (1994) "optimal restraint."

For an example, let us consider Kohut's (1984) well-known example of a "confrontative" intervention. In the third year of treatment, his analysand, a psychiatric resident who often drove "like a bat out of hell" (p. 74), was describing with anger and "a trace of challenging arrogance" his having received a speeding ticket. After forewarning him that he was going to give him the deepest interpretation yet, Kohut said firmly: "You are a complete idiot" (p. 74). After a second of silence, "the patient burst into a warm and friendly laughter and relaxed visibly on the couch" (p. 74). Why was this intervention facilitative? You will recall that the patient had been viewed as the genius in his family, causing his father to pull away and form an alliance with the elder brother. Kohut's "confrontation," I believe, provided a needed relational experience wherein Kohut, as a caring father, was not intimidated and avoidant of this man's superior attitude and braggadocio, but was able to take the patient on man-to-man. Perhaps Kohut's comment implicitly conveyed an understanding that the patient needed an involved father, but, more importantly, Kohut, through his comment was, in action, "as the patient needed him to be," in creating a developmentally requisite relational experience.[6]

With optimal responsiveness occurring within a dyadic interactional system, optimal is unique to each dyad and must take into account both patient *and* analyst. While optimal responsiveness captures well those particularly poignant situations when there is, indeed, a singular optimal response, that is, that no other response would do quite as well (Hazel Ipp, personal communication), "optimal," as pointed out at last year's conference by the Shanes (1994), Doctors (1994), and Kindler (1994), implies that there is a best response for each situation. In the majority of encounters, a number of responses could probably be equally facilitative, and even a broader range of responses could be variably facilitative. To suggest that there is one best response potentially places an added burden on the clinician, a burden that could encumber flexibility and spontaneity required in the analytic situation. I therefore propose the term *facilitative responsiveness* (borrowing from Winnicott's "facilitating environment"), which would include those special situations requiring a particular optimal response.[7]

What is it that we wish to facilitate in treatment? Bacal's (1990) answer is anchored in self psychology in that a response is optimal if the patient experiences it "as usable for the cohesion, strengthening and growth of his self" (p. 361). While I concur with this general goal, Lichtenberg et al. (1992) have recently posited a further specification of psychoanalytic goals.

We have conceptualized three fundamental goals for analytic treatment: a shared expansion of awareness, self-righting, and symbolic

---

[6] Bacal (1995) independently arrived at a very similar conclusion (p. 358).

[7] While optimal responsiveness addresses the broad range of the analyst's responses that occur in the analytic arena, the term has been criticized for underplaying initiative and for implying a one-way influence model. While the points are well taken from today's systems perspective, responsiveness does take into account the asymmetry of the analytic relationship in which the patient often takes the lead in action and focus. Perhaps a facilitating interaction more closely captures the complexity of a dyadic system. Regardless, we view the analytic system today as a complex interaction that involves far more than interpretation.

reorganization. The processes inherent in each goal are all interrelated. In psychoanalytic treatment we seek an expansion of awareness (through, for example, exploration and interpretation) that, in turn, gradually enables symbolic reorganization (that is, the establishment of new organizing patterns) that, in turn, facilitates self-righting (that is, regaining self-equilibrium or getting back on course developmentally). These processes may work in reverse order as well; namely, regaining self-equilibrium (perhaps through an analyst's implicit affirmation) can expand awareness—for example, of one's needs, expectations, and past experience—and incrementally add to symbolic reorganization. Thus, an analyst's response is facilitative if it contributes to these goals and there is a wide range of how facilitative a response might be.

NEEDS AND RELATEDNESS INVOLVING SELF, SELF-WITH-OTHER, AND OTHER

While self psychology has focused principally on selfobject needs, that is, the use of the other for self-regulatory purposes, the selfobject dimension of relatedness is only one dimension of relatedness (Stolorow, 1986; Shane and Shane, 1994). More recently, based on Stern's (1985) infant research and emanating from Winnicott's work (1965, 1971), there has been an emergent emphasis, both within and outside of self psychology, on the patient's need to relate to a separate other and to experience the other's subjectivity, what has been referred to as intersubjective relatedness (Benjamin, 1988; Aron, 1991; Hoffman, 1992; Shane and Shane, 1994), subject-to-subject relatedness (Jacobs, in press), or, my term, self-with-other relatedness (Fosshage, 1995b).

Based on Kohut (1984), the Shanes (1994) describe selfobject relatedness as involving the sense of self in relation to a self-regulating other. For example, when a patient is feeling depleted and discouraged, the need for implicitly validating understanding from the other may come to the fore; that is, selfobject relatedness becomes paramount. In describing intersubjective relatedness the Shanes (1994) first quote Stern: "It is an interactive state of 'I know that you know that I know,' and 'I feel that you feel that I feel'" (p. 11). Emde's (1988) description follows, which I sense to be a progressively fuller interest in the other's subjectivity: "I care to know and feel all about us, about you, about me, and about our 'we-ness'" (p. 286). For example, on those occasions when a patient is feeling more solid, he may desire to encounter more fully the analyst's subjectivity.

One day, for example, when an analysand, who was in the field and savvy about these issues, sat down and somewhat humorously, but pointedly, exclaimed: "Jim, I am going to ask you a question. Enough of this empathic shit, I want your opinion!" While I am aware that there are a number of ways of understanding this comment, I believe that she was addressing my proclivity (and, incidentally, hers when she functioned as an analyst) to understand from within her perspective. On this occasion, the patient desired input about herself from me as a person with a different subjectivity and perspective—input to be reflected on and considered. I, thus, gave her my opinion.

While Kohut and self psychologists have focused on empathic immersion, understanding from within the frame of reference of the patient, and its impact on self-consolidation, a number of object relational (e.g., Winnicott, 1971; Modell, 1984), relational (Benjamin, 1988; Aron 1991; Hoffman, 1992), and relational/self psychological (Slavin and Kriegman, 1992; Fosshage, 1995b; Jacobs, in press) psychoanalytic authors have focused on the developmental need of experiencing the analyst as a separate person with a distinct subjectivity. In discussing these issues, Slavin and Kriegman (1992) conclude: "We must, thus, clearly face the fact that an immersion in the patient's subjective world . . . must be complemented, at times, by what is, in effect, the open expression of the analyst's reality" (pp. 252–253).

While the distinction between selfobject and intersubjective relatedness is crucially important and offers considerable heuristic value to the clinician, it is not without conceptual problems that have significant clinical implications and, in my view, requires modification.

When, as an adult, an individual's motivation for attachment gains priority, attachment needs and forms of relatedness, in my view, are best conceptualized as ranging along a continuum involving self needs or concerns (what the Shanes call selfobject relatedness),[8] needs for or concerns about self-with-other (what the Shanes call intersubjective relatedness), and needs to focus on or concerns about the other. For example, in a state of self-fragility, self-concerns and the need for a mirroring or idealized other are in the forefront. In the mid-range of the continuum, when one is feeling more centered, concerns and desires about self-with-other will emerge, along with a mutuality and a different quality of intimacy. And at the other end of the continuum, a more exclusive focus on the concerns and subjectivity of the other has still another quality of relatedness that is more like a parent to a child, a teacher to a student, and a friend to a friend in need and is highlighted in Erikson's (1959) stage of generativity. Yet who the other is and what

---

[8] Self needs, in a broad sense, traverse the whole continuum of needs, concerns, and relatedness. Yet, when I refer to self needs here more narrowly, I am designating when one's sense of self and its regulation are in the forefront of experience and involves, more poignantly, the mirroring, idealizing, and twinship selfobject needs that Kohut delineated.

the other's subjectivity is are important throughout the entire range of self, self-with-other, and other concerns—it is a matter of degree and of focus. On those occasions when we are feeling vulnerable—for example, an important decision is about to be made—and self-concerns are in the foreground, the opinion of the other may be sought out to expand one's awareness (the self-with-other dimension) and to shore up the self (the selfobject dimension). Even when one's self concerns and the need for mirroring are in the forefront, it matters who the other is and what the nature of the other's subjectivity is—for example, how important is he or she to us and does the person like us or not?

Each experience of relatedness will tend to activate expectations and constructions based on lived experience. Thematic selfobject failures leave in their wake not only "deficits," that is, developmental impairments, but also problematic organizing patterns. Deficit theory (as Atwood, Brandchaft, and Stolorow, 1995, delineated at the same conference) tends to obscure our recognition of the formation of pathological structure. Viewing these concerns or forms of relatedness on a continuum and always emergent within an intersubjective matrix positions us clinically, as Stolorow, Brandchaft, and Atwood (1987) have stressed, to remain alert to the problematic organizing patterns that are triggered—a topic to which I will return.

When any of these various attachment needs are met, selfobject experience is generated. While we know well that an adequate response to a needed mirroring experience is vitalizing, to encounter another's subjectivity can also promote a selfobject experience. The so-called antagonistic or adversarial selfobject, as delineated by Wolf (1980) and Lachmann (1986), is, for example, one type of vitalizing experience with an intersubjective other. And generative acts of parenting a child and guiding and helping another can be vitalizing and self-enhancing. Accordingly, to speak of selfobject relatedness does not capture the range of relatedness that can generate selfobject experience.

Part of the problem is related to the term *selfobject needs,* for it is used to refer to the use of the other for self-regulatory purposes. Kohut designated three types of selfobject needs, namely, mirroring, idealizing, and twinship needs. *Selfobject needs* refers solely to those needs that occur in the attachment arena and, in addition, does not directly address needs for "self-with-other" or "other" relatedness. Lichtenberg's (1991) phenomenologically based reconceptualization of selfobject as selfobject experience accounts for an expanded range of experience that can be vitalizing, self-enhancing, and generative of self-cohesion (Lichtenberg et al., 1992). For example, selfobject experience may be generated through a mirroring or self-with-other encounter (in the attachment arena), through successful exploratory/assertive activity, through a sexual experience, through physiological regulation, and so forth. In light of this expanded range of potential selfobject experience, it helps us in our clinical work to be specific about the needs, taking into consideration the whole range of attachment needs and related motivational priorities (Lichtenberg, 1989; Lichtenberg et al., 1992) when designating the type of selfobject experience sought after and generated.

Thus, I propose that, rather than conceptualizing two forms of relatedness, we view relatedness on a continuum, ranging from core self concerns, self-with-other concerns, and concerns about the other. While we could use the terms *selfobject* and *intersubjective relatedness* to demarcate two points on the relatedness continuum, the use of the term *selfobject* is confusing since experience along the entire continuum of relatedness can result in selfobject experience. Moreover, even in selfobject relatedness, there is some intersubjective relatedness. I propose, instead, that we refer to self concerns, self-with-other concerns and concerns with the other—or self, self-with-other, and other relatedness—keeping in mind that these are foreground–background phenomena.

What are the clinical implications of this relatedness continuum? Regardless of where a person's needs or concerns fall on the attachment or relatedness continuum, clinically it is important to address both the concerns and the organizing patterns that are concomitantly triggered. To think in terms of selfobject relatedness, I believe, tends to position us disadvantageously to think of impairment, deficit, and the use of the other solely for self-regulatory functions. It tends to obfuscate the intersubjective dimension and the personhood of the other (Bacal and Newman, 1990). As a consequence, we are less prone to think of the problematic organizing patterns that were established as a result of thematic selfobject failure (Brandchaft and Stolorow, 1990; Brandchaft, 1994; Fosshage, this volume), what Brandchaft (1994) has more recently termed pathological accommodative structures. And, finally, when self-with-other relatedness emerges in the analytic relationship, the use of both listening perspectives will facilitate illuminating organizing patterns and their relational impact and will provide a fuller basis for needed interactive experience.

CLINICAL VIGNETTE

I present the following brief clinical vignette to illustrate the interweaving of selfobject ruptures and problematic organizing patterns, self and self-with-other dimensions of relatedness, and the analyst's use of the two listening perspectives to enhance understanding. Several years ago I had begun psychoanalytic treatment with a woman who was extremely sensitive, perceptive, and reactive. She was quite labile in mood and prone to fragile self-states. Easily feeling impinged upon, she experienced natural light in my office as painfully too bright, for which, at her request, I regularly adjusted the blinds. Both of her parents had been remarkably absent, with her mother often feeling overwhelmed. She had a prolonged incestuous relationship with her older brother and, when she would cry out to her mother for protection, her mother pushed her away with, "Leave me alone, you're killing me." She felt that her life had been saved by her previous analyst, who had been her first real caretaker. His move to another city unfortunately aborted treatment and forced her to find another analyst, a very painful process.

During a session toward the end of the first month that I wish to focus on, I experienced the room as uncomfortably warm and went to the window to adjust the ventilation. At the following session she related how upset she was with me for my getting up in the middle of the session, when she was talking, to stare out the window. Being taken aback by what, to me, was a very idiosyncratic perception and knowing that our capacity to share humor often helped her to regain perspective, I, in a somewhat humorous self-mocking vein, said, "The mark of a good analyst—get up in the middle of a session and stare out the window." In this instance, it was a misjudgment, for she was far too hurt with her particular framing of the event to join in. Instead, she felt invalidated and perhaps even ridiculed. Recapturing my empathic stance, I inquired about her experience when I had gone to the window (what Lichtenberg et al., 1992, call wearing the attributions). She had felt that I was uninterested in what she was saying. I reflected that her feeling that I went to stare out the window while she was talking and was uninterested in her understandably was quite hurtful to her. She appeared to feel better that I had heard, understood, and validated her experience, yet she was still consumed by the injury and her particular organization of the event. Clearly, she needed to be able to free herself from this particular pattern of experiencing the event in order to regain more fully her self-equilibrium. To that end, I inquired toward the end of the session if she would like to hear about my experience as to what prompted my going to the window. Possibly the use of the discrepancy of our experiences, I thought, would be useful in illuminating her view of the uninterested other and offering an alternative perspective. She declined.

In the following session 2 days later, she told me that she had not wanted to hear my point of view at the previous session and somewhat humorously, yet pointedly, remarked, "Jim, when I come into the room, just check your subjectivity at the door." I smiled and told her that I would try my best, although it could prove difficult on occasion. We then proceeded with her experience and were able to focus on how precarious she felt my interest in her was. At one point it dawned on me what was occurring when she felt overwhelmed by my subjectivity, and I interpreted in a gentle manner, "I think I understand that when I do something suddenly, like go to the window, or bring my subjective viewpoint in here, that it feels like I am taking up all the space in here, that there is no room for you, for your thoughts and desires, and I sense that you must have felt just that way with your brother." She notably relaxed and acknowledged that she thought I was right. Shortly afterward, she smiled and said, "Now, you can let me know what was happening for you at the window." I then explained that I was uncomfortably warm, had assumed she was too and did not ask her, thinking that it would be more disruptive, and had adjusted the window to get more air. She smiled and felt reassured.

In light of the rupture and her fragile self-state, she needed me to hear and understand her feelings—self-relatedness was in the forefront. It was also crucially important to make sense out of her experience by illuminating the particular relational scenario or organizing pattern that had been triggered—an aspect of self-with-other relatedness—for her to feel fully understood and to enable her to restore self-equilibrium. So long as she framed the events as indicative of my disinterest in her, she surely would be unable to feel fully restored. My interpretation of the transference in the here and now, and its origins, was based on both listening stances, that is, on my empathic grasp of her experience of me and on my other-centered experience as the intrusive, overwhelming other in relationship with the patient. Following the interpretation, she felt, through a sense of being heard and understood, sufficiently consolidated to be able to relate self-with-other more fully and inquired about my experience. Airing the discrepancies in our experiences further illuminated her particular organization as well as served as a basis for the establishment of an alternative perspective.

CONCLUSION

In conclusion, the emergent contemporary view of the psychoanalytic arena that increasingly is gaining momentum and definition is of two people, patient and analyst, interactionally engaged in pursuit of fostering the patient's development. Patients enter treatment hoping for the requisite developmental experiences. They also enter treatment with problematic expectations based on thematic lived experience. Traditionally, analysis has focused on the repetitive transferences or, what is called from a contemporary perspective, problematic organizing patterns. Self psychology has contributed to our understanding that an analyst must be sufficiently available so that patient and analyst can find a way of creating the necessary developmental experiences. While

52   Fosshage

understanding and explaining the problematic transferential experiences provides one basis for needed experience, patients often require more poignant interactions with analysts to create needed relational selfobject experience. Even the analysis of transference requires experience with the analyst that contrasts with deeply embedded convictions about the nature of reality (that is, patterns of organization) in order to enable their illumination. Accordingly, the range of responses required of an analyst has expanded far beyond the bounds of exploration and interpretation and is more adequately captured by the terms facilitative or optimal responsiveness. I have proposed that the use of both empathic and other-centered listening perspectives enhances understanding of a patient and enables an analyst to relate more flexibly and facilitatively, depending on whether a patient's self, self-with-other, or other concerns have motivational priority. Based on this understanding, an analyst uses a complex and subtle tapestry of verbal and nonverbal responses to facilitate expansion of awareness, psychological reorganization, and self-righting.

REFERENCES

Alexander, F. (1956), *Psychoanalysis and Psychotherapy*. New York: Norton.
Aron, L. (1991), The patient's experience of the analyst's subjectivity. *Psychoanal. Dial.*, 1:29–51.
Bacal, H. (1985), Optimal responsiveness and the therapeutic process. In: *Progress in Self Psychology, Vol. 1*, ed. A. Goldberg. Hillsdale, NJ: The Analytic Press, pp. 202–227.
—— (1988), Reflections on "optimum frustration." In: *Progress in Self Psychology, Vol. 4*, ed. A. Goldberg. Hillsdale, NJ: The Analytic Press, pp. 127–131.
—— (1995), The essence of Kohut's work and progress of self psychology. *Psychoanal. Dial.*, 5:353–366.
—— (1990), The elements of a corrective selfobject experience. *Psychoanal. Inq.*, 10:347–372.
—— & Newman, K. (1990), *Theories of Object Relations*. New York: Columbia University Press.
Balint, M. (1968), *The Basic Fault*. London: Tavistock.
Beebe, B., Jaffe, J. & Lachmann, F. (1992), A dyadic systems view of communication. In: *Relational Perspectives*, ed. N. Skolnick & S. Warshaw. Hillsdale, NJ: The Analytic Press, pp. 61–81.
—— & Lachmann, F. (1994), Representation and internalization in infancy: three principles of salience. *Psychoanal. Psychol.*, 11:127–166.
Benjamin, J. (1988), *The Bonds of Love*. New York: Pantheon Press.
Brandchaft, B. (1988), Critical issues in regard to empathy. Presented at the 11th Annual Conference on the Psychology of the Self, Washington, DC, October 16.
—— (1994), To free the spirit from its cell. In: *The Widening Scope of Self Psychology, Progress in Self Psychology, Vol. 10*, ed. A. Goldberg. Hillsdale, NJ: The Analytic Press, pp. 209–230.

—— & Stolorow, R. (1990), Varieties of therapeutic alliance. *The Annual of Psycho-analysis,* 18:99–114. Hillsdale, NJ: The Analytic Press.

Doctors, S. (1994), Notes on the contribution of the analyst's self-awareness to "optimal responsiveness." Presented at the 17th Annual Conference on the Psychology of the Self, Chicago, IL, October 21.

Emde, R. N. (1988), Development terminable and interminable: 2. Recent psychoanalytic theory and therapeutic considerations. *Internat. J. Psycho-Anal.,* 69:283–296.

Erikson, E. (1959), *Identity and the Life Cycle.* New York: Norton.

Fairbairn, W. R. D. (1958), On the nature and aims of psycho-analytical treatment. *Internat. J. Psycho-Anal.,* 39:374–385.

Ferenczi, S. (1932), *The Clinical Diary of Sandor Ferenczi,* ed. J. Dupont. Cambridge, MA: Harvard University Press, 1988.

Fosshage, J. (1991), Beyond the basic rule. In: *The Evolution of Self Psychology, Progress in Self Psychology, Vol. 7,* ed. A. Goldberg. Hillsdale, NJ: The Analytic Press, pp. 64–71.

—— (1992), Self psychology: The self and its vicissitudes within a relational matrix. In: *Relational Perspectives in Psychoanalysis,* ed., N. Skolnick & S. Warshaw. Hillsdale, NJ: The Analytic Press, pp. 21–42.

—— (1994), Toward reconceptualizing transference: Theoretical and clinical considerations. *Internat. J. Psycho-Anal.,* 75:265–280.

—— (1995a), Interaction in psychoanalysis: A broadening horizon. *Psychoanal. Dial.,* 5:459–478.

—— (1995b), Countertransference as the analyst's experience of the analysand: the influence of listening perspectives. *Psychoanal. Psychol.,* 12:375–391.

Frank, K. A. (1993), Action, insight, and working through: Outlines of an integrative approach. *Psychoanal. Dial.,* 3:535–577.

Freud, A. (1936), *The Ego and the Mechanisms of Defense.* New York: International Universities Press.

Freud, S. (1911–1915), Papers on technique. *Standard Edition,* 12:89–171. London: Hogarth Press, 1953.

Friedman, L. (1978), Trends in psychoanalytic theory of treatment. *Psychoanal. Quart.,* 47:524–567.

Gill, M. (1994), *Psychoanalysis in Transition.* Hillsdale, NJ: The Analytic Press.

Goldberg, A., ed. (1978), *The Psychology of the Self.* New York: International Universities Press.

Greenberg, J. & Mitchell, S. (1983), *Object Relations in Psychoanalytic Theory.* Cambridge, MA: Harvard University Press.

Guntrip, H. (1968), *Schizoid Phenomena, Object Relations and the Self.* London: Hogarth Press.

Hoffman, I. Z. (1992), Soome practical implications of a social-constructivist view of the psychoanalytic situation. *Psychoanal. Dial.,* 2:287–304.

Jacobs, L. (in press), "Subject-subject relating": An example of optimal responsiveness in intersubjectivity theory. In: *Optimal Responsiveness,* ed. H. Bacal. Northvale, NJ: Aronson.

Kindler, A. (1994), Discussion for self psychology conference. Presented at the 17th Annual Conference on the Psychology of the Self, Chicago, IL, October 21.

Kohut, H. (1959), Introspection, empathy, and psychoanalysis. *J. Amer. Psychoanal. Assn.,* 7:459–483.

—— (1977), *The Restoration of the Self.* New York: International Universities Press.

—— (1981), From the transcription of remarks presented by Heinz Kohut at the Conference on Self Psychology, Berkeley, CA, October.

—— (1984), *How Does Analysis Cure?* ed. A. Goldberg & P. Stepansky. Chicago: University of Chicago Press.

Lachmann, F. (1986), Interpretation of psychic conflict and adversarial relationships: A self-psychoanalytic perspective. *Psychoanal. Psychol.,* 3:341–355.

Lichtenberg, J. (1984), The empathic mode of perception and alternative vantage points for psychoanalytic work. In: *Empathy II,* ed. J. Lichtenberg, M. Bornstein & D. Silver. Hillsdale, NJ: The Analytic Press, pp. 113–136.

—— (1989), *Psychoanalysis and Motivation.* Hillsdale, NJ: The Analytic Press.

—— (1991), What is a selfobject? *Psychoanal. Dial.,* 1:455–479.

—— Lachmann, F. & Fosshage, J. (1992), *Self and Motivational Systems.* Hillsdale, NJ: The Analytic Press.

—— —— —— (1996), *The Clinical Exchange.* Hillsdale, NJ: The Analytic Press.

Lindon, J. (1994), Gratification and provision in psychoanalysis: Should we get rid of "the rule of abstinence?" *Psychoanal. Dial.,* 4:549–582.

Mitchell, S. (1988), *Relational Concepts in Psychoanalysis.* New York: Basic Books.

Modell, A. (1984), *Psychoanalysis in a New Context.* New York: International Universities Press.

Namnum, A. (1976), Activity and personal involvement in psychoanalytic technique. *Bull. Menn. Clin.,* 40:105–117.

Ornstein, A. (1974), The dread to repeat and the new beginning. *The Annual of Psychoanalysis,* 2:231–248. Madison, CT: International Universities Press.

—— & Ornstein, P. (1984), Empathy and the therapeutic dialogue. Presented at the Fifth Annual Psychotherapy Symposium on "Psychotherapy: The Therapeutic Dialogue," Harvard University, The Cambridge Hospital, Boston, MA, June 28–30.

Sander, L. (1977), The regulation of exchange in the infant–caretaker system and some aspects of the context-content relationship. In: *Interaction, Conversation, and the Development of Language,* ed. M. Lewis & L. Rosenblum. New York: Wiley, pp. 133–156.

—— (1985), Toward a logic of organization in psycho-biological development. In: *Biologic Response Styles,* ed. K. Klar & L. Siever. Washington, DC: American Psychiatric Press.

Sandler, J. (1976), Countertransference and role-responsiveness. *Internat. Rev. Psycho-Anal.,* 3:43–47.

Shane, M. & Shane, E. (1994), Self psychology in search of the optimal: A consideration of optimal responsiveness, optimal provision, optimal gratification, and optimal restraint in the clinical situation. Presented at the 17th Annual Conference of the Psychology of the Self, Chicago, IL, October 21.

Skolnick, N. & Warshaw, S. (1992), *Relational Perspectives in Psychoanalysis.* Hillsdale, NJ: The Analytic Press.

Slavin, M. & Kriegman, D. (1992), *The Adaptive Design of the Human Psyche.* New York: Guilford.

Stern, D. (1985), *The Interpersonal World of the Infant.* New York: Basic.

Stolorow, R. (1986), On experiencing an object: A multidimensional perspective. In: *Progress in Self Psychology, Vol. 2,* ed. A. Goldberg. New York: Guilford, pp. 273–279.

———— (1993), Thoughts on the nature and therapeutic action of psychoanalytic interpretation. In: *The Widening Scope of Self Psychology, Progress in Self Psychology, Vol. 9,* ed. A. Goldberg. Hillsdale, NJ: The Analytic Press, pp. 31–43.

———— (1995), Dynamic, dyadic, intersubjective systems: An evolving paradigm for psychoanalysis. Presented at the Division 39 spring meeting, Los Angeles.

———— Brandchaft, B. & Atwood, G. (1987), *Psychoanalytic Treatment.* Hillsdale, NJ: The Analytic Press.

Terman, D. (1988), Optimum frustration: Structuralization and the therapeutic process. In: *Learning from Kohut: Progress in Self Psychology, Vol. 4,* ed. A. Goldberg. Hillsdale, NJ: The Analytic Press, pp. 113–125.

Tolpin, M. (1983), Corrective emotional experience: A self psychological reevaluation. In: *The Future of Psychoanalysis,* ed. A. Goldberg. New York: International Universities Press, pp. 363–380.

Tolpin, P. (1988), Optimal affective engagement: The analyst's role in therapy. In: *Learning from Kohut, Progress in Self Psychology, Vol. 4,* ed. A. Goldberg. Hillsdale, NJ: The Analytic Press, pp. 160–168.

Winnicott, D. W. (1965), *The Maturational Processes and the Facilitating Environment.* London: Hogarth Press.

———— (1971), The use of an object and relating through identifications. In: *Playing and Reality.* Harmondsworth, U.K.: Penguin Books, 1974.

Wolf, E. (1980), On the developmental line of selfobject relations. In: *Advances in Self Psychology,* ed. A. Goldberg. New York: International Universities Press, pp. 117–132.

———— (1988), *Treating the Self.* New York: Guilford.

Chapter 5

Optimal Responsiveness and Analytic Listening: Discussion of James L. Fosshage's "Listening/ Experiencing Perspectives and the Quest for a Facilitating Responsiveness"

Howard A. Bacal

In his remarkably rich paper, Fosshage makes several contributions: first, the elaboration of his perspective, which he introduced recently (Fosshage, 1995a) on a dual mode of analytic listening; second, how this mode of listening facilitates the analyst's optimal responsiveness to the patient; third, the enrichment of our appreciation of the theoretical relevance and clinical utility of the optimal responsiveness concept; and fourth, with Lichtenberg and Lachmann, the further elucidation of its goals. Fifth, Fosshage proposes a particular spectrum as a guide to listening that implies a modification of certain guidelines for the analyst's

This discussion of James L. Fosshage's paper was read at the 18th Annual Conference on the Psychology of the Self, San Francisco, October 22, 1995, Panel 3.

optimal responsiveness that were recently offered by Morton and Estelle Shane (1996).

In contrast to the recommendation that has now become second nature to self psychologists, but that was revolutionary when Kohut (1959) first advocated it—namely, that the analyst should consistently maintain an empathic stance—Fosshage proposes that the analyst should instead adopt a *dual* perspective when listening to the analysand. He suggests that the analyst should vary his stance, back and forth, between an empathic vantage point and a position that he calls "other-centered," because this will provide more comprehensive data for understanding the patient. In particular, he has found that when a patient requires a more interactive kind of experience, the use of both listening perspectives is particularly useful in supplying data on which to base responses that will provide this sort of experience for the patient. He illustrates this way of listening with vignettes from his work with his patient, J. I will come back to these two modes of listening and their contribution to the analyst's responsiveness later in my discussion, in connection with a clinical vignette of my own.

Fosshage provides us with an extensive review of psychoanalytic perspectives on the therapeutic process and the analyst's contribution to that process, which includes virtually all the major revisionists of the classical model. Kohut initially articulated a traditionally classical theory about how analysis cures, namely, that psychological structure is constituted by an area of progressive neutralization of infantile impulses, and that it is formed by the introjection of innumerable experiences of optimal, as opposed to traumatic, frustration (Kohut and Seitz, 1963). In parallel, he used optimal frustration as the centerpiece of his self psychological explanation of the curative process when he considered the frustration of selfobject needs to be essential to the acquisition of self-structure (Kohut, 1984).

Kohut (1977) emphasized the transmutation into self-structure of necessary, though manageable and thus, "optimal," micro-frustrations. Wolf (1988, 1993) modified this view and emphasized the importance of the process of restoration of selfobject disruptions, which are ubiquitous, though not necessarily inevitable. Beebe and Lachmann (1988), Beebe, Jaffe, and Lachmann (1992), Fosshage (1992, 1995a, 1995b), Lichtenberg, Lachmann, and Fosshage (1992), Lachmann and Beebe (1992), and Stolorow, Brandchaft, and Atwood (1987) have emphasized the developmental importance and therapeutic centrality of mutual regulatory, or intersubjective, interactions. Similar views on what is central in the therapeutic process have been offered by Paul Tolpin (1988) in his description of "optimal affective engagement" and by Terman (1988) in his "dialogue of construction," where he explicitly argues against the validity of a theory of "optimal frustration." Marian Tolpin (1983) has emphasized the importance of the internalization of the ongoing selfobject tie, which I extended in my concept of a "corrective selfobject experience" (Bacal, 1990, 1995b; Bacal and Newman, 1990). More recently, Lessem and Orange (1993) have advanced the view that the emotional bond that develops as a result of interactions between the patient and the therapist constitutes the major curative determinant in psychoanalytic therapy, a view that is similar to my emphasis on the centrality of the selfobject relationship in the treatment process (Bacal, 1994, 1995b).

I am glad that Fosshage recognizes that Kohut, himself, belongs in his list of revisionists. I believe I am not the only one who doubts that Kohut's optimal frustration theory of analytic cure was Kohut's true theoretical position or the only one who wonders whether this was, toward the end of his life, a reconciliatory gesture to his classical analytic confreres. Indeed, my impression, gained from many discussions with him about the therapeutic process, as well as from my own experience of the way he practiced, was that Heinz personally believed that it was selfobject relational experience, in the context of a responsive ambience, that ultimately helped the patient. In effect, my conceptualization of the analyst's contribution to the therapeutic process as *optimal responsiveness* (Bacal, 1985) derives essentially from the way Kohut worked—not only with others, but also with me.

As many of you know, Kohut was inclined to write in quite long sentences, so one occasionally loses the thread of what he is saying and it is necessary to hunt back to the beginning of the sentence for the verb or for an important participle to properly understand him. Well, he tended to deliver interpretations in the same way, but, since I did not have the written text in front of me when he spoke, I would, not infrequently, lose track of his—sometimes quite complex—messages. This frustration, however, never required transmutation, because, for me, the optimal response was not in his words—it was, as Elliott Markson so aptly puts it, in the "music."[1] The words, so to say, simply carried the tune. The tune he played, over and over, harmonized with what I needed at that time: acceptance and optimism, delivered with warmth and kindness. What he said—and he offered many astute observations and explanations—was of secondary importance. I can barely recall any of it. I do remember, vividly, though, what he said once (probably more

---

[1] Markson (personal communication) was referring not only to the therapeutic quality of Kohut's communications, but to the quality of the therapeutic communications that any analyst's verbal communications may embody, which may transcend the meaning of the words themselves.

than once) during a particularly gloomy period when I was recounting one dismal experience after another, in response to which he would, for the most part, simply listen quietly and receptively. He said, quite seriously—and to me, at first, quite unbelievably—at the end of one of *my* long sentences, "Well, perhaps we can find something good, even in this!" In effect, this theme and variation constituted the essence of what he conveyed to me over some considerable period of time.

Although I was not conscious of it then, I was also learning from Kohut what the analyst's contribution to the therapeutic process should be. I was, in effect, learning about *optimal responsiveness.* I remember something else, too, which I would like to share with you. I recall the time when, just as I was sadly leaving Heinz's office at the end of a weekend—during which I had had three analytic sessions and was returning to Canada, not to see him again for another fortnight—he put his arm around my shoulder and gave me an encouraging, affectionate hug. This was, for me, the provision, as Lindon (1994) would say, of an experience that facilitated, as Fosshage would say, the progress of my treatment—and my life. That Kohut knew that this was what I needed and that he did this, rather than interpret the need for something like this, was another instance of Kohut's *optimal responsiveness.* In retrospect, I can now articulate, some 18 years after it happened, that it had specific and profound meaning for me—the offer of a shielding, fatherly presence—but at that time, I was not consciously aware of this interpretation, nor did I need to be. As Jim Fosshage puts it and to which he so vividly gives chapter and verse in his paper, "While communication of understanding is central to the analytic process and therapeutic action, it falls short . . . in capturing the full range of what patients seek and developmentally need and the complexity of the interaction that occurs within the psychoanalytic arena." Kohut ingeniously captured the essence of what this experience is when he coined that wonderful, but impossible, term *selfobject.*

I have suggested (Bacal, 1990) that the responses of the analyst that are optimal are those that facilitate a therapeutic selfobject experience, a view with which Fosshage would appear to agree.

Here is a summary of my most recent formulation of *optimal responsiveness,* which will be elaborated in a forthcoming book on the subject (Bacal, in press b) that will include chapters by a number of our colleagues.

The principle of optimal responsiveness conceptualizes the analyst's contribution to the therapeutic experience of the patient. As an encompassing principle that informs the therapist's work, the term *optimal responsiveness* is meant to have both theoretical and clinical significance.

Theoretically, it provides an alternative explanation for therapeutic effect to the optimal frustration/transmuting internalization hypothesis. That hypothesis states that the firming up or accretion of psychological structure results from the internalization—in effect, the taking over—of the analyst's functions when the patient experiences manageable, micro-frustrations of his or her selfobject needs. *Optimal responsiveness, in contrast, implies that it is the patient's selfobject experience in the context of a relationship with the analyst that is therapeutic, regardless of whether this experience occurs in the absence of disruption or in the process of restoration of the connection with the analyst that has been disrupted through the frustration of selfobject experience.* With his encouraging gesture, Kohut responded to his analysand's wordless appeal to lessen the impact of the traumatic experiences that he would once more have to face alone on another long break by protectively closing the painful distance between them, between the father and the son. Later, however, the optimal response consequent upon the occurrence of the traumatic experiences during the actual break, which were sometimes associated with a disruption of the selfobject bond between analysand and analyst, was interpretive understanding.

In my view, optimal responsiveness more accurately describes the analyst's therapeutic function than either optimal frustration or optimal gratification, both of which, I submit, are irrelevant, either as theoretical concepts or as practical guidelines, to psychoanalytic treatment. Optimal responsiveness asserts that, while the therapeutic function of the analyst may include frustration or gratification or so-called "neutrality," none of these are intrinsic to it.

Optimal responsiveness—both as a theoretical concept and as a clinical principle—centrally includes the view that the analyst's therapeutic function often constitutes much more—and sometimes much less—than what our theories and some of our teachers have told us it does. In other words, the optimal responsiveness concept accords analytic legitimacy to a broad range of responses that analysts *in fact* offer their patients when they are being therapeutic.

In addition, optimal responsiveness rests upon what I would call *a theory of therapeutic specificity: that the therapeutic process entails the operation of a more-or-less unique,[2] reciprocally active therapeutic system for each analyst–patient couple in which the*

---

[2] Doctors's (1995) view of analyzability, with which I would agree, is relevant here: "From a dyadic systems view . . . each dyad is unique and there are a range of different, successful analyses conceivable for any one person. The question expands beyond 'what the patient needs' or even 'what the analyst is capable of' to the question of 'goodness-of-fit in the dyad.' "

analyst's task is to discover and to provide what is therapeutic for that specific patient for the cohesion, strengthening, and growth of his self. That is, as dearly as we would like to have *general guidelines* about how to conduct therapy, the particularity of individual need, as well as the complexity of the dyadic therapeutic system that attends it—which both Doctors (1995) and Sukharov (1995) have emphasized—all underscore the limitations of generalizing about what is optimal for whom. A theory of therapeutic specificity also implicitly recognizes the deep reservoir of responsiveness within the personal self of the analyst, which analysts draw on when they are therapeutic to their patients.

Optimal responsiveness thus comprises the therapist's acts of communicating to his patient in ways that that particular patient experiences as usable. Therapeutic usability comprises responses that variously include the verbal and the nonverbal. The verbal includes a host of utterances in addition to interpretation, and much of the nonverbal entails what has been variously called the analytic atmosphere by Balint (1968) or the analytic ambience by Wolf (1976).

As John Lindon has vividly illustrated (Lindon, 1994), the analyst's repertoire of therapeutic responsivity can be intelligibly comprehended as a rich variety of provisions. While interpretation is an instance of such provision, it may not be as pervasively crucial as we would like to believe it is, and it may or may not be the predominant mode in which a particular analysand experiences his or her analyst to be helpful. The same may be said for empathy, an observation that Richard Tuch (1995) has also recently made. Everything the analyst says or does not say, does or does not do, is experienced as some kind of response by the patient. The term *empathy* is used in self psychology to denote both a mode of observation, as well as the provision of a certain kind of responsiveness by the analyst. Optimal responsiveness (which, because it implies specificity of responsivity embodies the notion of "optimal restraint" developed by Morton and Estelle Shane, 1996), may therefore *entail* the provision of empathy, interpretation, quiet acceptance, restraint, or forthright confrontation, and so on, but it is not, a priori, synonymous with any of them.

I would like to offer a caution about delineating goals or criteria for improvement for our patients. Fosshage quotes my stating that a response is optimal if the patient experiences it "as usable for the cohesion, strengthening and growth of his self." I stand by this, yet it should be recognized for what it is—a kind of metapsychological statement reflecting a general self-psychological understanding of what constitutes psychological health, as are the goals of "shared expansion of awareness, self-righting, and symbolic reorganization." I learned long ago, while I was involved, for many years, in doing outcome research in psychotherapy, that any generalizations, however relevant they may appear to be as criteria for assessing psychological improvement, must take second place to the *specifying* of dynamic criteria that are applicable to the *particular* patient and his illness (Malan et al., 1968). Although we are not at the stage when we can, with any confidence, predict the results of any particular intervention, we are, I think, as psychoanalysts, obliged to subordinate our generalizations about psychological health to the delineation of what is relevant for the *particular* patient's psychological organization in *that* patient's psychological life.

It is true, of course, what Fosshage suggests, that there is no one-only response that will be useful for the patient. But this observation does not vitiate the appropriateness of searching for what may be most helpful to the patient at that moment. This should not be a burden, not something that we need fear. It may sometimes be a challenging task, but it is almost always a vitalizing one, whose pursuit is fully consonant with the exercise of flexibility and spontaneity. When we discover what the optimal response might have been, as a result of putting our foot in it, as we all do, from time to time, the intersubjective analysis of what went wrong will now constitute what is optimal and will be as valuable as the experiences of the patient when the analyst's responses felt just right. This was the case in the example of Fosshage's work with the patient after he inadvertently caused a self-disruption by going to the window to adjust the ventilation and precipitated another one by referring humorously to something that he and the patient had understood previously together. It was also the case in the example I gave (above) in the interaction between Kohut and myself after the 2-week break had occurred. It is important to recognize that, when selfobject disruption occurs, the analyst's attempts *at the moment* to *provide* the selfobject function that was frustrated will usually not be effective; that is, an attempt to right the wrong, then, will usually not work, at anything beyond a superficial level. The responses that will be experienced by the patient as optimal, at that time, comprise the acceptance of the patient's experience as valid—"wearing the attribution," as Lichtenberg, Lachmann, and Fosshage (1992, pp. 191–195) put it—and the attempt to understand what went wrong.

The principle of optimal responsiveness, as I have described it, not only disciplines us to consider carefully what is best for our patients; it also frees us to be more of who we can be[3] in order to help them heal. In effect, the concept is intended to articulate a more comprehensive and accurate description of how good therapists actually work.

---

[3] I am grateful to Sue Mendenhall for drawing this to my attention.

I believe that, when Kohut gave me that encouraging hug prior to the break, he sensed that I needed him to provide me with a specific self-object experience—in effect, to be what I needed—and he was. I do not think he was acting a part, as Alexander advocated. Yet, as Kohut himself would later allow, this was a corrective emotional experience, or, as I would describe it, a *corrective selfobject experience* (Bacal, 1990). I am convinced that he deeply felt what he did and, from what I now know of his life, I have a hunch that when he was doing this for me, he was likely doing the same for himself. In effect, I think we do more of this with our patients than we readily admit. But I do not think we need be ashamed of it. Far from it.

In consideration of this, I would now like to pose a question for Jim Fosshage and for all of us. In order to fully know what I needed at that moment, did Kohut have to shift his listening stance between a concentrated attunement to my subjectivity and what Fosshage calls an "other-centered" listening perspective? Of course, only Heinz could properly answer this question. But consider this. He likely knew something of what I needed by empathically tuning in to the son in me. But did he also need to experience the "other" in the son–father dyad, in order to know that what was needed by the son was that the father would wish to be close and encouraging and protective to his son? I would agree with Fosshage that he did, but that the "other" was Kohut, himself, now the father, not only to me, but also to himself-as-son, at that moment. Thus, what I am adding here is that one of the ways that one can effectively pick up what Fosshage calls the other-centered perspective is to tune in to one's own subjectivity and to use it, carefully, in the service of understanding and responding to our patients. Thus, Fosshage's assertion that "when we speak of optimal responsiveness, we are referring to the analyst's facilitative contribution to an extremely complex dyadic relational system" concurs exactly with my own observations.

A recent Ph.D. thesis on optimal responsiveness and intersubjectivity by Estrella (1993) demonstrates the same complexity. Estrella studied the subjective and intersubjective experiences of psychotherapists that contributed to their optimal responsiveness with their patients. Estrella found that the mutuality of subjective experience between patient an therapist contributed to their attunement and empathic resonance. Seven of the nine psychotherapists in the study effectively "weaved their own [sense of their personal losses . . . into their responses to their patients." Estrella concludes that "the psychotherapist's attunement to his or her own subjective pain, and corresponding resonance to their particular patient's pain, may have contributed significantly to their being optimally responsive." The psychotherapists did not share their feelings of grief and mourning with their patients. Yet the identification, recognition, and emotional awareness of their losses seemed to put them on a highly sensitive level of self-awareness that contributed to their affective attunement towards their patient's traumas and corresponding emotional pain, which they could effectively integrate into their therapeutic interventions with their particular patients.

Finally, I want to say a brief word about Fosshage's suggestion for viewing forms of relatedness (reflecting attachment needs) on a continuum ranging from *self-concerns* through *concerns about self-with-other* to *concerns about the other*. Fosshage offers this spectrum as a lens through which we may see more clearly what the state of the patient's self may be with regard to relatedness. I would suggest, however, that we consider this schema, or spectrum, from another angle. I believe that it is preeminently useful in referring, not to a continuum of the patient's relatedness, but rather, to the patient's *subjective experience of concern on a continuum*, which ranges between self-concern and the other experiential positions of concern: self-with-other and concerns about the other. That is, regardless of whether we believe that all psychological experience is ultimately determined relationally or intersubjectively, the patient's subjectivity may or may not include, at any particular time, the *experience* of relatedness or the need for attachment. In other words, the self may or may not be motivated, in Lichtenberg's sense, or organized, if I may borrow Stolorow's term, in this sense, at the moment. For example, if the patient is organized around self-with-other concerns, the optimal response may usefully take this into consideration. At another time, the analyst may discover that the patient's self-state will best be responded to by respecting the patient's need to show concern for, or to give to, the analyst.[4] If the patient is not organized in these ways at the time but is, rather, organized around concerns for self, responses that include the other may be experienced as intrusive or disruptive. This, of course, has implications for the use of so-called "transference" interpretations.

Fosshage's view is that a dual listening perspective will assist the analyst in knowing where the patient is on this spectrum. I would agree, but, as I stated earlier, I would identify the *other* in this situation as the analyst. Insofar as the analyst is attuned to his own subjectivity as reflecting or resonating with the patient's *other*—as the patient experiences that other, or wishes that other to be—the analyst will hear more

---

[4] An important—sometimes essential—aspect of the patient's selfobject experience may comprise the experience of *providing it to the other*. The experience of giving, as Suttie (1935) has indicated, can be as important to the development of one's emotional health as the experience of receiving. Put in self-psychological terms, the discovery that one can give something valuable to one's analyst can be a vitalizing selfobject experience.

complex sounds about the patient's subjectivity. I believe that the analyst has more than a dual listening perspective. I posit that the analyst's mode of apprehending the patient shifts with his psychical distance from the patient and that these shifts, which are reflected in the analyst's subjectivity, are variously determined by the patient's expectations and by analyst's reactions to them (see Bacal, in press a).

How useful it will be, in practice, to know where the patient is on the Shanes' spectrum or on Fosshage's spectrum or on my modification of his spectrum as a guide to where the *analyst* might best be with the patient is a question that needs to be tested by further clinical work. I would, again, caution against placing too much weight on *any general guideline* for the analyst's optimal responsiveness.

Fosshage, too, appears to recognize that the selfobject needs of a patient may sometimes be surprising; that is, they may not quite fit our theories. He notes—though he is not the only one who has observed this—that, contrary to expectations, even when a patient is vulnerable and self-preoccupied, he or she may sometimes need the analyst to share more, not less, of his personal subjectivity in order to provide a therapeutic experience.[5] At other times, as Winnicott (1958) has observed, the patient simply needs to be alone in the presence of the other and needs to know that the analyst knows this.

REFERENCES

Bacal, H. A. (1985), Optimal responsiveness and the therapeutic process. In: *Progress in Self Psychology, Vol. 1,* ed. A. Goldberg. New York: Guilford, pp. 202–226.
—— (1990), The elements of a corrective selfobject experience. *Psychoanal. Inq.,* 10:347–372.
—— (1994), The selfobject relationship in psychoanalytic treatment. In: *A Decade of Progress, Progress in Self Psychology, Vol. 10,* ed. A. Goldberg. Hillsdale, NJ: The Analytic Press, pp. 21–30.
—— (1995a), The essence of Kohut's work and the progress of self psychology. *Psychoanal. Dial.,* 5:353–366.
—— (1995b), The centrality of selfobject experience in psychological relatedness. *Psychoanal. Dial.,* 5:403–409.
—— (in press a), The analyst's subjectivity: How it can illuminate the analysand's experience. *Psychoanal. Dial.*
—— ed. (in press b), *Optimal Responsiveness.* Northvale, NJ: Aronson.
—— & Newman, K. M. (1990), *Theories of Object Relations.* New York: Columbia University Press.
—— & Thomson, P. G. (1996), The psychoanalyst's selfobject needs and the effect of their frustration on the treatment: A new view of countertransference. In: *Basic*

---

[5] See also Lynne Jacobs (in press) and Lynn Preston (1995).

Ideas Reconsidered, Progress in Self Psychology, Vol. 12, ed. A. Goldberg. Hillsdale, NJ: The Analytic Press, pp. 17–35.

—— & Lachmann, F. (1988), Mother–infant mutual influence and precursors of psychic structure. In: *Frontiers in Self Psychology: Progress in Self Psychology, Vol. 3,* ed. A. Goldberg. Hillsdale, NJ: The Analytic Press, pp. 3–25.

—— Jaffe, J. & Lachmann, F. (1992), A dyadic systems view of communication. In: *Relational Perspectives in Psychoanalysis,* ed. N. Skolnick & S. Warshaw. Hillsdale, NJ: The Analytic Press, pp. 61–81.

Balint, M. (1968), *The Basic Fault.* London: Tavistock.

Doctors, S. (1995), Notes on the contribution of the analyst's self-awareness to "Optimal Responsiveness." Discussion of "Self psychology in search of the optimal: Optimal responsiveness, optimal provision, optimal gratification, and optimal restraint in the clinical situation," by M. Shane & S. Shane. Presented at the 17th Annual Conference on the Psychology of the Self, Chicago, IL, October 21, 1994.

Estrella, C. (1993), Optimal responsiveness: An exploratory study of the subjective and intersubjective experiences of psychotherapists. Unpublished Ph.D. dissertation, California Institute for Clinical Social Work.

Fosshage, J. (1992), Self psychology: The self and its vicissitudes within a relational matrix. In: *Relational Perspectives in Psychoanalysis,* ed. N. Skolnick & S. Warshaw. Hillsdale, NJ: The Analytic Press, pp. 21–42.

—— (1995a), Countertransference as the analyst's experience of the analysand: The influence of listening perspectives. *Psychoanal. Psychol.,* 12:375–391.

—— (1995b), Interaction in psychoanalysis: A broadening horizon. *Psychoanal. Dial.,* 5:459–478.

Jacobs, L. (in press), Subject–subject relating: An example of optimal responsiveness in intersubjectivity theory. In: *Optimal Responsiveness,* ed. H. A. Bacal. Northvale, NJ: Aronson.

Kohut, H. (1959), Empathy, introspection and psychoanalysis: An examination of the relationship between mode of observation and theory. In: *The Search for the Self, Vol. 1,* ed. P. Ornstein. New York: International Universities Press, pp. 205–232.

—— (1977), *The Restoration of the Self.* New York: International Universities Press.

—— (1984), *How Does Analysis Cure?* ed A. Goldberg & P. Stepansky. Chicago: University of Chicago Press.

—— & Seitz, P. (1963), Concepts and theories of psychoanalysis. In: *The Search for the Self, Vol. 1,* ed. H. Kohut. New York: International Universities Press, 1978, pp. 337–374.

Lachmann, F. M. & Beebe, B. (1992), Reformulations of early development and transference: Implications for psychic structure formation. In: *Interface of Psychoanalysis and Psychology,* ed. J. Barron, M. Eagle & D. Wolitzky. Washington, DC: American Psychological Association.

Lessem, P. & Orange, D. (1993), Emotional bonds: The therapeutic action of psychoanalysis revisited. Unpublished Manuscript.

Lichtenberg, J., Lachmann, F. & Fosshage, J. (1992), *Self & Motivational Systems.* Hillsdale, NJ: The Analytic Press.

Lindon, J. A. (1994), Gratification and provision in psychoanalysis. Should we get rid of "The rule of abstinence"? *Psychoanal. Dial.,* 4:549–582.

Malan, D. H., Bacal, H. A., Heath, E. S. & Balfour, F. H. G. (1968), A study of psychodynamic changes in untreated neurotic patients. *Brit. J. Psychiat.,* 114:510, 525–551.

Preston, L. (1995), Expressive relating: The intentional use of the analyst's subjectivity. Presented at the association for Psychoanalytic Self Psychology Conference, New York, April 22, 1995.

Shane, M. & Shane, E. (1996), Self psychology in search of the optimal: A consideration of optimal responsiveness, optimal provision, optimal gratification, and optimal restraint in the clinical situation. In: *Basic Ideas Reconsidered: Progress in Self Psychology, Vol. 12,* ed. A. Goldberg. Hillsdale, NJ: The Analytic Press, pp. 37–54.

Stolorow, R., Brandchaft, B. & Atwood, G. (1987), *Psychoanalytic Treatment.* Hillsdale, NJ: The Analytic Press.

Sukharov, M. (1995), The patient's empathic understanding of the therapist: A bilateral systems view of the empathic process. Presented at the 18th Annual Conference on the Psychology of the Self, San Francisco, October 21, 1995.

Suttie, I. D. (1935), *The Origins of Love and Hate.* London: Kegan Paul, Trench, Trubner.

Terman, D. (1988), Optimum frustration: Structuralization and the therapeutic process. In: *Learning from Kohut Progress in Self Psychology, Vol. 4,* ed. A. Goldberg. New York: The Analytic Press, pp. 113–125.

Tolpin, M. (1983), Corrective emotional experience: A self-psychological reevaluation. In: *The Future of Psychoanalysis,* ed. A. Goldberg. New York: International Universities Press, pp. 363–379.

Tolpin, P. (1988), Optimal affective engagement: The analyst's role in therapy. In: *Learning from Kohut Progress in Self Psychology, Vol. 4,* ed. A. Goldberg. New York: The Analytic Press, pp. 160–168.

Tuch, R. (1997), Beyond empathy: Confronting certain complexities in self-psychological theory. *Psychoanal. Quart.,* 66:259–282.

Winnicott, D. W. (1958), The capacity to be alone. In: *The Maturational Processes and the Facilitating Environment,* London: Hogarth Press, 1965, pp. 29–36.

Wolf, E. S. (1976), Ambience and abstinence. In: *The Annual of Psychoanalysis, Vol. 4.* New York: International Universities Press, pp. 101–115.

—— (1988), *Treating the Self.* New York: Guilford.

—— (1993), Disruptions in the therapeutic relationship in psychoanalysis: A view from self psychology. *Internat. J. Psycho-Anal.,* 74:675–687.

Chapter 6

Walking into the Eye of the Storm: Encountering "Repressed Memories" in the Therapeutic Context

Amy Eldridge

The clinical phenomenon of "repressed memory" has become a subject of controversy that extends far beyond the therapeutic context in which it originates. Problems occur as society struggles to determine the "truth" of such memories. Are they relics from the past, unburied in their original form from the depths? Does such an archeological metaphor fit the recall of memories as they occur in the therapeutic context? Or, as current theorists would suggest (Stolorow, Brandchaft, and Atwood, 1987), can "truth" actually be a concretized version of subjective experience? When memories resurface in the therapeutic context and are taken as pieces of truth beyond this context, a process occurs that is similar to that of the repressed memory in the personality structure: isolated, affectively charged pieces of experience are taken out of context and literalized as if they were solid pieces of "truth."

Making sense of the clinical phenomenon of "repressed memories" within the therapeutic context is a challenging endeavor. A very intriguing case will be presented that has led me to address the following questions in reference to "repressed memories." From a self-psychological perspective, what is a "repressed memory"? What is its relationship to dissociation? What is the impact upon the developing self? How does the therapeutic process contribute to the recall of such memories? What clinical response is therapeutic? In other words, can we understand the nature of the clinical phenomena of "repressed memories" within the theory of self psychology and therefore enhance the therapeutic process when such phenomena occur?

First, it is necessary to clarify the distinctions between repression and dissociation. Traditionally, repression has been associated with drive theory and thought of as a form of "forgetting," or containing, conflicted mental contents in order to preserve the integrity of the personality structure. Dissociation described a condition in which one set of mental contents was severed from the personality structure, not contained within it, resulting in a highly compromised personality structure lacking in essential integration between components. Kohut referred to "splits" within the personality. Horizontal splits involved repression of painful affect associated with the experience of selfobject failure, fostering self-cohesion. Vertical splits, similar to dissociation, threaten self-cohesion in that they allow two incompatible sets of experience and ideation to exist side by side. One side is discarded or disparaged in order for the other side to be maintained. The dissociated segment may or may not be available to consciousness (Goldberg, 1994).

Second, the concept of trauma must be examined, because the clinical phenomena of "repressed memories" has been linked to the treatment of trauma survivors. Kohut (1971, 1991) clearly stated that the experience of being cut off from selfobject responsiveness defines an experience as traumatic, rather than events themselves. Failure in selfobject responsiveness leaves the self vulnerable to the painful affect associated with the failure (not the trauma) and repression isolates the threatening affect, thereby protecting the self from fragmentation. While making reference to traumatic events and their impact on the self-structure, Kohut (1991) concludes:

> Extreme situations, such as the one to which inmates of Nazi extermination camps were exposed, demonstrate with special poignancy that the dangers which elicit the greatest fears in people are not associated with biological death, per se, but with the destruction of the self through withdrawal of selfobject support. . . . The prolonged exposure to a milieu that lacked all selfobject support created self-defects in at least some of the survivors, including the propensity toward profound disintegration anxiety that the mere passage of time will not cure [pp. 502–503].

Kohut thus recognized the potentially devastating effect of trauma on the self structure. However, by maintaining a focus on the experience of selfobject failure, Kohut did not address the problems inherent in integrating affect created by traumatic events themselves. Nor did he address the issue of memory and its relation to trauma. Kohut has left this level of investigation open to his followers.

TRAUMA AND MEMORY

Stolorow and Atwood (1992) refined Kohut's view on trauma, emphasizing the role of the selfobject in integrating affective experiences (rather than only causing, through failure, painful affect). "Our central thesis . . . is that early developmental trauma originates within a formative intersubjective context whose central feature is a failure of affect attunement . . . leading to a loss of affect regulatory capacity and thereby to an unbearable, overwhelmed, disintegrated, disorganized state" (p. 53). In their view, experience becomes accessible to consciousness only within an "affect integrating, containing, and modulating intersubjective context" (p. 53). When this is lacking, dissociation of the painful affect occurs; thus, the memory is deprived of symbolization and integration.

Palombo (1992) explains that such unintegrated experiences fail to become part of the life narrative since they fail to have meaning attached to them, which normally occurs through the developmental dialogue. "Failures in the integration of experiences result from the exposure to emotions that are overwhelming and that cannot be made meaningful to that person. It is in the nature of trauma that the person is overwhelmed by the intensity of the feelings stirred up by the experience and cannot make the experience sufficiently meaningful as to integrate it with the rest of his/her experiences" (p. 262). The result is an incoherent narrative, in his view equating with a lack of cohesion in the sense of self.

Studies of children who have undergone trauma, i.e., external occurrences that are, by their nature, too frightening, painful, and overwhelming for the self to integrate, shed light on the nature of what Ornstein (1994) refers to as "traumatic memories." Children tend to remain functional and coherent as they experience traumatic events. Their thoughts during such events tend to be both mundane and extreme. Mundane includes noticing the details of setting, worrying about eating lunch, and so on. The extreme are fears of dying, of literally being destroyed, and of being separated permanently from loved ones. Fear itself becomes an unbearable threat; the children wonder what horrible thing will happen next. It is as if one horrible occurrence irreparably breaks the child's feeling of safety, no matter how well the child is protected before and after the trauma (Terr, 1990).

Isolated trauma is often recalled in vivid detail. Repetitive trauma is more likely to be dissociated. Traumatized children become highly sensitized to external cues that suggest threat. Repetitively traumatized children develop defenses against reexperiencing trauma, both against remembering the past and experiencing future trauma. They tend to become "numb" and have no conscious presence as trauma (or anything that is similar to trauma; these highly sensitized children may overgeneralize in their defensiveness) occurs again. Yet the pain, the fear, the rage cannot be obliterated; the physical sensations, the affect associated, and the cognitive awareness are dissociated in order for the child to survive psychologically (Terr, 1991).

The dissociated content of the experience of repetitive trauma is powerful and overwhelming. It is stored in the form of visual images, body sensations, smells, insignificant details of the surround, and most strikingly, unshared affect. When the caretaker is not present during the trauma or is one of the traumatizers, the child is not able to gain the selfobject responsiveness needed to integrate, rather than dissociate, the experience. The defenses against reexperiencing the trauma through telling are too massive for the child to overcome.

From a self-psychological perspective, then, "repressed memories" can be defined as a clinical phenomenon associated with the experiencing of events that generate intense and overwhelming affect, the experience of selfobject failure in assisting in the integration of the affect, which results in dissociation of *both* the affect and the memory from self-structure. The memories are not actually repressed in the correct use of the term but are dissociated, that is, a vertical split in which the memories and affect are kept unconscious and separate from the self-structure. The dissociated content of memories and affect are not linguistically encoded; rather, they are stored in confusing fragments of sight, sound, and touch accompanied by intense affective states. This form of memory is extremely painful to recall and creates the experience of fragmentation.

THE TREATMENT PROCESS

The therapeutic process involves the remobilization of the unconscious. We are accustomed to patients sharing painful memories and the accompanying selfobject longings for understanding, protection, or whatever form of psychologically necessary response was missing. We recognize that our presence is a powerful influence in the therapeutic process, that what emerges is a jointly determined process on both the conscious and unconscious level for therapist and patient. To believe that the patient's memories are accurate defies our current state of knowledge; we recognize that these are subjective experiences shaped by the structures of the mind and influenced by the present context (Stolorow et al., 1987).

"Repressed memories" that result from the experience of childhood trauma and the defense of dissociation have a different quality from other memories. They are filled with details that do not tell the story. Most striking is that they often recur in response to very subtle elements of the therapeutic context, which the therapist may not be able to recognize. In other words, they appear to emerge out of context. Because they have been dissociated, they have not undergone the same types of revisions that other memories do as development proceeds and as new experiences are acquired. Often, the affect precedes the cognitive in its reemergence and is frightening and confusing. Ornstein (1994) notes that these memories have an inherent conflict in them; to remember will bring back the intense affective experience in relatively unaltered form, and they are experienced as "unspeakable and unsharable" (p. 136). Yet these memories, fragmented as they are, must be articulated in order for the self to be integrated.

The response of the therapist is vitally needed as the memories emerge. The patient is likely to feel as overwhelmed, threatened, and confused as in childhood. The affective experience of the patient is likely to be as intense as if the threatening events were occurring in the present and the patient is still the child. This is a terribly uncomfortable juncture therapeutically as the therapist witnesses and vicariously experiences the horror felt by the patient. The therapist may feel frighteningly bewildered; when the memories return spontaneously in the therapeutic session, they often seem disjunctive from the process and from what is known of the patient, so that conceptual understanding is lacking. At this juncture, the therapist may be tempted to introduce an explanation in order to regain some sense of order and coherence. Ideally, the therapist will draw upon the affective experience generated within and the knowledge base acquired. Understandably, the therapist may react to the intensity of the affect and the uncertainty and lose touch with the patient. To understand the process of integrating repressed memories, that pieces will emerge and sense will be made, can help the therapist tolerate the painful affect and ambiguity that goes beyond the ordinary.

CASE PRESENTATION

Several years ago, Nancy became my patient via her daughter. Nancy and her husband Frank were referred to me for consultation regarding their then 5-year-old daughter Susan. Susan was disrupting her kindergarten class and was thought to possibly be attention deficit disordered. In the context of our meeting regarding her daughter, Nancy struck me as a concerned, but strict, parent who worked many hours and seemed to respond to her daughter in a rigid autocratic style, rather than with warmth and understanding. She impressed me as competent and tough, but with very good intentions. Frank seemed much softer and gentler and as though he were protective of his daughter from the power of his wife.

After meeting with Susan several times, I observed her to be a very anxious little girl who was hungry for constant attention and approval. While playing, she openly disavowed her relationship with her mother, claiming that her real mother had left her father and that the mother she lived with was really her stepmother. She portrayed this "stepmother" as angry and punitive towards her and her father. She longed for her real mother who would be loving to them both.

When I met again with the Nancy and Frank, I shared this fantasy with them and wondered about its meaning. At this point, Nancy asked Frank to leave the room, which he readily did. Nancy looked at me and quietly said, "You know, don't you?" as if I had seen through her and knew the pain that she was in. Crying, she went on to say that her daughter is right; she is angry and punitive and almost at the end of her rope. She was the one who needed help desperately. She would do what was best for her daughter, but she thought that the problems were mainly hers. We invited her husband in, and she told him what she had told me. He seemed frightened by her upset and readily agreed that she should have help. I felt no choice but to respond to this poignant plea for help. I began to see Nancy on an individual basis.

Nancy is a large woman, in her late forties, who is about 50 pounds overweight. She is always impeccably groomed and attractively dressed. She works for a large manufacturing company in a middle management position. She is clearly bright, very articulate, and quite humorous. The power of her anger is palpable as she enters the room. It is communicated in her tone, her expression, her posture. The image that comes to mind is that of a guard dog, snarling and showing its teeth, protecting its turf. Less evident, but somehow conveyed is a sense of desperation. We quickly shifted to twice a week.

Nancy had been in therapy years before, after a divorce from her first husband. She had used a friendship type of relationship, combined with hypnosis to work herself out of a severe depression. She recognized that she had just touched the surface and that she needed to go further to understand why she felt so badly. She approached therapy as a job to be done, seeming to feel that she had no choice but to try, but with little conviction that it could help her change. She kept her distance, initially, and spent her time reporting on her anger. Anger was the dominant theme, as Nancy felt assaulted so easily. Any failure to recognize her importance provoked Nancy to angry tirades against the injurious party, whether it be another driver, her boss, her husband or her daughter.

Nancy gave me a sketchy history. She was the oldest of three children in a low-income military family. She described a stormy relationship with her mother, whom she experienced as condemning and uncaring. Her father was more loving, but ineffectual and unavailable because he was under her mother's power. She had a very unhappy childhood with many moves and felt burdened by having to help care for the younger children. She was overweight and isolated, unable to make friends or develop sustaining relationships outside her family. She went away for her first year of college and was then forced to return home, resentfully, because of finances. She completed college and taught for several years before marrying her first husband. Retrospectively, she felt that she married him because he paid attention to her and provided a way out of her home. She became pregnant right away with a daughter (now in her twenties) and later a son. She eventually left him when she discovered that he was having affairs (her children were about ages 8 and 10).

Nancy became suicidally depressed during the course of the divorce and consequently agreed that the ex-husband could have custody of her children. She found help and found a job and eventually moved to this area. After a number of years, she met Frank. Never truly in love with him, she married him because she thought she had no other possibilities for love. She has come to love him over the 10 years of their marriage. Their daughter Susan was planned because Frank wanted a child and she felt she owed it to him to give him one.

As I initially came to know Nancy, I found it difficult not to respond in a manner similar to that attributed to her mother: condemning and uncaring. She was really hard to feel any warmth towards, and I did not during the first few months, maybe more, of her treatment. She would enter my office already angry, critical of whomever she had encountered in the waiting room, haughtily listing their defects. She seemed to expect that I would feel the way she did, and together we would enjoy the ridicule. I always listened to her critique, one part of me repelled by her hostility and one part of me understanding that she was presenting herself to me for examination and acceptance. To question her reactions was to suggest that I was not in harmony with her and was experienced, at this early point in the treatment, as critical. Yet to agree with her would have indicated that I would respond to her difficulties in a condemning manner. I believed that my response to her criticisms of others would let her know how I would respond to her "faults." I wished to communicate that her observations were important and informative, so I listened and questioned from the point of view of learning about what she had seen. At the same time, I attempted to convey that I understood the plight of the person that she was describing by making gently sympathetic remarks. So, like her, I used my head to help me enter this treatment. I did not yet understand Nancy well enough to respond freely. I was cautious. Slowly, over the course of the first 6 months, the stage was set for her to open herself to me. And, abruptly, she did.

Nancy had presented several salient issues that she wanted to resolve: her relationship with her daughter, her weight, and her lack of progress at work. She felt that she was making some progress related to her daughter and this became a topic of discussion (albeit without insight). She felt that her weight issue was too emotionally charged for her to touch on initially. So, Nancy focused on her wish to advance professionally. She felt extremely frustrated at work. She had a number of positions at the same level with different companies and had not been able to move ahead, despite her clear competence. She began a diatribe about the sexism at work and her hopeless conviction that she was being blocked by power-hungry men from what she wanted. Again, she presented with the sense that I would share her bitterness towards men. After listening for quite a while, I made the suggestion that she, in some way, may be blocking her way and that she might be able to examine this and become aware of how and why it was happening. Before leaving the session, she walked over to me, put her arm around me and told me that she loved me.

Needless to say, I was taken aback and experienced this spontaneous display of affection as disjointed from the session. I think that I was polite and yet expressed some surprise at her reaction. She left very pleased. She approached the next session as usual and made no reference to the closing of the past session. After several moments, I brought it up, wondering what had led to her feeling so loving at that moment and what her thoughts had been about it past the session. She seemed surprised, but not hurt, by my questions. She explained that she felt hopeful that she could change with my help and had continued to feel a sense of pleasure about it. My suggesting that there was something within her to work on gave her a sense that change was possible. I experienced a warmth and softness to her that I had not seen before, yet it seemed so disconnected from the angry, powerful woman I was used to seeing. I filed this incident away as puzzling—not so much by the content, but by the affect. This warmth seemed to come out of a process within her that I was not privy to, certainly not a warmth acquired through any mutual sense of intimacy.

Our work was interrupted by a long planned vacation that Nancy and Frank took together. Upon her return, Nancy had much to tell me about her emotional reactions during the trip. She first recounted dining at the captain's table and feeling extremely out of place and uncomfortable. She recognized that she handled this by becoming critical and sarcastic and wondered why she behaved this way. Secondly, she had begun to have images of a slender beautiful woman who was gentle, yet able. She was able to describe her image in detail, emphasizing that the woman was thin, yet muscular and very feminine. She felt that this image was a vision of the woman she wanted to be, of the woman within her.

Her presentation suggested more than a fantasy; it was as if she felt that this visioned woman lived within her. She could see her and feel her essence and felt very excited by feeling her presence. She was hopeful that she could become like this instead of the angry woman at the captain's table. While I recognized this fantasy as representing the renewal of hope and, likely, the beginning of an idealizing transference, the form was intriguing and unfamiliar. She recognized this vision as herself, yet her experience was also as if this were someone else. No mere fantasy, this felt real to her.

As our sessions continued, she began to speak of feeling or not feeling this woman within. She told me she had read about multiple personalities and wondered whether this was what she was experiencing. She also knew that she was highly suggestible and thought she could be making up this experience and convincing herself. (She had easily taken to hypnosis in the past and thought of herself as someone who exaggerates. I believed it possible that her experience was shaped by the popular writings on multiple personality disorder, but I was not convinced. I thought it also possible that she was afraid of these feelings and what they might hold.) I suggested that we wait and see what developed, that we would come to know this better as our work continued. At this point, I was intrigued by her experience, but not disturbed. I truly believed that we would know in time, since I had confidence in the process and in myself. Although I was familiar with the existence of multiple personality disorder, I had not worked with anyone with the "disorder." I knew that this was possibly what would emerge, but I wasn't convinced.

The next few months were highly charged. Nancy began to elaborate on her past. Before the birth of her siblings and while her father was overseas, Nancy's mother experienced a severe depression. They moved to her maternal grandparents' home during this time. Nancy was about 5 years of age, although her memory was sketchy. She remembered this as the beginning of her unhappiness, because she felt terribly neglected and frightened by her grandfather's progressive illness. During one such session, Nancy abruptly shifted from talking about her past to shrieking in pain. She reported feeling tingling sensations and then shooting charges in her limbs. She was frightened and crying. I, too, was frightened. Somehow, we both knew that this was a somatic response to the memories, rather than a heart attack. I had witnessed other experiences of flashback before, but none so intense, so immediate. I held on to myself and calmly responded to her distress. When I likened her description to receiving a shock, she recalled sticking her finger in an outlet deliberately while at her grandmother's and being severely shocked. She struggled to understand why she would try, at such a young age, to hurt herself.

In the sessions that followed, Nancy recalled being sent to school (at about age 8) with a runny egg sandwich for breakfast to eat on her walk, and how she would stuff it in her mouth despite her distaste for it and would end up at school with egg all over her, overweight and alone. (This seemed a metaphor for her lonely childhood in which she felt lost and depleted, and the need to take whatever was offered. I imagined that this was connected to her sense of being suggestible.) She spent a number of sessions wondering why it was that her mother did not care for her and how angry she was at her mother for treating her this way. Again, a flash of memory surfaced. She recalled a car trip with her mother and her siblings. Her mother stopped for gas. Nancy went to the washroom and when she returned, the car was gone. Her mother had left her there. She recalled crying frantically. A kind man, who turned out to be the sheriff of the small town that they were passing through, came to her rescue. He comforted and assured her that, if they didn't find her mother, he would take her home and he and his wife would care for her. She recalls liking that idea and calming down. Shortly after this, her mother reappeared, explaining that she had not noticed that she had left without her daughter until stopping again for gas. Nancy did not believe this story—she felt that she was deliberately left behind and that her mother had thought better of it and come back for her. Nancy recalled wishing that her mother had not come back and that the man would have kept her. I noted to myself her desperateness to have someone protect her.

She felt enormous pain after recalling this incident, believing that her mother truly did not want her. She sobbed through the telling of the memory as if it were happening anew. The depth of her sadness mirrored the previous depth of her anger. For the next 6 months, she continued to have recollections, usually beginning shortly after entering my office. She felt as though she saved them until I was present, not able to bare the feelings alone. The somatic memories returned. She once again experienced the painful "shocked" feeling, but this time, memories emerged. She recalled fragments of sexual abuse, committed by her mother's uncle while they visited his home. The shocking feeling came as he tried to penetrate her, but was unable to because of the strength of her hymen. (She had to have it surgically opened before she could have intercourse.) She would close her eyes and describe the room, the smell, the feelings as if it were occurring in the present. She recalled the gruesome details, from the length of her uncle's fingernails to the stimulating sensation of orgasm. She experienced nauseating shame at having been aroused by these experiences. She then recalled a neighbor watching them and masturbating—and could see herself floating above the table that she was lying on, escaping. She recognized that she dissociated during the abuse—that she lost contact with her own body.

These recollections had great meaning for Nancy. She now understood why she masturbated so frequently as a child and how often she "tempted" her mother to catch her in the act. She also understood the roots of the great shame she felt and hatred for her body. She felt it betrayed her by being aroused; she experienced extreme loss of control and, ultimately, disconnection from her body. She explained that she often looked in the mirror and was surprised by the overweight image that she saw, as if it were somebody else in the mirror. The slimmer woman she had envisioned earlier more fits her internal image of her body. Her powerful sexual longings seemed, at one level, an attempt to connect with her body again.

As Nancy's story unfolded, I felt deep concern and compassion for her. Her suffering was excruciating to behold, as memories were exposed, layer by layer in my office. I found that I needed great comfort myself, often assuring myself that my presence during these recollections would help. I did not dread the sessions because I felt very committed to her. Fortunately, she was my last appointment of the day, so that I could regroup after engaging in this intensely painful process.

Outside my office, Nancy found that she was barely able to contain her rage. She became concerned about driving, since she often took this as an opportunity to respond challengingly when someone dared to cut her off or something similar. She was viciously angry at home and at work. She had shared her recollections with her husband and he tried valiantly to be supportive. As she became worn down (as were others, I'm sure), we decided that antidepressants should be considered. She readily took to the suggestion and acted upon the referral. Nancy was very frightened of her potential for violence, her out-of-control rage, and the chronic sense of hopelessness that she felt. She found that Prozac was very helpful. While the pain and anger continued, she felt increased control and energy.

Nancy once again began to experience others within her. She did not feel that they were separate personalities, nor did she ever feel that she was anyone else but herself. Rather, she felt fragments of personalities within her. First, she experienced a "saviour," a male protector who kept her alive. She recalled that he had appeared when she had been suicidal in the past and she thought that he was an angel. Then, a spunky child appeared who was not afraid of anyone and then a lost child, frightened and alone. Hidden within her, she described the child who escaped from the abuse, who retained "goodness" hidden away in a beautiful cave-like place, afraid to come out. Next came an angry, spiteful, bitter girl.

As these images appeared to her, she struggled to bring them into herself. We would discuss their attributes and work to understand why they were put aside and why she found it difficult to take them in. As an example, Nancy recalled a vague memory of running away from home and becoming lost and frightened. She could picture the alley that she found herself in and could picture herself as very small, close to age 5. She was looking for her father. She cried out in fright as she realized that she was lost and in a dangerous area. She was immobilized. Next she recalled a "spunky" girl taking over and leading her back to the street. She liked this girl because she was not afraid. My comments reflected the fear that she felt and the way in which she managed to find the wherewithal within to help herself, even at this young age. But she left behind the feelings of this lost little girl and replaced them with fear-lessness. She could not recall why she ran away to find her father; she just knew that was who she was seeking. We imagined, together, that this memory may have coincided with the period of her mother's depression. Nancy believed that this was her first experience of dissociation.

This felt like a period of reconstruction, not dissimilar to recalling events with affect and understanding as one does in therapy. Instead, Nancy recalled fragments within her, which, for her seemed to encapsulate memories and affect together. Unlike other recollections, these fragments lacked context. They were presented as movie images with affect. Nancy's feelings were so vividly portrayed that I felt as though I were watching them on large screen with surround sound stereo. My struggle was to help her understand these images that were so disconnected in time and place. I had to rely on a loose sense of her history and an acute sense of the process between us to offer any understanding. There were many gaps in the reconstruction. When we stretched to try to piece recollections together in a narrative, it felt as though we were writing fiction, since there were no data to rely on. Rather than the story being clear, Nancy seemed to benefit from bringing together pieces within her. This seemed to be her way of becoming more integrated, and I adjusted my stance.

CLINICAL DISCUSSION

As I respond to others, I responded to Nancy along the lines of developing a relationship in which understanding of her issues was possible and integration at the emotional and cognitive levels could take place—allowing her a more stable, yet flexible, sense of herself. These basic principles led me to see Nancy as struggling with a lack of integration in a particular form—on a continuum with more ordinary discontinuities in experiencing the self. I understood that Nancy's initial hostility was defensive, that she had experienced chronic neglect, as well as traumatic abuse. She had developed a strong exterior but felt painfully empty and disconnected inside. Sex, food, and anger had become sources of stimulation for her, shaped by her history, to keep her feeling alive and connected. The breakthrough of love that she felt for me early in the treatment was the first sign of her dissociative experiences and of the potential inside.

The dissociative defense kept many of Nancy's experiences of self in isolation from one another. Rather than discrete personalities, Nancy's images seemed to reflect experiences of self that had been dissociated defensively and therefore existed as if they were separate entities. As Schafer (1992) points out, a person creates many narratives of self, which are then ordered into a supraordinate narrative that is complete, coherent, and consistent. (It is possible that the multiple personality disorder is further along in the continuum of incoherence in that the multiple narratives of self become experienced as concrete, coherent realities.) In the therapeutic context, the gentle, loving, creative aspects of Nancy's self, captured in images dated as to age and appearance, could be retrieved and strengthened. The process indicates that they were not the outcome of further integration and development (as is often the hoped for outcome of therapy), but rather already constructed pieces of Nancy's psychological structure that were unavailable in the present relational context as experienced by Nancy. She was always on guard, ready for assault, and had long ago hidden these treasures to keep them safe.

As described in the case, the intense moments (hours, weeks, months) in which Nancy experienced frightening flashes of affective memory were excruciatingly painful to behold. While I recognized the "flashback" phenomena, I was unprepared for its power and the confusion that is created in the patient–therapist dyadic experience. To vicariously experience was not difficult; tolerating the experience was. I can imagine that structuring the "recall" through hypnosis is very appealing in such cases. I can also imagine that any suggestion that I made to Nancy in this vulnerable state would have been quickly accepted by her in order to defocus from the pain and to build another defensive structure (note her readiness to construct a memory about being shocked). I found it very difficult to tolerate the lack of coherence and continuity—sense was not easily made so I had nothing to hold onto myself. I should explain that I knew what was occurring clinically and that I knew of theoretical and treatment approaches, but the intellect was only a foothold against the storm. I was challenged to stay with the affective experience and to trust that, by doing so, my presence would be felt and the structure of the experience would change accordingly. Instead of feeling overwhelmingly alone and undefended, Nancy would now have a sense of a caring person with her, and the selfobject function needed to help her tolerate and integrate her experience would be available through the transference.

An important element in the therapeutic response, as in other cases, involves the creation of a more coherent narrative (Palombo, 1992). When working with dissociative phenomena, the memories that emerge are more apt to begin with an affective "flashback" experience akin to walking into an intense action thriller in a high-tech movie theater without knowing the plot. Even as the affect diminishes, memories may be incomplete and focused on mundane details that do not provide much context. Because of the longstanding dissociation, these memories may be hard to place in the life narrative—the patient may not even know when and if traumatic events occurred. Often, just fragments are presented. In order for the patient to gain a sense of psychological integrity, somehow the patient must be able to make sense of these experiences and integrate them with the life narrative as already developed. Clearly, the narrative may be greatly disrupted by the occurrence of these memories, and greater confusion and anxiety will be understandable reactions. Also, the patient, like the traumatized child, becomes fearful of any further recall that may be traumatizing. The need for coherence may help the patient to continue to recall bits and pieces until some level of "understandability" is obtained. The transference helps sustain the patient through this process and the therapeutic milieu becomes the context in which the flashbacks are imbedded.

The therapist's knowledge and experience will help shape the patient's understanding; this is an inevitable and beneficial part of the therapeutic process. However, interpretations and explanations should be offered cautiously and on the basis of sufficient data so that the patient does not foreclose the painful exploration process in favor of the therapist's wisdom. Rather than trying to determine the "validity" of the memories and insert them into the patient's history, they are treated metaphorically.[1] In Nancy's case, the memories were often iconic and

---

[1] Schafer (1992) states: "It is especially important to emphasize that narrative is not an alternative to truth or reality; rather it is the mode in which, inevitably, truth and reality are presented. We have only versions of the true and the real. Narratively unmediated, definitive access to truth and reality cannot be demonstrated" (p. xv). I therefore recognize that the memories that surfaced in Nancy's treatment were not replicas of historic events but were constructed out of images and affect that occurred in the context of those moments in treatment. However, my belief in the reconstructed memories was critical to Nancy's treatment.

unnarrated. My words about the affect experienced and the patient's response to the affect allowed her to develop a greater understanding of herself and, perhaps more importantly, experience herself as being understandable. Theoretically, my comments focused on my understanding of her efforts to maintain psychological integrity, to defend the self against what were felt to be annihilative assaults. While gaps in memory remain, coherence was derived from the experience of knowing and understanding, in the context of the therapeutic milieu, that which had been dissociated. This process allowed her to continue to the therapeutic work in a more typical fashion as more familiar defenses and transference issues came to the foreground.

CONCLUSION

In this chapter, I have tried to describe and discuss the clinical phenomena of "repressed memory" as it presents itself spontaneously in the therapeutic setting. The uniqueness of this type of memory lies in its structure and in its clinical presentation. Clinical responsiveness is made difficult by the following: (1) the "memory" is often stimulated by an extremely subtle response to the treatment context which neither therapist nor patient will be able to identify or anticipate; (2) the first presentation of the memory may be affective and frighteningly intense; (3) the affective aftermath of the experience will be greater fear and confusion rather than relief; (4) the context of the memory may not be readily available for recall (if ever), making integration of the memory very difficult without writing a highly fictionalized account; and (5) the therapeutic process of vicarious introspection is akin to walking into a tornado in its fullest intensity. Successful treatment requires that the therapist and patient persist in allowing memories to resurface and that the therapist refrains from distancing so that the selfobject transference holds and maintains the patient through the recall process. This process diminishes the intensity of the affect. Finally, the therapist and the patient must co-construct a meaningful narrative in which these memories are able to

---

I am not certain that she could have integrated the affect and the fragments of memory had I not believed her. In other words, I doubt that I would have provided the needed selfobject experience. On the whole, I did believe her. The form and the presentation of Nancy's memories suggest that she was traumatized. Her issues and symptoms fit the pattern of an abuse survivor, as I know it. She seemed to present other incidents in ways that I found to be believable. The validity of the story for therapeutic purposes was strong (see Perlman, 1993). Outside of therapy, a different level of validity is generally called for. For example, family members often require substantiation of the memories (or at least some details of the memories) from others. Legal validity is even more exacting as "evidence" is required to prosecute.

undergo structural transformation and become elements of the patient's self-experience.

REFERENCES

Goldberg, A. (1994), *The Problem of Perversion*. Hillsdale, NJ: The Analytic Press.
Kohut, H. (1971), *The Analysis of the Self*. New York: International Universities Press.
—— (1991), Selected problems in self psychology. In: *The Search for the Self*, ed. P. Ornstein, Madison, CT: International Universities Press, pp. 489–523.
Ornstein, A. (1994), Trauma, memory, and psychic continuity. In: *A Decade of Progress: Progress in Self Psychology, Vol. 10,* ed. A. Goldberg. Hillsdale, NJ: The Analytic Press, pp. 131–146.
Palombo, J. (1992), Narratives, self-cohesion, and the patient's search for meaning. *Clin. Social Work J.,* 20:249–269.
Perlman, S. (1993), Unlocking incest memories: Preoedipal transference, countertransference, and the body. *J.Amer. Acad. Psychoanal.,* 21:363–386.
Schafer, R. (1992), *Retelling a Life*. New York: Basic Books.
Stolorow, R. & Atwood, G. (1992), *Contexts of Being*. Hillsdale, NJ: The Analytic Press.
—— Brandchaft, B. & Atwood, G. (1987), *Psychoanalytic Treatment*. Hillsdale, NJ: The Analytic Press.
Terr, L. (1990), *Too Scared to Cry*. New York: Basic Books.
—— (1991), Childhood traumas: An outline and overview. *Amer. J. Psychiat.,* 148:10–20.

Chapter 7

Mature Selfobject Experience

George Hagman

This chapter will explore the nature and function of mature selfobject experience in human psychology and in analytic treatment. Self psychology began with the clinical study of narcissistic character disorders. It was during his analysis of these patients that Kohut identified the archaic transferences, the study of which led to all subsequent elaborations of self-psychological theory and practice (Kohut, 1971). The keystone of Kohut's clinical edifice was and remains the concept of the selfobject. Since 1971 an enormous literature has expanded on Kohut's observations and theories. An important facet of this discussion has been the changing nature of selfobject experience throughout development and maturation. Most self psychologists have focused on archaic selfobject relating; however, it is recognized that selfobject experience plays a part in psychological life throughout the life span. Developmentally advanced levels of selfobject experience have been referred to as mature selfobjects. In spite of the importance of this concept in our understanding of human psychology beyond the earliest stages of childhood, it has remained poorly developed. In his last work, Kohut (1984) moved the concept of mature selfobject relating closer to center stage. Others have recognized its importance, but they have not elaborated on Kohut's points beyond a superficial level.

Selfobject experience develops on a continuum, the earliest (archaic) forms being centered on the core and emergent sense of self, the later forms uniting an increasing articulated sense of self with a growing recognition of the subjectivity of the other (Winnicott, 1971; Stern, 1985; Benjamin, 1988, 1991; Aron, 1991; Hagman, 1996). Archaic selfobject experience centers on the emergent sense of a core and subjective self with the other functioning as a facilitator of this process. Mature selfobject experience requires the capacity, desire, and ability to

---

The author wishes to thank Peter Zimmerman, Ph.D. for his assistance in the writing of this chapter.

expand self-experience so as to include the other. From this point of view mature selfobject relating involves an intertwining of "self-centeredness" and "other-centeredness." This capacity to recognize the other as an independent center of subjectivity is the hallmark of mature selfobject experience.

Another area is the impact of the recognition of the other on the elaboration of the self (Schachtel, 1959; Winnicott, 1971; Modell, 1984; Benjamin, 1988, 1991; Eigen, 1993; Hagman, 1996). Although much has been said about the role of archaic selfobject experience in facilitating the unfolding of the self's innate program, less has been said regarding the function of selfobject experience in the self's development beyond the innate and the archaic. Maturity involves movement beyond a personal program to include truly new and even surprising areas of self-expansion. A skilled, resourceful, and creative engagement with others is essential for the elaboration of the mature self. The initial notion of the selfobject did not include a provision for the "creative" impact of the other on self-experience. My claim will be that it is through the recognition of otherness within mature selfobject experience that "new" self-experience occurs, adding to the self in often unpredictable and surprising ways. When recognition of otherness is lacking, the self may remain poorly elaborated or stunted.

LITERATURE REVIEW

Kohut's initial conceptualization of the selfobject was limited to its archaic form. Essentially prestructural, the selfobject was understood to provide support for the emergent nuclear self. Transmuting internalization involved the breaking down of the psychological components of the selfobject accompanied by their internal structuralization. In Kohut's early model, maturation involved the replacement of dependence on selfobjects (invariably archaic in nature) with autonomous psychic structure. However, over time Kohut realized that autonomy was highly qualified, and he postulated a continuing role for selfobjects beyond archaic needs. In 1977 he wrote: "The psychologically healthy adult continues to need the mirroring of the self by self-objects (to be exact; by the selfobject aspects of his love objects) and he continues to need targets for his idealizations" (p. 188). However, Kohut later found that selfobject experience evolves over time. In 1984 he wrote: "The developmental advances that characterize psychological life must, in our view, be seen in the changing nature of the relationship between the self and its selfobjects" (p. 47). In that work he referred to a *specific* use of the term selfobject when applied to *archaic* selfobjects and a *general* meaning of the term "as that dimension of our experience of another person that relates to this person's functions in shoring up our self" (p. 49). The experience of the mature selfobject he described as "an experience in depth: when the adult experiences the self-sustaining efforts of a maturely chosen selfobject, the selfobject experiences of all the preceding stages of his life reverberate unconsciously" (pp. 49-50). Whether these mature selfobject experiences involve mirroring, idealization, or twinship, Kohut believed that selfobject responsiveness was crucial.

In addition, Kohut pointed out that while the differentiation between object and selfobject is necessary, the distinction is not always clinically fruitful. He stated: "The mutual influence of the two intertwining sets of experiences (of object and selfobject) one upon the other deserves intensive study. Echoing Freud, I have emphasized that object love strengthens the self. . . . Furthermore, it is well known that a strong self enables us to experience love and desire more intensely (Kohut, 1984, p. 53). Kohut saw the use of others to strengthen the self as a capacity of adulthood whose selfobject milieu "composed of his family, his friends, his work situation, and last but not least, the cultural resources of the group to which he belongs" (p. 71).

Kohut stressed that the developmental progression from archaic to mature selfobject experiences involved "the replacement of a merger experience with the selfobject by the experience of empathic resonance from the side of the selfobject." In that work (Kohut, 1984) Kohut viewed empathic resonance as a quality of the explaining phase of analysis when there is an "empathic bond on a mature level" that is retained and "even deepened in its scope via the analyst's imparting his . . . insights to the patient" (p. 185). In spite of the growing recognition of the analyst's subjectivity, he or she retains selfobject functions for the patient. For Kohut the use of mature selfobjects did not preclude more archaic forms of relating; he stated: "During periods when the person's self is exposed to extreme stress, his ability to avail himself temporarily of archaic modes of narcissistic sustenance via archaic self-selfobject processes of support is an asset of his personality organization and a quality that is not only compatible with, but specifically characterizes the mature self organization" (Kohut, 1984, p. 185).

Since the publication of *How Does Analysis Cure?* some authors argued for the restriction of the selfobject concept to Kohut's specific definition. These authors (Goldberg, 1988; Wolf, 1988; Lichtenberg, 1991) made a sharp distinction between the selfobject experience and the object experience. For example, Lichtenberg (1991) noted: "A selfobject experience is thus a reference not to actual interpersonal relations or to internalization of functions but to affect-laden symbolic representation" (p. 472). Wolf (1988) echoed Lichtenberg: "Precisely defined, a selfobject is neither self nor object, but the *subjective* aspect of a self-sustaining function performed by a relationship of self to objects who by their presence or activity evoke and maintain the self and the experience of selfhood. As such the selfobject relationship refers to an intrapsychic experience and does not describe the interpersonal relationship between self and other objects. It denotes the experience of imagoes that are needed for the sustenance of the self" (p. 184).

However, other authors attempted to avoid a reductionist definition of the selfobject and/or a rigid differentiation between the concepts of object and selfobject. In 1991 Paul Ornstein argued for the lack of a "sharp dichotomy" between the mature selfobject and a love object; he said: "these are experientially thoroughly intertwined, and almost unrecognizable as qualitatively different" (p. 27). He continued: "If love is a capacity of a healthy self, can love not be fully amalgamated with other needs and wishes in relation to that other whom we now describe in our conceptualizations as a mature selfobject?" These mature selfobjects "whose qualities and organization includes its own center of initiative as well as the recognition of a separate center of initiative in the other" (p. 27). Thus Ornstein subsumed within the concept of the mature selfobject a complex experience of mutual recognition between persons. The selfobject concept includes not only the experience a person has of their self, but also the needs of the self of the other viewed from the "emotional vantage point of the self" (p. 25).

In their discussion of the importance of self-delineating selfobject experiences, Stolorow and Atwood (1992) described a developmental continuum: "from early sensorimotor forms of validation occurring in the pre-verbal transactions between infant and care giver, to later processes of validation that take place increasingly through symbolic communication and involve the child's awareness of others as centers of subjectivity" (p. 27). They further noted how "new forms of validation become possible once the child becomes aware of others as experiencing subjects" (Stern, 1985). In this phase, the caregiver's acts of participatory identification with the child's subjective states increasingly become communicated through verbal and other symbols, permitting the gradual evolution of a symbolic world of self and other experienced by the child as real (p. 28).

Recently, Bacal (1994) expanded on this perspective. He stated: "The selfobject is a multifaceted concept that implies not only the experience of need and experience of function provided by the other, or object, but also the experience of a relationship. . . . My conceptualization of a selfobject relationship is an intrapsychic experience of another who can be counted on to provide essential selfobject functions" (p. 404).

In a related sense Shane and Shane (1990) viewed the capacity to offer to another an opportunity for a selfobject experience as the hallmark of mature selfobject relating. The clearest example of this is the mature capacity of the analyst to hold out the potential for a selfobject experience to their patients. Essential to the facilitation of the clinical process is the analyst's willingness and ability to experience the transference (which implies the recognition of the patient's subjectivity) as reflectively serving selfobject functions. In other words the analyst's mature capacity to be a "good enough other" through the provision of opportunities for selfobject experience to the patient also promotes the development of the creative and unique self-experience of the analyst (a point also made by Bacal [1995] p. 403).

To my mind, the most accurate, useful, and experience-near viewpoint has been the recognition of the intertwining experience of object and selfobject as argued by Kohut in his general definition of the selfobject and subsequently elaborated by Ornstein, Bacal, Stolorow, and the Shanes. In fact, even for Kohut, but most especially these more recent authors, the capacity to recognize the independent center of initiative and subjective experience of the other, simultaneously with its selfobject function, is a developmental advance characteristic of maturity. To this end the remainder of this chapter will elaborate on this view of the selfobject experience as represented by the concept of mature selfobject relating.

MATURE SELFOBJECT RELATIONS

As an introduction to my discussion of the characteristics of mature selfobject relating I will briefly overview the concept of the archaic selfobject experience and review recent findings regarding the developmental progression towards maturity.

Development of the Capacity for Mature Selfobject Experience

The archaic selfobject is the experience of an object's function in the emergence and/or in the maintenance of a core sense of self (Kohut, 1977, 1984; Wolf, 1988; Stern, 1985). The well-functioning archaic selfobject is experienced as attuned seamlessly and harmoniously with the self; Kohut understood this as an experience of *merger*. There is a naive confidence in the availability of the archaic selfobject experience that is "taken for granted." There is also a tight restriction in its function to areas that are related to the maintenance of self-viability and the facilitation of the emergence of inborn tendencies for self-organization. Although Stern argued persuasively for the mutuality of the parenting relationship, it is probable that the infant experiences the archaic selfobject as functioning *without personal effort or agency.* In addition there is probably only a rudimentary recognition of the otherness of the object as an independent center of subjectivity. This one-sidedness of the archaic selfobject relationship is characteristic; it is experienced as functioning solely to meet the infant's needs. These needs are related to the actualization of physical and psychological capacities and the regulation of physiologic and affective states; by this means, the primary organization and affective tone of self-experience crystallizes. In sum, the child's experience of the archaic selfobject tie is *self-centered;* as of yet the infant has not acquired the capability to decenter, to include recognition of the subjectivity of the other in self-experience.

While an archaic experience of "being-at-one-with" an idealized or mirroring other has been found to be essential to the establishment of a cohesive and vital self, the creative elaboration of mature selfhood throughout the life span depends on the capacity to recognize the intersubjectivity of the selfobject bond, and it is through this creative tension (Winnicott, 1971; Benjamin, 1988) between recognizing the other and asserting the self that self-experience is elaborated and continually renewed. In the absence of these renewing experiences, development may cease, resulting in arrest, fixation, and stasis. Winnicott (1971) argued powerfully that the recognition of otherness is essential for useful engagement in the social world (which includes psychoanalysis). He wrote: "A world of shared reality is created which the subject can use and which can feed back other-than-me substances into the subject" (p. 94). It is through this process that the ability to love, to empathize, and to be an other to the other arises.

Jessica Benjamin (1991) placed the capacity for other-recognition at the center of her developmental model: "The other must be recognized as another subject in order for the self to fully experience his or her subjectivity in the other's presence. This means, first, that we have a need for recognition and second, a capacity to recognize others in return, mutual recognition. But recognition is a capacity of individual development that is only unevenly realized" (p. 45). Utilizing Winnicott's theory of the use of the object (Winnicott, 1971), Benjamin described a dialectical process of negation and recognition through which the developing child finds pleasure in the experience of the mother as a subject. Benjamin (1991) stated: "The capacity to recognize the mother as a subject is an important part of early development" (p. 46) (also see Aron, 1992).

In support of Benjamin's argument, nonanalytic researchers such as Hoffman (1984), Trevarthen (1979, 1980, 1992), Compos and Stemberg (1981), Butterworth (1991), and Damon (1996) have identified the development in late infancy of the capacity to move beyond the "global empathy" of the newborn (Hoffman, 1984) to a point where "the infant's empathic reactions increasingly become channeled into sympathetic feelings for people that the infant cares about. The infant begins to realize that other people are independent beings who have their own happy and unhappy feelings" (Damon, 1996, p. 206). Cole characterized these developments, which he places between the ages of 6 and 9 months, as "a new biosocial-behavioral reorganization of life" (Cole, 1996). Colin Trevarthan (1979, 1980) used the terms *primary intersubjectivity* and *secondary intersubjectivity* to refer to the same phenomena while stressing the developmental sequencing of other-recognition capacity.

From the point of view of psychoanalytic developmental research, Daniel Stern (1985) confirmed the fact that by the ninth month infants exhibit a capacity to recognize the mother as a subject distinct from themselves. Stern stated: "Infants gradually come upon the momentous realization that inner subjective experiences, the subject matter of the mind, are potentially sharable with someone else" (p. 124). From that point a central feature of the infant's reality is the perception of the mother as subject. In fact Stern described how the recognition of intersubjectivity develops along with the awareness of the self's own subjectivity. For Stern the pleasure of intersubjectivity unfolds spontaneously as an inherent part of the infant's experience of the world. Affective attunement and empathy are other forms of intersubjective sharing—the core experiences that contribute to the crystallization of a cohesive self (an earlier form being "core relatedness" a later form being "verbal relatedness" [Stern, 1985]).

Kohut (1984) relates the capacity for recognition of the other's subjectivity to the increasing structuralization of the self through an incremental process of "transmuting internalization." Under normal developmental conditions Kohut explained how accompanying the healthy structuralization of the self (cohesive, strong and harmonious) there is a "shift in self-selfobject relations that is of great significance, namely, a gradual shift from the self relying for its nutriment on archaic modes of contact in the narcissistic sphere . . . to its ability to be sustained most of the time by the empathic resonance that emanates from the selfobjects of adult life" (p. 70).

Mature Selfobject Experience

The developmental progression towards more mature forms of selfobject relating involves the experience of an increasingly complex set of functions than those that characterize archaic forms of selfobject relating.

1. The Experience of Relationship

Mature selfobject experience is invariably of a relationship with an other (see Bacal, 1994); rather than simply happening (as with archaic selfobject relating), mature selfobject experience requires the participation of the person in securing, using, and nurturing relationships with others to meet selfobject needs. As we will see, this sense of the differentiation of the object from the self is fundamental to the mature selfobject experience and is the touchstone concept for distinguishing mature from archaic forms of selfobject relating.

2. Mature Confidence

In the previous section I noted the naive confidence in the object, which is characteristic of archaic experience. In contrast, the confidence in the availability of mature selfobject experiences is learned. Most importantly, it is confidence in the continuity and restoration of selfobject functions in spite of actual and/or anticipated failures, which is characteristic of mature selfobject relating. The philosopher David Hume spoke of how our daily functioning depends on assuming things will occur based on experience. For example, we assume the sun will rise each morning. We do not question such basic assumptions; to do so would make living intolerable. The archaic selfobject experience is assumed as the sunrise is, or as is the firmness of the floor as we slide out of bed in the morning. Mature selfobject experience is felt to be less reliable, but we acquire confidence that, in spite of uncertainty, our selfobject needs will be met within a range of reliability and adequacy (Bacal and Newman, 1990). Thus we achieve the capacity to tolerate uncertainty while at the same time holding on to the selfobject tie. To adapt Winnicott's idea, we acquire confidence in the "good-enough" mature selfobject functioning.

3. Flexibility of Function

Kohut (1984) noted how mature selfobject relating is characterized by flexibility. Over time, the mature person will experience fluctuations in selfobject need. During times of loss, frustration, or stress the mature person may experience the reactivation of archaic needs for mirroring, companionship, or seamless attunement with an idealized other. Unlike the archaic selfobject experience, which is restricted to the specific emergent needs of the core self, mature selfobject relating is flexible and the person has a capacity to use selfobject experiences in variable ways or to secure the needed selfobject experiences from others.

4. Personal Agency

The active procurement and usage of mature selfobject experiences presupposes a sense of agency on the individual's part. Rather than being the recipient of selfobject ministrations from caretakers (archaic relating), the maturely functioning person acts within the selfobject milieu to "make it happen." This is in contrast to Kohut's early model of the individual's mature self as an autonomous structure crystallized from the transmuting internalization of selfobjects. Rather, the mature person, as a result of their confidence in the availability of selfobject experiences and their skills in securing and nurturing selfobject responses, is an active agent in the construction, regulation, and maintenance of their selfobject milieu.

5. Other Recognition

Kohut, Ornstein, and others have stressed how, in mature selfobject relating, the other is experienced as a separate and distinct center of initiative. Benjamin (1988, 1991) and Aron (1991, 1992) have argued for the concept of recognition of the subjectivity of the other as a key aspect of mature development (see also Hagman, 1996). Slavin and Kreigman (1992) view this capacity as biologically inherent and locate its source in evolutionary processes. In archaic selfobject relating, the subjectivity of the other is only dimly perceived and almost certainly plays little, if any, part in the experience of its key functions. In contrast, the recognition of otherness is fundamental to the mature selfobject experience. This is a more specific aspect of the relationship quality that we discussed in #1. As Kohut noted, in the explaining stage of analysis, the analysand gradually recognizes the analyst as another person separate from themselves, with a unique perspective and center of experience; this recognition is an essential precondition for mutative interpretation. However, Kohut stressed that the analyst *still* retains selfobject functions for the analysand. This is the area of *intertwining* that he, and later Ornstein, wrote about. Mature selfobject relating is virtually defined by the simultaneity of the recognition of otherness with the continuing experience of selfobject functioning. From this dialectical process, the rest of the mature selfobject characteristics follow.

6. The Experience of Reciprocity

It is understood that even the earliest forms of selfobject experience
involve some level of a give-and-take process of mutual recognition and
reciprocity (Spitz, 1965; Trevarthen, 1979, 1980; Stern, 1985; also see
Slavin and Kriegman [1992] for a discussion of the evolutionary basis of
reciprocal altruism). However, others experienced as providing archaic
selfobject functions are felt to do so selflessly—the self of the other is *not*
experienced as a primary factor in archaic relating. On the other hand
mature selfobject relating involves the *central experience* of reciprocity.
In mature selfobject relating the recognition of otherness is an integral
part of the experience, and the person involved will reciprocate based
on their assessment of the other's needs. Of course, when there is
regression to archaic usage, reciprocity may be temporarily suspended;
when mature levels of relating are restored, the experience of mutual
engagement resumes.

7. The Capacity to be Empathic

Many studies have argued that empathy is a developmental achievement
that is an outgrowth of more archaic processes. Early forms of infant–
parent interactions that can be characterized by specific forms of coordinated and responsive behaviors are (from this perspective) early prototypical forms of affective and behavioral attunement similar in appearance to empathy (Condon, 1984). However, there is agreement that
true empathy is a characteristic of maturity (Terman, 1980). Most importantly, empathy requires the recognition of the other as an independent
center of subjectivity, while at the same time there is an experience of
intersubjectivity. This allows for an empathic stance that is centered both
"within" and "without" the other's mind. In addition, the recognition of
otherness leads to the utilization of both "objective" and "subjective"
modes of observation, which, in combination, allow for an in-depth,
stereoscopic experience of the selfobject-other. Whether one person can
in fact know vicariously the inner life of another is hotly debated;
nonetheless, it is clear that however the process of mature empathy
occurs, a central characteristic is the intertwining of the experience of
self and other. To this end I believe that the mature selfobject experience involves a sense of empathic connection that contains a simultaneous recognition of self and other, characterized by cognitive/affective
sharing.

8. Self-Transformation

The archaic selfobject experience facilitates the unfolding and elaboration of the inherent program of the emergent self—it does not necessarily add anything new. With maturity the experience of relationship, recognition of subjectivity and differentiation, and reciprocity leads to the inclusion within the self of other-than-me experience. The boundary of selfhood expands to include an other who is an independent center of subjectivity, which means that experiences will occur that are not predictable and that introduce new, and even surprising, elements into the self.

This quality of surprise has been lacking in self-psychological models. It is the engagement with an other, *recognized as such,* that the self is elaborated in creative and unpredictable ways. Because of this the mature selfobject experience is transformational. We change, we become different and acquire new qualities of self through engagement with the subjectivities of others who simultaneously serve selfobject functions. This experience of transformation is at the heart of Kohut's model of interpretive change, which I touched on above (and will be discussed more extensively below). New, not-self elements are assimilated and accommodated to by the self, which is transformed in the process.

9. Altruism

In their work *The Adaptive Design of the Human Psyche* (1992) Slavin and Kriegman argue that altruistic motives are central to human psychology. In other words, concern for others is not secondary to some inherent self-interest, but a primary adaptive orientation which underlies the fundamentally relational nature of intrapsychic life. Self psychologists have also stressed that the ability to be a good-enough other (i.e., to offer the opportunity for a selfobject experience) is the most developed capacity of mature selfobject relating. The Shanes (1990) write: "The range of experiences in adult life where one serves the needs of another, where that other's emotional requirements are perceived to have priority over one's own comprises a state of being we call *otherhood.* It is a general term that defines the many adult relationships wherein empathy and healthy altruism are seen as prerequisite to performing functions on behalf of another person" (Shane and Shane, 1990, p. 489). They continue: "Otherhood requires, what Buie (1981) refers to as *full adult empathy.* He says, It is object centered, not self centered. Adult (object centered) empathy (as opposed to self centered empathy) is concerned with much more than the other person's giving, nongiving or threatening attitudes towards oneself (pp. 281–307). Buie adds that in adult empathy there is a capacity to learn about one's objects in their own right" (p. 287). However, the Shanes expand on Buie's object-based perspective's implications for self-experience. They continue: "Whenever we fulfill an other's need to shore up or maintain the other's self or to satisfy the other's libidinal desires—that is, to perceive the other as an object in its own right—we are concomitantly experiencing the other as serving to satisfy our own needs, namely, as selfobject" (p. 490). And further: "The capacity to serve as a self-regulating other (selfobject) becomes an essential attribute of good-enough otherness" (p. 490). Hence, altruism characterizes the most advanced forms of mature self-object relating. In other words, in instances of altruism, offering a self-object experience to another functions as a selfobject experience for the self. I am not suggesting a naive and sentimental form of charitableness, but a deep and elaborate ongoing state of engagement with others in which self-interest and self-experience, as well as altruism and other recognition, are intertwined flexibly and purposefully in experiences that encompass a multiperson psychological field.

FORMS OF MATURE SELFOBJECT RELATING

The following is a brief review of the varieties of mature selfobject experiences. Rather than considering each in depth, my intent is to offer a survey that conveys the different forms of selfobject relating throughout life.

Friendship

Since the times of Homer and Aristotle, friendship has been viewed as a bedrock of society. Contemporary psychodynamic models include the capacity to form and sustain enduring, mutually beneficial friendships as a defining feature of healthy maturity. In diagnostic assessments the absence of friendship in a person's life can be indicative of severe psychopathology. On the one hand the prevalence of stormy and/or exploitative/abusive "friendships" has been found to be characteristic of borderline and narcissistic character disorders. On the other hand, the absence of motivation toward (and capacity for) friendship typifies the emotional lives of many schizophrenic patients.

Enduring friendship requires the reciprocal recognition of the other as an independent center of subjectivity encompassing a range of unique interests and motivations. At the same time there are experiences of intertwining perception, feeling, understanding, values, and interests. Friends "support and appreciate each other's narrative constructions of shared experience" (Galatzer-Levy and Cohler, 1993, p. 157). The quality of self-experience can be profoundly influenced by the vicissitudes of friendships. Being with "best friends" is commonly experienced as a celebration. The support of friends has been found to be essential to health and social adaptation. Hence, friendships are often the most meaningful and important of relationships.

The similarities between the above description of friendship and mature selfobject relating should be clear. The experience of friendship is the quintessential mature selfobject relationship. While the twinship or alter-ego nature of the friendship experience is easily recognizable, friends may also serve idealizing, mirroring, or self-delineating functions. Invariably, there is confidence in friendship and flexibility of mutual caring and support. Friendship is felt to be freely chosen by each partner. A good friend recognizes and attends to the separate and distinct subjectivity of the other, while at the same time relishing the experience of mutuality. Effective friendship is reciprocal, characterized by a mutually beneficial give and take. Empathy, the experience of being understood, is essential. Galatzer-Levy and Cohler (1993) noted in friendship: "The mutual appreciation for some core aspect of the other as an essential experience of friendship" (p. 158). Friendship also alters the partners as they engage with each other, allowing "other than me" experiences to be included in the life of the self. And finally the ability and willingness to place the needs of the friend before those of oneself (deliberately and without self-defeating motives) are considered the finest qualities of a good friend.

Obviously, what I am describing is an ideal. The difficulties of friendship are the frequent subjects of psychoanalytic inquiry. The experience of selfobject failure and the activation of archaic needs can threaten the reciprocal foundations of almost any friendship. Rather it is the capacity and willingness to engage in friendship and to work to sustain and nurture such a relationship that characterizes mature selfobject relating.

Mature Love and Sexuality

Early attempts to engage in loving sexual relationships are oftentimes tumultuous and short. Once again, the young person experiences himself as alternately passionately merged with the adored and/or admiring other and entranced by the other's uniqueness and independence. The ability to securely combine satisfying togetherness with an alluring differentiation is vulnerable to disruption. Transitory obsession, narcissistic rageful outbursts, and time-limited depressive or manic withdrawal are common and perhaps normal responses to disruptions in these still maturing forms of love (Person, 1988) .

Mature love and sexuality is characterized by a more balanced, less disruptive passion. Mature lovers indulge and cultivate the mutual gratification of selfobject needs: sharing idealizations, mirroring grandiosity, and being alter-egos. However, their capacity to enjoy and cultivate sensuous experiences of convergence is accompanied (and enhanced) by the continued capacity to recognize the independent subjectivity of the loved other. Person (1988) notes: "One may seek merger, but one seeks it with an Other. If one were successful in achieving complete and total merger there would be no other . . . when the pursuit of merger is unchecked, the lover becomes either a slave or tyrant" (p. 137). Earlier, Benedek (1984) described how lovers become "mutually a part of the self-system of the other" (p. 111). The classical view of love and sex as regressive phenomena misses the continued engagement in advanced levels of relating that characterizes mature sexual passion. "Good sex" is not solely a primitive fusion experience, but a skilled and articulate dialogue between persons who share an ability to attune physical desire, fantasy, and self-assertion with other-recognition—just as expert dancers remain exquisitely attuned to the flow and tension of their partner's cues and responses. In these instances sex can be considered to be a mature selfobject experience.

The experience of mature romantic love serves to enhance and nurture self-experience. Person (1988) notes: "Insofar as love mobilizes the individual to act for another rather than directly for the self, it serves as an agent for individual change. The lover is enabled to move out of the solipsism of his own consciousness and to embrace another consciousness as a separate and equal center to the universe" (p. 121). The experience of engagement with the loved one's unique subjectivity adds to the sense of self. Once more Person wrote that: "Love being directed outward, toward an Other, gives one, quite literally, a sense of direction, hence a purpose and value which are lacking in isolated individuals. This sense of direction and meaning further alters the sense of self, enabling one to feel capable of becoming something even more" (p. 122).

Marriage

> Research from very different perspectives have found that marital intimacy includes closeness; warmth; deep understanding of the other; sharing of ideas, information and feelings; fostering reciprocal personal growth; feeling needed and making the other feel needed; giving and receiving help and affection [Galatzer-Levy and Cohler, 1993, p. 254].

In all cultures commitment to a marriage has profound implications for self-experience (Benedek, 1984). Marriage as an institution, an experience, and an idea serves a pervasive self-referencing function for all adult members of our society. Self-esteem, social role and status, and access to broad ranges of selfobject experiences in one's culture can be directly affected by marital status. For married persons the experience of the relationship with one's mate can either function to sustain, enhance, and nurture self-experience or, on the other hand, serve to deplete, damage, or fragment the self (Ringstrom, 1994). Among the infinite variables that determine the quality of a marriage, elements of mutuality, recognition of individual subjectivity, and shared commitment are central. "Intimacy is experienced in the attunement to the other's needs and the enjoying of addressing them" (Ringstrom, 1994, p. 182). Marriages where the partners serve largely archaic selfobject functions may persist, but not thrive. The traditional asymmetrical power structure of marriage where the psychological and practical benefits accrue largely to the male partner has resulted in all to familiar partnerships of stagnation and oppression rather than sustained mutual self-enhancement and growth (Benjamin, 1988). From the point of view expressed in this chapter, the capacity of marital partners to engage with each other in a reciprocal, mature selfobject experience will be one of the factors that determine a marriage's viability and its self-sustaining, self-nurturing, and self-transformative function. Ringstrom (1994) noted: "Personal evolution in the relationship is linked to spouses' increased capacity for attunement to one another and to their discovery of ways to be responsive without losing and individual sense of self" (p. 182). Galatzer-Levy and Cohler (1993) also found the fundamental basis of a healthy marriage in the spouses' "shared understanding of the meaning of experience" (p. 254). The analysis and resolution of impediments to spouses' mutual recognition of each other's subjectivity, as well as intersubjectivity, is often key to effective marital treatment. "Spousal dysfunctional adaptation all have their origins in the spouses' experiencing one another as incapable of being understanding and responsive to the other's emotional needs" (Ringstrom, 1994, p. 163).

Parenting

Parents who are able to function in empathic merger with the forming self of the child, allow the use of their psychic organization as the child's own, and at the same time, phase specifically in tune with the child's changing needs, accept the child's separation, as a center of perception and initiative. This support of the forming and firming narcissism in the child is the developmental task of parenthood. The continuing transformation of their own narcissism is the developmental process of parenthood. . . . The forming and firming narcissism within the child and the further transformation of narcissism in the parents is essentially a twin process and may best be described as a double helix . . . a two-way process in which parental psychic structure also undergoes transformation [Elson, 1984, p. 299].

Self psychology has contributed much to our understanding of the function of the parent in self-development during childhood (Terman, 1980; Kohut, 1982; Elson, 1984; Muslin, 1984). In 1982 Heinz Kohut argued for the central position of the experience of parenting in human life. He stated: "Man's deepest and most central joy, that of being a link in the chain of generations. . . . Healthy man experiences . . . with deepest joy, the next generation as an extension of his own self. It is the primacy of the support for the succeeding generation, therefore, which is normal and human" (p. 403). Effective parenting depends on the capacity of the adult to empathize with their child. "The experience of parenthood commonly reshapes people's experience of themselves and others. The process begins with the discovery and working through of the fact that their actual baby is different from their preexisting fantasy baby. To perform the function of essential other for the baby, parents must be both irrationally committed to her and at the same time responsive to her—able to know and value" (Galatzer-Levy and Cohler, 1993, p. 42). Clinical self-psychological theory and research has emphasized the pathogenic impact of the parent's empathic incapacity as well as the damage to the self resulting from the parent's use of the relationship with the child for the satisfaction of archaic selfobject needs (Elson, 1984). Muslin noted how some parents are "not able to share the inner mental life of his child" (p. 323). A healthy parenting relationship depends on the mutuality of selfobject relating; however, the reciprocity between parent and child is experienced differently by each participant. The child, especially in earliest childhood, experiences the parent in archaic terms (which have been discussed above). The quality of the selfobject experience for the parent is related to their ability to make available selfobject experiences for their child, which means that the most mature selfobject experience of parenthood occurs at times when the parent fully and clearly recognizes the otherness of their child, as they orient their selves towards the satisfaction of their child's selfobject needs. In his discussion of the attributes of healthy fatherhood, Muslin (1984) noted: "The father is someone who can give to his progeny with joy, the joy of gift giving, the joy of vicariously experiencing what he has or has not had, the joy of being witness to the beauty of the unfolding maturation of his children . . . the self revels in the unfolding of his/her charges" (p. 323). I am not talking of self-negation; both Winnicott (1971) and Benjamin (1988, 1991) have instructed us regarding the parents' need to sustain and protect their own subjectivity simultaneous with devotion to child care. On the other hand, it is also true at times that in some instances parents may value the welfare of their child above their own self-interest (or more precisely the child's interests become those of the parent); in these instances the altruistic element in mature selfobject relating is most prominent. However, normally, a good parenting experience for both participants involves the mutual ongoing satisfaction of selfobject needs (more in the archaic range for the child and in the mature range for the adult). Good enough parents must be able to accept their child's idealization, mirror their child's grandiosity, and/or be their child's alter-ego. Stressing the role in the provision of selfobject functions to the child, Muslin (1984) adds that "one must be able to experience these functions as abiding self-pleasure—the joy of being the provider of worth to another" (p. 323). Albert Solnit (1984) conveyed the richness of parent–child reciprocity when he noted:

> In nurturing and representing the dependent child, parents fulfil vital needs of the child and at the same time they have the opportunity to continue the unfolding of their own adult development. The mutuality, of course, arises not so much from what is originally associated with the blood-tie, but more out of the hour-to-hour, day-to-day care of the child by the parents and the response of the child to the parents. These inter-actions establish resonating bonds and affectionate, empathic attach-ments that constitutes the primary psychological relationships between parents and their children [p. 230].

Creativity

"The main *motivation* at the root of creative experience is man's need to relate to the world around him. . . . It is . . . apparent in the artist's lifelong effort to grasp and render something which he has envisaged in the encounter with the world. . . . In such acts of relatedness man finds both the world and himself" (Schachtel, 1959, p. 241).

Creativity is regarded as one of the most valued of human capacities. Traditionally, psychoanalysts have emphasized the role of regressive states, the primary process and the interaction of presymbolic and symbolic cognition in the creative process. Winnicott has explored the nature of the creative play that can occur in the potential space between illusion and reality. It has been my finding that the most skilled, refined, and accomplished creative efforts are made possible through the artist's engagement with the object of their creative efforts in a mature selfob-ject experience. The self-experience of the artist is enhanced and vital-ized when her self-expressive interests converge with the expressive potential of the medium in the context of a specific aesthetic culture (medium and cultural aesthetic convention together make up an art form). For example, great painting cannot occur in the absence of the artist's understanding of the nature of paint, color, canvas, and composition, as well as the historical and contemporary context of painting as an art form. Raw expressiveness has little aesthetic value without first being processed through a skilled, reciprocal dialogue in which the inherent nature of the art form is recognized, respected, and then brought into dynamic interplay with the subjectivity and expressive interests of the artist. In this light, the "object" of the artist's creative efforts (for example, the art forms of painting, sculpture, film, etc.) can be understood to possess its own subjectivity, and the creative selfobject experience to be a dialectic in which the self of the artist and the independent subjective nature of the art form are engaged through the artist's effort and skill. Carl Rotenberg (1988) writes:

> Once the artist begins a work, he surrenders to it as though the work were dominating him, demanding a solution to its own ambiguities, and requiring completion. The artist experiences the selfobject functioning of the art work as alive, active, interpretive, and eventually having transformational capabilities, to the extent that the inner puzzles of the artist are worked out through this externalization [p. 209].

> The interplay is quite human, even though the particular medium that fosters it is inanimate [p. 211].

In the artwork self-experience and other-experience are intertwined. This engagement will result in true creation if the artist maintains his or her capacity to recognize the intersubjective nature of her aesthetic experience. If the artist attempts to disregard the essential nature of the medium or if the artist experiences his or her self as stifled or otherwise suppressed by the challenges posed by his or her specific art form, the creative endeavor will be inhibited at best, doomed to failure at worst. Therefore, the capacity of the artist to engage with his or her chosen art form in a mature selfobject relationship characterized by agency, confidence, flexibility, recognition, reciprocity, and altruism (artists frequently place other areas of self-interest second to their art) is essential to high levels of aesthetic accomplishment. I would like to add that the capacity to engage in mature selfobject relationships is limited with some individuals to areas of artistic effort and that the experience of pleasurable or vitalizing attunement that characterizes successful creative efforts does not necessarily characterize all phases of the creative process. In fact the torment of many creative personalities can be explained by their repeated encounters with selfobject failure (followed hopefully by restoration) as they pursue increasingly elusive and complex aesthetic challenges. (The suffering of Beethoven is a good example of this type of tormented creative experiencing; Mozart's self-confidence, pleasure, and ease of composition is an example of the opposite.)

CLINICAL IMPLICATIONS

An excellent example of the working through of an archaic selfobject tie and the development of the capacity for mature selfobject relating can be found in Kohut's The Two Analyses of Mr. Z (1979). In the early part of the second analysis it became clear that Mr. Z's persistent doubts about the truth of early memories of the mother's psychosis were motivated by fears concerning "the loss of the mother as an archaic selfobject. A loss that . . . threatened him with dissolution, with the loss of a self that at these moments he considered to be his only one. His doubts, his tendency to take back what he had already recognized and revealed . . . prevented him from fully acknowledging what he in fact experienced and knew" about her (p. 418). Eventually, Mr. Z moved beyond the delusion-like convictions regarding his mother's strength and power with the support of an idealized transference and the activation of an early selfobject tie to his father. At the end of the analysis Kohut noted the fundamentally changed nature of Z's relationship to his parents. He stated: "I was impressed by his expanded empathy with and tolerant attitude towards the shortcomings of his parents. Even with regard to the distortions of the personality of his mother . . . he could now express a modicum of understanding, even compassion. And he was able to see, without a trace of the idealizations with which he had begun his first analysis, the positive features of her personality. On the firm basis of his separateness and maleness, he could acknowledge that, despite her serious psychopathology, she had given him a great deal" (pp. 442–443). Kohut further noted that Z came to see that his "greatest assets" came from this woman whose deep flaws he had come to admit, and (most significantly for our argument), despite the breaking of the deep merger ties with the mother and the accompanying recognition of her full subjectivity, Z "retained his most significant talents and skills," a sign of the continued importance of the selfobject tie to the mother for Mr. Z's mature self-experience.

As was the case with Mr. Z a primary goal of analytic treatment is the development of the patient's capacity to establish and utilize mature selfobject relationships. Over the course of analysis most patients engage in various forms of selfobject relating in an effort to repair and more fully elaborate various sectors of self-experience. The analyst's experience of the patient is key to the understanding and facilitation of this process. The competent analyst should possess the ability to sustain mature selfobject relating over time and to restore the mature tie when it is lost due to selfobject failures occurring in treatment. In other words, the analyst works to experience the patient as serving mature selfobject functions, and it is the analyst's internal model of mature relating that acts as a reference for his or her understanding of the patient's transference. For much of the analysis this is a "one-sided" process as the analyst accepts and facilitates the patient's less mature, and often archaic, transferences. From this perspective, the countertransference reflects the analyst's experience of the fluctuations in the mature selfobject tie. Kohut's point regarding the countertransferential burdens of work with archaic transferences can be explained, I believe, as the analyst's experience of the periodic or sustained failure in mature selfobject experience due to the patient's lack of recognition of the analyst as an independent center of subjectivity. In fact during periods when the analyst serves an archaic function, all of the areas of mature relating become attenuated, as the center of the shared analytic universe shifts decisively to the patient. Kohut describes how the analyst must tolerate this negation. Optimally, the analyst does not resist, but facilitates the process *in the patient's interest.* On the other hand, the use of self as an effective therapeutic instrument serves an important selfobject function for the analyst. At times, he or she engages the patient in areas of archaic relating, and at other times he or she resists (perhaps even interferes with) the unfolding of the patient's transferences—these are common aspects of the countertransference that the analyst must address and utilize by means of self-analysis, supervision, and/or psychoanalysis proper.

When viewed from the perspective of a complete analysis, most of the transference relationship is not experienced on an archaic level but possesses a variable degree of maturity. Kohut (1984, pp. 184–185) emphasized this point when he distinguished between the "archaic bond of identity," which characterizes the "understanding aspect" of the analyst's activity and the "greater objectivity" and differentiation of the "explaining aspects." In fact most patients retain the capacity to recognize the analyst as an independent center of subjectivity, and they continue to engage in reciprocal interactions—to a greater or lesser extent. Our interest as analysts is in the vicissitudes of this baseline of mature relating, which is in most cases only unevenly achieved and maintained. All transferences result in some degree of variability in the patient's capacity to recognize the subjectivity of the other, to be confident, to reciprocate, and so on; this is what is expected and welcomed. Understanding the dynamics of these selfobject transferences, specifically the relationship between the patient's inner vulnerability and his or her experience of the analyst, is our central concern. However, an important implication of the mature selfobject experience concept is to encourage the analyst to focus attention not only on the inner function or meaning of the selfobject experience, but also its grounding in the relational context that becomes intertwined with the patient's experience of self. In practical terms the analyst must highlight through interpretation who he or she "is" to the patient and what the patient's experience is of what he or she "does" if they are to resonate empathically with the patient. When the patient becomes capable of mature selfobject relating, the analyst's empathy (traditionally viewed as a mirror) inevitably comes to include for the patient some expression of the analyst's own subjectivity. Empathy in this case is inclusive of "me and you"—the "us" of the analytic dyad (the "Analytic Third" described by Ogden in 1994). This does not mean that the analyst seeks to center the treatment on his or her self, but it does mean that eventually the analysis comes to involve the mutually constructed meaning of the interaction *as experienced by the patient*. At this point the analyst emerges from behind the metaphorical mirror to explore the patient's often accurate perceptions of and justifiable reactions to themselves (Aron, 1991).

The termination of an analysis arrives when the patient begins to experience an adequate level of stability in their mature selfobject experiences. This may result from the resolution of some self-crisis and the return to a previous level of functioning or the successful completion of a previously thwarted developmental process. In any case, the patient feels generally satisfied with their relationships in which there is a renewed (or "new") experience of mutuality, confidence, recognition, and empathy, as well as the opportunity for further growth. As Kohut stressed, clinically, the patient can achieve mature selfobject experiences through persons and/or activities (such as work or art). Ultimately, the central goal is the restoration of a vital and cohesive experience of self richly and productively intertwined with the world.

REFERENCES

Aron, L. (1991), The patient's experience of the analyst's subjectivity. *Psychoanal. Dial.*, 1:29–51.

———— (1992), Interpretation as expression of the analyst's subjectivity. *Psychoanal. Dial.*, 2:475–507.

Bacal, H. (1994), The selfobject relationship in psychoanalytic treatment. In: *A Decade of Progress, Progress in Self Psychology, Vol. 10*, ed. A. Goldberg. Hillsdale, NJ: The Analytic Press, pp. 21–30.

———— (1995), The centrality of selfobject experience in psychological relatedness. *Psychoanal. Dial.*, 5:403–410.

Benedek, T. (1984), The family as a psychologic field. In: *Parenthood*, ed. E. J. Anthony & T. Benedek. New York: Little, Brown, pp. 109–136.

Benjamin, J. (1988), *The Bonds of Love*. New York: Pantheon.
—— (1991), Recognition and destruction: An outline of intersubjectivity. In: *Relational Perspectives in Psychoanalysis,* ed. N. Skolnick & S. Warshaw. Hillsdale, NJ: The Analytic Press, pp. 43–60.
Buie, D. (1981), Empathy: Its nature and limitations. *J. Amer. Psychoanal. Assn.,* 29:281–307.
Butterworth, G. (1991), The ontogeny and phylogeny of joint visual attention. In: *Natural Theories of the Mind,* ed. A. Whitten. Oxford: Blackwell, pp. 223–232.
Cole, M. (1996), Interacting minds in the life-span perspective: A cultural-historical approach to culture and cognitive development. In: *Interactive Minds,* ed. P. Baltes & U. Staudinger. Cambridge: Cambridge University Press, pp. 59–87.
Compos, J. J. & Sternberg, C. R. (1981), Perception, appraisal, and emotion: The onset of social referencing. In: *Infant Social Cognition,* ed. M. E. Lamb & L. R. Sherrod. Hillsdale, NJ: Lawrence Erlbaum Associates, pp. 273–314.
Condon, W. S. (1984), Communication and empathy. In: *Empathy II,* ed. J. Lichtenberg, M. Bornstein & D. Silver. Hillsdale, NJ: The Analytic Press, pp. 35–58.
Damon, W. (1996), The lifelong transformation of moral goals through social influence. In: *Interactive Minds,* ed. P. Baltes & U. Staudinger. Cambridge: Cambridge University Press, pp. 198–220.
Eigen, M. (1993), *The Electrified Tightrope*. Northvale, NJ: Aronson.
Elson, M. (1984), Parenthood and the transformations of narcissism. In: *Parenthood,* ed. R. Cohen, B. Cohler & S. Weissman. New York: Guilford, pp. 297–314.
Galatzer-Levy, R. M. & Cohler, B. (1993), *The Essential Other*. New York: Basic Books.
Goldberg, A. (1988), *A Fresh Look at Psychoanalysis*. Hillsdale, NJ: The Analytic Press.
Hagman, G. (1996), Flight from the subjectivity of the other: Pathological adaptation to childhood parent loss. In: *Basic Ideas Reconsidered, Progress in Self Psychology, Vol. 12,* ed. A. Goldberg. Hillsdale, NJ: The Analytic Press, pp. 207–219.
—— (1997), Clinical implications of the concept of mature selfobject experience. Paper presented to the Annual Meeting of the Psychology of the Self.
Hoffman, M. L. (1984), Interaction of affect and cognition in empathy. In: *Emotions, Cognition, and Behavior,* ed. C. E. Izard, J. Kagan & R. B. Zajonc. Cambridge: Cambridge University Press, pp. 1–41.
Kohut, H. (1971), *The Analysis of the Self*. Madison, CT: International Universities Press.
—— (1977), *The Restoration of the Self*. Madison, CT: International Universities Press.
—— (1979), The two analyses of Mr. Z. *Internat. J. Psychoanal.,* 60:3–27.
—— (1984), *How Does Analysis Cure?* ed. A. Goldberg & P. Stepansky. Chicago: University of Chicago Press.
Lichtenberg, J. (1991). What is a selfobject? *Psychoanal. Dial.,* 1:455–479.
Modell, A. (1984), *Psychoanalysis in a New Context*. Madison, CT: International Universities Press.
Muslin, H. (1984), On the resistance to fatherhood: Consideration on the self of the father. In: *Parenthood,* ed. R. Cohen, B. Cohler & S. Weissman. New York: Guilford, pp. 315–325.
Ogden, T. (1994), *Subjects of Analysis*. Northvale, NJ: Aronson.

Ornstein, P. (1991), Why self psychology is not an object relations theory: Clinical and theoretical considerations. In: *The Evolution of Self Psychology, Progress in Self Psychology, Vol. 7,.* ed. A. Goldberg. Hillsdale, NJ: The Analytic Press, pp. 17–30.

Person, E. (1988), *Dreams of Love and Fateful Encounters.* New York: Norton.

Ringstrom, P. (1994), An intersubjective approach to conjoint therapy. In: *A Decade of Progress: Progress in Self Psychology, Vol. 10,* ed. A Goldberg. Hillsdale, NJ: The Analytic Press, pp. 159–182.

Rotenberg, C. T. (1988), Selfobject theory and the artistic process. In: *Learning from Kohut: Progress in Self Psychology, Vol. 4,* ed. A. Goldberg. Hillsdale, NJ: The Analytic Press, pp. 193–213.

Schachtel, E. (1959), *Metamorphosis.* New York: Basic Books.

Shane, M. & Shane, E. (1990), The struggle for otherhood: Implications for development in adulthood of the capacity to be a good-enough object for another. In: *New Dimensions in Adult Development,* ed. R. Nemiroff & C. Colarusso. New York: Basic Books, pp. 487–498.

Slavin, M. O. & Kriegman, D. (1992), *The Adaptive Design of the Human Psyche.* New York: Guilford Press.

Solnit, A. (1984), Parenthood and child advocacy. In: *Parenthood,* ed. R. Cohen, B. Cohler & S. Weissman. New York: Guilford, pp. 227–238.

Spitz, R. (1965), The evolution of dialogue. In: *Drive Affects, Behavior. Vol. 2,* ed. M. Schur. Madison, CT: International Universities Press, pp. 170–192.

Stern, D. (1985), *The Interpersonal World of the Infant.* New York: Basic Books.

Stolorow, R. & Atwood, G. (1992), *Contexts of Being.* Hillsdale, NJ: The Analytic Press.

Terman, D. (1980), Object love and the psychology of the self. In: *Advances in Self Psychology,* ed. A. Goldberg. Madison, CT: International Universities Press, pp. 349–364.

Trevarthen, C. (1979), Communication and cooperation in early infancy: A description of primary intersubjectivity. In: *Before Speech,* ed. M. Bullowa. New York: Cambridge University Press, pp. 321–347.

——— (1980), The foundation of intersubjectivity: Development of interpersonal and cooperative understanding in infants. In: *Changing the Subject,* ed. J. Henriques. London: Methuen Press, pp. 79–110.

——— (1992), The self born in intersubjectivity: An infant communicating. In: *Ecological and Interpersonal Knowledge of the Self,* ed. U. Neisser. New York: Cambridge University Press, pp. 32–52.

Winnicott, D. W. (1971), *Playing and Reality.* New York: Basic Books.

Wolf, E. (1988), *Treating the Self.* New York: Guilford Press.

Chapter 8

The Shame Experiences Of the Analyst

Ruth Stein

In a recently published paper, Fonagy and Target (1995) tell us of a patient with a congenital deformity of the spine, who, unkempt, unshaven, and dirty, declined with contempt any help from the analyst, while at the same time asking for it, and sneeringly rejected an interpretation involving his dependency on the latter. This patient started an analytic session by suddenly taking off his shirt to reveal his deformed back, leaving it exposed for the entire session. "I felt revulsion, confusion, and then shame," writes Fonagy (p. 489). His comments about the patient's attempt to preempt his anxiety of rejection "by trying to control the feelings of those around him" (p. 489) met with derision, although Fonagy sensed that his interpretation had been true; the patient, however, refused to accept the analyst's empathy with "the sense of injustice and hurt which seemed to drive his bitter hatred." But then Fonagy (1995) had the idea of telling him: "It seems that you feel safer when someone is uncomfortable" (p. 489). "To this the patient readily agreed," writes Fonagy (1995, p. 489).

This is one of the few mentions in the literature of a shame experience of the analyst, which is, however, not further discussed. I think that precisely at the moment that Fonagy sensed more directly the patient's

---

Paper presented at the Annual Conference of Self Psychology, San Francisco, October 1995.

I am grateful to Jonathan Slavin for the care and thoroughness with which he read an early draft of this paper, to Anna Gelman and Rina Kretch for their collecting for me examples from their clinical work, to Raanan Kulka, Rina Lazar, and Itamar Levy for their understanding and ideas; and to my discussant, Barnett Malin, for his helpful suggestions for reorganization of the chapter.

shame and discomfort and could apprehend and interpret the patient's defense against shame (rather than his dependency or his sense of injustice), the analyst could come empathically near the patient's experience and could find ready acceptance in the patient's heart. Now a clearer picture could emerge: that of "a persecutory, cruel but damaged object (represented by [the patient's] . . . back), and a figure seen as shamed, uncomfortable and weak [which was sometimes the analyst and sometimes the patient]" (p. 489).

In this chapter, I want to discuss some manifestations and consequences of the experience of shame in the analyst. My inspiration for discussing shame came from Kohut's writings and was further supported by the intersubjective approach that takes into account the influence of the observer, the analyst. This approach suggests that the analyst in fact also turns to the patient with selfobject needs (Stolorow and Atwood, 1992, p. 247), although usually in a less archaic form. This growing mutuality of analyst and patient (Aron, 1992, 1996; Casement, 1985, 1990) enlivens our notions about the shame of the analyst, in addition to that of the patient. Recent findings and knowledge gained from developmental research on shame (Schore, 1991; Tyson and Tyson, 1990), which deeply connect with self psychology's view of shame as a response to selfobject nonresponsiveness (rather than as a simple reaction formation against drives), all contribute to an expanded, modified conception of our habitual notions of shame. The perspective of relational theory (e.g., Mitchell, 1988) powerfully informs my approach as well, providing such notions as the need of the patient to have his experience reclaimed and revitalized and his disordered subjectivity healed, and the analyst's knowledge, which is not only about the mind, but which is personal *and* not idiosyncratic. Such knowledge as the analyst has, grounds her beliefs about the patient in her own subjective experience (Mitchell, 1993). And last, the background for this chapter is my longstanding interest in affects (Stein, 1990, 1991, 1993, 1994, 1995, 1996), together with ideas that emerged during work with my patients. In this chapter, therefore, I will suggest that understanding and acknowledging moments of shame in the analyst and discerning their varieties may greatly help us become free to tap new dimensions in our clinical work.

In what follows, I shall present different varieties of the experience of shame in the analyst, which, for heuristic reasons, will be differentiated into four kinds. The first two, which I shall call "resonant shame" and "introjected shame," are the analyst's responses to the patient's shame and shamelessness, respectively, whereas the last two, "shame of lack" and "shame of excess," pertain more to the analyst's self-experience and will be followed by some of my views on the analyst's selfobject function and its links with shame. I shall then attempt to point to some reasons why the shame experience of the analyst has not been discussed until now, adumbrating the analyst's changed position as a major factor responsible for this state of affairs. In presenting some varieties of the analyst's possible shame experiences, I shall begin with two types of shame, which derive from the intersubjective interaction between the two analytic partners.

THE ANALYST'S RESONANT SHAME

There are situations where the contemporary analyst, less invisible and freer than the classical analyst, with all her lesser susceptibility to shame and with her greater freedom, as I shall try to show later, may resonate with the patient's shame so powerfully, may feel the reverberations of this particular kind of pain that wants to hide, as to consciously or unconsciously feel ashamed and embarassed herself. The contagious quality of shame may then shift the analyst's attention from containing and "metabolizing" the patient's experience, toward withdrawing into her own feelings of guilt and shame about witnessing the patient's shamed feelings and gestures. Or the analyst may unconsciously altogether block feeling any shame, with its potentially paralyzing threat and eventual spiraling into resourcelessness. The patient, on his part, may wish not to embarass his analyst, and thus both patient and analyst may collude in not recognizing or misrecognizing painful aspects of their actual, mutual experience (Lewis, 1971). In this way, shame is probably one of the principal factors contributing to the analyst–patient collusions, because in the case of shame, the comfort one usually gets from sharing feelings does not apply. This is a specific feature of shame: recognizing and resonating with the other's shame feelings can be embarrassing and painful. Sometimes silence is the most empathic route; at other times, suitable words have to be found in an effort not to withdraw in the face of the patient's shame and help him with it. Lawrence Friedman (1992) convincingly, though indirectly, touches on how the analyst's dispassionate attitude toward the patient's most painful passionate (embarrassing) feelings and acts strongly impresses the patient (p. 12). I read Friedman as saying that the analyst's calmness and her nonjudgmental attitude in the face of delicate, shameful feelings can put an end to the mutual reverberations of shame. Such an inner attitude, where the analyst is both immersed in the patient's experience and overcomes it, presupposes maturity and freedom from shame, which the patient will sense and usually experience as helpful with his own shame. It is in the context of the resonating and amplifying power of shame that we can read Freud's admission that he could not bear being looked at by his patients 8 hours a day (in Schneider, 1987, p. 207). Freud (1915) also said that transference love functions as a resistance to treatment and serves to put the analyst "in painful embarassment" ("*peinliche Verlegenheit*," p. 124). Let me give an example of what I mean by that.

Case A

I had a patient who, at the beginning of his treatment, would come in, sit down, and fix me with a direct, wordless, frozen stare, which lasted for what seemed to me unending moments. I felt extremely uncomfortable and self-conscious, yet I tried not to look away because I had the feeling he needed me to be there for him by looking back at him with a steady, friendly, yet unsmiling look and to sustain my discomfort and embarrassment at being looked at in such a way. All this time, I was trying to figure out, first to myself, and later with him, what his stare meant. I felt like I was being swallowed up by his eyes, almost made into a senseless object, and I was alarmed by his lack of reserve or compunction or feeling of proportion about his rather bizarre stare. After some weeks, he felt secure enough to tell me he stared at me out of great fear, fear that made his eyes glued on to my face—his fear of therapy, of me, and of what we were about to discover in the depths of his soul. It then became clear that what he called his fear was another name for his chronic shame about himself, which he tried to counterphobically overcome by this stare. With time, the intensity of his stare lessened somewhat, and it then assumed a different function: it now expressed his intense need for contact, especially physical contact, and it was his way of feeling in deep touch with me. After much therapeutic work, this stare disappeared or, rather, was transformed into verbalizable recollections, wishes, fantasies, and new emotional experiences. I believe that by my not shying away from his gaze and hiding and by my wordless, concrete mirroring of his excited stare, he was enabled to gradually calm down from his excited fear and be able to reflect about what was happening to him.

A different variety of the analyst's shame is illustrated by Fonagy's example. This is the kind of shame the analyst experiences with perversions; we could name it "counterperverse shame."

THE ANALYST'S SHAME AND PERVERSION

Shame may be experienced by the analyst when she becomes strongly enmeshed in transference–countertransference gambits of certain patients, who may show amazing shamelessness.

Case B is an example communicated to me by a colleague. From the beginning of her treatment, this patient started a kind of "exposure contest" with her therapist, where she would inquire, spy, and pry upon her analyst's whereabouts. This narcissistically disturbed woman who felt overly shamed and humiliated by the analytic procedure, reacted by intruding upon her analyst's life in the same way she felt the analyst had done to her. The analyst would at such moments feel unpleasantly surprised and invaded, and gradually she became aware of feeling increasingly embarrassed and ashamed. In the concrete words of this colleague: "It is as if such a patient were saying, "You are my analyst, therefore I am entitled to get into everything that is yours, even into your pants.'" The analyst felt, like one may typically feel in such cases, a blend of revulsion, of being coerced against her will, of helplessness, and of being titillatingly manipulated and frustrated, all of these reactions leading to shame feelings.

The countertransference to perverse enactments or even to the (always enactive) descriptions of perverse scenes is typically that of a listener or spectator who is being coerced to participantly witness a vicariously shaming scene or event and being made to feel the shame that should be normally involved. The analyst then experiences what may metaphorically be called the "missing" shame of the patient, the shame the perverse patient "should" experience but fails to when he degrades and desecrates himself, often projecting it into the analyst by his arrogant and devaluatory attitude. "Witnessing such a scene [the prototypical perverse scene in which humiliation is used for achieving control]," writes Nathanson (1992), "we tend to avert our own gaze and cry out our wish that the protagonist be shielded from our view" (p. 318). It is intriguing to note that with perverts we may be ashamed both of their excess and shamelessness, and of the image they create of us as limited, "square," ridiculously naive, lacking—in sophistication, wit, or glamor. The analyst who receives the pervert's gaze feels shame by being looked at in this way. In my experience, such enactments and feelings are particularly likely to happen with perverse patients, who characteristically tend to evince high degrees of shamelessness (Khan, 1979; Bonnet, 1981; Chasseguet-Smirgel, 1984). When we are coerced and enmeshed into an enactment of a perverse relationship, we have to bear and carry the patient who abandons shame that is felt as threatening to his self. Perversity is the refusal of differentiation, a struggle against boundaries (the pervert does not experience and use shame to maintain limits); it is the abnegating of the experience of the other person as separate and as entitled to his own privacy.

The two apparently contradictory situations, that of resonant shame and that of perverse shamelessness, point to an interesting phenomenon, namely that *the danger of collusion, falseness, or impasse is averted if one of the analytic partners experiences shame:* either the patient experiences shame with the analyst managing not to resonate too closely with his shame, or the analyst feels shame, by having to temporarily carry the perverse patient's shame. If both partners feel too ashamed, painful themes will be bypassed, whereas if both partners have no shame, various perverse or narcissistic enactments are likely to happen. Thus, shame is an exquisitely subtle and complex marker of the boundaries between normal and abnormal curiosity and exposure.

In addition to resonant shame and projected shame, which are varieties of the analyst's experience of reverberating, projectively identifying, or containing mental contents of the patient, there are two other, rather self-directed, types of shame experiences of the analyst, namely, shame of lack and shame of excess.

SHAME OF LACK

Shame is usually regarded as awareness of one's lack, failure, or defect. The classical examples are those of the analyst being made to feel aware of her shortcomings, mistakes, or inefficiency.

Since these cases are the most familiar and thought about, I shall go into a more subtle, less articulate, but no less important, phenomenon of shame: shame that regulates surplus of excitement, which has a tendency to be perceived and experienced by the excited person as loss or lack of control. Freud (1905) conceptualized shame as a superego counterforce or reaction formation against overstimulation of the exhibitionistic drives, which has potential ego-disruptive effects. Schore (1991) writes that "shame signals the self system to terminate interest-excitement in whatever has come to its attention" (p. 194). Excitement, as Kohut and contemporary relational theorists say, is not necessarily sexual or sexually derived but is a much broader affect. Spezzano (1993), for instance, says that, given the inevitable uncertainty about the future and the lack of any absolute (foundational) knowledge nowadays, one should regard excitement as the best guide to our actions (p. 157). This broadened psychoanalytic view of excitement makes the affect that deals with excitement, namely shame, a central phenomenon of self-experience. Indeed, Kohut (1971) speaks of defenses against dangerous excitement: excitement that cannot be contained arouses shame to block it. However, if the analyst is inhibited by shame (about the patient's excited erotic transference, for example), she will unconsciously repudiate it and thus be unable to empathically attune to the patient's excitement, fear, and desire and to help put these feelings into words, narratives, and transference fantasies. On the other hand, as shame is a means of regulating excitement when the analyst's excitement cannot be controlled and modulated "naturally"; that is, in case the analyst cannot contain disruptive affects, her (conscious or unconscious) shame might help her modulate or suppress these feelings rather than act them out and harm analytic developments. In this sense, shame in its mature and subtle forms is a powerful protection that sustains self-respect, dignity, and integrity, and the signal of shame serves these ends. Analytic competence lies in the analyst's becoming clearly aware of her shame and in analyzing and overcoming it to be creatively free to intervene therapeutically and not project it onto the patient, because only when the patient does not get back the projected shame of the analyst can he moderate and mollify his own shame and self-rejection (cf., Speziale-Bagliacca, 1991, p. 31 and Sandler, 1992, p. 196).

SHAME OF EXCESS

The shame the analyst experiences upon realizing she has been too expressive, ardent, or unrestrained; her reserve about the patient's exuberance and idealizations; but also the analyst's feelings of having passed from an intense affective state to a decidedly less intense one (for instance, the intimacy that builds within a session, which suddenly comes to an end when the hour is over) are all instances of what I call "shame of excess."

There is obviously something fearful about excitement for analysts, and we have learned to link spontaneity and excitement with an anti-analytic attitude because of its attributes of arousal, nonreflective directness, and nearness to impulsivity and notions of acting out and loss of professional control. But it is the exquisite blend of spontaneity and reflection that marks the art of analysis. It is the unique combination of deeply thinking and feeling without succumbing to the action tendencies inherent in strong affect that yields psychoanalytic understanding and wisdom.

This latter way in which shame functions, what I have called "shame of excess," is a profoundly important but ignored aspect, which is being now discovered and articulated by many researchers on shame. It has to do with the idea that shame is not necessarily caused by some fault, lack, or negative quality: one can experience searing shame at points of high expectations, excitement, or pleasurable feelings.

Thus, the more the analyst can experience and tolerate such states of excitement without becoming too aroused or anxious, the more she will be able to be in touch with her inner knowledge of herself and of her patient. Kohut (1971) beautifully describes the psychic pain of such a self-deflation, and Schore (1991) spoke of it as a rapid reduction of interest-excitement, a sudden decrement in mounting pleasure. In Kohutian terminology, shame is related to an empathic break between the mirroring selfobject and the grandiose self. Kohut tapped a process that is ubiquitous and occurs often and mostly automatically, when he spoke of empathic failure as lack of in-tuneness (of the caretaker or analyst to the child or patient) and showed its vicissitudes within narcissistic patients, as well as within everybody. He even spoke of empathic failures as mini-traumata, which replicate, on a smaller scale, "the dedifferentiating influx of unneutralized narcissistic libido" (1971, p. 152). What I would like to add here is that the analyst, too, can at certain moments experience empathic failure of her own toward herself or of her patient toward her and feel ashamed.

Let me illustrate what I have in mind with an event that took place at a party I was attending, where I spotted an ex-patient of mine whom I liked, but whose analysis I estimated to have been not very satisfactory. At the end of this analysis, I had felt that perhaps more could and should have been done to help her. Seeing her, I felt quite interested in her and curious about how she had fared after the analysis. I greeted her and asked her how she was, but as I was addressing her, I somehow realized that my hailing was unwelcome and that she was not reciprocating my interest in her: it was all completely different from what I had expected it to be. At that very moment, I felt my interest in her and even slight enjoyment become embarassing and inappropriate manifestations, my look an unwelcome intrusion, and my greeting a flat movement, left hanging in midair. She did not say a word, but her countenance expressed what I took to be some kind of condescension through which she seemed to wordlessly signal the futility, uselessness, and worthlessness of my query, or so I thought. I did not say anything further, and I remained with this extremely unpleasant experience throughout the evening and remembered it for many weeks. Only months later, upon incidentally meeting her on the street, did we clear up this matter. As I again politely inquired about her well-being, she flippantly replied that I had not seemed so interested when I had asked her the same question last time, so why was I asking now. It soon became clear that she had felt so embarassed by my unexpected presence at the party and my open interest in her that she could not bring herself to say a word: instead, in her discomfort, her face involuntarily became a grimace of shame. It was a tremendous relief for her to learn that my withdrawal after addressing her was not out of indifference to her, but because of the way I had interpreted her wordless answer to my question. With myself, I then wondered what it had been that had not let me see her shame and led me instead to read her response as a shaming gesture toward me. Reflecting upon it, I realized that the part that came from within myself that had contributed to this situation was my self-criticism (partially a result of identifying with her own criticism of herself and of me and partially my own feeling of dissatisfaction with my analytic work with her). As to her part, I realized that what had been misleading me was that the expression of her face did not look like that of an embarrassed adult. It was the face of an openly ashamed child, with one shoulder lifted, eyebrows raised, the mouth pulled down at the corners, the head a little tilted aside, all a blatant and childish expression of shame. Aided by knowledge of my self-doubt about her, I understood it as referring to the same aspect of our past enterprise, the analysis, as the one I had been worried about. I did not realize that the clues of worthlessness her face emitted were directed toward herself. She had been unable to contain her excitement on seeing me, and her facial signs of shame, unexpectedly intense and uncontrolled, were read by me as a gesture of a put-down, as her attempt to communicate that our connection was without value and even contemptible in her eyes. I could not see that this expression referred to her own inner state, to her self-perception and self-image. I could not see that her drooped head (Tomkins [1963] ascribes it to sudden loss of tonus in the neck that is a physiological accompaniment of shame) and the contours of her lips were not signs of dislike, but a sign of the utter shock of her shame of me, who represented for her at that moment, transferentially perhaps, the shaming other. Rather symmetrically, she was for me at the same moment the shaming other, and I felt ashamed by her wordless affect display and ashamed of my unsuspecting directness (and shameless-ness). This encounter, brief, but under very loaded circumstances, was enough for both of us to put us into months of unpleasant feelings of being rejected; each of us privately felt, with the sure knowledge of the flash of recognition of a face, a similar feeling that could be dissipated only at a later encounter. A short time afterwards, this woman resumed analysis with me, which this time reached parts of her that had not been accessible in the past.

Thus, we have come a long way from the common-sense, familiar connotation of shame as the reaction to the exposure of something faulty or lacking in oneself. In addition to such "shame of lack" and in addition to shame or lack of shame that is transmitted the way affects are transmitted, through resonance (and attunement) from one person to another, or through projective identification there is shame as shock about exuberance and excess. These different varieties imply different kinds of subtle, delicate balances of intimacy and distance. All inter-weave with various inner states in the analyst and patient and produce blends of restraint with varying degrees of comfort.

THE ANALYST AS SELFOBJECT, THE USE OF THE OBJECT

It is arguable that the potential for shame may provide one sort of answer when we ask ourselves what draws us as analysts to fulfill our patients' selfobject needs. What (in addition to our competence-seeking work ego and our reparative commitments) makes it so attractive, so deeply moving (at least for some types of analysts), to be prepared to steadfastly mirror some of the most "absurd" or "extravagant" needs of our narcissistic patients? Why should the analyst desire to serve and be used as a selfobject (provided it is something different than the echoes of masochistic submission, analytic grandiosity, and rescue fantasies)? Is it only to assuage our own sense of loneliness by deeply connecting, immersing ourselves and merging with another human's inner world, and identifying with the empathic reception we are giving him? May it not also be that the attracting power of this therapeutic activity for analysts lies in the fact that by following, by "shadowing," the patient with sensitive dedication, we in a sense fulfill a longing to shed our occasionally burdensome selves and identities (cf., Lichtenstein, 1977, p. 187) and, thus, to protect ourselves against the pains and errors born of our initiative and difference? May we not be nourishing the fantasy that, by being empathically immersed in the patient's experiential world, we can spare ourselves our own exposure, our coming forth and showing ourselves in our naked individuality, and that, moreover, we can enjoy the opportunity given to us of making good our strayings from the patient's inner perceptual rules by the clarification of our empathic failures with him? In this sense, being an analytic selfobject is holding on to a banister, a support; it is molding oneself according to the shape and contours of the selfobject needed by the patient.

Some take this even further (as have done Ferenczi and Winnicott, each in his own way) and have added the context of being prepared to be "used." Here we are talking of giving ourselves over, in a sense, so the patient can use those of our functions that he needs for his own growth (Bollas, 1987). There is something pleasurable as well as embarrassing in being used. Perhaps it is embarrassing because it is pleasurable, the pleasure deriving from the temptation inherent in giving oneself over and faithfully following the other's intimate movements and strivings—as if, in a sense, giving up the right to have one's embarrassment existent and active.

There are analysts who are particularly sensitive, and sometimes actually embarrassed, when the patient needs them to express happy recognition of his achievements or warm or enthusiastic reception of some of his experiences or even claims. They may feel that their balance is threatened. They may feel ashamed either through projective identification (identification with the praise-dependent patient's projections) or because of the feeling that, by expressing recognition of the patient's narcissistic strivings or feelings, they will seem awkward or foolish or become diminished in their own or in their patient's eyes. This, in my experience, accounts for mistakes by omission made by the analyst who lacks the inner freedom to "celebrate" the patient (Bollas, 1989) when it is analytically or therapeutically needed. Such an analyst will instead feel pressured and will unwittingly use her interpretations to ward off this felt pressure. What I am saying is that serving as a selfobject may potentially defend against the analyst's (effortful) responsibility for her individuality and the shame that is liable to follow, but I am also saying that evading functioning as a selfobject for the patient may likewise be a defense and for the same reasons. From the patient's perspective, the analyst's avoidance of "celebrating" him, of recognizing his achievements or qualities, is experienced as a much needed affirmation that is not forthcoming at vulnerable moments. The analyst, who is ashamed to happily or calmly recognize or "celebrate" the patient, is then experienced as censuring and condemningly judgmental, and the outcome of the analyst's withdrawal is that, rather than valuing the differences between self and other and remaining confident and proud, the patient then feels obliged to wipe out this difference by various means (such as narcissistic withdrawal, devaluation, or some of the defensive self states described by Kohut).

Another difficulty analysts may have, as Kohut observed (e.g., 1971, p. 266), is to let the patient admire and idealize them when he needs it, without attempting to interpret it as a defense. Kohut explains it as the analyst's fear of his own grandiosity getting out of hand when stimulated by the patient's idealization of him. I read it as the analyst's fear that the patient's idealization might break through her protective shame barrier. She may consequently redouble her efforts to hold it in check, at the same time reinforcing her shame-rooted avoidance of such interventions. It is as if the analyst feared the danger of believing the patient and forgetting all shame. In other words, the analyst's counterresistance to being idealized may stem from her fear of accepting (introjectively identifying with) and believing both in her aggrandized size and the patient's feeling himself as small, and thereby indeed perceiving him as small and shameful. This is another instance of how the unworked-through, excessive shame of the analyst, resulting from insufficiently integrated grandiosity and narcissistic devaluatory tendencies, tendencies that need and "absorb" shame for their regulation and control, may interfere with therapeutic work.

WHY THE ANALYST'S SHAME IS NOT DISCUSSED

With recent attention to the analyst's emotional responsiveness, it is surprising that the literature on the shame of the analyst is practically nonexistent. There are no descriptions of how it feels for us analysts to really be proven wrong, of the subtle discomfort we feel when we sound off track, of the apprehension and anxiety in appearing ignorant or mistaken, and of having to grope occasionally for the right words, metaphors, and intuitions, only to be corrected by the patient. Even though there are numerous recent essays and books on shame, products of the intense interest sparked lately by this affect, shame has not found its way to metapsychology or to other nuclear psychodynamic explanations, in contrast to the affects of anxiety and guilt that have always held a basic and constitutive role in psychoanalytic theory. Kohut's theorizing is in some sense an exception, and when he could overcome his discomfort and shame when being reprimanded and chastized by Miss F, he gave birth to his groundbreaking theory. Another recent exception is Andrew Morrison's (1994) recent paper. In addition to the difficulties in grasping this complex and sometimes paradoxical affect, an affect that can arouse the desire to hide or to be angry and attack, an affect that is a central regulator of all other affects and that involves the whole self, there are the emotional dynamics of the analyst who experiences such an affect, dynamics that have impeded analytic attention from being granted to the analyst's shame.

Sandor Ferenczi wrote that "we analysts must admit to ourselves that we are much indebted to our patients for their sharply critical view of us, especially when we promote their development, which helps us gain considerable insight regarding . . . our own character" (in Dupont, 1988, p. 26). Ferenczi, writes Anthony Bass (1993), "came to realize that stalled analyses often foundered on the shoals of the analyst's own artificiality of behavior, his feigned friendliness, part of a posture or facade intended to mask or deny countertransferential feelings and responses *at odds with the analyst's preferred self-image*" (p. 155, italics added). Bass mentions Wolstein (1992), who wrote that "the psychoanalyst may . . . adopt a professional attitude of expertise—attitudinalize, so to say, a therapeutic facade . . . but . . . a patient's capacity to perceive the unconscious psychic experience of others, including the psychoanalyst, does not shut down by virtue of taking the socially defined role of patient" (pp. 185–186). Hoffman (1983) writes that the idea of patient and analyst generating plausible hypotheses about each other makes the analyst more aware not only of her actual impact on the patient, but also of the contrast between this impact and her imagined, wished-for stance—and the impressions it generates.

SHAME AND THE ANALYST'S NEW POSITION

Now our question becomes more specific: What happens to the analyst's shame feelings in this new, less elevated, less distanced position? Does such a position entail that she will experience more, or less, shame? Apparently, the analyst now is less protected and more exposed to scrutiny, both her own and that of her patient's; she can conceal less embarrassments under so-called neutrality; she can hide less behind the mask of the blank screen; she cannot act any more like the cold, infallible surgeon, who operates upon a patient whose view is taken to be dazed by his own analytic regression. The analyst and her foibles are exposed, often taken into the midst of the analytic discourse and not always dismissed as the patient's tranference, but seen as the patient's occasionally valid perceptions of his analyst. The analyst is more aware of being grasped by the patient, while at the same time being more sharply aware of not knowing what her gesture or interpretation will mean to an individual patient at a particular moment (Schafer, 1983; Hoffman, 1996). Having become aware of this lack of certainty, a great many of us analysts become more humble—even as our experience and accumulated knowledge have increased.

But intriguingly, this humbleness goes hand in hand with more legitimation to be fallible. The analyst's fallibility is being more acknowledged than in the past (cf. Cooper, 1993). No longer occupying such an authoritarian position, the analyst assumedly tends to be more tolerant and less ashamed about exposure of her shortcomings (see Morrison's [1994] beautiful example; other examples are unforeseen events, loss of control, evident mistakes one makes, and certain countertransferential reactions, a central instance of which may be reactions to an erotic transference). When the analyst knows that she is bound to have countertransferential feelings and that it is not inappropriate to experience them, she will feel less ashamed; she will have acquired more degrees of freedom, and a greater range will open for her in the space between acceptable feelings and those she will feel she has to defend against. In short, the "new" analytic position is more revealing and thus more conducive to shame but is at the same time more permissive, even relieving, in that it encompasses the analyst's proneness to error and uncertainty as legitimate and natural aspects of her analytic attitude.

SUMMARY

This chaper addresses varieties of the shame experiences of the analyst, in the wake of the great interest recently shown in the affect of shame as a central regulator of self states and as a marker of boundaries. Four

different varieties of the shame experiences of the analyst are presented
and discussed and illustrated with the help of clinical material: two
object-related types of shame, namely resonant shame and introjected
(or vicarious) shame, and two self-directed types, namely shame of lack
and shame of excess, are described. It is further suggested that changes
in the analyst's position make for a different relationship of the analyst
to her shame in interesting ways.

REFERENCES

Aron, L. (1992), Interpretation as expression of the analyst's subjectivity. *Psychoanal. Dial.*, 2:475–507.
—— (1996), *A Meeting of Minds.* Hillsdale, NJ: The Analytic Press.
Bass, A. (1993), Review essay: *On Learning from the Patient,* by Patrick Casement. *Psychoanal. Dial.*, 3:151–167.
Bollas, C. (1987), *The Shadow of the Object: Psychoanalysis and the Unthought Known.* London: Free Association Books.
—— (1989), *Forces of Destiny.* London: Free Association Books.
Bonnet, G. (1981), *Voir–Etre vu.* Paris: Presses Universitaires de France.
Casement, P. (1985), *On Learning from the Patient.* London: Tavistock.
—— (1990), *On Further Learning from the Patient.* London: Tavistock.
Chasseguet-Smirgel, J. (1984), *Ethique et Esthetique de la Perversion.* Paris: Champ Vallon.
Cooper, A. (1993), Interpretive fallibility and the psychoanalytic dialogue. *J. Amer. Psychoanal. Assn.*, 41:95–126.
Dupont, J., ed. (1988), *The Clinical Diary of Sandor Ferenczi.* Cambridge, MA: Harvard University Press.
Fonagy, P. & Target, M. (1995), Understanding the violent patient: The use of the body and the role of the father. *Internat. J. Psycho-Anal.*, 76:487–502.
Freud, S. (1905), Three essays on the theory of sexuality. *Standard Edition,* 7:123–245. London: Hogarth Press, 1953.
—— (1915), Observations on transference love. *Standard Edition,* 12:157–171. London: Hogarth Press, 1958.
Friedman, L. (1992), How and why do patients become more objective? Sterba compared with Strachey. *Psychoanal. Quart.*, 61:1–17.
Hoffman, I. Z. (1983), The patient as interpreter of the analyst's experience. *Contemp. Psychoanal.*, 19:389–422.
—— (1996), The intimate and ironic authority of the psychoanalyst's presence. *Psychoanal. Quart.*, 65:102–136.
Khan, M. M. R. (1979), *Alienation in Perversions.* New York: International Universities Press.
Kohut, H. (1971), *The Analysis of the Self.* New York: International Universities Press.
Lewis, H. B. (1971), *Shame and Guilt in Neurosis.* New York: International Universities Press.
Lichtenstein, H. (1977), *The Dilemma of Human Identity.* New York: Aronson.
Mitchell, S. A. (1988), *Relational Concepts in Psychoanalysis.* Cambridge, MA: Harvard University Press.

—— (1993), *Hope and Dread in Psychoanalysis*. New York: Basic Books.

Morrison, A. (1994), The breadth and boundaries of a self-psychological immersion in shame: A one-and-a-half person perspective. *Psychoanal. Dial.*, 4:19–36.

Nathanson, D. L. (1992), *Shame and Pride*. New York: Norton.

Sandler, J. (1992), Reflections on developments in the theory of psychoanalytic technique. *Internat. J. Psycho-Anal.*, 73:189–198.

Schafer, R. (1983), *The Analytic Attitude*. London: Hogarth Press.

Schneider, C. (1987), A mature sense of shame. In: *The Many Faces of Shame*, ed. D. L. Nathanson. New York: Guilford, pp. 194–213.

Schore, A. N. (1991), Early superego development: The emergence of shame and narcissistic affect regulation in the practicing period. *Psychoanal. & Contemp. Thought*, 14:187–249.

Speziale-Bagliacca, R. (1991), Psychic change: Developments in the theory of psychoanalytic technique. *Internat. J. Psycho-Anal.*, 72:27–32.

Spezzano, C. (1993), *Affect in Psychoanalysis*. London: The Analytic Press.

Stein, R. (1990), A new look at the theory of Melanie Klein. *Internat. J. Psycho-Anal.*, 71:499–511.

—— (1991), *Psychoanalytic Theories of Affect*. New York: Praeger.

—— (1993), Conceptual developments in the psychoanalytic theory of affects. *Sichot, Israel J. Psychother.*, 8:5–14 (in Hebrew).

—— (1994), Conceptual developments in the psychoanalytic theory of affects. Part II: Clinical and theoretical implications. *Sichot, Israel J. Psychother.*, 9:6–22 (in Hebrew).

—— (1995), The role of affects in the process of change in psychotherapy. *Israel J. Psychiat.*, 32:174–183.

—— (in press), Two principles of the functioning of affects. Paper read at the Israel Psychoanalytic Society, March 29, 1996.

Stolorow, R. & Atwood, G. (1992), *Contexts of Being*. Hillsdale, NJ: The Analytic Press.

Tomkins, S. S. (1963), *Affect, Imagery, Consciousness, Vol. 2*. New York: Springer.

Tyson, P. & Tyson, R. L. (1990), *Psychoanalytic Theories of Development*. London: Yale University Press.

Wolstein, B. (1992), Resistance interlocked with countertransference. *Contemp. Psychoanal.*, 28:172–190.

Chapter 9

The Nondifficult Patient and the Nondifficult Analyst: Resolving the Impasse of Intersubjective Pseudoconjunction

Marc L. Miller

In a recent paper, Dr. Martin Livingston (1996) introduced the term *nondifficult* to describe a category of patients who, in contrast to so-called "difficult" patients (Brandchaft and Stolorow, 1988), present "no threats to the analyst's identity, organizing principles, or sanity" (Livingston, 1996, p. 142) in the course of psychoanalytic treatment. These are patients who have been generally neglected in the literature and are usually ignored in supervisory sessions. Their treatment tends to meander along, often for extended periods of time, with both therapist and patient ostensibly content to meet week after week, month after month, with the therapist often feeling bored, and occasionally wondering whether any changes are really occurring, but unable or unwilling to do anything that might disrupt the mutual security that this type of therapy situation provides.

As analysts, weary from our all-too-frequent stressful encounters with "difficult" patients, managed care representatives, and often the significant people of our personal lives as well, we can all identify with the experience of welcoming the respite offered by a "nondifficult" patient. After a while, however, we may become aware of a sense of boredom

---

An earlier version of this paper was presented as a discussion of M. Livingston's (1996) paper, on March 2, 1996, at a workshop sponsored by the Training and Research Institute for Self Psychology in New York, NY.

and complacency: the analytic encounter somehow lacks "vitality," because the most vital parts of the patient seem to be dissociated from the intersubjective encounter. As Livingston realized in working with his patient, Mrs. A, the therapist's subjective experience of boredom is the indicator that "should serve as a warning sign" (Livingston, 1996, p. 143) that an impasse is occurring. Though less "noisy" and far less likely to threaten the treatment with "premature termination" than those arising with "difficult" patients, these "quiet" impasses are no less crucial for us to understand and learn to address more effectively.

In order to begin the process of clarifying the intersubjective issues underlying such an impasse with his patient, Livingston followed the recommendation given by Stolorow and Atwood (1992), "that inquiry must include the therapist's continual reflection on the involvement of his own personal subjectivity in the ongoing therapeutic process" (p. 121), by embarking on a project of self-supervision, which involved "tak[ing] detailed notes which would include [his own] subjective experiences" (Livingston, 1996, p. 143) during the course of the therapy process. The goals of his self-supervisory project were "to deepen [his] understanding of what was taking place, sharpen [his] own self awareness, and revitalize a treatment process that felt stuck" (p. 143). Livingston provides a fascinating account of his thoughts and feelings, in addition to the actual verbal content, during the eight analytic sessions presented, as he is quite candid in recording his conscious subjective experiences in his self-supervisory notes. In sharing this record with his colleagues in the psychoanalytic community, he has provided us with invaluable data that illuminate the intersubjective nature of the analytic process.

In the discussion that follows, I examine some aspects of the analytic treatment of nondifficult patients, attempting to clarify and expand upon some of the ideas introduced by Livingston and to illustrate the complexities inherent in the therapeutic process by utilizing the actual data (the session notes) he has provided. My comments include my personal thoughts/associations/reactions to what Livingston has written, coming from my own subjective vantage point *outside* of the therapeutic dyad. This perspective has advantages and disadvantages as compared with that of the analyst. On the one hand, I was not there and must depend entirely on what has been reported to us, whereas the analyst's experience of what happened in those sessions is, in many ways, far more complete. On the other hand, the analyst, as part of the transference–countertransference (intersubjective) matrix, is inevitably drawn into intersubjective patterns and enactments about which he can only aspire to gain anything close to complete reflective self-awareness. Blind spots based on one's own subjectivity, which are impossible for any analyst to avoid, constitute the limitations of self-supervision: as analysts, our capacity for self-reflection is limited to those experiences that are, or can readily become, accessible to our conscious awareness. Hence, we are all *inevitably* limited by our own subjectivity. Therefore, an observer viewing from a vantage point outside the dyadic matrix, whose subjectivity is not interacting with either participant's subjectivity directly, may be better able to "see" certain aspects of what is happening than either of the actual participants themselves. This assertion does not imply an absence of subjective bias: I make no claims at being any more objective than anyone else, but it *does* suggest a greater likelihood that certain intersubjective patterns will be seen more readily by the nonparticipant than by either of the co-participants engaged in the process. In my opinion, this in no way diminishes the insights and contributions of the actual analyst: if the analyst were not as engaged and involved in the intersubjective experience, the therapy would indeed have remained lifeless and nontherapeutic; it is via the relationship, which includes many dimensions, that growth of self-structure, resolution of conflict, and increased self-awareness are fostered. With these considerations in mind, I will now address several issues raised for me in reading Livingston's paper.

Livingston utilizes the concepts of *intersubjective disjunction* and *intersubjective conjunction,* terms first used by Atwood and Stolorow (1984), to explain the differences between those impasses that typically develop with difficult patients and those that typically develop with nondifficult patients. In a very interesting way, Livingston has utilized these terms somewhat differently than their originators; I think these differences are worth looking at more closely.

Stolorow and Atwood (1992) discuss intersubjective conjunction and intersubjective disjunction as follows:

> The first of these [conjunction] is illustrated by instances in which the principles structuring the patient's experiences give rise to expressions that are assimilated into closely similar central configurations in the psychological life of the therapist. Disjunction, by contrast, occurs when the therapist assimilates the material expressed by the patient into configurations that significantly alter its meaning for the patient. Repetitive occurrences of intersubjective conjunction and disjunction are inevitable accompaniments of the therapeutic process and reflect the interaction of differently organized subjective worlds [p. 103].

In other words, intersubjective conjunctions occur when the analyst's understanding of the patient's subjective experience essentially coincides with the patient's actual subjective experience, and intersubjective disjunctions occur when the analyst's understanding of the patient's subjective experience is essentially discrepant from the patient's actual subjective experience. Stolorow and Atwood (1992) see these processes occurring without conscious awareness or as being what they refer to as "prereflectively unconscious." Conjunctions and disjunctions can become either helpful or harmful to the therapeutic process, depending on the therapist's ability or inability to become "reflectively self-aware" of his/her own organizing principles being activated in the therapy interaction. Stolorow and Atwood focus their attention on how the *therapist* assimilates the expressions of the *patient's* subjective experience (i.e., the transference).

Their recommended treatment strategy is for the therapist to strive to maintain a stance of "sustained empathic inquiry," that is, "to seek consistently to comprehend the meaning of the patient's expressions, his affect states, and, most centrally, the impact of the analyst from a perspective *within* rather than outside the patient's subjective frame of reference" (p. 93). While Stolorow and Atwood's intersubjective perspective clearly recognizes the essentially interactional, mutually influencing nature of the therapy relationship, they orient their discussion of these issues primarily from the point of view of the therapist striving to maintain empathic connection with the patient's subjective experience: Does the therapist's experience correspond or diverge from the experience of the patient? How does this impact on the patient? And what should the therapist do to foster a reconnection?

Livingston orients his perspective more from the other side of the equation, placing more emphasis on the subjective experience of the therapist (i.e., the countertransference). He focuses us on the therapist's subjective reaction when the patient's experience of the interaction either corresponds or diverges from the experience of the therapist. In the case of difficult patients, he sees intersubjective disjunction as occurring when "the patient's experience of the situation (and especially of the analyst) is sharply at odds with that of the analyst" (Livingston, 1996, p. 141). The perspective of the analyst's subjective experience of the disjunction is reflected in the observation that "this is particularly uncomfortable when the patient attributes qualities to the analyst that are disowned and thus become an onslaught on the analyst's sense of his own identity" (Livingston, 1996, p. 141). When the patient's attributions coincide with disowned (self-dystonic) or dissociated aspects of the analyst's personality, the analyst (in the absence of reflective self-awareness) will be unable to "accept and then explore the patient's attributions" and will be more likely to respond in a manner that "invalidates the patient's experience" (p. 141), inducing a disruption in the selfobject matrix.

In contrast, Livingston sees nondifficult patients as being "*very skillful* at not placing this uncomfortable demand on the analyst" (p. 142, italics added). In this context, Livingston utilizes the term *intersubjective conjunction* to describe the situation involving "the patient [who] experiences the therapy setting, and particularly the analyst, only in a manner that coincides with the analyst's self experience" (p. 142). In this case, Livingston is giving the conjunction concept a very interesting twist, as he sees the conjunction as the result of something the patient is *actively doing*, either with or without conscious awareness. Looked at this way, the intersubjective conjunction in the treatment situation results from the patient's selective editing of her own self-experience to accommodate to the analyst's self-experience. For this kind of patient, this is the price deemed necessary to maintain the needed selfobject connection with the Other.

Livingston's nondifficult patient is thus seen as *creating* a conjunction to avoid conflict and disconnection. Stolorow and Atwood's (1992) conceptualization of intersubjective conjunction seems to assume a *preexisting* correspondence between the patterns of subjective experience of patient and therapist. I would suggest the clarification that, in the case of the nondifficult patient, those situations that are initially actually intersubjective *disjunctions* (reflecting lack of congruity between the experiences of patient and therapist) are transformed by the patient into what would more accurately be described as *pseudo*conjunctions, whereby the patient's actual subjective experience is sacrificed in order to conform with the experience of the Other, to eliminate the danger of loss of the needed selfobject connection.

Atwood and Stolorow's (1984) discussion of the intersubjective context in which psychopathology is originally established offers a developmental paradigm for the process occurring in the therapy situation that Livingston (1996) is describing:

> When the psychological organization of the parent cannot sufficiently accommodate to the changing, phase-specific needs of the developing child, then the more malleable and vulnerable psychological structure of the child will accommodate to what is available. A number of pathological outcomes are possible. The child may develop a defensive "false self" . . . , an "identity theme" . . . that serves the archaic selfobject needs of the parent, in order to maintain the needed tie at whatever cost to authentic self-experience [p. 69].

This, in essence, is the person who grows up to become a nondifficult patient. In the therapy situation, the patient's "skill" at modifying her own interpersonal behavior and perhaps even her conscious subjective experience so as to pose "no threats to the analyst's identity, organizing principles, or sanity" (Livingston, 1996, p. 142), thereby avoiding disruption of the selfobject connection between them, can thus be seen as an intersubjective (transference–countertransference) reenactment of the pattern established long before in the patient's life, vis-à-vis the significant early caretakers.

Livingston's case record illustrates and illuminates many issues pertaining to the analytic treatment of nondifficult patients and to the intersubjective nature of the analytic treatment process in general. Before proceeding with my close examination of the sequences of interactions and subjective reactions reported by Livingston, I want to reiterate that it is not my intention to scrutinize the analyst's work for the purpose of criticizing and pointing out "mistakes" or to suggest that I would have done things "better" if I were the treating analyst. On the contrary, I believe that it is in the nature of the intersubjective process of psychoanalytic treatment that the treating analyst, whoever he or she may be, cannot help but become engaged in patterns of interaction about which it is impossible to have complete reflective self-awareness as the process unfolds. A great deal can be clarified about the treatment process with the nondifficult patient by following the advice of Brandchaft and Stolorow (1988) in their original paper on "the difficult patient," namely "that the intersubjective field within which such behavior takes place should now be . . . minutely studied" (p. 105). It is in this spirit that I turn now to Livingston's account of the analytic process in his work with his nondifficult patient, Mrs. A.

Similar to Kohut's analyses of Mr. Z (Kohut, 1979), Mrs. A had an initial period of treatment with Livingston prior to his acquaintance with the insights of self psychology and after a 5-year hiatus returned for an analysis that benefited from his understanding of self psychology (and intersubjectivity). Of the earlier therapy Livingston states that a "strong empathic bond was sustained with very little experience of rupture and repair" (Livingston, 1996, p. 144), and interpretation remained at the "understanding" (rather than the "explanation") level. He explains his analytic stance as follows:

> It seemed important to allow a lengthy period of sustained empathic responsiveness and to allow the patient to progress at her own pace. She seemed very appreciative and insistent on this, and became very anxious at any attempts to explore her perceptions of me in any depth. In other words, I think that a prolonged and uninterpreted idealizing transference was unfolding that provided an essential nurturing experience and perhaps also failed to sustain a position of empathic inquiry into our relationship [p. 144].

Because of his assessment of the patient's fragility, as expressed by her becoming "very anxious at any attempts to explore her perceptions of [the analyst] in any depth" (p. 144), Livingston adapted a stance of acceptance, nurturance, and avoidance of any inquiry that might be experienced by the patient as anxiety-provoking, especially regarding their relationship. Yet, in spite of this approach, the treatment ended very precipitously, "without plan or discussion," "interrupted when the patient's acting out resulted in a serious financial disaster of which she was intensely ashamed" (p. 144). Livingston does not tell us the nature of Mrs. A's "acting out," nor does he employ his current understanding to speculate on the intersubjective issues (including both his own and the patient's contributions) underlying the events leading to her premature termination.

When Mrs. A returns 5 years later, she does so "on a four times a week basis after her father's death left her financially comfortable" (Livingston, 1996, p. 144). Regarding the period between her return and the first session reported to us (4 months into the treatment), Livingston does not tell us whether he and Mrs. A discussed and explored her feelings and fantasies about the previous treatment, especially the precipitous termination 5 years earlier, how the patient decided to return to her former therapist after so long a time, what she imagined he felt about her "acting out," about her leaving, and about her return, and so on. If such issues were addressed, it would have been very interesting to learn what was said. If such issues were not addressed, I would assume that this choice reflected the analyst's continued assessment that the patient's fragility and need for "sustained empathic responsiveness" still precluded more direct inquiry into her intersubjective experience. In any case, not long into this treatment Livingston reports becoming aware of feeling a sense of comfort that borders on complacency, and recognizing that "the very nondifficulty along with a lack of vitality in the sessions should serve as a warning sign" (p. 143) of a treatment impasse, he embarks on his self-supervisory project.

He begins his self-supervisory notes with a session 4 months into the new treatment. His initial description of "the atmosphere in this session" as "friendly and warm while lacking any sense of aliveness" (p. 144) captures his awareness that, despite the experience of comfort and superficial pleasantness, something is wrong. The patient begins by talking about a situation outside of the treatment relationship: her boss, about to lose her job, "tr[ies] to make the patient her ally" (p. 144). This extra-analytic anecdote might be explored in several ways. Opting to stay with what is closest to the patient's awareness and therefore least threatening, the analyst could inquire about the patient's subjective experiences in regard to this situation with her boss. Alternatively, the analyst might explore the anecdote as an allusion to the transference, following Gill's (1982) recommendation, and might try to clarify possible transference implications: for example, the boss might represent the analyst, who has already once lost his "job," and who may be seen by her as trying to keep it now by making her his ally, that is, by maintaining a "friendly and warm" atmosphere, or perhaps, in a reversal of roles, it might be she who fears being "let go" by the analyst and therefore must try to make *him* her ally. Perhaps a more gradual transition, from surface to depth (Josephs, 1995), starting with the initial exploration of the situation with her boss, and then gradually exploring the possible treatment implications, might have been particularly helpful in beginning to open up the blocked therapeutic process.

Interestingly, Livingston does not intervene at all; instead, he reports that his "mind wanders." When his "attention returns," it is "after a long silence," when Mrs. A "reports that she is 'doing something to herself'" (Livingston, 1996, p. 144). At this point, roused from his reverie, Livingston encourages the patient to say more: she clarifies that she has been "'numbing herself' so as not to feel anything or think anything" (p. 144). Now, aware of his own "lapse of attention," Livingston wonders whether the patient is *reacting to his lapse* and asks "if she has any awareness of what triggered her doing this to herself" (p. 144). He notes that "she is visibly embarrassed and remains quiet" (p. 144), but he does not ask her to say more about this experience. Instead, his "thoughts turn inward" once again. In the face of what seems to me to be a critical moment in the session, the analyst's immediate response is a shift in awareness from the immediacy of the interpersonal interaction to his own introspective reflection upon the relationship: he reflects upon how "comfortable" he feels with Mrs. A, with "no pressure to be anything more than a warm accepting listener or sometimes just a presence in the room as she sits in silence for varying amounts of time," "never impatient or frustrated with her" and without "any need to push her" (p. 144).

As I tried to understand what might be going on for Livingston that he is aware of only the most pleasant feelings toward his patient while being so complacent, lacking in vitality, subject to lapses of attention, and avoidant of inquiry into the intersubjective process, it occurred to me that Livingston might be manifesting the subjective experience of being a *nondifficult analyst*, the intersubjective counterpart of the non-difficult patient. Within the context of the intersubjective field comprising both patient and analyst, a pattern of mutual relating seems to have been established whereby *both* coparticipants unconsciously collude to minimize provoking anxiety in the other and, thereby, avoid threatening the integrity of the selfobject bond. From Livingston's notes we can observe the process (the implications of which remain prereflectively unconscious to him) from the analyst's subjective vantage point: he avoids arousing any anxiety in the patient (by avoiding inquiry into her experience of the therapy relationship), his awareness retreats inward (away from interactions that might result in potentially disjunctive interactions), and his conscious feelings regarding the patient remain consonant with the maintenance of such a nonthreatening stance (only positive affects are experienced consciously, while negative affects are dissociated).

Lulled as he is by the complacency inherent in this process, it is very much to Livingston's credit that he now questions what is happening intersubjectively, especially about his role in inducing her to numb herself: he "wonder[s] aloud if her numbing herself might be related to a subtle sense she might have of fluctuations in [his] attentiveness or in her own sense of connectedness" (p. 145). For the first time, the analyst had directly focused attention on what might be going on intersubjectively, and this does indeed mark "the beginning of a shift" that can potentially allow the two participants to clarify and alter their pattern of interaction. Livingston's hypothesis of what is happening appears to be that Mrs. A's numbing herself is a response to his inattentiveness, which he assumes she experiences "as a selfobject failure." Livingston tells us that he now "sense[s] the possibility that her defensive numbing might well be a protection against experiencing a painful loss of [his] attunement rather than seeing [his] lapse as a response to her numbness" (p. 145). The recognition of this possibility marks an important shift in the analyst's awareness, as it permits him to empathically explore *the patient's* subjective experience, rather than considering only his own. This should not be taken to mean that one perspective is "right" and the other is "wrong": these two alternative perspectives are not mutually exclusive, because they reflect the subjective experiences of the two coparticipants in the dyad, who are continuously reacting to each other, in an ongoing system of mutual influence, but the analyst cannot be open to the patient's perspective until "de-centering" from his own.

In response to Livingston's questioning whether her numbing herself might be reactive to her perception of fluctuations in his attentiveness or in her own sense of connectedness, Mrs. A indicates that "she has a sense of when she began to close off," but "hesitates to express it further." She "then briefly reassures [him] that it is in response to her own inner thoughts and not to any action of [his]" (p. 145). At this point, the analyst makes an interpretation based on what he assumes is the operative "organizing principle," namely that Mrs. A never attributes blame to him, but rather tends to direct blame at herself. He interprets "that perhaps her reluctance to see [his] contribution to her distress is related to a fear of losing her sense of being connected to [him]" (p. 145). While this interpretation may be "correct," I believe it to be premature, because it has not yet been established via inquiry and exploration that the patient has been experiencing "distress" or that she has actually experienced the analyst as inattentive. Mrs. A responds to the interpretation by confirming her "wish to be more connected" but does not comment directly on his assumption that she is protecting him from blame for his lapses of attention. Instead of directly stating how she *does* experience him, she shares a fantasy, a less direct form of communication, which "she often has in sessions," but which she has never verbalized until now. Her fantasy is of "a thousand people staring in silence, waiting for her to say the right thing. She wants very much to satisfy them, but feels totally inadequate and has no idea what they want" (p. 145). This fantasy, I believe, concretizes Mrs. A's experiential dilemma in the therapy situation: when Livingston's attention floats off in his silent reveries, she (who is lying on the couch, unable to view him) experiences him not as inattentive and detached (as he has assumed, based on his own self-experience), but rather as "staring in silence, waiting for her to say the right thing" (p. 145). She desperately wants to "say the right thing," "to satisfy" him, but in the absence of ground rules and feedback from him, she is left feeling "totally inadequate." Mrs. A wishes to achieve a synchrony between the Other's expectations and her behavior, which was referred to earlier as creating an intersubjective pseudoconjunction, but unable to discover what the demanding, yet inscrutable, Other requires of her, she feels disconnected and alone and retreats into a state of numbness.

Mrs. A's fantasy reflects a subjective experience of the analytic relationship which is definitely discrepant from Livingston's assumptions about her experience; this discrepancy suggests the underlying presence of an intersubjective disjunction, in which "the therapist assimilates the material expressed by the patient into configurations that significantly alter its meaning for the patient" (Stolorow and Atwood, 1992, p. 103). Faced with this discrepancy, in a manner characteristic of a nondifficult patient, Mrs. A does not risk directly challenging her analyst's assumptions about what she is experiencing, but she does introduce her fantasy of the "thousand people staring," as an indirect communication of her intersubjective experience. I believe that the reason she can verbalize this fantasy now for the first time, although she has often thought of it in sessions before, is that the analyst has begun to expand the sphere of discourse to address the intersubjective experience. While Livingston's conscious understanding of the fantasy's intersubjective meaning has not yet crystallized in his conscious awareness, he is left questioning whether his "comfortable acceptance of her pace [constitutes] a nurturant acceptance—the provision of a needed selfobject experience, or could it also, in part, interfere with the inquiring part of sustained empathic inquiry?" (Livingston, 1996, p. 145).

This question highlights the dilemma faced by self psychologically oriented analysts, since we tend to think of our possible roles in the treatment situation as falling into two major categories: either we can provide "a needed selfobject experience" by being accepting and nurturing, which the patient is likely to experience as selfobject attunement, or else we can take an inquiring stance, which, by seeking to clarify those aspects of experience that are not being talked about and tend to be self-dystonic, inevitably generates anxiety in the patient and risks jeopardizing the integrity of the selfobject bond. Faced with this choice, especially with patients we assess as having vulnerable self-structures (this applies to both difficult and nondifficult patients), we usually opt for the stance that avoids threatening the selfobject bond and that generates the least anxiety (for both the patient and the analyst).

The "bipolar conception of transference" offered by Stolorow, Brandchaft, and Atwood (1987, p. 101) is a helpful basis for understanding the choices faced by the analyst in the treatment situation. In the view of these authors, transference can best be understood as encompassing two "poles" or dimensions of intersubjective experience, with one pole representing "the patient's longing to experience the analyst as a source of requisite selfobject functions that were missing or insufficient during the formative years," and the other pole reflecting "the patient's expectations and fears of a transference repetition of the original experiences of selfobject failure," which "becomes the source of conflict and resistance" (p. 102). These two experiential dimensions are seen as alternately occupying the foreground or the background of the patient's experience in the analytic encounter, largely dependent upon "whether or not the analyst's interpretive activity is experienced by the patient as being attuned to his affective states and needs" (p. 102). Stolorow and his colleagues suggest a treatment approach that recognizes the inevitable oscillations of these dimensions of transference. As long as the selfobject dimension remains intact, with one of the selfobject transferences having been activated and sustained, the process of "psychological structure formation" proceeds. When the patient experiences the analyst "as unattuned, foreshadowing a traumatic repetition of early selfobject failure, the conflictual and resistive dimension of the transference is frequently brought into the foreground, while the patient's selfobject yearnings are, of necessity, driven into hiding" (p. 102). When the analyst seeks to clarify the patient's subjective experience of the analyst-as-failing-selfobject, "demonstrating his attunement to the patient's reactive affect states and thereby mending the ruptured tie, the selfobject pole of the transference becomes restored and strengthened and the conflictual/resistive/repetitive dimension tends to recede into the background" (p. 102).

With the nondifficult patient, who assiduously avoids disjunctive encounters with the analyst, the part of the sequence outlined by Stolorow and his colleagues (1997) which entails "the conflictual and resistive dimension of the transference" being overtly expressed in the foreground by the patient is very unlikely to occur: the conflictual dimension of transference is avoided through the creation of intersubjective pseudoconjunctions, in order to prevent any disruption of the selfobject bond. Josephs (1995) offers an alternative viewpoint that illuminates a limitation of the approach suggested by Stolorow and his colleagues and that clarifies the situation involving the nondifficult patient. Josephs states:

> If in the foreground the patient is experiencing selfobject attunement while in the background experiencing a repetitive reenactment, the possibility does not seem to be entertained by Stolorow and his colleagues that the experience of selfobject attunement can serve multiple functions other than [only] self-restorative ones. Perhaps the experience of selfobject attunement as a compromise formation serves in part as a defense against exploring the background repetitive dimensions of the relationship, and at some point in the analysis the defensive function of needing a perfectly attuned relationship with the analyst could be interpreted [p. 134].

While the "nondifficult" patient maintains the experience of seemingly perfect selfobject attunement with the analyst, the price she has to pay for doing so is the repetitive reenactment of the experience of creating intersubjective pseudoconjunctions, sacrificing her genuine sense of self. As Josephs comments, "Self psychologists tend to assume that if they are being empathic and are overtly experienced by the patient as meeting selfobject needs, they are probably not covertly participating in the enactment of a pathological object relation from childhood. Perhaps while overtly experiencing something genuinely new, the patient could still be covertly reexperiencing something old" (p. 134).

Josephs recommends a treatment approach that balances empathic attunement *and* interpretation of unconscious or self-dystonic aspects of experience (which would certainly include the propensity for avoiding disjunctive interactions), by conducting a process of empathic inquiry addressing intersubjective issues sequentially from those closest to the "surface" of conscious awareness, namely those most self-syntonic, to those closer to the "depth" of unconscious, self-dystonic experience. The complication in following Josephs's recommendation is that to the degree the analyst may be unaware of his own complicity in the intersubjective enactment, he will be unable to recognize the need for investigating and interpreting what is being enacted. However, if the analyst strives to maintain a consistent stance of sustained empathic inquiry, seeking to clarify the patient's subjective experience within the intersubjective matrix of the treatment situation even when unclear about what is "really" going on himself (which reflects the inevitable limitations of our own subjectivity), then many previously unknown facets of the intersubjective situation will gradually become clarified.

As the therapy process continues, Livingston encourages Mrs. A to talk about her reaction to his inattentiveness, but instead, gradually, with great hesitancy in overcoming her resistance to expressing how she truly feels, she clarifies that what she *is* experiencing is fear of his "disapproval or disdain" (Livingston, 1996, p. 147) and that her numbing herself protects her from feeling afraid. In the third session reported, a major breakthrough occurs following "another long silence." Eventually, the patient smiles and breaks the silence by stating that she feels uncomfortable "whenever she experiences [Livingston] paying attention to her" (p. 148). In contrast to what he has been assuming, Mrs. A has been unaware of his periods of inattention; as she has been lying on the couch during silences, she has felt very uncomfortable, with conflicting and confusing feelings, assuming that he *has* been "paying attention to her." She expresses her ambivalence about his attentiveness by saying, " 'It is as if I want it very much and at the same time I don't want it' " (p. 148). This statement is followed by a series of verbalizations that seem to reflect regressive, dissociated experiences. She " 'hear[s] a child's voice . . . mimicking' " the tone of an adult, saying,

> " 'Leave me alone—stop pestering me.' Then it becomes a little girl's voice, clearly frightened and pleading to be left alone. Finally it sounds like a warning" [p. 148].

Obviously terrified, Mrs. A "looks up at" Livingston and says, " 'This is a crazy place—a place I don't go.' " With the session ending, seeking reassurance, she asks, " 'If I let the voices speak, will they ever go away?' " (p. 148). Livingston reports feeling conflicted about how reassuring he should be: he chooses to empathically verbalize "how scary it is to explore this place," but holds back from more direct reassurance about the voices, for fear that this might "dilute the unfolding process." He does not comment on his thoughts about Mrs. A's "voices." My own thoughts were of a child's experience of being abused, perhaps sexually, confused about her feelings, very frightened, and "pleading to be left alone." In the present of the therapy situation, she is terrified to go to that "crazy place," but with her analyst accompanying her, she has begun the journey.

The following day's session begins with Mrs. A expressing her fears of going crazy, experienced as fragmentation/disintegration, which she verbalizes as being " 'afraid I will fall apart and be all in pieces' "

(p. 149). Her dependence on the analyst's selfobject presence, her simultaneous fear of his abandonment, and her self-protective wish to be self-reliant are expressed when she says, "'I won't be able to put myself together and then you will leave before I can. I'll be all alone and apart. It is much too scary when I am alone. I have to get a grip on myself—to keep together'" (p. 149). The intensity and "poignancy" of her words leaves Livingston "inwardly frightened" (a feeling we can all empathize with), and he tries to "contain" this feeling "without communicating any fear" to her. Mrs. A "relates a fantasy she has had of asking [him] to promise that [he] won't leave her while she is in pieces" (p. 149), obviously seeking his reassurance that he will not abandon her through this frightening process. Eventually, "the focus sharpens onto [their] relationship," especially on Mrs. A's ambivalence about closeness versus distance, that is, wanting Livingston "not too near, yet not too far away." She explains: "'It is as if I look up every now and then to be sure I haven't pushed you to where you will be unreachable. It is like I want to be sure you are on the shelf, but your attentiveness can't get too close because then I would feel all this crazy stuff coming out'" (p. 149). In this session, Mrs. A clarifies her conflict about her connection with her analyst: she needs to know that she is not all alone through the therapy process, but *too* much closeness threatens the integrity of her sense of self (which, again, hints at a history of sexual abuse). She then expresses the fear that she will be seen by her analyst as "manipulative and pulling [his] strings" (p. 149), explained as "dishonest controlling." Livingston responds by telling her that he "see[s] she feels very vulnerable in exposing her need to control the distance between [them]" and he reassures her that he views "her exploration of these needs [to be] certainly an honest expression (rather than a disguised manipulation)" (pp. 149–150). While reassuring, this intervention does not clarify the meaning of her transferential fear/expectation that she will be blamed (being seen as "manipulative") for doing what she needs to do (assertively stating both her need for closeness and her need to protect herself from too much closeness). That she expects to be blamed by the analyst, a male authority figure, again reminds me of the experience of the abused child who is blamed (for being "bad," seductive, or manipulative) by the abusive adult.

The final interaction of this session raises some difficult issues. "As the session ends, she asks shyly if 'all this is really okay'" (p. 150). Livingston, wishing to "respond simply and directly to her request for reassurance . . . tell[s] her with an enthusiastic warmth, 'Yes, it is very okay—in fact exciting'" (p. 150). While I agree with Livingston's decision to directly reassure his patient, who is venturing into very "scary" material, I wonder about his final words ("in fact exciting"), which suggest to me an intrusion of countertransferential material that could frighten this patient. On one level, close to his conscious awareness I would guess, Livingston appears to be expressing his own excitement and enthusiasm at the turn the treatment process has taken over the past week: since he instituted his self-analysis and his interventions have more consistently focused on intersubjective issues, the quality of the therapy has indeed changed dramatically and is certainly no longer "boring." On this level, his statement may convey to his patient that the way to please him is to continue to produce "exciting" material. Left unanalyzed, this interaction could represent a reenactment of the child–parent pattern typical of the nondifficult patient, who seeks to avoid displeasing, and simultaneously seeks to please, the potentially rejecting parent-figure. On another level, the word *exciting* has obvious sexual connotations, which, given the possibility of a history of sexual abuse, could be experienced by the patient as anything but "reassuring." I wonder whether, at an unconscious level, the analyst may have "picked up on" the patient's sexual abuse history and, without any conscious awareness, may be participating in an unconscious intersubjective enactment by unwittingly behaving in a sexually seductive manner. While the issue of abuse, sexual or otherwise, has not been manifestly mentioned by either the patient or the analyst, how these words impacted on the patient's psyche remains unclear.

These possibilities highlight the difficulties inherent in self-analysis. Josephs (1995) offers a discussion of countertransference that I find extremely helpful. He suggests that "countertransference, like transference, could be classified as either self-syntonic or self-dystonic. Self-syntonic countertransference has ready access to awareness, whereas self-dystonic countertransference tends to be repudiated" (p. 172). He cites Racker (1968), who

> discussed the problem of the analyst's resistance to the countertransference resulting in a counterresistance that parallels the patient's resistance to the analytic process. For a patient's perception of the analyst's personality to be self-dystonic, it does not matter whether that trait is "really" present in the analyst's personality but is operating unconsciously or whether the patient is largely projecting a trait onto the analyst that the analyst does not actually possess. Either way, it is dystonic from the syntonic sense of self and therefore threatening [p. 171].

Unlike the difficult patient, who overtly attributes dystonic traits to the analyst, the nondifficult patient will avoid such attributions; however, it seems inevitable that at an unconscious level the nondifficult patient expects the analyst to treat her the way her early traumatizing caretaker(s) did, and this attribution can be communicated outside of either participant's conscious awareness. Josephs goes on to say that "regardless of the relative accuracy or inaccuracy of the patient's perceptions of the analyst [conscious or unconscious], the analyst's natural role responsiveness . . . to the patient's role expectations makes it likely that the analyst does in at least some subtle way act in a manner congruent with the patient's perception of him or her" (p. 172).

Even the most conscientiously introspective analysts (of whom Livingston is clearly an example) will probably have great difficulty, or simply be unable, to consciously recognize those aspects of their countertransferential self-experience which are most self-dystonic. For Livingston, the possibility that he may be enacting the role of exploiter of his patient (whether at the level of wanting her to keep him excited in the sense of entertained and not bored, let alone at the level of exploiting her sexually) has to be a self-perception that would be extremely unacceptable to his conscious, syntonic sense of self-identity. It is therefore little wonder that he remained unaware that there might be something disturbing about telling Mrs. A that what is going on between them is "in fact exciting." As for Mrs. A, it would certainly be consistent with her role as a nondifficult patient for her to suppress, or dissociate, any experience of the analyst that might be disturbing to *his* syntonic sense of self.

In the next session reported, Mrs. A shows remarkable self-awareness as she talks of "making a 'deal' not to bring up anything which might make [Livingston] uncomfortable in return for being able to keep [him] at just the right distance" (Livingston, 1996, p. 151). They "shared a chuckle over her need to reassure [him] that it was about her father and not really about [him]" (p. 151), and then "she began to explore the genetic roots of the 'deal' in a way which was both clearer and emotionally more connected than ever before" (p. 151), going "back and forth between observations of her experience with [him] and her role in not upsetting each family member from early childhood through recent years" (p. 151), clarifying how this organizing principle has operated, and still operates, in her relationships. She explains how neither her adoptive father (with his violent temper, sense of disgust, and threats of "'send[ing] her back to the Indians'" [p. 151]) nor her adoptive mother (whose priority was protecting her schizophrenic sister, and who relied on Mrs. A to function as *her* selfobject) could ever be relied upon for support or safety, and how she learned that "it is not safe to let anyone too close" (p. 151). With her analyst's empathic help, Mrs. A has apparently gained considerable awareness of this organizing principle. What is less clear is whether, at the same time, in being such a "good patient" throughout this session, she has felt the need to play the role of the compliant "good girl" trying to please and appease her father/analyst.

Her need to please and avoid displeasing Livingston is expressed at the start of the following session, as Mrs. A begins by "expressing a fear that [he] will become bored and give up on her" (p. 152). Livingston tries to clarify whether she is reacting to something he has done, but she exonerates him and expresses "how important" it has been to her "that [he] had never given up on her," which has enabled her "to keep coming even when she feels hopeless and discouraged" (p. 152). In saying this, she is expressing her positive experience of the selfobject dimension of the transference. Simultaneously, I believe, she is denying the conflictual/resistive/repetitive dimension of the transference. What she says coincides with the analyst's self-syntonic view of himself as nurturant, patient, and supportive; what she denies is designed to relieve him of seeing himself as a failing, or conditional, selfobject, a view that she senses he would experience as self-dystonic. As the selfobject dimension takes firm hold of the foreground of the intersubjective matrix, Mrs. A is able to talk meaningfully about several important experiences of abandonment, physical and emotional, by her birth-mother and by her adoptive father (whose death meant that she would never get his approval, despite all her efforts to do so). Livingston maintains his role as the empathic selfobject, affirming her feelings of hurt and loss, mirroring her strength ("of never giving up"), and clarifying her underlying sense of "yearning and [feeling] unfulfilled" (p. 152). Mrs. A "is obviously moved" as she feels so understood by, and connected to, her analyst but then begins "to feel overwhelmed" and tries "to understand it all." Livingston tells her "that sometimes it might be more important to just experience her feelings and [not] . . . to understand and keep it 'under control' or even to put in words the sadness [he] could . . . see on her face" (pp. 152–153). Mrs. A cries "quietly for a while" and "as she was leaving rested her head on [his] shoulder in a very peaceful embrace" (p. 153). Livingston is the soothing, nurturing father, providing those selfobject functions that her own father never did, and never could, provide. This moment is very tender and loving, for both patient and analyst, and Mrs. A seems comfortable with the closeness. But we know that she has very conflicted feelings about closeness (emotional and physical), and it would be very surprising if the experience of this embrace does not stimulate, at some level, dysphoric feelings as well as pleasant ones.

Mrs. A begins the next session already expressing the other side of her conflict about closeness. She verbalizes the pressure she is feeling to figure out "ways to distract [him] or to occupy [him]" (p. 153) to keep him at a distance from her. Her imagery is very clear: "'It's like I am a lion tamer and you are the lion on a box. I have my whip and a chair and I have to watch you very carefully'" (pp. 153–154). After a brief pause and Livingston's encouragement to continue, she adds, "'I'm not allowed to say these things. If I do, or do anything at all to make you uncomfortable, then you will pounce. You will be on top of me—pinning me down and biting'" (p. 154). Once she says it, Mrs. A spends "the rest of the session center[ing] around how hard it is for her to see [Livingston] this way" (p. 154), but she holds onto her duel view of him, as both the person "she trusts more than she has ever trusted anyone," and, simultaneously, as the "lion" who "will pounce upon her if she breaks the deal and fails to keep [him] comfortable" (p. 154). These two views, again, reflect both the selfobject and the conflictual/repetitive dimensions of the transference. Then Livingston "tell[s] her the story of a man who keeps snapping his fingers . . . [to] keep the lions away" (p. 154). The man's "friend exclaims that there are no lions within thousands of miles" and "his smug reply is, 'See, it works!'" (p. 154). While this story is funny, and both patient and analyst "laugh together," I wonder why Livingston is being so "smug" about Mrs. A's fear of lions.

Mrs. A returns the next day with the saying "'A sated lion is no danger to anyone'" (p. 154). She soon reports feeling "'a clear physical tension in [her] body'" and declares to her analyst, "'I am ready to fight you'" (p. 154). Something very powerful is going on for her, as she now seems able to hold onto her negative attribution of her analyst as the potentially dangerous predator who she must muster up the courage to fight. But quickly she begins to equivocate, as she fears being seen as "crazy" and feels a need to protect Livingston from "feel[ing] blamed for her fears." He tries to keep her focused on his role as the provoker of her fears, but quickly recognizes that his attempts at helping her to "talk about what [he] might be doing to trigger her fear seem counterproductive at this point" (p. 154). Despite his efforts, "she responds by again assuring [him] that the feelings are within her" (p. 154). In her next statement, Mrs. A redirects the focus of the aggressive attribution to herself, saying, "'The lion could be in me too. I erase parts of me that could be dangerous. I keep a grip on things'" (p. 154). While what she is saying about herself here is undoubtedly accurate (namely, regarding her own aggression, her self-erasing tendencies, especially regarding her aggression, and her need to maintain control), this shift strikes me as a retreat from her earlier attempt at experiencing her analyst in the role of the lion. This retreat is motivated, I believe, by her characteristic need (typical of the nondifficult patient) to protect the analyst from a self-dystonic (negative) attribution.

Livingston, following the content rather than the process, responds with his understanding "that she is afraid of her own wanting and hunger as well as the other person's" (p. 154). He says, "'What I hear you saying is that it is the hunger which feels dangerous'" (p. 155). She immediately responds, "'Sure, if I'm the meal'" (p. 155). This response and the fear that follows clarify beyond any doubt that what is affectively most salient for her at this moment is her fear of the *Other's* aggressive "hunger," not of her own: she fears being the lion's victim. Livingston, recognizing that this is the right moment to renew his efforts at helping her directly assign attributes to him which she fears he might experience as self-dystonic, asks "if she 'has ever seen [him] as hungry in some way'" (p. 155). This question is right on target. She responds after a long pause: "'It isn't really hungry—at least that's not the word. The word is different, but it has all the feelings we are talking about as hunger. Your interest scares me. You look at me with intensity and interest. I want it and it is very scary" (p. 155). Mrs. A has now been able to state very directly how she has been experiencing her analyst's "intensity and interest," and now he has been able to hear her very clearly. At this moment of revelation, the intersubjective disjunction that had been silently present, underlying their relationship for quite some time, entered the realm of conscious discourse: the analyst, who had experienced his "intense empathic listening stance" as "nurturing and wonderful," now understood that his patient had experienced his "intensity and interest" as potentially very dangerous, like hunger of the unsated lion. Her discomfort with the "intensity" of his look touched on a self-dystonic aspect of himself: Livingston shares (with us, not the patient) his association to himself as a voyeuristic "little boy . . . interested in an aunt's beautiful inner thigh" (p. 155); he thought he had successfully sublimated this part of himself into his empathically attuned therapeutic stance, but he now realized that, perhaps, the sublimation was not as complete as he had thought. Until now, Mrs. A had protected him from this awareness, but now Livingston was able to accept the information and tolerate the resulting mixture of feelings: "a bit confused and hurt," at the narcissistic injury inherent in this process of discovery, but also "excited and optimistic" at the positive results of his self-supervision.

His ability to "contain [his] own process" and "simply continue to listen attentively" (p. 155) permitted her to stay with her feelings and associations, including feelings of shame and confusion, self-blame for "encouraging the interest" (of which she says, "'I want it and I don't want it'" [p. 156]), and fear that her wanting will be "misinterpreted," leading to feeling "humiliated." She questions "whether these feelings relate to something that happened," remembers "always [feeling] uncomfortable with [her] parents' friends who 'really loved [her]' and remembers that "their interest scared [her]" (p. 19). These memories call to my mind what Ferenczi (1933) called the "confusion of tongues between adults and the child," namely how the "tenderness" desired by the child is misinterpreted as "passion" by sexually abusive adults. Whatever the source of these childhood fears, they were invalidated by her mother, who responded to her pleas not to go visit these people by telling her she "was silly" and saying "of course [you] want to see them." The abused child, faced with such adults, has no recourse but to dissociate her own self-experience while overtly complying with the adults' expectations of her (cf. Ferenczi, 1933; Miller, 1979; Herman, 1992; Davies and Frawley, 1994; Brothers, 1995). Such a child is very likely to become a nondifficult patient. As this final reported session ends, Livingston apparently has not considered the possibility that his patient may have been sexually abused. But he *has* provided the empathic encouragement and sense of safety that has permitted her to risk articulating these feelings; he has communicated his willingness to tolerate hearing what she really feels, however painful it may be to him, and this has provided the "holding environment" needed for her to take the risk of saying what had previously seemed impossible to risk saying.

As I tried to demonstrate in my discussion of Livingston's paper, the analyst's task in resolving the typical impasse in the psychoanalytic treatment of the nondifficult patient is an extremely difficult one: it requires the analyst to have the courage to face aspects of self-experience that may be self-dystonic (and therefore associated with anxiety and shame) in order to enable the patient to feel safe enough to risk the dangers she associates with overt intersubjective disjunctions. As the intersubjective matrix is established in the treatment situation, it is inevitable that *both* coparticipants become engaged, without conscious awareness, in enactments that encompass the psychodynamics of *both* coparticipants. The analyst's struggle to achieve reflective self-awareness is *always* limited by his own subjective blind spots.

While my detailed discussion of Livingston's case has highlighted what I believe to be *his* particular blind spots in relating with *this* particular patient, I wonder whether this case may exemplify a rather pervasive problem encountered in the work of many self psychologists (including many who also subscribe to intersubjective theory). In our self-syntonic investment in being "good self psychologists," namely "empathic," attuned, attentive, and accepting of our patients, we may unconsciously remain unable to truly acknowledge and tolerate our patients' anxiety in relation to us as "bad" or "persecutory" objects (for example, our being experienced as blaming, disdainful, overly attentive, abandoning, or otherwise threatening). We may, therefore, too readily give verbal reassurance of our "actual" goodness, while failing to express empathy for their *need* for reassurance in the face of their experience of us as "bad."[1] Such "false" reassurance, rather than genuinely relieving the patient's anxiety, tends to drive it further into dissociation, further from the realm of intersubjective discourse.

However, the greater our honesty, courage, and determination to be *truly* open to hearing what the patient is *really* feeling about us, but dreads telling us, the greater the likelihood that the treatment process can gradually unfold, and important insights for both patient *and* analyst can be gained.

REFERENCES

Atwood, G. & Stolorow, R. (1984), *Structures of Subjectivity: Explorations in Psychoanalytic Phenomenology.* Hillsdale, NJ: The Analytic Press.

Brandchaft, B. & —— (1988), The difficult patient. In: *The Intersubjective Perspective,* ed. R. D. Stolorow, G. E. Atwood & B. Brandchaft, Northvale, NJ: Aronson, 1994, pp. 93–112.

Brothers, D. (1995), *Falling Backwards.* New York: Norton.

Davies, J. M. & Frawley, M. G. (1994), *Treating the Adult Survivor of Childhood Sexual Abuse.* New York: Basic Books.

Ferenczi, S. (1933), Confusion of tongues between adults and the child. In: *Final Contributions to the Problems and Methods of Psycho-Analysis.* New York: Brunner/Mazel, 1955, pp. 156–167.

Gill, M. (1982), *Analysis of Transference, Volume I.* New York: International Universities Press.

Herman, J. L. (1992), *Trauma and Recovery.* New York: Basic Books.

Josephs, L. (1995), *Balancing Empathy and Interpretation.* Northvale, NJ: Aronson.

Kohut, H. (1979), The two analyses of Mr. Z. *Internat. J. Psycho-Anal.,* 60:3–27.

Livingston, M. S. (1996), Countertransference and curative process with "nondifficult" patients. In: *Basic Ideas Reconsidered: Progress in Self Psychology, Vol. 12,* ed. A. Goldberg. Hillsdale, NJ: The Analytic Press, pp. 141–158.

Miller, A. (1979), *Prisoners of Childhood.* New York: Basic Books, 1981.

Racker, H. (1968), *Transference and Countertransference.* New York: International Universities Press.

Stolorow, R. & Atwood, G. (1992), *Contexts of Being.* Hillsdale, NJ: The Analytic Press.

—— Brandchaft, B. & Atwood, G. (1987), *Psychoanalytic Treatment.* Hillsdale, NJ: The Analytic Press.

---

[1] I thank Dr. Lawrence Josephs for clarifying this point to me (personal communication).

Supervision

From Parallel Process to Developmental Process: A Developmental/ Plan Formulation Approach to Supervision

Thomas Rosbrow

In this chapter, a developmental approach to supervision will be elaborated. The developmental approach applies to two complementary levels: as a model for the actual process of supervision, the interaction between supervisor and supervisee, and as a specific theory, the *plan formulation model*, which is used within supervision to understand the dynamics of the patient and of treatment.

Understanding psychoanalytic supervision as a developmental process is an obvious idea, because supervision is an intense mentoring experience with significant effects on the analyst's identifications and actual functioning. There have also been many excellent writings applying a developmental model to treatment and contrasting this approach to a more traditional defense-resistance approach (see Shane, 1977, Schlessinger and Robbins, 1983; Thoma and Kaechele, 1986; Emde, 1990; Settlage, 1992). However, this model has not been applied in any

Originally published in *Psychodynamic Concepts of Supervision*, edited by M. Rock. Northvale, NJ: Aronson, 1996; reprinted with permission of the editors and publishers.

thorough way to the supervisory relationship. Like any significant formative relationship, both parties learn and change together. Along with the effects of the relationship on the supervisee, this is also a process with marked effects on the professional identity and clinical work of the supervisor. The meaning and effects of supervision on the supervisor is then another previously undiscussed area worth more attention. Looking at the developmental meanings of the relationship for both supervisee and supervisor will be one aim of this essay.

The initial impetus for this essay was to look at supervision from the perspective of the theory and research of the San Francisco Psychotherapy Research Group (formerly the Mt. Zion Psychotherapy Research Group) (Weiss and Sampson, 1986). This is the theory that will be used to look at a case within supervision. Using the Research Group's plan formulation model provides an open, evolving framework for looking at both the patient's core psychodynamics and the patient's movement in treatment. It provides a developmental model of psychopathology and treatment, which delineates the patient's progressive, adaptive capacities. Formulating a plan entails thinking within the patient's own frame of reference, the same stance used in self psychology (Rosbrow, 1993).

If supervision is truly a significant developmental process, what are the effects on the supervisor as well as on the supervisee? This question will be examined by looking at the effect of doing supervision on the supervisor's self-analytic process. Finally, the crucial importance of "being real" in supervision will be discussed.

FROM PARALLEL PROCESS TO DEVELOPMENTAL PROCESS

Recent developmental theories converge in seeing the infant/person/ patient as a constructive, intentional agent. Seeing the person as intentionally, if unconsciously, struggling to overcome crippling beliefs derived from traumatic experiences and interactions contrasts with the view of the patient as ruled by unconscious resistances, clinging to infantile or archaic fixations or gratifications. The concept of resistance has been criticized as an atavistic relic of an earlier time when patients relied on the analyst's authority to elicit confession of secrets. By terming the patient's difficulties in relaxing and communicating resistances, the analyst suggests that the patient willfully chooses (even if unconsciously) to withhold and obstruct the process of treatment. For example, resistance–defense interpretation was criticized by Wolf as being part of a nondemocratic atmosphere where the analyst instructs the patient on how and when to disclose (Wolf, 1991). Others have similarly advocated the replacement of the "basic rule"—to say everything that comes to mind—with an easier encouragement to talk as freely as possible (Bowlby, 1988).

Ideas about resistance are particularly relevant to a discussion of supervision. The concept of the parallel process has been a dominant, probably *the* dominant, idea in the literature on supervision since its introduction by Ekstein and Wallerstein in 1958. It is prominently featured in current writing in supervision (see Caligor, Bromberg, and Meltzer, 1984). Before critiquing the parallel process concept, I have to say that Ekstein and Wallerstein's (1958) book remains surprisingly fresh and readable and has ideas that are, to my mind, very germane to current problems. The authors repeatedly advocate that the analyst's autonomy must be cultivated and respected. They warn against the supervisor's looking for adherents rather than nurturing the originality of his or her supervisees. The supervisee's need to identify too readily can dovetail with a supervisor's vanity, hampering genuine learning. The result is "to produce dependent admirers' rather than independent coworkers" (pp. 58–59).

The main thrust of the book, however, is quite different. Their thesis is that the supervisee unconsciously identifies with aspects of a patient's resistance, which resonates with his or her own neurotic difficulties, and then enacts these problems via "parallel process" with the supervisor. The supervisee's "problems about learning" with the supervisor stem from unresolved characterological difficulties. Though the authors go to great lengths to distinguish these learning problems from therapy issues, the distinction appears to be only one of different labels—calling it a learning problem rather than a character problem.

For example, speaking of a supervisee's initial skepticism, they state, "Overt skepticism can be dealt with as a resistance just as any other. . . . The acknowledgement of this difficulty in the student is a foreshadowing of the particular way in which he will resist being taught" (p. 154). In the following passage where they describe "learning problems," their emphasis on the supervisee's character is clear:

> The major obstacle to the smooth growth of psychotherapeutic sensitivity and competence (and hence, of improved clinical service as well), is the mobilization during the process of learning of idiosyncratic patterns that determine the way in which a given individual learns—the ways in which mastery is sought and the specific difficulties that limit its effectiveness. These "learning problems" encompass the whole complex of ways of acting and responding within the psychotherapy situation that are determined not by the objectively ascertained needs of the patient but by the characteristic, automatic—and therefore, at times inappropriate—patterns of response of the would-be helper [p. 137].

The task of supervision is then to unknot the supervisee's neurotic inter-action with patients and within supervision. They declare that this is the great bulk of work with beginning therapists and that technical skill cannot be taught *at all* until these problems are clarified:

> Only through unraveling the learning problems that he experiences with his patient, that therapist can come to see the other side of the thera-peutic interaction, the technical-skill problems posed by the disturbed mental processes of the patient. This will be a rather late achievement in the training process of the young therapist. It may even seem that this achievement is not a part of the process of learning, but rather is the end-product of successful learning [p. 173].

The identificatory phenomena highlighted in parallel process thinking certainly occur, and I am not loathe to interpret them when needed. But putting the therapist's identification with unconscious resistance and characterological "learning problems" at the conceptual center of the supervisory experience, as many writers have, infantilizes and patronizes the therapist. Loewald has talked about the "differential" between analyst and patient, the experienced difference in psychological knowl-edge and mastery between them (Loewald, 1980). He emphasizes that some gradient is necessary between the two, because the analyst must have a higher level of understanding and organization in relationship to the patient's problems. But he underlines that the gradient does not pertain to their relationship as two human beings, that the gradient is specific to the task at hand. A parallel process orientation can stretch the gradient between supervisor and supervisee to a dangerous degree. The supervisor is then in the postion of the omniscient interpreter/ therapist, while the supervisee is in the position of the unknowing patient.

TEACH OR TREAT—A FALSE DICHOTOMY

The literature on supervision also discusses in a similar authoritarian-tinged vein the "teach or treat" question—what balance to take between being purely "educational" in supervision, that is, focused on the patient, and analyzing the therapist's countertransference problems (e.g., Flem-ing, 1971; for a contemporary discussion, see Sarnat, 1992). The teach or treat question suggests that teaching technique and psychodynamics to the supervisee is suspect and constantly runs the risk of avoiding the "real stuff," the supervisee's problematic countertransference.

Using a developmental approach, one looks at this matter from a different angle, which does not split up teaching and treating—for therapy or for supervision. In therapy, the analyst naturally provides information and knowledge in any number of ways depending on the person's needs, blind spots, conflicts, or deficits. He or she does so both in making interpretations and also at times serving as a "developmental object"—taking on parental or caretaking functions, sometimes literally, sometimes symbolically (Modell, 1990). The therapist does this for a multitude of reasons, for example, to protect the patient from danger or to serve as a model of identification.

The teach–treat dilemma is a false dichotomy that imagines there should be a pure interpretive technique rigorously applied to the dynamics of the analytic situation, untainted by contaminating advice, support, or encouragement. In supervision, the dilemma concept suggests at one point that the supervisee is a student who receives instruction and then shifts to becoming a patient who receives interpretation (or, is "treated" like a "patient" most of the time, offering up countertransference for analysis by a supervisor/analyst). The educational process and the therapeutic process are split and polarized. The split is well illustrated in the last quote by Ekstein and Wallerstein, where technical learning can only follow work on the supervisee's characterologically based problems.

In a developmental approach, the process of learning in supervision is itself mutative and, in a broader sense therapeutic. The supervisee learns from the supervisor through instruction, affective experience, and identification. By listening to and formulating about patients, the supervisee also unconsciously, as well as consciously, self-reflects, associates, and deepens self-awareness. A great deal of the supervisee's anxiety can be resolved when he or she feels a better understanding of the case: good education diminishes countertransference.

The therapist's intense emotional reactions can often be understood within a formulation of the patient's life and identifications. Often, the therapist, unconsciously, either identifies with aspects of the patient's self or with qualities of the patient's primary objects. These are often termed *projective identifications,* or in Weiss's terms *passive into active tests.* The supervisee does not usually have to "go on the couch" to look at these processes.

The supervisor works to make the supervisee feel safe to bring up countertransference feelings at a level of depth that is comfortable to that person. Those reactions to patients that stem primarily from the supervisee's own life, the supervisee's transferences to a patient, can more readily, and genuinely, be discussed at the supervisee's initiative. As in treatment, this type of self-disclosure, if it happens, takes place over a long period of time.

The supervisee is encouraged, at times, to stretch and try unfamiliar ways of relating and intervening. The supervisor needs to be empathic to the supervisee's hesitance to do things differently, but also respect the supervisee's inevitable real differences of opinion and different ways of working. This acceptance of difference is also mutative for the supervisor, who gets help in mastering his or her own needs to be in control and omnipotent by respecting the supervisee's individuality and initiative.

USING A PLAN FORMULATION

The basic assumptions of the plan formulation model about pathogenesis and therapeutic change, derived from detailed empirical observations and research, are common to other psychoanalytic developmental theories derived primarily from clinical and research observations of infants, children, and caretakers (Rosbrow, 1993). These assumptions involve the person's (or infant's) basic healthy strivings for activity, self-regulation, and mastery (see Lichtenberg, 1989; Emde, 1990; Leichtman, 1990). In treatment, the patient works to accomplish specific forsaken developmental goals and to gain insight into how these goals were abandoned. In the crucial sequence of the plan formulation, the *patient works unconsciously to disconfirm pathogenic beliefs by testing them with the analyst.*

The following vignette illustrates, albeit sketchily, how to make a plan formulation about a case. Put briefly, a plan formulation constructs a picture of the patient's unconscious plan for treatment, what the patient is inferred to be seeking from treatment. This construct includes the patient's *unconscious goals*, the *pathogenic beliefs* that stop her from accomplishing the goals, the *tests* the patient will unconsciously enact with the analyst, and insights that would help the patient.

Pathogenic beliefs refers to how a child comes to understand and interpret painful events and interactions. Weiss emphasizes the significance of *the sense of personal responsibility* in the formation of pathogenic beliefs. Because of childish egocentrism and paucity of life experience, a child is prone to interpret himself or herself to blame for environmental failure and mistreatment. If a parent is chronically angry and threatening, the child can infer that he or she is irritating and deserving of punishment. Or if a parent is listless and unhappy, the child can infer he or she is draining and demanding. Feeling responsible for the caretaker's failings, the child may unconsciously decide to compromise normal developmental goals, assuming his or her desires and strivings provoked the caretaker's wrath, withdrawal, or any other traumatic parental attitude. A pathogenic belief is the specific hypothesis the child constructs; for example, "If I was less demanding and weak, then my mother would not be so exhausted and overwhelmed." These beliefs are formed unconsciously, and subsequently the person uses them to avert psychic danger. If the child believes his or her demandingness drained a parent, the child might decide, unconsciously, to ask for as little as possible from others and present a front of pseudo-strength, while warding off feelings of need and disappointment.

While these beliefs are compelling and neurotogenic, the individual also unconsciously seeks experience with others that might contradict a belief and give an opportunity for resumed development—Weiss defines this as *testing* of the environment, a universal phenomenon. I have argued that in another part of the person's experience, he or she knows, or remembers, "evidence" that he or she is not at fault—a view shared by Bowlby (Rosbrow, 1993). However, given the strength of the beliefs, the individual's view of the outside world usually confirms his or her beliefs. Sometimes in development, an experience with another person is so strikingly different from what is expected that a person's view of the world can be dramatically changed. This can happen with a friend, a mentor, or a lover, especially when the other person's different qualities are experienced in extremely stressful or significant circumstances.

The patient's strivings to work through and discard specific pathogenic beliefs are constructed as the patient's goals for treatment and typically can be inferred during early sessions. In treatment, the patient continuously tests the therapist in two important ways. One is by simply scanning assiduously, mostly unconsciously, the character and behavior of the therapist and comparing him or her with significant others. The second way is by reenacting key relationships with the therapist, again unconsciously, and finding out whether the therapist represents a new object, with all that implies for resumed development and working through of repressed, traumatic experiences.

VIGNETTE

This vignette also illustrates how supervisor and supervisee may differ over dynamics of a case, but still use the framework of the plan formulation to look at the effects of the supervisee's interventions. The supervision is a reciprocal, mutually enriching process, where both parties work and learn together.

The supervisee, an experienced clinician with a different, well-formed theoretical orientation, usually refrained from interventions that, to her, suggested advice-giving or intrusions into the patient's life. The patient quickly posed a dramatic test that called for the analyst to inevitably either directly respond to the crisis in the patient's life, or else let the patient self-destruct. This vignette illustrates how differing styles of responding to a patient can be accepted and understood.

In this case, the patient, Ms. A, was a professional woman in her twenties, employed in a blue-chip financial institution, who was contemplating a serious breach of professional ethics, with the potential for scandal and public disgrace. Ms. A's mother was a bitter, cut-throat businesswoman, a female version of the real-estate sharks in David Mamet's *GlenGarry GlenRoss*, who sneered at people who played by the rules as losers and wimps. During childhood, the mother frequently ridiculed and humiliated Ms. A verbally and, at the least, threatened her physically. She had been, and still was, detached, disinterested, and unsupportive of the patient's professional strivings. The patient was aware at rare moments of feelings of hurt and anger towards her mother but was typically obsessed with her current preoccupations with little insight. Ms. A presented herself as greedy and impulsive but was shocked at her frequent rejection by others. She described her female therapist as an establishment type from a more privileged, educated background, with a mixture of respect, envy, and class animosity—one of the super straight, seemingly moral authorities she scorned and feared.

From a plan formulation perspective, the patient was currently posing a major test on multiple levels. She was testing to see if the therapist would permit her to destroy her new-found success and agree with her view of herself as debased and despicable. From her mother's contemptuous attacks, she had developed the pathogenic belief that she was loathsome and weak and that she did not deserve to be happy either professionally or personally. She also felt that if she shined, her mother would be hurt and enraged. At the same time, she identified with her mother out of loyalty and guilt (see Weiss, 1986; Modell, 1984 a, b). Imitating her mother's psychopathic tendencies in an exaggerated way was an act of fealty. Her toying with scandal and disgrace could involve a need, out of survivor guilt, to keep herself bitter and failed like her mother just at the time that respectability and security were potentially hers. Ms. A's professional aspirations and actual vocational choice, a field involving very strenuous ethics, suggested that she desperately wanted to individuate from her mother and feel respectable and socially responsible. These aspirations are inferred to be the patient's unconscious goals.

The current crisis pushed the therapist to explicitly demonstrate if she wished the patient failure, akin to the mother, or whether she was a new object who believed in the patient's talents and wished-for self and would not let Ms. A destroy her hard-won professional success. Demonstrating this did not feel easy to the therapist, since Ms. A presented her imagined professional indiscretions in a provocative, defiant, ego-syntonic manner. The therapist had grounds to fear that, if she confronted the patient about the risks involved, Ms. A would perceive her as judgemental and intrusive and confirm Ms. A's transference perceptions of her as obsessively moralistic and hostile towards her. If the negative transference intensified, Ms. A. could become paranoid and untreatable. The therapist also had reservations, out of her own well-founded ideas, about intervening in ways that could be construed as telling the patient what to do.

The supervisor's advice was to spell out to Ms. A the dangers of her behavior in a full, lengthy fashion. This would include the present danger of professional disgrace, the therapist's concern about this, the hypothesis of unconscious guilt and identification with her mother, and the possible implications of this interpretation making the patient regard the therapist as excessively moralistic versus the therapist's interest in circumventing disaster for Ms. A. This type of intervention would give the patient the "big picture."[1] Even if the dynamics were rebuffed by Ms. A, which was likely, the seeds could be planted for future use.

The therapist chose to intervene in a quite different manner, sympatico with her own style and convictions. At a certain point when Ms. A was characteristically plotting and scheming, the therapist calmly queried her about her proposed actions and their potential consequences. She wondered how Ms. A was assured her actions would work out beneficially, rather than backfire on her—she was not in a position to calculate the odds. At the time, Ms. A responded to these comments by pausing thoughtfully and then going on with her usual obsessive ruminations.

The therapist saw herself, at this particular point in treatment, addressing a defect in the patient's reality testing. Her intervention reflected this frame of reference that was more germane to her. At the same time, the therapist's intervention was also a response to—and a translation of—the supervisor's recommendations and exhortations. Although the therapist was not very interested in, or in agreement with, the formulation of the patient's pathogenic beliefs and goals, she came to agree with the idea that the patient's actions constituted a test that had to be addressed for the patient's sake and for the treatment to proceed.

This therapist had a strong need to work in her own way. She found a way to speak to the patient that incorporated supervisory input but expressed her own nuanced position. A parallel process view might see the therapist displaying her problems in learning through her need to

---

[1] I am grateful to Harold Sampson, who introduced me to using a "big picture" approach in two ways: (1) to construct a broad overview of what the patient is striving to accomplish in treatment and; (2) to, at crucial moments in treatment, impart this total picture to the patient.

assert her autonomy and do things differently, and wonder about the parallel nature of her identification with the patient. One could apply a testing model and wonder how the supervisee might be testing the supervisor by disagreeing and asserting herself, and what would be a passed test for the supervisor. I do not advocate using a testing model for the supervisory process, however, though this idea has been fruitfully discussed by members of the research group. To do so would bring back the problems I discussed as inherent in the parallel process literature—a patronizing emphasis on the therapist's patientlike inadequacies and character problems.

Rather than looking at the supervisee's actions as tests, they can be seen as constituting the supervisee's own plan for supervision—a way of understanding the supervisee's goals and needs at a crucial point in professional development. Often the supervisee's plan will involve complex needs to both identify with the supervisor, learn from the supervisor, and at the same time be his or her own person. The supervisor felt that the therapist had to have her needs for autonomy respected in order to take in the supervisor's help. At the same time, the therapist could not overidentify with the patient's need for autonomy, or then she would let the patient self-destruct out of an overzealous interest in being nonintrusive. The supervisor dealt with this situation by repeating his understanding of the patient's testing over numerous sessions, while also observing and listening to the therapist's different ways of handling the patient with interest—respecting the therapist's autonomy, while asserting his own, different point of view. For each supervisee, the supervisor has to find a way to be "optimally responsive" (Bacal, 1985).

In following sessions, it became clear that Ms. A had dropped her scheme as unwise, without explicitly crediting this decision to the therapist. Over the next few months, she continued to feel aggrieved and entitled, but no longer contemplated endangering herself. Most marked was a shift in affect, noticeable to both Ms. A and her therapist; Ms. A began to consciously experience depression and emptiness, along with feelings of shame and inadequacy. This shift suggested a marked lessening of defense, and the beginning capacity to bear unpleasant emotions. Her psychological mindedness increased subtly as she, with difficulty, started to acknowledge her sense of frustration and limitation. Ms. A understood her experienced depression as a gain in awareness and began to look at relevant childhood memories. Ms. A's caustic perception of the therapist's moralism became tempered by grudging respect for the therapist's integrity.

This vignette illustrates the two issues of how to apply a theory and how to work together with different theories. Ms. A's potentially ruinous scheme is inferred to constitute a major test with implications for her real life, her capacity to self-reflect in treatment and with significant transference meanings. After this situation was addressed, the patient rapidly, albeit subtly, grew in her capacity to protect her self from acting self-destructively, and in her budding ability to externalize less and self-reflect. This positive shift, following the therapist's response to an inferred test constitutes a "passed test," in Weiss's terms. The patient unconsciously processes the therapist's reaction, feels reassured, and perceives the therapist in a new, more protective light, and then can work in treatment with more confidence and openness.

Regarding working with different theories, the therapist made a different type of intervention than the supervisor suggested, a reflection of both stylistic and theoretical differences. We cannot predict how the patient might have responded to the proposed intervention. But the way the therapist spoke to the patient "passed the test" regardless, by calling the patient's attention to the therapist's concern and perception of the self-destructive dangers of the patient's actions. The plan model, if used flexibly, can explain the effects of various modes of intervention, by formulating what the patient is asking (or "testing"), and then seeing how the patient responds to the therapist's actions.

This method looks at process—the patient's psychological minded-ness, capacity to experience affects, and so on—rather than at content, as a way of retrospectively appraising therapeutic action. It is not impor-tant whether the patient "agrees" with an intervention, but how the patient's psychological work is affected. Others writing on supervision have similarly emphasized the need to look at the clinical evidence to see the effects of an interpretation or intervention, rather that relying on theory (Ekstein and Wallerstein, 1958; Haesler, 1993). The plan model does the same thing but more systematically, as the research has used process measures to look at the effect of interventions both immediately and more long term (Weiss, 1993). The plan model can respect and give clarity to inevitable differences in approach. From the point of view of theoretical pluralism (Bernardi and Bernardi, 1993), people of different orientations can work together and learn from one another using this framework.

Regarding differences stemming from a personal manner, the super-visee can learn more about what is curative or enhancing about his or her own "personal equation." Perceiving what works in therapy stem-ming from the person's natural way of being is an important function for supervision. This self-awareness is a key element in knowing how to use oneself fully in doing treatment. This heightened positive self-awareness can make the analyst appreciate more easily, with less narcissistic vulnerability, when these same traits do not work in other situations or with other patients.

For the supervisor, learning repeatedly that "there is more than one way to skin a cat" is a valuable lesson against theoretical rigidity or personal omnipotence—pulls and pitfalls for anyone doing treatment. Seeing how other styles or ways of thinking work helps me to stretch or improvise more freely when my habitual way of working does not connect with a certain patient. My potential repertoire can include images of how others make contact and facilitate a patient's growth.

At the same time, I am not just espousing modesty and eclecticism. When a supervised treatment is going well and has become more open or changed course in response to supervisory input, the supervisor can powerfully experience a sense of conviction of the "rightness" of what he or she espouses. This strengthened self-feeling of confidence and effectiveness is valuable and sustaining and can paradoxically allow one to tolerate the equally important feelings of doubt and uncertainty inherent in our work.

During supervision, the supervisor constructs a complex representation of the patient and has the opportunity to add depth and detail to the representation over time. The same capacity to make representations of other unseen people, the important people in a patient's life, is an important part of the analyst's empathic capacities. Doing supervision greatly stimulates the analyst's ability to represent and visualize another's reality.

SUPERVISION AND SELF-ANALYSIS

For some time, the attainment of the self-analytic function has been a sine qua non of a successful analytic treatment, particularly for an analyst (e.g., Fleming, 1971). Today, analysts are describing in ever finer detail actual experiences of self analysis (Barron, 1993), or self inquiry (Gardner, 1983). This movement towards more open scrutiny and elaboration of the analyst's personal associations and lived experience inside and outside of sessions is stimulating and salutary. Reading this literature heightens the analyst's awareness of barely conscious thoughts and feelings that persist as a stream parallel to the patient's associations.

Typically, the self-analytic activity is explained as a final internalization of the analyst's own analysis—the internal structure formed through a successful analysis, in large part through identification with one's own analyst. I can talk to myself, ask myself questions, as my analyst did with me. While this is undoubtedly true, the effect of supervision on the development of the self-analytic function is both obvious and subtle. As analysts, our self analysis is constantly activated, indeed demanded, in our work with our patients. Doing treatment, I have time and space to systematically observe my associations and self reflect. What is sometimes referred to as self supervision is inseparable from self analysis. In this process, thoughts about a patient flow seamlessly into thoughts about one's own life and psychology. How we hear and categorize our patient's material is centrally involved with what we have learned and experienced in supervision, perhaps as much as in our own treatment. This is especially so when long-term relationships with important mentors have taken place. My organization of my patient's material then becomes the first step, the impetus for my ongoing self-analytic work.

Doing supervision then allows the supervisor the opportunity for deeper self-analytic work through his contact with the supervisee and the supervisee's patients. While listening to patients, the analyst is usually aware of a concurrent track of associations related to the analyst's own life and concerns. When doing supervision, the analyst more often has associations related to his work-life with patients, rather than about his personal life. When I associate to a patient during supervision, it prods me to think about what affinities and differences there are between my patient and the supervisee's patient. Later, I'm prodded to think more about my own patient, which then leads into self-analysis as well. While writing this article, I've become more aware of how listening to a supervisee describe a patient reminds me of a present patient of my own. Suggesting, with the benefit of the supervisor's distance, an intervention that is helpful with the supervisee's patient, then encourages me to try something new with my own patient. Usually, the situations have a common thread, but the actual patients and interventions are quite different. Listening to the supervision material triggered a network of associations and actions with unintended beneficial effects on my own clinical work and self-reflection. I imagine this is a background phenomena for supervisors, which has been little explored or acknowledged.

I was supervising a case of a very depressed woman with a history of physical abuse, which was mentioned only at the beginning of a long-term treatment. At a certain point, the patient was becoming increasingly numb, withdrawn, and unproductive, in work and in therapy, and the therapist was feeling helpless and alarmed. I suggested introducing to the patient the idea that her chronic feelings of numbness and hopelessness might relate to her rarely discussed childhood trauma and encouraging her discussion of these experiences. Over some time, introducing the topic stirred up the patient in many ways and opened up current secrets and symptoms she had been unable to touch in treatment, specifically severe bulimia. While supervising this case, I found myself consistently thinking of a seemingly quite different patient I was treating, a man with some depression, but bothered primarily from sexual and professional inhibitions that he was steadily overcoming. His treatment was at times plodding but, overall, was moving along and in no state of crisis. I wondered for awhile why I was thinking about him and what was happening now in his treatment.

I realized that the common thread(s) related to his own tendency to be flat and undescriptive and that I felt—without usually realizing it—a certain ennui about his treatment. Though there was not a parallel trauma in his history, he shared with the other patient longstanding difficulties in self-regulation—with her, bulimia, and with him, restlessness, difficulties sleeping, and organizing himself. My ennui stopped me from pursuing various leads in his material, which could foster his self-reflection and his taking more responsibility for getting his life on track. Thinking about these parallels helped me to make a renewed, refreshed effort with him, which has enlivened our work. This is an undramatic, everyday example of how supervision affects, often preconsciously, the supervisor. My guess is this goes on all the time with supervisors.

Thinking about supervision has highlighted for me the intrinsic, deeply reciprocal value of the supervisory relationship. When supervision works, both parties can grow and benefit enormously, more than is commonly understood. After being supervised, the analyst is fortunate if supervision becomes part of a person's professional functioning. The supervisor owes a debt of gratitude towards his or her supervisees for extending his capacity to listen to himself and to his patients. All analysts must undergo, enjoy, and struggle with the need for continuous self-analytic scrutiny. Doing supervision constantly rejuvenates and assists the analyst's capacity for self inquiry.

For the supervisee, the potential gains are much greater. When supervision works, the supervisee first gains the conceptual tools needed to harness that person's intuitions and unique therapeutic style. Then, through careful observation of the treatment process by supervisor and supervisee, the supervisee gains a different, sharper picture of his or her own idiographic character and how it affects patients. By underscoring key moments in treatment, when the patient poses unavoidable tests and the analyst successfully "passes the test," resulting in discernible shifts in the patient's therapeutic capacities, the supervisor constructs for the supervisee a picture of his or her actual strengths and style of working. Having his or her creativity understood and described, made conscious, by the supervisor helps the supervisee establish a clearer sense of personal agency and identity as an analyst. After supervision, the analyst retains a supervisory introject that consists of a distillation, or fusion, of the teachings and relationships with important supervisors.

BEING REAL

For the supervisee to "complete supervision," to feel finished, to be able to internalize the supervisor, the quality of the relationship is paramount. Impossible to "teach," but possible and important for the supervisor to model, is a manner of openness, honesty, and "realness." By that, I mean the supervisor should relate to the supervisee without pretension, airs of superiority, or artifice. Winnicott stressed the crucial importance of the analyst's aliveness and realness (Winnicott, 1962). He saw it as an antidote to the patient's false-self compliance with the analyst, repeating the person's environmental trauma with parents who demanded or appeared to psychologically need overcompliance (Winnicott, 1960).

Until a certain point down the road in the supervisee's training, it is inevitable for the (relatively) new analyst to be, at times, stiff and lacking in spontaneity. While mastering new skills and anxieties as an analyst, the supervisee will often be pulled to act like he or she imagines one should, rather than as oneself. While inevitable, this constrained way of being, often based on imagined rules, runs counter to what both patient and analyst need—for the analyst to relate in a natural, genuine manner (see Heimann, 1989). A supervisor can help the supervisee understand and utilize his or her own "personal idiom" (Bollas, 1992) in two ways. One is for the supervisor to relate to the supervisee in a frank, real manner, while respecting differences of opinion and character. The other is to help the supervisee recognize when his or her own spontaneous, true-self relatedness has a mutative effect with patients and how to use this part of him or herself more freely.

REFERENCES

Bacal, H. (1985), Optimal responsiveness and the therapeutic process. In: *Progress in Self Psychology, Vol. 1,* ed. A. Goldberg. New York: Guilford, pp. 202–227.

Barron, J., ed. (1993), *Self-Analysis.* Hillsdale, NJ: The Analytic Press.

Bernardi, R. & Bernardi, B. (1993), Does our self-analysis take into consideration our assumptions? In: *Self-Analysis,* ed. J. Barron. Hillsdale, NJ: The Analytic Press, pp. 29–46.

Bollas, C. (1992), *Being a Character.* New York: Hill & Wang.

Bowlby, J. (1988), Attachment, communication, and the therapeutic process. In: *A Secure Base.* New York: Basic Books, pp. 137–157.

Caligor, L., Bromberg, P. & Meltzer, J., eds. (1984), *Clinical Perspectives on the Supervision of Psychoanalysis and Psychotherapy.* New York: Plenum Press.

Ekstein, R. & Wallerstein, R. (1958), *The Teaching and Learning of Supervision.* New York: Basic Books.

Emde, R. (1990), Mobilizing fundamental modes of development: Empathic availability and therapeutic action. *J. Amer. Psychoanal. Assn.*, 38:881–914.

Fleming, J. (1971). Freud's concept of self-analysis: Its relevance for psychoanalytic training. In: *Currents in Psychoanalysis*, ed. I. Marcus. New York: International Universities Press.

Gardner, R. (1983), *Self Inquiry*. Hillsdale, NJ: The Analytic Press.

Haesler, L. (1993), Adequate distance in the relationship between supervisor and supervisee. The position of the supervisor between "teacher" and "analyst." *Internat. J. Psycho-Anal.*, 74:547–555.

Heimann, P. (1989), On the necessity for the analyst to be natural with his patient. In: *About Children and Children-no-longer*, ed. M. Tonnesman. New York: Tavistock Routledge.

Leichtman, M. (1990), Developmental psychology and psychoanalysis. I. The context for a revolution in psychoanalysis. *J. Amer. Psychoanal. Assn.*, 38:915–950.

Lichtenberg, J. (1989), *Psychoanalysis and Motivation*. Hillsdale, NJ: The Analytic Press.

Loewald, H. (1980), On the therapeutic action of psychoanalysis. In: *Papers on Psychoanalysis*. New Haven, CT: Yale University Press, pp. 221–256.

Modell, A. (1984a), On having more. In: *Psychoanalysis in a New Context*. New York: International Universities Press, pp. 71–82.

—— (1984b), On having the right to a life. In *Psychoanalysis in a New Context*. New York: International Universities Press, pp. 55–69.

—— (1990), Play, illusion, and the setting of psychoanalysis. In: *Other Times, Other Realities*. Cambridge, MA: Harvard University Press, pp. 23–43.

Rosbrow, T. (1993), Significance of the unconscious plan for psychoanalytic theory. *Psychoanal. Psychol.*, 10:515–532.

Sarnat, J. E. (1992), Supervision in relationship: Resolving the teach-treat controversy in psychoanalytic supervision. *Psychoanal. Psychol.*, 9:387–403.

Schlessinger, N. & Robbins, F. (1983), *A Developmental View of the Psychoanalytic Process*. New York: International Universities Press.

Settlage, C. F. (1992), Psychoanalytic observations on adult development in life and in the therapeutic relationship. *Psychoanal. & Contemp. Thought*, 15:349–374.

Shane, M. (1977), A rationale for teaching analytic technique based on a developmental orientation and approach. *Internat. J. Psycho-Anal.*, 58:95–108.

Thoma, H. & Kaechele, H. (1986), *Psychoanalytic Practice 1*. New York: Springer-Verlag.

Weiss, J. (1986), Part I. Theory and clinical observations. In: *The Psychoanalytic Process*, ed. J. Weiss & H. Sampson. New York: Guilford, pp. 3–138.

—— & Sampson, H. (1986), *The Psychoanalytic Process*. New York: Guilford.

—— (1993), *How Therapy Works*. New York: Guilford.

Winnicott, D. W. (1960), Ego distortion in terms of true and false self. In: *The Maturational Processes and the Facilitating Environment*. New York: International Universities Press, 1965, pp. 141–151.

—— (1962), The aims of psychoanalytical treatment. In: *The Maturational Processes and the Facilitating Environment*. New York: International Universities Press, 1965, pp. 166–170.

Wolf, E. S. (1991), Advances in self psychology: The evolution of psychoanalytic treatment. *Psychoanal. Inq.*, 11:123–146.

Chapter 11

The Drift Toward Contemporary Self Psychology: Supervision on the Cusp of a Change In Theory

Kenneth L. Koenig

What time can achieve, human intelligence cannot.
—old folk saying

Much has been written about and presented at various conferences regarding the upheaval in psychoanalysis in the last 25 years or so. This paradigm shift represents a great change in emphasis in the analyses that are now conducted (Ornstein and Kay, 1990; Skolnick and Warshaw, 1992; Shane and Shane, 1993; Sucharov, 1992). It is my aim to provide another view of this phenomenon, as a psychoanalytic supervisee, initially during the early 1970s and again in the mid-1990s.

In this chapter I trace my process of retrospectively supervising a case that I had once analyzed under supervision in the early 1970s. I also review a series of papers that my supervisor had written through the years of her work on early parent loss. I will comment on related issues of the relationship between theory and technique. These emerged during my review because I had noticed a difference in the analysis when I was able to intuitively work in a more contemporary style. Lindon (1991) has illustrated that various theoretical approaches may lead to satisfactory analytic results. My observation is that the progression toward contemporary theory (which includes a psychology of the self and a modern developmental perspective) has encouraged technique that helps guide analysts toward remaining attuned to the patient's central affect states. This allows us to more consistently interpret from within the patient's point of view and enables the profound and unique sense of being understood by another. At times, when I serendipitously used this approach with my case in the 1970s, the analysis seemed to progress successfully. When I did not, it foundered. In addition to summarizing my findings, I will also try to show the value of this unusual type of review process in that it enabled me to work through my own issues dealing with my prior analytic training experience.

I began the supervised analysis of Sally in 1973 while a candidate at the Denver Institute of Psychoanalysis. Sally had experienced a double parent loss at the age of four, involving a car–train accident in which her parents were both killed and she was injured. Sally was hospitalized with minor facial cuts and then, upon release, went to live with relatives. During her late teens she met and married a U.S. serviceman and they moved to the United States. A few years later, at the age of 24, Sally applied for low-fee analysis through the psychoanalytic institute. She complained of a longstanding "feeling of depression" that began after she got out of the hospital following the accident. She also described an exploitative affair in which she had been involved and could not end. This was her immediate reason for seeking treatment. My assigned supervisor on this case was Dr. Joan Fleming, who specialized in the treatment of parent loss cases and had written extensively on this subject since 1963. (At that time in Denver, supervisors were assigned to you, an interesting parallel to the prevailing power arrangement in the psychoanalytic endeavor itself.) I worked with Sally for one and one-half years, at which time she ended the analysis and moved to another town.

Some time after the completion of this case, my training was interrupted in the mid 1970s, and it was not until 1993 that I reentered formal psychoanalytic training, this time as an advanced candidate at the Institute for Contemporary Psychoanalysis in Los Angeles. I had discontinued my training in the 1970s because of what I perceived to be the adverse educational atmosphere at the Denver Institute at that time and, in my mind, the questionable effectiveness of much of what I was being taught to do. Subsequent events, communications, and publications have since confirmed my convictions (Levy, 1994; Mayerson, 1994, personal communication; Schwartz, 1994). However, at the time, this series of events was personally quite traumatic. I has precious little peer support for my perception of the training atmosphere that existed, and I was left with a myriad of doubts about the efficacy of my work. I knew nothing of the professional and personal struggles of Kohut with the political forces within the psychoanalytic power structure. Later, when I did learn of his travails, Kohut (1982) eventually provided a figure with whom I could identify in my own struggle.

I recalled as one of the positive highlights of this early training experience the case that I had treated with Dr. Fleming. Now, during the training program at my new institute I felt that I had acquired enough additional self-understanding, supervision, experience, and perspective to go back and examine our work with Sally in detail, this time from the contemporary viewpoint I was consolidating and in an atmosphere that encouraged this kind of open exploration. I would have the benefit of many years of hindsight and clinical experience using psychoanalytic self psychology and the intersubjective perspective that I had learned in less formal settings such as annual conferences on the psychology of the self. In addition, like many analysts, I was amalgamating other relational approaches and modern developmental theory into my own unique blend of theory and technique.

Psychoanalysis seemed so different to me now than it did then. I wondered what it was that my old institute was training me to do and what, in fact, I was actually doing with my patients. What was the impact of the theoretical perspective that I had then and now? What were the "deficiencies" I could find in the old work and what was effective? When did my work with Sally (and my other control case) not feel "right" as it seemed in many instances? I had the good fortune to have retained intact all the process notes with Fleming's supervisory comments jotted in the margins, as well as all my case writeups, and presentations. In addition, this process was greatly aided by the fact that Dr. Fleming had documented in a number of papers over a span of years the ongoing development of her concepts for working with parent loss cases.

CASE REVIEW PROCESS

To begin with, I encountered my first big obstacle, myself. Re-reading these old notes became an exceedingly painful and embarrassing experience. I immediately focused on what I felt was my lack of understanding of the process of creating an unfolding dialogue, my inept and clumsy attempts to apply what I imagined at the time was appropriate analytic technique and a classical-style abstinence, and my inadequate ideas of establishing ongoing periods of empathic attunement with Sally. When I did comment, rather than exploring her affects in a way that allowed for an enhancement of her curiosity, I asked leading questions or made quasi-authoritative or challenging statements that seemed to limit her personal exploration and sense of owning the process. I could notice right away that I felt that I had to "make" the analysis happen rather than trusting in a developmental thrust (i.e., self-righting tendancy) within the patient to guide us. This created a hierarchical relationship between us and often put her on the defensive. The general tenor of many of the sessions reflected a kind of removed, distant atmosphere for which I, as I reviewed the notes, now held myself responsible (although at the time I recall holding her responsible). The review became, to some extent, unbearable, and I found my attention wandering. It took a great effort to push through these notes with a useful level of concentration. The fact that this analysis was occurring under close supervision by an experienced supervisor who was an expert both in supervision (Fleming and Benedek, 1966) and in parent loss was minimally consoling. I realized that part of what was occurring was related to my youth and lack of analytic experience. Hirsch (1993) has convincingly illustrated how factors of age and sex of the analyst and patient affect the countertransference patterns in the analytic dyad, which are, in turn, likely to affect both the process and the eventual outcome. However, there was ample evidence in my case notes that many problems in·Sally's analysis were due to the theoretical model that we were utilizing.

As I delved further, I began to notice that there was an encouraging trend to the sessions. This involved certain, albeit infrequent, sessions or moments within a session in which I could see that I was able to break the bonds of my standard approach and, in spite of prevailing analytic practices (or my own inexperience), make better empathic contact with my patient by just "being myself," that is, addressing her in a less formal, more natural, and affect-responsive fashion. Sally would then respond by becoming calmer, more organized, and more of a partner in the analytic enterprise. I felt that this phenomenon might be something that I could document. My increased attuned responsiveness at these times was made feasible with this patient because it fortuitously seemed in concert with some of Dr. Fleming's (1972) convictions. She taught that the analyst working with a developmental arrest first needs to diagnose the level of the arrest and then use special technical interventions to overcome certain initial resistances supposed to have been caused by the arrest such as a difficulty in "giving any significant meaning to the analyst" (p. 40). These interventions involved the use of what Fleming called "explanatory empathy," which emphasized making it obvious to the patient that the analyst was "with them" and, at times, offering direct help with their "reality testing" (Fleming, 1973, personal communication).

I appear to have used these notions to support my own convictions about how I *preferred* to conduct the analysis. I remembered being in great conflict over this at the time because the supervision of my other control case emphasized a more traditional analytic approach, that is, the strict maintenance of analytic abstinence and the search for recovered and reconstructed memories, especially at the oedipal level. I kept feeling as though what I was learning in my supervision with Dr. Fleming could, and should, be routinely applied to my work with my other control case. Unfortunately, I was chastised by my other supervisors when I would act on this conviction. It is important to remember that there was no substantial body of theory within which these ideas were well integrated. Dr. Fleming's techniques were primarily conceptualized for use with parent loss cases alone. She attempted to maintain a fit for her ideas as they evolved, within the well-established body of general psychoanalytic theory, but it is clear to me in retrospect that she could have benefited from greater theoretical latitude than was available at the time.

As psychoanalytic thinking progressed, Fleming, as an early dedicated developmentalist, did begin to draw heavily upon Margaret Mahler's work. When I re-read Fleming's later papers, I was also impressed that many of her formulations (when translated into comparable language) came quite close to approximating those of Heinz Kohut. For example, in a paper on the development of object constancy in adults, Fleming (1975) described a patient who clearly requested a mirroring response from her, which she provided, and then used Winnicott (p. 754) in depicting the dialogue between a mother and infant in support of her approach. She described the major defensive use of disavowal by these patients. She talked (1972) of the use of fantasy in her patients to maintain "a feeling of needed wished-for relationships" (p. 27) without apparent awareness of similar object relations concepts or the selfobject transference. Reference to Kohut's work does not appear in her major writings on parent loss although she did come from the same institute. Goldberg (1995, personal communication) speculates that because of a deep professional enmity between Fleming and Kohut and because of theoretical differences, for example, on the origin of the trauma in parent loss, Fleming never credited him in her writings. Only after she moved to Denver in the late 1960s did she seem to feel free to incorporate his ideas into her work. She then did so within the framework of other more mainstream theories, particularly Mahler's. Political differences, as well, may have interfered with her more openly acknowledging her use of Kohut's revolutionary contributions.

I noticed that as Dr. Fleming tried in vain to keep her ideas grounded in the prevailing drive-oriented theory and practice of the time, the internal logic of her arguments broke down or seemed to fall short of explaining the clinical approaches she was advocating. In one of her papers, Fleming (1972) outlines two important therapeutic actions with which I became familiar in our work with Sally: (1) the use of the word *we* by the analyst in referring to "himself and the part of the patient's ego which is consonant with reality," and (2) the importance of interpreting the "avoidance of mourning work and the consequent arrest in development" by "well-timed confrontation with the denial of a loss and an effort to help the patient recall memories about the dead parent" (p. 41). Estelle and Morton Shane, in a 1990 paper on object and selfobject loss, comment on the first approach by noting that, "It is as if [Fleming] feels the need to force an object relationship rather than address the patient's perceived lack of support in the past, in the present, and in the transference" (p. 118). Concerning the second special technique the Shanes observe, "It seems to us that the patient's defenses against the unbearable, inevitable permanency of the loss are thus directly assaulted" (p. 117). Hence, in a way, Fleming's prescribed analytic activity reinforced my old convictions that I had to "make" the analysis go forward by imposition of my "objective reality" rather than affectively tracking the patient's own directional progress. In addition, the Shanes identify what was not recognized by Fleming at that time, that is, the possibility of retraumatization in the present of the patient by the analyst. Instead, Fleming attributes the patient's withdrawal responses and other attempts at self-protection as directed only toward the pain of the past. It became clear in my review that some episodes of withdrawal occurred after my ill-timed interventions around Sally's losses. Thus, by repeatedly "forcing" this point of view on her in the analysis, I was often not sensitively attuned to the affects and meanings in Sally's current experience. At those times, mysteriously it then seemed, a rupture in the relationship would occur. I could now see that my behavior had replicated traumatic experiences Sally had experienced in the past with unattuned surrogate parents after her loss. My treatment approach remained grounded in a one-person psychology, a monadic view of the analytic relationship that limited my ability to analyze Sally's here and now affective responses.

The Shanes suggest that the selfobject concept provides a far greater specificity than does object loss in pinpointing the injuries sustained by the self with early parent loss. The selfobject concept also provides better guidance toward the therapeutic steps needed for repair. The child suffers a double loss in an early parent loss. In addition to the object loss itself, the child also experiences the loss of future self-regulating selfobject functions the deceased could have provided. Treatment utilizing the selfobject concept can now address these double losses with a greater degree of specificity. For example, the Shanes (1990), following Kohut, pinpoint the lack of post-loss provision of an "adequate supportive environment to strengthen the child's total self and aid in dealing with his defensive avoidances," which allows the child to "spontaneously mourn the death of an important loved one" (p. 119). Periodically, Sally would complain bitterly about the lack of help provided by her stepfamily in grieving the loss of her parents, but our theoretical viewpoint did not help me to appreciate the importance of acknowledging my failures in this regard as the analysis evolved.

Needless to say, Sally's analysis was, at times, tumultuous. I followed her through the end of one affair, the end of her marriage, into another affair with her boss, and finally through the breakup of that affair. Subsequently, she moved with her young daughter to another town, for both of them to be closer to her supportive ex-mother-in-law and to obtain a much higher paying position utilizing her full skills. By the end of the review, I was pleasantly surprised to realize that she was, after all, able to creatively make good use of whatever requisite attuned responsiveness I and others in her surround did provide, even though it was less than optimal by today's standards. She seemed to benefit more from the analysis and show more remarkable resilience than I would have noted at the time it was conducted or imagined at the beginning of my view.

REVIEW OF FLEMING'S PAPERS

Reviewing Joan Fleming's writings revealed a microcosm of a steady and rapid development of analytic theory through those years and added immeasurably to my understanding of the evolution of her teaching. As I read these five papers ranging from 1963 to 1975, I also realized that I was witnessing the personal growth of my highly idealized supervisor since changes in prevailing theory (and, perhaps, political circumstances) were giving her an opportunity to reexamine her basic ideas about the process of psychoanalysis. A close comparative reading of her five papers enabled me to tease out the movement of her ideological shifts.

Two papers were published in 1963 (Fleming, 1963; Fleming and Altschul, 1963). In the first, with Altschul (1963), they wrote that the patient's resistance to giving the analyst any meaning in the present was related to efforts to protect the fantasy that the parent(s) was still alive. The prescribed therapeutic task was to "break through the defensive denial of loss and to complete the work of mourning. The mourning process had to be set in motion before an analyzable regressive transference neurosis could develop" (p. 420). Within this ideology, it was the analyst's task, as the arbiter of reality, to repeatedly confront the patient with the reality of the death of the parent and its effect in all its variegated forms. Arrest was seen as "largely due to the absence of a libidinal object whose presence was necessary for the ego's growth towards normal maturation" (Fleming and Altschul, 1963). In her paper on the evolution of the parent loss research project, while describing the analyst's role, Fleming (1963) states: "If the student learns well and becomes skillful in psychoanalytic technique, he also learns to make more accurate observations, to control his own personal intrusion, and to make the psychoanalytic situation more constant as a controlled observational situation" (p. 94). Later she states: "He must further maximize his objectivity and self-observing skill because in a research situation he must also observe his own process of observing, question its accuracy and reliability, recognize its errors and try to correct them by a maximal tolerance for change and organization" (p. 95). A view of a relatively detached analyst prevailed in Fleming's early thinking. This notion preserves the lofty correctness of the position of the analyst and supports his objective view of the analytic process. In contrast, Mitchell (1993), writing from a contemporary relational view, states, "Our era is postscientistic—we no longer can maintain a deep confidence that science, objectivity, and technological competence themselves can serve as an orienting framework providing meaning and understanding" (p. 18). Of course, the roots of some of these issues, the detached analyst-observer versus the participating analyst, go back to the Freud-Ferenczi controversy early in psychoanalytic history (Haynal, 1988).

By 1972, after she moved to Denver, in a paper on the development of the working alliance in parent loss cases, Fleming (1972) gingerly begins to incorporate the concept of empathy into her writings. She quotes Rado (in delivering the Sandor Rado Lecture in 1971) as describing "the effective therapeutic principle as the methodical use of human influence and emphasiz[ing] the responses of the therapist which must be in tune with the needs and the hopes of the patient" (p. 23). She adds, "He does not mean indiscriminate gratification but rather an empathic tuning in on the same wavelength for a diagnostic under-standing which allows the therapist freedom to choose responses in line with therapeutic goals appropriate for a given patient" (p. 23). There follows a warning that to maintain the "constancy of the analytic situa-tion and the basic model as described by Eissler [is] of great assistance" (p. 24). Fleming here was careful to support the prevailing more tradi-tional analytic caveat against the "overgratification" of the patient.

Later in the same paper Fleming cites Khan (1960), describing the treatment of a patient with some aspects of early object deprivation as part of her childhood experience. Khan's description of the therapeutic role he assumed during this period of analysis is quoted: "to be there, alive, alert, embodied, and vital, but not to impinge with any personal need to translate her affective experiences into their mental correlates" (p. 38). To me, this sounds very close to a position Kohut had evolved in his work with Miss F. Kohut saw this as the patient's need throughout analysis to seek out experiences that were growth promoting. Fleming, in contrast, saw Khan's technique as representing a symbiosis temporarily needed to build a working alliance so that an analyzable traditional transference neurosis could eventually be established and analyzed. This limited view of transference prevented Fleming from going that one step further in helping me to achieve a greater comfort with acknowledging my role in providing certain empathic "gratifications" to my patient throughout the whole analysis. In retrospect, approaching the transference from this perspective left me as an analyst of that time with only two paradoxical choices. I had to accept and potentially "overgratify" the patient's object needs (and thereby overstep the boundaries of accepted analytic practice). Alternatively, I was required to confront these needs and (to quote Fleming, 1972) correct "this defensive distortion of reality and a long continued belief in magical thinking" (p. 42), thereby acting in a manner that felt incongruent with my clinical intuition.

In a paper on diagnosis in parent loss (Fleming, 1974), Fleming strongly advises the clinician to think of the possibility that "an event in the environment, the death of a parent, may have a profound effect on a child's development which could result in serious pathology" (p. 440). She once again advocates that in the first phase of the analysis the therapist "meet the needs and supply the developmental experiences unintegrated by the adult child before what blocked the growth process has been removed" (p. 444). In this paper, by way of illustrating the basic diagnostic concepts of parent loss that she had postulated, Fleming reevaluates three of her older cases, which she felt she incompletely analyzed before her understanding of the concept of arrested development or uncompleted mourning. In summarizing the second cases she notes that even though she doubted that the patient reached "a real maturity" by the end, "My constancy and the analytic relationship provided her with experience which she never had had with her father. She was able to make use of this in a way which permitted growth toward positive . . . relationships" (p. 448). This shift toward a decreased emphasis on interpretation and greater importance on a therapeutic effect of the analytic relationship itself, while certainly not highlighted by Fleming, seems quite significant to me in light of the tone of her final paper on the subject of parent loss.

By the mid-1970s, toward the end of her career, Fleming's thinking (1975) was heavily influenced by separation-individuation theory. Under the sway of this approach, her efforts at theorizing had become more sophisticated. Much of this involves illuminating the concept of parent loss in the context of object relations theory. Fleming uses this theory to express her recognition of the importance of the reciprocity in the relationship between parent and child. Beebe and Lachmann (1988) and others have later detailed this mutual regulating system. Fleming (1975) concludes her paper by asking

> Is it possible that the structural changes we hope for from the psychoanalytic experience can be facilitated by the responses from the analyst other than interpretation in the usual sense of the term? My experiences in trying to understand the clinical phenomena that commonly appear in the course of psychoanalytic therapy have led me more and more insistently in this direction. No adult is really a baby, and an analyst is not his parent. Nevertheless, the object need in many adults reproduces in many ways the functional relationship between mother and child—the diatrophic feeling without which the analytic process meets with difficulty [p. 749].

What first struck me about this statement is Fleming's (1975) use of this new theory to extend her finding toward all psychoanalytic patients, not just those with early parent loss. She goes on to talk of "reciprocity of relatedness," "an element of the experience [in analysis] that builds configurations that each of the parties involved learn to perceive as object and subject—you and I. The important element here is the feeling of being approved of, of being valued" (p. 749). After a cogent case example, Fleming was able to acknowledge the increased self-cohesion that her patient felt after a series of exchanges involving "provisions" she had made and found a way, using Mahler's theory, to account for these changes in the patient (i.e., "an intensified regressive need for symbiosis") (p. 755). This permitted Fleming to tolerate and allow this behavior and to incorporate it into the analytic interchange without having to interpret or disrupt it. Later in this chapter, she compares this approach with that of child analysis and makes the point that, with a child, certain enactments are allowed, and "interpretation accompanies the action or follows it when appropriate" (p. 755). She states, "I have been increasingly impressed with the fact that we expect our adult patients to possess a degree of maturity on their psychosocial developmental line that would almost preclude any need for analysis. Often, without that degree of maturity we do not think of them as analyzable" (p. 756). When I compared these statements with what Fleming had written only a few years before, I found her comments to be exemplary of the development of her own capacity, as new theoretical approaches became available, to review and reflect on her previous ideas, to face their shortcomings, and to begin to modify them, to use her words, "with a sense of enlightenment that I value, however retarded it has been" (p. 750). She had found a way, despite even political ramifications, to modify her theoretical writings to more accurately reflect an approach that seemed to yield better therapeutic results.

DISCUSSION

Mitchell, in his Editorial Philosophy (1991), attempts to describe why psychoanalysts have "enormous difficulty listening and speaking meaningfully to each other" (p. 1). He concludes:

> In today's world of psychoanalytic heterodoxy, theoretical perspectives cannot persuasively claim a unique access to universal truths. Psychoanalytic models seem more clearly to be particular perspectives, personal (although sometimes shared) visions, embedded in the daily crucible of clinical experience, in an ongoing effort to explain both one's patients and oneself to oneself. We need to learn to regard differences in theoretical perspectives not as unfortunate deviations from one accurate understanding, but as fortunate expressions of the countless ways in which human experience can be organized [p. 6].

My experience, as documented in this chapter, leads me to be in fundamental agreement with his position. I believe that supervisors should, at the present state of our theoretical development, advocate theoretical pluralism. In the hands of someone who believes in his or her favorite, perhaps pure, but usually amalgamated, approach, their theoretical position may offer the tool that allows that particular patient–therapist dyad to proceed with successful analysis. The subjectivity of another analyst may not allow for optimal use of that particular theoretical structure. Some of the problems that I encountered in my work with Sally could be written off as due to my youth, my psychoanalytic inexperience, or my personal countertransference problems. Yet, as I have shown, many of these problems could have been averted by my access to self psychology theory and some other contemporary approaches we now teach. I believe that today's students are often better able than I was to provide their patients with requisite attuned responsiveness because of the theoretical advances we have made in the interim.

SUMMARY

Engaging in this project has given me a sense of mastery over the traumatic experiences of my analytic past. It has also enlarged my perspective. I have a better sense of myself as embedded within a historical process of shifting paradigms taking place within the analytic community (as was Joan Fleming in her time). Robert Jay Lifton (1993) states,

"What we call the self—one's inclusive sense . . . of one's own being—is enormously sensitive to the flow of history" (p. 2). Fleming's approach had its limitations, but now, with hindsight, I can see her strengths more clearly. I can admire her efforts to change and expand her thinking and her bold attempt to examine and reexamine her work in light of newer ideas and learning experiences and, as she wrote (1963) "to try and correct them by a maximal tolerance for change and reorganization" (p. 95). I am impressed perhaps, somewhat awed, by the burden of political and ideological forces that shape our current thinking and the inherent difficulties, as Goldberg (1990) has shown, in freeing ourselves from them. And finally, I am also, once again, impressed by the vulnerability of the supervisee to the supervisor. Supervising is a position of great inherent responsibility that has made me all the more grateful for the open-minded and helpful approach of the supervisors I encountered in the second phase of my analytic training.

My personal psychoanalytic experience seems to be a metaphor for how effective change in a theoretical perspective offers the patient–analyst dyad increased leverage in the clinical situation. For example, for my therapeutic growth to occur, I needed to find a learning situation with greater latitude. I needed a vitalizing, affirming milieu in which to encounter further training and case experience with a wider variety of theories. I required an atmosphere of respect in which I could develop the self-cohering, solid relationships with teachers that I admired. I needed an environment that provided me with exposure to a style of work that was more compatible with my own, within which I would be encouraged to develop my own style. When I was finally able to find this setting, I could take this journey into the past. I believe that my experience parallels what many survivors of early parent loss need as well, that is, to find some sense of themselves within a new and healthier interactional environment, an optimal self-selfobject milieu, and then they can go back and complete the mourning and other work necessary for personal growth.

REFERENCES

Beebe, B. & Lachmann, F. (1988), Mother–infant mutual influence and precursors of psychic structure, In: *Frontiers in Self Psychology: Progress in Self Psychology, Vol. 3*, ed. A. Goldberg. Hillsdale, NJ: The Analytic Press, pp. 3–25.

Fleming, J. (1963), The evolution of a research project in psychoanalysis. In: *Counterpoint: Libidinal Object and Subject,* ed. H. S. Gaskill. New York: International Universities Press, pp. 75–105.

—— (1972), Early object deprivation and transference phenomena: The working alliance. *Psychoanal. Quart.,* 41:23–49.

—— (1974), The problem of diagnosis in parent loss cases. *Comtemp. Psychoanal.*, 10:439–452.

—— (1975), Some observations on object constancy in the psychoanalysis of adults. *J. Amer. Psychoanal. Assn.*, 23:743–760.

—— & Altschul, S. (1963), Activation of mourning and growth by psychoanalysis. *Internat. J. Psycho-Anal.*, 44:419–431.

—— & Benedek, T. (1966), *Psychoanalytic Supervision.* New York: Grune and Stratton.

Goldberg, A. (1990), *The Prisonhouse of Psychoanalysis.* Hillsdale, NJ: The Analytic Press.

Haynal, A. (1988), *The Technique at Issue: Controversies in Psychoanalysis from Freud to Ferenczi to Michael Balint.* London: Karnac Books.

Hirsch, I. (1993), Countertransference enactments and some issues related to external factors in the analyst's life. *Psychoanal. Dial.*, 3:343–366.

Khan, M. (1960), Regression and integration in the analytic setting. *Internat. J. Psycho-Anal.*, 41:130–146.

Kohut, H. (1982), Introspection, empathy and the semi-circle of mental health. *Internat. J. Psycho-Anal.*, 63:395–407.

Levy, M. (1994), Three perspectives on Denver's dark ages. *Amer. Psychoanal.*, 28:4a–5a.

Lifton, R. J. (1993), *The Protean Self.* New York: Basic Books.

Lindon, J. (1991), Does theory require technique? *Bull. Menninger Clinic*, 55:1–21.

Mitchell, S. (1991), Editorial philosophy. *Psychoanal. Dial.*, 1:1–7.

—— (1993), *Hope and Dread in Psychoanalysis.* New York: Basic Books.

Ornstein, P. & Kay, J. (1990), Development of psychoanalytic self psychology: A historical-conceptual overview. In: *Review of Psychiatry, Vol. 9*, ed. A. Tasman, S. M. Goldfinger & C. Kaufmann. Washington, DC: American Psychiatric Press, pp. 303–320.

Schwartz, I. G. (1994), Three perspectives on Denver's dark ages. *Amer. Psychoanal.*, 28:4a.

Shane E. & Shane, M. (1990), Object loss and selfobject loss: A consideration of self psychology's contribution to understanding mourning and the failure to mourn. *The Annual of Psychoanalysis*, 18:115–131. Hillsdale, NJ: The Analytic Press.

—— (1993), Self psychology after Kohut: One theory or many? *J. Amer. Psychoanal. Assn.*, 41:777–797.

Skolnick, N. & Warshaw, S. (1992), *Relational Perspectives in Psychoanalysis.* Hillsdale, NJ: The Analytic Press.

Sucharov, M. (1992), Quantum physics and self psychology: Toward a new epistemology. In: *New Therapeutic Visions: Progress in Self Psychology, Vol. 8*, ed. A. Goldberg. Hillsdale, NJ: The Analytic Press, pp. 199–211.

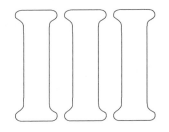

Sexuality

Chapter 12

The Self and Orientation: The Case of Mr. G

R. Dennis Shelby

One of the more controversial aspects of the ongoing reconsideration of the phenomenon of homosexuality within psychoanalysis is the assertion by Isay (1989) that only gay and lesbian clinicians should treat gay and lesbian patients. Responses to this position were immediate, have been rattling in the halls of psychoanalytic institutes, and continue to appear in publications. For example, Goldberg (1995) basically states that this position values familiarity over technique. While MacIntosh (1994) purports to convey the evenhandedness of the psychoanalytic community, ultimately, the work conveys considerable ambivilence as to whether homosexual desire can be viewed as genuine versus defensive in nature.

Since human beings are capable of using a wide array of activities in a defensive manner, it becomes problematic to assert that all homosexual desire is "genuine." Clearly, there is a difference between homosexual acts and a homosexual orientation. And clearly there are men whose erotic fantasies and potential to form relationships are oriented towards men. With this population it is more appropriate to look at sexualization or defensive use of sexuality within the context of their orientation. This is the population of men that this chapter addresses.

The assertion that only certain people should treat certain people clearly intersects with the larger question of what is curative in psychoanalysis or psychotherapy. Though technical issues are raised, the issue

Paper Presented at the 18th Conference on the Psychology of the Self, San Francisco, CA, October 1995.

181

of competence is raised as well. Of course, no one likes to have their work questioned, if not devalued, and I cannot ascribe wholeheartedly to Isay's position, ultimately because it would besmirch my own analysis. However, I am cautious when it comes to referring a gay or lesbian patient for psychotherapy or psychoanalysis. The question here is what is it that I think about, or intuit, when it comes to recommending a therapist for a gay man?

Isay's position is based on several assumptions. The first and perhaps central is the assumption of the lack, or relative lack, of hostility both conscious and unconscious on the part of gay or lesbian clinicians in relation to their gay and lesbian patients. A second assumption appears related to the role of identifications in the "curative" process of psychoanalysis and intensive psychotherapy.

From a self-psychological perspective, these assumptions must be reconsidered and reframed. First, the absence of hostility is not the same as mirroring. Second, from a self perspective, we tend to view the self-object transferences and consequent transmuting internalizations as "curative" rather than the establishment of "healthier" identifications and subsequent representations of self and other. So let us rephrase the question of gay and lesbian clinicians treating gay and lesbian patients. Let us ask, "What are the influences or potential influences on the self-object transferences and the consequent influence on the rekindled development of the self?" as well as, "Is this solely based on the orientation of the clinician?"

The case of Mr. G is quite long and complicated. It was impossible to address the highly significant impact of HIV and its transformations over the course of 8 years of treatment and the emergence of the selfobject transferences within the confines of a single paper. The themes related to HIV in this case are elaborated in the chapter "Mourning Within a Culture of Mourning" by Shelby in Cadwell, Burnham, and Forstein (1994).

What started out as a couple case quickly turned into helping Mr. G mourn the loss of his partner to AIDS, a mourning process highly complicated by his own HIV infection and identifications with his deceased partner. Subsequently, a considerable revitalization of the self evolved through the mobilization of selfobject transferences. As with many of my cases, Mr. G was in treatment twice a week for 6 years, terminated, and then returned a year and a half later in the wake of a failed relationship. The original transferences were mobilized quickly, and many themes were reworked in greater depth.

I initially saw Mr. G and his partner as a couple. They were referred because of difficulties they were having managing the impact of his partner's diagnosis of AIDS. AIDS was still fairly new to Chicago then.

The anxiety, uncertainty, and terror of the disease were heightened by its newness and were greatly impeding the couple's ability to talk to each other about the disease and abour their many fears. Mr. G was relieved and excited to have the forum of couples work. His partner was somewhat suspicious and reluctant. Gradually, a dialogue between us opened up, and the two men were able to sort out several miscommunications that had resulted in hurt and anger. Unfortunately, after the second session, Mr. G's partner developed a second infection of pneumocystis and died several weeks later. While his partner was hospitalized, I maintained contact with Mr. G and the family, visiting the hospital several times. Mr. G took great comfort in my presence, yet made it clear that he did not want to talk in detail about the intensity of his affects. We all knew that it was a matter of time before his partner's death. I maintained a quiet, reassuring presence.

Following the death and funeral, Mr. G spent the next month, which coincided with the Christmas holidays, at his parent's home in a neighboring state. He called me during his first day back at his office. His voice trembled and he began to cry; he did not understand what was happening to him and he was afraid he was "losing it." We made an appointment for later that evening. In my office, he was repeatedly overwhelmed. He related that while at his parents' home he had felt shaky but not to the degree he was currently experiencing. After returning to his home and work, he began to feel intense waves of sadness and anxiety. He missed his partner deeply and was terrified of facing life without him. Mr. G had never lost a person so central in his life; he had no idea of what mourning was like and was afraid that he was indeed losing his mind. I pointed out that I did not think he was losing his mind, that in a way, his mourning had been put "on hold" while he was at his parents', but now that he was back in his own environment, alone, where reminders of his partner's absence were acutely evident, the process was beginning.

Mr. G quickly formed an intense attachment. In the early months of our work together, the treatment relationship was used to modulate, sustain, and organize his often intense and shifting affect states. He experienced his sessions as a place where his feelings could be tolerated and understood, where he could be less afraid of being overwhelmed to the point of no return. In many a session, he was barely consolable, yet by the end of the hour he was calmer. The dominant image of him during the early months was that of a lost and terrified little boy surrounded by a terrifying world where no one looked familiar. As he associated, I listened for the fragmentation and the dominant affects, while trying to ascertain the dimensions of the now-lost selfobject constellation of his relationship.

Invariably, the fragmentations were triggered by a memory, a photograph, or a pattern of responsiveness that could no longer be repeated in its familiar and sustaining way between the two men. I affirmed the centrality of his loss, his pain, sadness, and confusion as he attempted to function in a world that "no longer made sense." Mr. G kept in close contact with his partner's family. There were many phone calls in which they shared their mutual grief. However, his own parents appeared to be in a quandary about why their son was so grief-stricken. Mr. G's parents had known of the relationship and had been very supportive during his partner's illness, death, and funeral. Mr. G related his growing anger over feeling discounted by them. During a phone call his father implied that it was "time to get over it." Mr. G angrily replied, "How would you feel if Mother dropped dead?" His father apologized, and Mr. G was delighted that he had succeeded in getting his father to understand him. This was also the beginning of a wider dialogue with his parents regarding his homosexuality, a topic that had not really been discussed in his family of origin despite a great deal of contact and involvement in the family by him and his partner.

As the time since his partner's death progressed, Mr. G's affects gradually became more stable and predictable. Approximately 6 months after his partner's death, the families and Mr. G gathered to disperse his partner's ashes. The chosen site was a family vacation home located in remote woodland that had been a favorite place of his partner's since childhood. Mr. G dispersed a portion of the ashes in each of his partner's favorite places on the property. As he did so, he carefully photographed each place. On his return, he brought the photographs to the session. He related that I had been such a central part of his mourning that he wanted me to somehow participate in the dispersing of the ashes.

Shortly after, Mr. G became increasingly preoccupied with his own antibody status. He had been tested during his partner's first episode of pneumocystis. He had put his own antibody status in the back of his mind while he tended to his partner and again while he was preoccupied with the early phases of mourning. Now the impact of being positive was beginning to surface. He began to feel increasingly damaged, ill, and doomed. Being positive began to feel like "a monkey on my back—an angry screaming monkey digging in his claws; I can't get to him to rip him away."

Mr. G also became very anxious about his attachment to me. He wanted to cut back to once a week; he was over the hump now, the dispersing of the ashes was a watershed. He feared becoming dependent and was terribly anxious about how much a part of his life I had become. I attempted to work with his anxiety, but it became clear that he could not tolerate much interpretation and agreed to try once a week. That lasted less than several days, because Mr. G found himself becoming acutely disorganized and we were back to twice a week.

A long account of his difficulties with the relationship with his partner followed. Despite how central he had become in his life, Mr G was very reluctant to let the relationship deepen and was highly ambivalent. Mr. G related his guilt at the pain he must have caused his partner owing to his reluctance to commit to the relationship. He related how the "devotion" in his partner's eyes made him anxious, and he had tried to get away from it during the early months and periodically throughout the relationship via anonymous sex in tea rooms. A dominant memory was his leaving on a European vacation with a friend. His partner could not afford to go and the trip was planned before they had met. As the plane took off, Mr. G was overwhelmed and began to cry. He realized how in love he was, but also how desperately he was trying to flee. He was miserable throughout the holiday and could not wait to return. Mr. G also confessed to a sexualized element in the transference. He relates that when he first saw me, he felt a sexual attraction; he worried that once again he had hurt his partner. Mr. G wept as he related that many times during the years they were together he would begin to feel confined and pressured. He would visit tea rooms during the day, and then he arrived home, he felt guilty and would then be angry and devaluing of his partner. He was also convinced that he had infected his partner, that he had become infected either through his tea room visits or during the year that he lived in San Francisco; and that he had passed it on to his partner and killed him.

Several telescoping memories were presented that evolved into central themes of the treatment. There was a maternal memory of being in perhaps first grade or kindergarten, and there was a birthday party after school. His mother arrived at the school to pick him up with a present for the child. Mr. G became overwhelmed, was fearful of going to the party, and focused on the gift—wanting to know what was inside the package. He wanted to see the gift; he did not want to go the party and give it away, so he began to sob. He recalled his mother telling him that he would not have to go and could see the present if he danced for her. He related performing an agonized dance as he wept and his mother chuckled. As I responded to his humiliation, I wondered why his mother responded in such a way, why she could not help him "bridge" to the larger world. As we explored this, what emerged was a picture of a family that was almost enmeshed. His parents were second-generation Greek Orthodox in a town that was dominantly white midwestern Protestant but also had a reasonably large Greek community.

Mr. G's family owned a popular restaurant and though his father was "host to the town," there was very much the sense of sticking with the family and with other Greeks. There was a strong sense of being outsiders, a bit suspicious, and second class in comparison to the WASPs and needing to stick to one's family and to the social life that revolved around the church. He recalled his mother as being very shy and retiring. Mr. G also associated to going off to college. His parents tearfully left him in his dorm room. He became increasingly anxious and overwhelmed. His parents did as well and turned back after an hour on the road. Parents and son ran to each others' arms when he opened his door.

The other memories were paternal in nature. He recalled how his "big burly uncles" loved to toss him in the air and catch him. Mr. G was terrified of this activity, but it seemed to him that the more he protested, the more he was subjected to the game. It got to the point where he would run and hide when they arrived for a visit. His father, older brothers, and uncles were all into hunting, fishing, and sports. Mr. G hated all of these, yet felt forced to go along until they "finally gave up on me." He felt horribly anxious and inadequate and had a nagging sense that something was missing, that he did not have what the other boys and certainly not what the men had, that something was terribly wrong and he was defective. He was more drawn to math and science at which he excelled and was quiet and shy in temperament.

A particularly painful memory was being "drug along on a duck hunting [or duck murdering as he called it] expedition." It was cold, and the men were huddled and drinking in a duck blind in a swamp. Mr. G became bored and wandered off. He found a butterfly cocoon. Excitedly he ran back with his treasure, joyfully saying, "Dad! Dad! I found a cocoon!" Mr. G tripped over some equipment, causing a large crash that scared away a flock that had been slowly coming into range. He painfully recalled the exasperated looks on his father's and uncles' faces. Mr. G was humiliated and deflated. Once again, he had messed up. He just did not have what the men had; something was missing. Throughout this phase of his treatment, Mr. G used the phrase *weird and different* to describe his experience of self during latency. There was a particularly virulent inflection as he said the word *weird*.

As he related this, it was clear that he had also incorporated the old "homosexuality is caused by close-binding mothers and hostile distant fathers and is evidence that the person is sick, sick, sick" school of thinking that he had encountered as he searched the library as a late adolescent in an effort to understand his sexual feelings. The horror was still quite evident in his eyes as he described his anxious and secretive search in the library, only to discover writings that confirmed, if not enhanced, his worst fears. I countered that I did not think that his child-hood experience caused his homosexuality, but I did think that it left him with a great deal of pain, humiliation, and self-doubt. And how sad it was that when he searched the library in hopes of reassurance and understanding, what he encountered only made him feel worse, if not solidified his sense of being defective.

As Mr. G's history evolved, I was puzzled by several twists and turns. Though he had excelled in science and math in high school, as he was "coming out" in college, he switched his major to design. When I asked about this, he related that he did not think that, as a gay man, there would be any place for him in science, and besides he did have a creative side to himself that he wanted to explore. After meeting his partner, he left design, went back to school in computer science, and was now designing computer programs. He was very happy in his current profession since it blended the creative and science/math aspects of self.

Toward the end of college and shortly afterward, Mr. G became involved in relationships with two different, highly chaotic, borderline-ish drug-abusing men. He still trembled recounting the second man whom he met after moving to San Francisco—the chaos, the suicide attempts, the drugs—but also the wild, exciting sex. He returned to the Midwest, essentially to get away from this particular man, who attempted suicide as Mr. G packed his car to leave. I was struck by the contrast of the quiet, unassuming, almost elf-like Mr. G and the chaos of these first relationships.

Mr. G and his partner tended to keep to themselves. There was very much a twinship flavor to their lives. Both men quickly left their social networks of gay men behind, save for one or two friends that lived in distant cities. There was a dominant sense of "you and I against the world." Every weekend was the same routine—exploring plant, fish, bird, and rock stores, gradually assembling a huge collection of all four. An incident had occurred shortly before Mr. G met his partner, where he felt publicly humiliated at a party. The humiliation was apparently so great that he retreated from his rather extensive social network. As I listened to Mr. G, it appeared that he had experienced several massive fragmentations followed by lengthy seclusions several times in the course of his life—upon coming out, after leaving San Francisco, after the inci-dent in his social network, and now after his partner's death.

Mr. G's antibody status and his assumption of impending death were woven throughout the course of treatment; as this early phase was unfolding, he was also struggling with the acute sense of being damaged and doomed and that he had transmitted the infection to his beloved partner and killed him. At this point Mr. G's longstanding sense of being defective regarding his lack of masculine confidence, as well as his anxiety and self-doubt about his homosexuality, the devastating loss of his partner to AIDS, and his own HIV infection had combined to form an acutely damaged and defective sense of self. I found myself wondering if and how this would unravel.

We were now in another period of acute isolation, but this time he was solidly in treatment and we could begin to understand the complexity of the near collapse of his self. Mr. G basically went to work, came to sessions, spent time in his apartment, or visited his family. Weekend errands—a once favorite time with his partner—were torturous for him. On several occasions, he had full-blown panic attacks when he saw other male couples out shopping together and fled home to the safety of his apartment. Just as the now-lost relationship had the flavor of "my partner and I against the world," it now felt like "Mr. G and I against the world."

Very gradually, Mr. G's intense preoccupation with his antibody status declined. He gave away many of his partner's belongings, moved to an apartment more suitable for one person, and subscribed to several publications in order to keep abreast of developments in the treatment of HIV infection. As Mr. G made the move to his new apartment, there was a strong sense of using the treatment relationship as an anchor, while I mirrored each little step he took and responded to the sadness of giving up certain belongings of his partner and his need to hold on to others.

By coincidence, we were both moving to the same building. (The building was so huge that it is its own voting precinct.) When I told him that I too would be living in the building, Mr. G appeared curious, but nonplussed. Over the course of the year I lived there, our paths crossed perhaps four times. One incident proved to be initially traumatic for Mr. G, but we were able to make good use of it.

One evening I was working out in the gym. Mr. G was taking one of his few friends that he maintained contact with on a tour. They encountered me in the gym, we exchanged greetings, and they went on their way. In the session that followed, Mr. G was quite shaken. He told me that he felt he had intruded on my life, that he had done something very wrong, gone to a place he did not belong at all. He was afraid that I would be angry at him for disturbing me. He was quite shocked to find instead of being angry with him, that I was concerned about his anxiety and fear about a possible disruption in our relationship.

Many sessions followed in which he related his pain and anxiety over not "being like" the other boys or his uncles or his dad and the questioning looks from uncles and cousins at family gatherings when he did not want to play ball or watch sports, Gym class was specially traumatic, because he was picked last for team games, always had to take left field, and prayed the ball would not get hit in his direction.

In adolescence, gym became even more tortuous; he was terribly embarrassed to be naked around the other boys, feeling his penis was so much smaller and being stimulated by the other boys' nakedness, contrasted by his tremendous fear of becoming aroused and the other boys consequently discovering his "secret" for which he surely would be attacked. The pain Mr. G was reliving was quite exquisite; many times he wept as he recalled the painful isolation, sense of being damaged, and the ever-present sense of being vulnerable to attack. His older brother was a star athlete, winning many trophies and seeming to have what he didn't. He both admired and was intimidated by his older brother, and a nagging sense that his brother, who was now married and had several children, was superior to him persisted to the present day.

Mr. G was quite taken by my empathic responsiveness to his pain, though the fear of my attacking him for his "defects" was often lurking in the background as he related numerous incidents of humiliation and isolation and the "terrible secret" that he did not quite understand at that point in his life. "Weird and different, weird and different" was used repeatedly in an almost mantra-like manner. Mr. G was quite intrigued by my stance that the issue was not that he was defective, but rather that he was "temperamentally different" and that the issue was what was *not* happening between him and his father and uncles and brother that left him feeling different and defective, that for reasons we did not understand yet, he had trouble maintaining a sense of "traction" with the men in his life.

Rather than preclude an elaboration of his shame and humiliation over his sexuality, I believe this stance actually widened the scope and depth of our ability to explore the complex and painful affects surrounding the gender- and later sexual-related aspects of self. As the treatment progressed, it became clearer how affects regarding his painful sense of inadequacy as a boy later became intermingled with affects regarding his growing awareness of same-sex desire and in late adolescence his exploration of his sexuality.

Gradually, Mr. G's waiting room presentation shifted. Where before I had encountered him waiting anxiously, if not desperately, for me, he now appeared delighted and eager when I came to get him. We settled into a pattern of Mr. G telling me about the details of his latest projects at work, his latest computer upgrades, and the process of creating a new life for himself. He reflected on his delight and need to fill me in on the details of his life. I responded that perhaps he never felt that anyone was really interested in what he was interested in. This coincided with Mr. G talking more and more openly with his parents and sibs about his homosexuality, his experience growing up, and his struggles with being HIV positive. He eventually talked to his father about the duck-hunting incident. His father reported to be shocked by Mr. G's experience of the event. Father related that he was so proud of his son's gifts for math and science that he was delighted that his son, perhaps a future scientist, had "made a discovery." His father related that he was also a bit intimidated by his son's precociousness in areas that he just did not understand. Mr. G was quite taken aback by this. Rather than telling Mr. G he was disappointed, his father professed to being proud of him. It began to appear that perhaps his father had been unable to mirror his son's talents simply because they were in areas that his father did not understand or wherein he himself felt intimidated.

A repetition seemed to have confirmed this. Mr. G began to associate to wanting a laser. He had always wanted one as a child. Now they were quite affordable. He went into minute detail about how he could set it up with a series of mirrors so that the beam would go all the way around his apartment. I found myself drifting off and thinking, "Yeah so?" Mr. G quickly deflated and sadly and anxiously associated to how horrible it felt when people "strobed out" as he was talking about an exciting project or discovery. Over and over again, he would be excited about laser beams or some other esoteric discovery he had made in his science classes or magazines, only to have his father "glaze over." I apologized for repeating the same pattern. Mr. G was shocked that I apologized for my lack of responsiveness. He appeared to begin to believe that there may indeed be a connection between his despair and a lack of responsiveness on the part of others.

The treatment settled into a rather quiet phase of Mr. G telling me about his life both past and present; the periodic fragmentations around the loss of his partner became few and far between, his CD4 counts were stable, and I moved to the country, to a little town that Mr. G drove past on the way to his parents' home. (He knew of this via the change my in phone number.) Mr. G continued to maintain a high degree of isolation, socializing and spending holidays and vacations with his parents, sisters, and their children. He was delighted by how much more engaged he felt with his family—happy, spontaneous, and at times delighted. Periodically, he would reflect on how much more alive and hopeful he felt. The outside world, though, was still highly intimidating, and socialization outside of his family was negligible.

Following one of his trips home, he related how every time he drove by the exit for the little town I lived in, he wondered about my life. He would find himself smiling as he drove past the exit and wondered how I lived my life as a gay man. Did I have a partner? How did I manage life in a small town? How did I socialize? What did I do with my free time?

Mr. G never asked specific questions nor demanded any answers but was clearly delightfully curious.[1]

During this phase of the treatment he recalled a painful memory that had to do with being all alone with his confusing sexual attraction to men. I do not recall my exact response, but his response to mine was, "You know, I really wish I had had a gay uncle. Someone who could say, 'It's OK, relax, it's not that you are bad, you are just going to be gay.' As we talked about this, Mr. G related that somehow we had found a way to get into an incredibly painful part of his life and offer him a different way out, one that did not leave him feeling bad and defective but, rather, hopeful and more and more confident. Mr. G came to feel that he was not so much hiding out at his parents' as actively participating in the family life in a fuller way than ever before, yet a nagging sense of distance that appeared related to his being gay persisted, despite the many talks he continued to have with parents and sibs.

HIV suddenly intruded into this relatively blissful period of the treatment. Mr. G's T-cells dropped considerably. Just as he had achieved a degree of equilibrium secondary to the disruption caused by the decline in lab values, he developed a severe and extremely painful case of shingles. He canceled several sessions, often just before they were to begin, saying he was not feeling up to leaving his home. After the third cancellation, I gently insisted that he come in. He had spent the last 10 days holed up in his apartment, groggy on pain medication and attempting to keep at bay the terror he felt. He later related that he feared if he sat across from me, he would experience the terror full force.

In the course of the session, he indeed did experience considerable intense affect, mingled with considerable relief. He related that he felt intense terror; he kept being flooded by images of his partner on his death bed. He alternately felt acutely alone, isolated, terrified, and enraged. In the session, he repeatedly experienced these states and affects. He experienced himself as in the process of dying. The events that he had feared for so long were now happening. He too was dying, just like his partner, and it had come too soon, much too soon. Though his physician had explained that the shingles were not necessarily HIV-related, he experienced them as the "beginning of the end." At the end of the hour, with some surprise, he reported, "You are still here and I am still here. There were times when I felt you slipping away, but we are both still around."

---

[1] Recalling Kohut's *The Two Analyses of Mr Z*, I assumed his curiosity reflected a structure-building process.

After this experience with me, Mr. G attended sessions regularly, but a pronounced withdrawal was evident for several weeks. In part, this was related to the ongoing pain that proved very difficult to manage and the withdrawal of someone just not feeling well. The other crucial aspect was his preoccupation with the death of his partner and his own death. He was avoiding contact with his family because he experienced their concern as overstimulating. Mr. G felt their concern and anxiety was a confirmation that he was indeed seriously ill and dying. I quietly but firmly pursued him during this period. Gradually, the terror, withdrawal, and preoccupation with his partner eased as we were more firmly able to establish his symbolic connection of his symptoms to the ripping away of his relationship with his partner, and he was once again able to take considerable comfort in his family relationships. Eventually he related the experience to that of his partner calling to him as Captain Ahab, entangled in the harpoon lines, beckoned to Ishmael from Moby Dick, with myself on the other hand calling him back. There was also a transference connection: his wish that in the context of the idealizing transference with me which he experienced as very sustaining, that if he did everything right, he would not get sick. Thus the emergence of symptoms also represented a transference disappointment. This same sequence was experienced several months later in a much milder and less protracted form when Mr. G's T-cells declined to the point where his physician recommended he begin taking AZT.

Mr. G's social isolation worsened in the face of his beginning AZT. I had done some work with a large HIV social-educational-support organization and had observed noticeable improvements in several patients once they had gotten involved in this and other groups. Mr. G had read about the group and was curious. He made several attempts to attend the meetings. He frequently became anxious and overstimulated, however, especially if anyone attempted to strike up a conversation. Frequently, he made plans to attend but then fell asleep and missed the meetings. He was at once chagrined by this behavior and relieved. In the transference, he would both ask me for help and then dare me to do anything about it. Lengthy discussion of this dynamic did not result in enabling Mr. G to attend the meetings.

Associating to his memory of the birthday party and his mother's failure to help him move into the larger world, I suggested that he might want to join the group I was forming for seropositive men. He was anxious but interested. I took a neutral stance. He eventually decided not to join, but periodically asked about the group. Several months later an opening was available for the group and I told him. Again he was anxious but interested. This time I casually remarked; "I just might insist that you join." Mr. G laughed and the next week announced that he wanted to give the group a try.[2]

In the first several sessions he experienced considerable anxiety around revealing that he was a surviving partner and experienced several group members' responses as attacking and overstimulating, but was also surprised that there was another surviving partner in the group. For several weeks his individual session (which followed the group a day later) was spent in helping him to organize his experience of the group and the acute vulnerability he experienced. Very quickly, his anxiety diminished and he became an active member. A year or so into the group, as several members were talking about their experience of isolation and how it had changed since joining the group, Mr. G remarked, "Looking back, being so isolated was like being dead."

By his sixth year of treatment, Mr. G had become an integral member of the group and developed a friendship with another member. In the course of the group, the partner of another member died. Mr. G repeatedly reached out to the grief-stricken man, conveying his understanding of the depth of his loss. His friend enlisted him to help lead a smaller group for men who needed extra help and support while they were joining the larger support/educational organization for men who test positive. During a session following one of these groups, Mr. G related that a young man who was very shaken, anxious, and overwhelmed had come to the group, and he had spent a great deal of time with him, listening to him, reassuring, and answering his many questions. Mr. G reflected with a sense of amazement and accomplishment on the fact that he had helped someone with being HIV-positive, an issue that he himself had felt so helpless about. I pointed out that he had also helped a group member mourn, another experience that he had left him feeling helpless.

Mr. G and his new friend became inseparable. They had much in common; both had backgrounds in design, and both were delighted to have someone to pal round with. Eventually, the friend talked Mr. G into going on vacation with him. Mr. G was excited and anxious. This was the first vacation other than visiting his family that he had taken since his partner's death. They were going to Key West, and he still found himself anxious at times in crowds of gay men. He worried that he would find his old fears of "weird and different" emerging and ruining his vacation. As the trip approached, Mr. G confessed that he had been watching people rollerblade and wanted to learn. Something about

---

[2] I realize this may seem unusual. Had Mr. G not been HIV-positive in addition to so isolated, I would not have undertaken such a maneuver.

seeing people glide so effortlessly was grabbing him, and he wanted to experience that feeling. But how to do it? He did not consider himself at all athletic. In a way he felt rollerblading beyond his ability, almost forbidden, but he wanted to try.

I recalled his fascination with the many ski trips I had taken over the course of his treatment. (He knew about this because I had returned from one with my arm in a sling.) I pointed out that I had learned to ski as an adult and had to take lessons. I offered that perhaps he could find someone to teach him to rollerblade. Mr. G paused and associated that it seemed the other boys just did athletic things well and that there was no practice or teaching involved—you either had it or you didn't, and he assumed he didn't. He then associated to the long hours of practice his older brother devoted to his various sports: "Gee, I guess someone was helping him learn and get better at what he did." By the time he left for vacation, he had secured a pair of rollerblades and pads and had lined up daily lessons. He returned from his trip delighted and triumphant. To his amazement he had picked up rollerblading quite easily, having taken lessons in the morning and spent the afternoons blazing around the island, intoxicated by the feeling of freedom and exhilaration.

In this last phase of his treatment, Mr. G was on a roll. On a visit to his parents, he came across his highschool yearbooks. As he read the inscriptions, he saw clear and convincing evidence that others viewed him quite differently than he had assumed. He was clearly well liked, in some cases idealized; was considered funny, brilliant, and outgoing, and was voted "most likely to succeed." "Who was this person?" he asked. Again, he was amazed and shaken. The disparity between others' experience and his remembered experience of himself was considerable. Two distinct but highly interrelated lines of association followed. The first related to his questioning if he had "made himself over" in the wake of his partner's death (his assumed responsibility and his own seropositivity). Had the severe damage to his self-esteem resulted in his remaking his own history? The second line was related to his emerging sexuality. Back in highschool, it had been a deep, dark secret that no one else knew, certainly not the people writing in his yearbook. What would they have written if they had known about it? He realized that these two areas of meaning had converged. His partner's death and his own infection had concretized his secret, evolving sexual orientation and his sense of being weird, and different, if not evil.

Over the next few months, Mr. G reestablished contact with several old highschool buddies who also were gay. To his delight he was warmly received. Mr. G's friend who had helped him bridge to the larger world was diagnosed with PCP and CMV. Mr. G found himself very engaged with his friend, spending many hours at the hospital talking with and caring for him. He said that the whole experience of his friend's diagnosis and illness was a very calming and reassuring, rather than a disorganizing and evocative, experience. Mr. G found himself feeling considerably less frightened of illness and death.

Mr. G's brother visited him for several days. While he found himself having a great deal of fun and enjoying the visit immensely, he also found himself engaged with his brother in long conversations about death and dying and trying to make sense of these experiences. His brother, a professional firefighter, faced death every day. He had had numerous "close calls" and had lived with the deaths of colleagues and people he had hoped to save. Again, Mr. G found the conversations calming and was delighted at the depth to which he and his brother could understand each other. To his surprise, the old sense of inferiority did not intrude.

On a family vacation, while water skiing with his 12-year-old nephew (whose father had abandoned his family years before), he noticed the boy beaming at him as they skied side by side across the lake. The boy had then followed Mr. G around the entire weekend asking questions about computers, life in a big city, and so on. Mr. G was intrigued. Why was his nephew so curious about him? It was almost as if the boy were looking up to him. I pointed out that uncles are often very special people in boys' lives; the boy did not have a father and perhaps was hungry to have an adult male in his life. Perhaps his nephew was seeing and feeling things that Mr. G himself had trouble seeing and feeling. Mr. G reflected and said, "I guess I thought of myself more as the weird gay uncle that no one would want around their kid." I pointed out that I doubted his nephew saw the weird gay uncle. It seemed to me that the boy saw a man with a lot to offer, things that he desperately needed. By the way, I asked, if you were such an unathletic, wimpy kid, how is it that you learned to water ski? Mr. G laughed and was chagrined. Water skiing was the only athletic thing that he had learned to do well as a child, and he had completely forgotten about it. He had been skiing with his family during the summers all through the course of his treatment, but never mentioned it.

Mr. G's relationship with his nephew blossomed and I think proved very healing for Mr. G. His nephew called often, to ask him to come to his football and baseball games; Mr. G was delighted by the invitations and took his role as uncle very seriously. Mr. G gave his nephew his old computer and proceeded to teach him basic programming. There were several visits to the big city that they both found delightful. Mr. G was profoundly moved that he was able to give something to his nephew that he felt had been so missing in his own life as an adolescent. The rollerblading continued and he taught his nephew to blade, as well as compute. Mr. G also joined a gym and began to work out. He had attempted to join a gym several years earlier but found himself flooded with anxiety similar to that of his youth. This time, his nephew had taken him to the local YMCA during a visit. Rather than being torturous, he found the experience invigorating and joined a gym on his return to the city.

He delightedly reported an incident that his mother had told him about. His parents happened to be in a neighboring town during a gay pride parade and stayed to watch the festivities. When someone made a derogatory comment about the fags, his father flew into a rage, grabbed the man by the collar, and angrily said, "My son is gay; don't you dare say fag around me!" Mr. G pleased, reflected, "I guess he is on my side after all."

Parallel to this revitalization in his own life, the group was winding down. After 3 years, the members found themselves marveling at how engaged they had become in their worlds and how much life had come to a stop before joining the group. Best of all, despite the deaths of two members, everyone else was quite alive. A member remarked, "Since we are all doing so well, why in the hell are we still in this group; let's get out there and live." Mr. G began to discuss his own termination as well. He felt like a different person and was amazed when he compared the man he was when he walked into my office so many years ago with the man he had become. His job was taking him out of town more frequently, he found himself not longing for his sessions while away and was delighted with the work group he was involved in. He was excited and challenged by the projects he was involved in, which had become increasingly complex and now involved a worldwide computer network.

Mr. G chose to diminish the frequency of sessions over several months. The dominant affect state during this time was one of accomplishment and delight in the way he had come to feel about himself. During this termination phase, the friend Mr. G had met in the group died. Mr. G had actively participated in the process and was with his friend when he died. While he was terribly saddened by the loss, he was not acutely disorganized and again felt a sense of accomplishment and satisfaction.

As I assessed the course of treatment, I had my doubts over whether there had been sufficient work that would allow the formation of a successful relationship for Mr. G. However, Mr. G, primarily because of his HIV infection, was not thinking in terms of a new relationship; rather, he was enjoying life as he was now experiencing it and feeling more capable of managing the impact of the infection and great potential for eventual acute illness.

REPRISE

Mr. G returned to treatment approximately 1½ years later. The precipitant was a traumatic breakup with a man with whom he had had an intense relationship for several months. The relationship began very quickly, was passionate, and ended just as suddenly as it began. Mr. G was acutely distraught, tearful, and barely consolable. (Whether this was a factor or not, the breaking down of the relationship coincided with the time of year of his partner's decline and death 8 years before.) Mr. G related the details of the relationship. The man was 15 years younger, they had met at a workshop for HIV-positive people, and he had just found out that he was positive. They began seeing each other, and a passionate, intense dialogue was established very quickly. There was a great deal of intense sexual activity that Mr. G found exhilarating. Because both were positive, they felt freer and less restricted. They spent every free moment together and Mr. G found himself falling in love. He also found himself feeling intensely vital and confident. There was very much the flavor of a highly masculine union. The manner in which Mr. G related the nature of the relationship and the fact that his partner had just found out that he was HIV-positive led me to believe that there were many sexualizations at play. In the wake of its disruption, the old feelings of weird and different, of being defective, unmasculine and depleted were flooding in once more.

Trouble began when his partner auditioned and was tapped for a lead role in a theatrical production. Mr. G's first response was to panic when his friend related the extent of the rehearsal and performance schedules, which would sharply curtail their time together. Mr. G became increasingly anxious, clingy, and at times angry as rehearsals began and their "time together dropped off to nothing." Several angry interchanges occurred within the previously blissful and invigorating dialogue centering around the friend's preoccupation with the production and lack of concern over the decreased contact. While Mr. G settled down somewhat by opening night, I got the sense that something had been irreparably damaged for his friend. Mr. G feeling guilty for his distress, sent a huge bouquet to the dressing room. He was delighted to find that the man had referred to him as his partner in the program. After the play and at the party that followed however, his friend was cold and aloof. He later let Mr. G know that he was embarrassed by the size of the bouquet, which was huge in comparison to the arrangements the other cast members received. Mr. G was left feeling that he had messed up and he began to panic, totally confused by now, desperately wanting to do the right thing, but not being sure just what that was. Rather than return home together that night as he expected, his friend refused. Mr. G was devastated. There was a series of tense and anxious phone calls and a meeting where his friend told him that he was having second thoughts. In a panic, Mr. G called me.

Initially, he made it clear that he hoped I would be able to help him get a grip on things so that the relationship would be saved. If he could settle down, get a handle on the intensity of what he was feeling, then perhaps it could be salvaged. He feared that his distress was only pushing his friend farther and farther away. As we talked about the history of the relationship and his panic at the disruption owing to the play, Mr. G began to settle down, though several sessions later, the friend definitely terminated the relationship in a terse phone call. Mr. G was devastated and again barely consolable. His distress reminded me of the exquisite distress of a lost and abandoned small child, much the way he had appeared through the year following the death of his partner.

Mr. G became acutely preoccupied with his lost mate, desperate for the union they had once had, angry at its loss, angry with himself that he had wrecked it, confused that he had gone from being the "partner" mentioned in the playbill to "tossed away." During these early sessions, my approach was very much aimed at tending to his deep distress and attempting to modulate his intense and shifting affect states, though responding to the depths of his distress and letting him once again attach to me in the face of devastating loss.

The anxious preoccupation ended quite suddenly. Mr. G came in one day and was horribly embarrassed and humiliated. He confessed to calling his lost mate's answering machine repeatedly, just to hear his voice, but hanging up without leaving a message. His friend traced the calls, angrily called him up, and told him to stop or else he would accuse Mr. G of stalking him. He was horribly afraid to relate the incident to me, fearing further humiliation. Mr. G was greatly relieved when I responded to his longing and emptiness, that perhaps hearing the voice was his way of trying to soothe his devastation, by getting a semblance of the lost union.

As Mr. G's preoccupation continued to wane, several themes from the previous treatment were revived, and we were able to work with them with an affective intensity quite different from the previous work. Affects were much more available and had a richness and aliveness, and there was a greater fluidity to his associations. The first theme revolved around his long-standing sense of being damaged, his lack of masculine confidence, his unease and anxiety around men in general, and his sense of being different, "weird," and humiliated. The second theme revolved around the great separation, the gulf he continued to feel around his homosexuality, that constituted a central aspect of Mr. G's self and his family relationships. The third theme was a more consolidative, confident, joyful and vital sense of self that, while shaken by the breakup was still very much intact, operative, and striving.

The loss of the intense masculine union left Mr. G feeling anxiously inadequate but did not flood him in the way he so often was in the previous treatment. It seemed as though we were fast-forwarding through the earlier themes around his lack of masculine confidence, and longing for a connection to other men that would leave him feeling vital and confident. As he filled me in on the qualities of his lost mate, I got the sense that the man was desperate for mirroring himself and was acutely disappointed and consequently a bit paranoid when Mr. G did not sit back and beam at his being chosen for the play, no matter what the consequences for their time together. Mr. G was surprised by my thinking, being sure that the man had discovered something masculinely defective in him.

One day Mr. G came in and reported that he had been out with some friends over the weekend and had had a wonderful time. He had felt happy and spontaneous and had enjoyed the friendly, bantering conversations. "But," he added, with a hint of shame, "it was in a bar." I responded, "A playground is a playground." Mr. G fell quiet but was clearly thinking. Eventually, he reported, "I keep flashing back and forth between the way I felt the other night and that little kid out in left field praying that the ball would not be hit toward him." Mr. G went on to associate about "that weird little kid" in a way that had a highly split off and alienated flavor. There were multiple references to "him," "that," and "he" along with a great deal of sad affect. Eventually, I said, "You know, your sadness is yours; it is part of your history." Mr. G paused and said, "Oh my God, what have I been doing. That little kid is me, not some alien creature. I need to embrace him, not push him away." (Mr. G had, at one point in his treatment, become quite enamored with John Bradshaw, though the metaphors were not my personal ones, I was not going to argue.)

In the following session, Mr. G reported that the intervening week had been quite intense. He went home for a family reunion and found himself alternately engaged with his family and absorbed in the family albums looking at photographs of himself as a young child. He found himself feeling very engaged as he saw pictures of himself, as though he were seeing them for the first time. He also was surprised by how frail and small his "big burly uncles" had become, for it was the first time he noticed that he was taller than his father and the once-ominous uncles.

Themes emerged centered on around the gulf Mr. G felt between him and his family as well as in the two highly chaotic relationships he found himself in the midst of as a young man. Interestingly, his parents were quite aware of his distress over the recent breakup and were quite responsive and concerned about his distress. Mr. G contrasted his current experience of his parents and how as a young man his "terrible secret" had been something he had hidden from them at all costs. He related how tortuous and painful his "coming out" process was. There were no campus gay and lesbian student associations back then to provide a sense of belonging. Only a very "creepy and seedy" bar and the various campus tea rooms in which he periodically engaged in anonymous sex. And there were the ominous books on homosexuality in the campus library.

Mr. G went on to recall how one evening he had engaged in anonymous sex in a tea room and had become acutely overwhelmed, anxious, and confused. He desperately called home to hear his parents' reassuring voices. He related, "I can still see myself standing in that phone booth trembling, so scared, so confused." I remarked on how desperately he needed to hear their reassuring voices and then asked, "What did you talk about?" In a plaintive voice he replied, "Oh the weather, my classes." I then replied, "How sad that it just was not possible to tell them what was really going on." Mr. G burst into tears, "I wanted to tell them so bad, but it just seemed too terrible; I could not tell them that I was one of those people in the books."

The following semester, Mr. G dropped his science courses and enrolled in design. He truly felt there was no place for him in the sciences, and he had met several gay students in the design department, one of whom became a friend that he has maintained contact with to this day. But he also felt a gulf between him and his parents as he pursued his life as a gay man in much the isolation that he felt as a child. Mr. G reflected that he felt there was no way that his terrible secret could "fit in" to the closeness and warmth he felt from his family. While his homosexuality, on one hand, felt like a continuation of "weird and different," it also had a great deal of excitement, adventure, and danger now associated with it. Mr. G also wondered if the phone booth was also "when I said good-bye to the kid that everybody seemed to like in the yearbooks."

Mr. G wound down the second treatment, much as his first, gradually diminishing sessions over several months. He began dating a man, this time taking it slowly and, to his surprise, enjoying the process of gradually getting to know the man to be delightful, intriguing, and an adventure to be savored. When he left treatment, there was a solidity and calmness about Mr. G that was quite striking. I saw him a month later blazing down the lake front with another man, and I found myself wondering if that was his new boyfriend. My last communication from him was a Christmas card that conveyed a joyful vitality and awe. In it was a note that read, "Thanks for all your help. 1995 is looking much more exciting and hopeful than 1994."

SUMMARY

Much can be said about this case, and the case says a great deal on its own. Returning to the question that I began with regarding the potential influence on the selfobject transferences when both the patient and therapist are gay or lesbian, the "gay uncle" transference immediately comes to mind. It seems to me that in this case it was a variation on, or form of, the idealizing–mirroring transference that Anna Ornstein elaborated on in her 1983 paper. Basically, the need to experience mirroring from the idealized parent in order to transform archaic narcissistic structures into more consolidated and differentiated masculine and feminine structures. I am not glorifying traditional masculine and feminine roles, nor do I think of gender in structural metaphors. I do think, however, that the transference enabled renewed vitality and confidence in Mr. G's gender-related aspects of self. In part, this particular transference manifestation in Mr. G was also based on responsiveness to his struggle to make sense of his homosexuality, the pain that had accumulated over the years, the splitting off of this aspect of self, and ultimately mirroring of his essential goodness and validity as a gay man. It would be pure folly to assert that idealizing, mirroring, and alter ego transferences are more fully elaborated when both patient and therapist share the same orientation. One still has to have the technical capacity to allow the elaboration of and work with or within transference configurations.

The "gay uncle" transference was a transference: not a "reality" and certainly not a prescription for the treatment of all gay and lesbian patients. (No other patient has voiced this longing in such a clear way.) But it does seem to me that it evolved in response to my basic stance as a clinician toward Mr. G. What it enabled was his experience of a modulating, sustaining, and affirming other into woefully unmirrored and, the evidence suggests, split-off aspects of self. Perhaps the basis for psychoanalysis's ambivalence towards homosexuality (as conveyed in MacIntosh, 1994, and elsewhere) is the long-held assumption that homosexual desire is defensive in nature, rather than a legitimate form of human sexuality. On the other hand, to assume that all gay and lesbian clinicians have worked through the consequences of their homosexuality on their self-development creates problems as well. Each position can lead to problems in empathic responsiveness towards the patient's longings and needs. Ultimately, it is the transference and responsiveness to the patient; rather than the orientation of the therapist, that is central in the renewed development of the self.

Returning to an earlier point, however, the absence of hostility (especially perhaps the "professed absence of hostility") is not the same as mirroring. It is still an absence. What has been noticeably absent in self psychology's periodic references to homosexuality over the years has been the permission to mirror the homosexuality and its many nuances of our homosexual patients. And one does have to wonder about the absence.

So what is it that I consider when referring a homosexual patient for clinical work? The capacity to mirror the homosexual aspects of self, to distinguish between a sexualization and an orientation, the capacity to allow an idealizing transference to evolve and flourish, and the ability to recognize that questions about the genuineness of the patient's homosexual orientation may recapitulate earlier and ongoing problems in the selfobject milieu. But there also must be the technical ability to recognize sustain, and work with all of the above.

A self is a truly complex and multifaceted phenomenon. The clinical endeavor is a complex and multifaceted phenomenon as well. Sexuality and orientation are integral aspects of the self, however, and the consequences for an unmirrored self can be considerable.

REFERENCES

Goldberg, A. (1995), *The Problem of Perversion*. New Haven, CT: Yale University Press.

Isay, R. (1989), *Being Homosexual*. New York: Farrar, Straus and Giroux.

Kohut, H. (1979), The two analyses of Mr. Z. *Internat. J. Psycho-Anal.*, 60:3–27.

MacIntosh, H. (1994), Analyzing homosexual patients. *J. Amer. Psychoanal. Assn.*, 14:1183–1208.

Ornstein, A. (1983), An idealizing transference of the oedipal phase. In: *Reflections on Self Psychology*, ed. J. D. Lichtenberg & S. Kaplan. Hillsdale, NJ: The Analytic Press, pp. 135–147.

Shelby, R. D. (1994), Mourning within a culture of mourning. In: *Therapists on the Frontline*. ed. S. Cadwell, R. Burnham & M. Forstein. Washington, DC: The American Psychiatric Press.

Chapter 13

Discussion of Shelby's "The Self and Orientation: The Case of Mr. G"

Brenda Clorfene Solomon

Dennis Shelby continues his pioneering work on homosexuality by asking: How does the analyst's sexual orientation influence the potential selfobject transferences when the patient is homosexual? What unique countertransference reactions occur in the analyst when the patient is a male homosexual? Does the therapist's sexual orientation limit his or her potential to participate in the unfolding of the developmentally necessary and previously missing selfobject experience that provides pathways to the most vitalized, healthy sense of self?

There has been an absence in the self psychology literature of the mirroring selfobject transferences as they emerge in homosexual patients. I agree with Shelby's conclusion, "Sexuality and orientation are integral aspects of the self. Ultimately, it is the transference and responsiveness to the patient rather than the orientation of the therapist that is central in the renewed development of the self."

Important questions for considering the specific nuances of analyst/patient orientation include: What if this patient, Mr. G, had been treated by a heterosexual woman? a heterosexual man? a lesbian? Would there have been different selfobject configurations? How might they coconstruct the psychoanalytic dialogue?

In order to approach this, I will first offer my personal response to being asked to discuss Shelby's provocative questions. Next, I will briefly review the case and consider the patient as suffering from a narcissistic behavior disorder. The concept of compensatory structures will be mentioned. Finally, I will make some preliminary remarks on analyst sexual orientation and countertransference.

When the originally planned discussant, Bert Cohler, Ph.D., discovered that he was going to be out of the country and unable to participate, he asked me to pinch hit. When I heard the topic: self and orientation, treatment of a male homosexual, I admit, my initial response was, "Why me?" As I reflected on my *atypical* knee-jerk reaction, I thought analyzing it might lead me to understand more about my own organizing themes and countertransference to this subject. I thought, what experience do I have with male homosexuality? I thought about my evolution and enlightenment as a therapist learning about homosexuality.

To start at the beginning, when I was a psychiatric resident in the mid-1960s, an admired male colleague asked me to be a group therapist coleader in what was then thought to be a single-symptom homogenous group of male homosexuals. Gradually, I realized my participation was based on my fantasy that these attractive, competent male homosexuals had just not yet met the right woman! My grandiosity, not yet analyzed, was that I would be that woman who could change these men's orientation. These patients became my teachers and provided me a window into my naive countertransferences to homosexual men. Ten years later, I served as cochair with Nanette Gartrell, M.D., for the American Psychiatric Association's Committee on Women. Dr. Gartrell was then, as now, a researcher and activist for the Gay and Lesbian Caucus. She was also a fine teacher. Since then I have analyzed four lesbians, three of them mental health professionals. These women have been remarkable educators for their analyst.

I have been the chairperson for the American Psychoanalytic Association's Workshop on Psychoanalysis and AIDS. Since 1992, Bert Cohler and I joined the Special Issues for Homosexual Candidates Workshop of the American Psychoanalytic Association. Cohler and I then formed an ongoing workshop on homosexuality at the Chicago Institute for Psychoanalysis. Most recently, I am serving on the Chicago Institute's selection committee, which in 1995 selected its first openly gay candidate, Dennis Shelby. I am now writing a chapter in a planned casebook of narcissistic behavior disorders, which will detail the treatment of a lesbian whose perversion, I contend, is heterosexuality.

So over the past quarter of a century, my immersion in analytic theory has transformed my idea that I just had to be the perfectly attuned women and all those gay men in my therapy group would change their orientation. Now I know that only when a therapist is able to live comfortably with the conviction that homosexuality is a natural developmental endpoint for some individuals will she or he be able to conduct an analysis that is finely attuned and exploratory. At the same time the therapist must be capable of affirming the homosexual's capacity to love and be loved within his or her sexual orientation

(Corbett, 1993). In addition, an analyst must also not ignore the question of whether homosexuality is ever defensive, as many have considered.

Corbett recently recognized that by focusing solely on the gay male experience, he is participating in the overrepresentation of the male homosexual in the psychoanalytic literature, in contrast to the female homosexual. He recognizes the limits inherent in his solely focusing on the male, which could be seen as symptomatic of the phallocentrism, or perhaps more precisely, the gynophobia that characterizes so much of the psychoanalytic developmental literature. But he, as I, also recognizes the limits of our own clinical experience. At this time I have not had extensive experience in the treatment of gay men. Corbett, as do I, looks forward to analyses of homosexuality that address the similarities and differences in the gay male and female experience (p. 353). The development of homosexual women is glaringly underestimated through the virtual lack of any representation within the psychoanalytic canon but new publications are in press.

A chapter in the book *Lesbians and Psychoanalysis: Revolutions in Theory and Practice,* edited by Glassgold and Iasenza (1995), led me to wonder about the meaning of my revealing my sexual orientation in this discussion. The issue of disclosure is openly discussed in intersubjective circles. When did Shelby's patient learn of his therapist's homosexuality? What did that mean to Mr. G? Was it interpreted? With that question in mind, I shall segue into the case of Mr. G, an exposition that Shelby considers a reconstruction of a damaged self. Shelby summarizes Mr. G's themes: (1) a longstanding sense of being damaged, lack of masculine confidence, unease and anxiety about feeling weird, as well as (2) his homosexual, previously secret self.

In brief review, Shelby presents the psychotherapy of Mr. G, who was seen twice weekly for a total of 6 years, and then returned for a reprise of 2 years after an interruption. Mr. G came into couple's treatment with a partner, who soon died of AIDS. Shelby, both because of who he is as a person and because of his professional expertise, courageously initiated a visit to the couple as the partner was dying in the hospital. As a therapist, Shelby understood that his initial task was to help modulate, sustain, and organize his patient's shifting affects during the mourning process. The patient fantasied "losing it" and fragmenting. There was mounting evidence that Mr. G's family could not tolerate intense painful affects. This first period of mourning diminished as Mr. G brought his therapist photographs of his dispersal of his partner's ashes. Mr. G also wanted Shelby to participate in this dispersal step. This was evidence that the patient could now tolerate and voice the importance of his connection to his therapist.

Only after 6 months of treatment, when Mr. G's selfobject connection had deepened, was the patient ready to turn from mourning to the significance of his own HIV positive status, which he seemingly had disavowed. However, a familiar pattern of protective behaviors ensued when the patient attempted to bridge his feelings about his own HIV, guilt about his fantasy of infecting his partner, and his acknowledgment of sexual feelings for Shelby. Because Mr. G was not quite ready and unable to manage his overstimulated state, he characterologically *behaved* by canceling, withdrawing, and isolating himself. The therapist handled these behaviors (pathological organizing patterns) empathically, understanding Mr. G's fragility in regulating painful affects and attachments. Shelby held onto, perhaps stated, his conviction that via a healing selfobject connection, Mr. G was capable of growth. A relevant genetic screen memory then confirmed that Mr. G's mother had sabotaged his developmentally appropriate growth of dealing with the outside world when at 5 years he was invited to a party. Withdrawal and humiliation were encoded as the mother insisted that the crying child dance for her. Compensatory attempts to connect to idealized men failed as Mr. G told of his experience with his father and burly uncles who were into "duck murdering" and seemingly could not relate to his interests in cocoons and nature. Perhaps this screened an early unconscious awareness of the butterfly hidden inside himself.

In latency, Mr. G was already feeling weird and different, so by adolescence he was trying to find himself in the library. Everything he read pathologized homosexuality.

A twinship connection characterized Mr. G's young adult relationship with his partner. That a similar twinship was reestablished in therapy is seen in Mr. G's description of "It's Mr. Shelby and I against the world." That both men uncannily moved to the same condo building may seem more evidence of this twinship. Who knows what we can communicate unconsciously. What turned out to be developmentally transmuting was Mr. G's fortuitous experience of meeting his athletic, gay therapist in the gym, a place of many previous traumas. That Shelby could optimally respond and not criticize led to a deepening of an idealizing transference.

Shelby makes possible my hunch that a silent merger/mirror transference was also in place as he described his glazing over as Mr. G endlessly described the laser he wished to purchase. The beams would go all around the apartment by a series of mirrors. Was this the symbolic expression of a revitalized, archaic grandiose self? Did Shelby experience countertransference boredom, the glazing over because of the merger? How was this interpreted?

As in many narcissistic behavior disorders, the idealizing pole was easier to identify because of the patient's curative fantasy of becoming the gay uncle for his young eager nephew just as Shelby had become the idealized other for him.

When Mr. G's T-cell count lowered and shingles developed, he used old behaviors of isolation and withdrawal and became preoccupied with death. His family's concern felt scary and overstimulating to him. The therapist's gentle, but firm, empathic pursuit of his patient resulted in his return to treatment. Only then did Mr. G reveal his magical, unreal belief that his therapeutic (selfobject) connection would prevent T-cells from diminishing.

Shelby was able to gently encourage Mr. G to join a seropositive support group that he was leading. Understanding the mother's failures at helping the patient enter the larger world, Shelby, in what might be considered affect regulation reeducation (Modell, 1993) playfully insisted that his patient try this group. The twinship experience of this group was mutative. Mr. G's new vitality was captured in his learning to rollerblade, an activity in which he could freely exhibit his accomplishments. Only then could he appreciate that his past defensive isolation felt like death. His self was in the process of being made over. A previously secret, now proud, sexual self was evolving. He no longer had a sense of inferiority. Mr. G initiated termination by diminishing the frequency of his sessions.

The reprise after one and a half year's interruption was precipitated by a breakup with an actor–lover. (How soon after termination had this romance begun? Was this a replacement selfobject for the therapist?) This was a devastating loss handled by the patient's phone stalking of his former lover. Mr. G again required the help of his therapist. (Did Mr. G reenact his mother's intensity with his lover?) Mr. G's devastation raises questions about whether there were, in fact, structural changes from the first treatment. One would expect that structural changes would have been more stable.

Goldberg, in his important 1995 book, considers the treatment of narcissistic behavior disorders (NBD). He defines narcissistic behavior disorders by their psychological structure, explaining the function of the behavior. He details how behavior such as sexualization, such as Mr. G's visiting tea rooms and phone stalking (as opposed to sexuality), can aid in self-cohesion. Splitting mechanisms are used extensively so patients with narcissistic behavior disorder experience a reality self alongside a more archaic, primitive self. There are different self-states that develop from both sides of the split. For an enduring structural change, Goldberg asserts that bridging interpretations have to be made in order to heal the split between the two selves.

Goldberg (1995) defines such analysis of NBDs as reconstruction:

> Reconstruction, rather than restoration, is a radical concept because it implies dismantling something and erecting a new structure. We become architects of personality as well as the healers of disease. If we see the multipotential of the self, we can allow for a growth responsive more to one selfobject or to one form of selfobject than to another. The task of understanding our patients when they are NBDs is to make the necessary connection to both parts of the personality, to become part of the person's life, and so, inevitably, to become different ourselves [p. 190].

The diffuse vulnerability of an NBD is seen in Mr. G's handling of the tensions of everyday life. So, too, the failure to experience and tolerate affects is a measure of the general fragility of his self. Gradations of emotionality depend on the structuralization, which is a result, at a minimum, of the parent's responsiveness to the needs of the child during the earliest moments of tension regulation. The further failure of idealization leads to a lack of the structure building needed for controlling action and affect and allows for the sexualization that overwhelms the self. All the sexual dynamic problems of the oedipal phase (for either homosexual or heterosexual children) are of necessity superimposed on this fundamentally fragile structure. There is inadequate structuralization of either pole. The defect in idealization leads to sexualization (Goldberg, 1995, p. 94).

It is incumbent upon us to develop a theory that respects variation in human development. I agree with Goldberg (1995) that homosexuality needs a psychology, and it also needs a psychopathology since homosexuality, just as heterosexuality, can be in the service of a disordered development. In some cases of male homosexuality, it seems that early problems in development with the mirroring selfobject—that is, the parental responsiveness to the atypical masculine presentation—lead to a pursuit of the idealized selfobject for a structure of compensation. This configuration may itself be defective, and that deficiency may be handled, or defended, by sexualization. When homosexuality is seen as a compensatory structure, a particular selfobject transference develops in psychoanalysis. Goldberg finds that this transference configuration is an idealizing one, and it is often the site of various levels of sexualization. The sexualization of the transference usually subsides after a period of stability, and the major work of psychoanalysis is to rehabilitate this sector or pole of the self. What emerges is a more or less stable configuration that assumes the status of a compensatory structure. Profound defects in the grandiose pole of the self are readily apparent, but Goldberg claims it is usually not possible to engage this pole in psychoanalysis. If there appears to be some therapeutic work in this area, the resultant self-configuration remains primarily that of an idealized pole that serves as a compensatory structure and thereupon severely limits a full analytic experience with the pole of ambitions and exhibitionism.

Is Goldberg correct that, for some homosexual men who present with narcissistic behavior disorders, the grandiose self is too damaged to be rehabilitated by a mirroring transference in treatment? Or is this especially likely to be concluded by some heterosexual male analysts? If my diagnosis of Mr. G as an NBD is correct, has there been significant restructuring along the mirroring selfobject transferences as well as the idealizing? What are the implications of reprises in treatment? Is this just a temporary regression? Or is it evidence that the selfobject connection to Shelby had been stabilizing and filling in the deficit but not resolved (i.e., is interpretation necessary)? Do the reprises indicate compensatory structures or is that an unnecessary concept, as Fossage suggested in 1994? Or should I be considering Mr. G an NPD, not an NBD with a split self?

Thinking about Mr. G and his secret self, I am reminded of how Scott Goldsmith (1995) likens this aspect of the homosexual boy to that of a double agent. The homosexual boy is required to present himself as a boy with the opposite sets of object choices. The homosexual child growing up in a society where gender-role behaviors are rigidly defined and where gender is felt to dictate the gender of the love object is often faced with feelings of shame, humiliation, and self-hatred when he and others sense his gender-role atypicality and erotic feelings (Frommer, 1994). There is no other developmental circumstance that is fully comparable to the experience of the child who senses this difference but lacks the cognitive perspectivability to understand it and the emotional support to cope with it. He becomes a double agent in his own home, harboring one set of feelings while called upon to enact another. Not feeling authentic, he feels an impostor in his everyday life. Do homosexual men therefore need to employ splitting more than other men because of what gets mirrored as masculine?

With this in mind let's turn to the question: Is a gay therapist more likely to be able to adequately mirror a homosexual patient? Authors such as Anna and Paul Ornstein (1995), Alan Kindler (1993) and Judy Kantrowitz (1995) recently wrote about the beneficial aspects of the patient–analyst match. Each pair has its own nonreplicable characteristics. The interdigitation of the particular organizing principles of the analyst and patient may be therapeutically beneficial and determine the depth and range of work in any specific area. The subtle aspects of character and conflict of both and their interplay constitute a central therapeutic factor in therapy. I believe that character very much determines theory preference. Like it or not, just as politics are personal, theory preference is also personal. Our patients choose us because of who we are and how they hope we can offer a healing experience, that is a new beginning.

One might think that we, as enlightened self psychologists with a depathologized view of homosexuality, would naturally adopt an empathic stance, but it is a mistake to assume that the analyst operates from a position of neutrality regarding homosexuality merely because he or she adopts an empathic stance. Recent concepts of intersubjectivity that have reshaped traditional thinking about transference and counter-transference suggest that, whether or not the analyst behaves as if he were neutral, the patient is nonetheless influenced by the intersub-jectivity of all the analyst's feelings, whether or not they enter the treatment through overt verbal communication. How the analyst thinks and feels about homosexuality inevitably influences how he or she inquires into, formulates, and interprets homosexual experience with the patient.

An affirmative stance on the part of the therapist that emotionally communicates to the patient the therapist belief that homosexuality is a natural developmental endpoint for some is viewed as the correct appli-cation of self-psychological technique with homosexual patients. The analyst becomes fully interested in understanding the developmental ex-perience of the patient without searching for an etiological explanation to account for the homosexuality. What becomes primary is a fuller in-quiry and reconstruction of the childhood experience: As Shelby did, the therapist acknowledges and labels for the patient the presence of his developmentally appropriate homosexual self in childhood and helps him identify, understand, and interpret the disavowed expansive aspects. The failure to regulate painful affects based on humiliation and differ-ence came alive in the treatment. In NBDs, when there are inevitable failures in the selfobject bond, behaviors such as tea room visits can be understood as regression to sexualizations, which slowly gives way to fantasizing rather than behaving. This split can be interpreted within the selfobject transferences. The therapist understands the child's lonely attempts to negotiate a developmental experience in a homophobic setting and the emotional vulnerabilities that were formed. This affirming empathic stance conveys a positive mirroring of his homosexual child-self and its right to be. I believe that the sexual orientation of the analyst is not necessarily an impediment to this therapeutic goal.

However, as self psychologists, we should not deny that classical idea that homosexual desire also *may* be defensive in nature. In this chapter, Shelby seems to ignore that possibility.

Despite all the risks of generalizations, I will consider some general-izations about particular therapist/patient pairing that may benefit or hamper the establishment of stable selfobject transferences. Many homosexual patients are most comfortable working with therapists who are themselves homosexual (Isay, 1991). The reasons are obvious, given the homophobia of the culture at large and patients' concerns that any therapist might have a pathologized view of homosexuality. In addition, the sexual orientation of the analyst plays an important part in the nature of the intersubjective experience that gets created between the patient and the analyst. The analyst who knows something about the patient's experience firsthand may convey his understanding of that experience in a way that is different for the empathic analyst who does not. The patient may use this understanding to form a twinship or may feel mirrored more easily than with a heterosexual therapist. This may, in fact, be a positive advantage for the patient. However, this point raises the question of whether firsthand experience is necessary for optimal empathy. Can vicarious introspection lead us to optimal responsiveness or is firsthand experience inevitably an advantage? Must one be a parent to understand the joys and sorrows of parenting? Must one be black to understand the experience of racism in America? I think not. But one must be educated and analyzed to his or her personal organizing principles about such matters.

We might envision specific transference/countertransference issues that are particular to homosexual patients in therapy with a male homosexual analyst. The analyst and patient may each be continuing to struggle with his own homophobia so that a stable idealizing transference and authentic mirroring are hampered. A negative defective twinship can result and become an impasse. When therapist and patient have the very same characterological and experiential factors, it may be felicitous but it may also be deleterious. For example, male analysts, whether homosexual or heterosexual, are not immune to anxiety and shame about some aspects of their selves. Tolerating passivity and what some label feminine aspects are necessary ingredients in doing analytic work.

Stolorow and Atwood (1992) are among others who conclude that the intersubjective situation can facilitate or obstruct the progress of therapy, depending in large part on the extent of the therapist's ability to become reflectively aware of the organizing principles of his subjective world. In the 1960s I was unaware of my organizing principles, how my own heterosexual bias and gender grandiosity had made me unable to fully appreciate the subjective experience of my male, homosexual patients. Two analyses later, learning from my talented patients, immersing myself in self psychology and the homosexual literature, I have been transformed. As you may have intuited, I am heterosexual, but over the past 30 years, I believe I have become capable of mirroring the homosexual's unique struggle.

Therapy can be a healing and transforming process for both therapists and patients. Through empathic attunement coupled with the analyst's awareness of her or his own subjectivity, the patient has the opportunity to find a mirror that reflects back an affirmation of her (his) many strengths and the value of homosexual self.

As I reviewed the literature and thought about Shelby's significant contribution to Mr. G, I recognize theirs was a felicitous pairing of therapist and patient. However, it is not necessarily better for a gay therapist to treat gay patients. There are specific meanings to each pairing whether the therapist is a woman, man, hetero- or homosexual. These can always be analyzed from a self-psychological perspective. What is of primary importance is that the therapist be analyzed, having examined her or his theories about homosexuality and be ever-vigilant about her or his countertransferences. These are the minimum requirements for a therapist to be empathic with the experience of the homosexual growing up in twentieth century America. I am grateful to Dennis Shelby for the opportunity to discuss his work.

REFERENCES

Corbett, K. (1993), The mystery of homosexuality. *Psychoanal. Psychol.,* 10:3.

Fosshage, J. (1994), Compensatory structures or primary: An alternate view. Paper presented at the 1994 Annual Conference on the Psychology of the Self, Chicago, IL.

Frommer, M. S. (1994), Homosexuality and psychoanalysis: Technical considerations revisited. *Psychoanal. Dial.,* 4:215–233.

Goldberg, A. (1995), *The Problem of Perversion.* New Haven, CT: Yale University Press.

Goldsmith, S. (1995), Oedipus or Orestes? Gender identity development in homosexual men. *Psychoanal. Inq.,* 15:112–124.

Glassgold, J. & Iasenza, S., eds. (1995), *Lesbians and Psychoanalysis.* New York: Free Press.

Isay, R. A. (1991), The homosexual analyst: Clinical considerations. *The Psychoanalytic Study of the Child,* 46:199–216. New Haven, CT: Yale University Press.

Kantrowitz, J. (1995), The beneficial aspects of the patient–analyst match. *Internat. J. Psycho-Anal.,* 76299–314.

Kindler, A. (1993), Life used to be so easy. *Psychoanal. Dialog.,* 3:367–370.

Modell, A. (1993), *The Private Self.* Cambridge, MA: Harvard University Press.

Ornstein, A. & Ornstein, P. (1995), Marginal comments on the evolution of self psychology. *Psychoanal. Dialog.,* 5:421–425.

Stolorow, R. & Atwood, G. (1992), *Contexts of Being.* Hillsdale, NJ: The Analytic Press.

Chapter 14

The Self in Orientation: Issues of Female Homosexuality

Betsy Kassoff

I want to begin by telling you a story. Less than a decade ago, a young self psychologist made a pilgrimage to a faraway seashore. It was summer. She went to learn more about her work from famous teachers who came from all over the world to this celebrated seaside. There would be classes in the morning and then everyone who wanted could go to the ocean in the afternoon. The young self psychologist was quite impressed by the teachers and the gathering. She had come with her partner, also a self psychologist, also a woman, and they decided to go to different workshops and then to come back together. After the first day of classes, they met in their room and decided quickly to drive to one of a number of nearby beaches frequented by their people, the women who love women and the men who love men. They both were quiet until they reached a place on the shore where, as far as they could see, women's heads touched women's heads and male knees knocked casually against each other. Then they both breathed a sigh of relief and turned to each other. Were they doing it in your workshop? they each asked the other. Yes and yes was the answer. And the doing it was the making of negative remarks about their people. Not even subtle negative remarks, which they were used to screening out, but serious ones couched in professional jargon like perversion and derailed development. Did you say anything? No and no. They hung their heads. The following days they went to workshops together. When remarks were

---

Presented at the Self Psychology Conference, San Francisco, CA, October 1995.

made, casually, devaluing their people, the language they used for healing being used to demean, one or the other of them would raise their
hands. Language began to be more careful but no one talked to them.
They would go back into their hotel room, look at themselves in the
bathroom mirror, and wonder. Am I this way because. . . . They must
know. They seem so sure. The women touched each other less and felt
their strength dimming. And then they would go to the beach of their
people and feel cleansed again by the company and by the sun and the
sea. Not soon enough, they went home to their own town, ringed by the
ocean and a bay, where their people had achieved enough numbers and
power so that they could call themselves self psychologists and lesbians
in the same breath. But they never forgot that, outside of their magic
ring of water, it would be much harder. And they never went to that
faraway seashore again, even though the lobster was excellent and the
ocean was warm.

I tell this story, which is about myself, to try and help you empathize
with the experience of being lesbian in contemporary times—not to
sympathize, or to know intellectually, but to empathize, which all of you
know is the central tool of self psychology in the analytic task. Empathy
requires the capacity to attune affectively and to understand intellectually
(Ornstein and Ornstein, 1985). It is my experience that there exist systematic countertransference problems for most therapists in empathizing
with lesbian clients. Psychoanalytically informed therapists have particular challenges, having been trained in a model of homosexuality as a
pathological developmental outcome. That model has been rebutted, but
not replaced. Most rebuttals have been by gay men (Isay, 1989; Shelby,
1994; Frommer, 1994) who posit the thesis that homosexuality (for men
in particular, although for women by inference) is genetically determined
and thus should be relegated to the status of endowment as opposed to
volitional behavior (Shelby, 1995). Politically and personally, it may be
easier to accept someone with a genetic difference that cannot be
changed, such as skin color, than it may be to accept a difference such
as sexual orientation, which for some people may be chosen and, thus
technically, could be "unchosen" or renounced. This dilemma of choice
in the etiology of sexual orientation permeates the psychoanalytic literature even today (Frommer, 1995). The assumption of this chapter is that
currently there is no clear cut scientific/objective explanation for homosexual or heterosexual identity formation. Given the prevalence of com-
peting cultural theories, for some persons homosexual identity is understood as a biological given and for others is construed as a choice. For
those who subjectively perceive homosexual identity as a choice, many
determinants come into that choice including personal experience, cultural and familial supports, the perceived availability and consequences

for homosexual experiences, and the range of gender role behaviors understood to be allowed in heterosexual relationships (Burch, 1993).

The central point of this chapter is that lesbianism is an integral aspect of the self for lesbian clients. This will mean different things to different clients in different therapies, inevitably. However, the social status of female homosexuality, which of course varies between women of different races, classes, ages, and geographical locations (Gould, 1995), shares a common denominator. That denominator is the experience of difference from a dominant norm of heterosexuality. How that difference is internalized, known, felt, and transformed into meaning takes many forms. But a central piece is the experience of difference as deficiency. It takes a great deal of psychological sophistication to tolerate fluctuations in self-esteem resulting from deficient or inaccurate mirroring, as we all know. Even with the resources of multiple selfobject supports, when a particular selfobject milieu fails to attune, the cohesion of the self is tentative. For example, I am a reasonably educated, confident, psychologically resilient person with the blessing of many supportive colleagues and friends. But I felt bad at that conference at the seashore. Bad about myself. Ashamed for being a lesbian, even though in many ways I am a professional lesbian: out for most of my adult life, an activist. I could leave that conference for a more supportive environment and encapsulate the experience as a bad week and not representative of my life. But most of our clients don't have a sense of those options. Very few of them had that sense growing up. And so inevitably the work of repairing the self with lesbian clients includes understanding injuries related to selfobject failures acquired in the consolidation of homosexual identity, how lesbian identity may differ from gay male identity, and it is about the vicissitudes of a healthy relationship to sexual orientation as one aspect of self-experience.

To begin to think about this, we need to define some terms. *Gender identity, gender role,* and *sexual orientation* are all terms used in most psychoanalytic discussions of homosexuality. For the purpose of this discussion, I am using gender identity similarly to the term of *core gender* to indicate one's sense of biological sex—am I male? am I female? Gender role identity is the sense of one's masculinity or femininity according to the signifiers assigned as masculine or feminine in a particular context. Sexual orientation (often retermed affectional preference by lesbian/gay activists) is not defined here as percentage of homosexual behaviors/fantasies as in a Kinsey-like scale, but as a self-assigned identity that may or may not conform to overt behaviors but is usually based on a perception of oneself as being capable of falling in love with a person of the same biological sex. Much of the psychoanalytic literature about homosexuality has been preoccupied with issues of etiology. I am much less interested in this issue except to assert an understanding of homosexuality as an alternative developmental outcome to heterosexuality and bisexuality. I do not see this outcome per se as indicating developmental derailment or biological difference. This is also different from our colleague Shelby's (1994) understanding of homosexuality as an aspect of temperament. It is my observation that there may be some differences between gay men and lesbians regarding this issue, which affect our construction of etiological theory. Anecdotally, many of us know many men who self-attribute homosexuality as genetic and as identifiable to them as soon as they had a construct to organize their perception around. Some women share this self-perception of themselves as having been "born lesbian," but there are also a large number of women who have lived heterosexually but found heterosexuality constricting in terms of gender role identity options for women in relationship to most men. The reason this issue is relevant in this discussion is in reference to working clinically with lesbians and understanding their developmental dilemmas. In addition, I feel the clinical example of women choosing to work through their homosexual longings with the outcome of lesbian identity has something to contribute to a general understanding about the concepts of gender identity, gender role identity, and sexual orientation.

Carmen de Monteflores (1989) describes a number of psychological strategies all of us use to manage those parts of our identities in which we are seen as different from the dominant culture. One such strategy that most of us know well is *passing,* or taking on the language and manners of the dominant culture in such a way that nondominant identity becomes invisible. For gay men and lesbians, passing requires subordinating homosexuality to the status of a superfluous or social detail of identity. The self-talk of this identity sounds like: *I'm gay but so what. What I do in my own bedroom is private. I'm the same as you except for the gender of the person I have sex with.* For example, to pass in this particular moment would require me to assert that whether my patients and myself are gay-identified is irrelevant to our clinical work, that a self psychologically informed therapy unfolds itself similarly regardless of the sexual orientation of the patient or the analyst. Obviously, I'm choosing not to pass in this moment. On the other side of the continuum of strategies de Monteflores describes is *specialization;* that of construing all experience through the lens of specialness—in this case that everything about my therapy with a lesbian client has to do with her lesbianism and my lesbianism. In this moment I'm not choosing this strategy either. At this moment in historical time and place, lesbians and gay men have, I believe, some strategies available to them that were unavailable at the time de Monteflores wrote her article. Relational theorists and constructivists have articulated another option, the option of understanding that our identities, our selves, are formed in a context and are contextually mediated. In one context I may choose to pass, and then my homosexual identity is in the background. In another I may choose to focus on the specialness of my lesbian identity, and then my nonhomosexual identity is in the background. If we accept that the self is formed in an intersubjective and social context, this context is an aspect of any therapeutic relationship. Just like other aspects of the therapeutic relationship that come under the scrutiny of analysis, the sexual orientation of the therapist and the client, the attitudes and beliefs they both hold about sexual orientation, and the times and cultures that have shaped their views must be understood as aspects of the selfobject relationship which are contextually mediated.

How we view aspects of our identity, our selves, has much to do with the mirroring we receive about those aspects, as well as the capacity of those around us to serve idealizing functions—containing, protecting, explaining—when we are injured about displaying aspects of ourselves. These aspects of self are compromised for those of us—and this is all of us—who have grown up learning not only that homosexuality is not the norm, but is deviant. *Gay men are sissies and want to be women. Lesbians are ugly and want to be men.* To be homosexual is, at worst, a crime punishable by disowning and death and, at best, is a tragic or pitiable outcome. While most of us would disavow these ideas as our conscious contemporary perspective, we have assimilated them into our "unconscious organizing principles" (Stolorow and Atwood, 1987) and will continue to reorganize our experience along similar lines until we have intellectually and emotionally reorganized the construct of homosexuality.

One of the consequences of recognizing antihomosexual bias, and as a result reorganizing the construct of homosexuality clinically, may be the capacity to enter into the subjective experience of the client and ascertain whether their presenting issues have any relationship to etiological factors from an experience-near vantage point, as opposed to assuming that their homosexual identity per se is inevitably relevant clinical material. Another impact of redefining homosexuality as an alternative, but seriously stigmatized, developmental outcome could be sensitivity on the part of the clinican to the possibility of shame about homosexual identity on the part of the homosexual client, shame due to selective misattunement by significant others who have been influenced by dominant cultural values around the issues of gender role and sexual orientation. When a client's self-esteem or self-cohesion has suffered from a lack of selfobject functions affirming the lesbian/gay self and attuned responsiveness to injuries to that aspect of the self, self psychological theory would posit that there will be resulting vulnerabilities and disavowals of sectors of experience, which will be remobilized in the transference and rehabilitated in a successful therapy.

In order to prioritize the selfobject dimension of the transference as opposed to the repetitive or reenacting dimension of the transference, the therapist (straight or gay) will need to examine his or her prereflective beliefs about masculinity and femininity, straightness and gayness, biology and destiny. Attitudes about what maleness and femaleness delineate, why one would choose to act on homosexual impulses given social attitudes, whether sexual impulses are drive-based or fragments of relational needs, permeate the theoretical assumptions of both psychoanalysis and sociology. The ideas of social construction, that gender, gender role, and sexual orientation are constructed by those viewing it, add another layer to this issue. One of the great contributions of self psychology has been its capacity to acknowledge the problem with experience-distant hypotheses about client experience and to support the therapist in entering into an experience-near relationship with the client. We all know that this demands more of the therapist in using the countertransference material that emerges. There may be certain client presentations, such as homosexual erotic transferences, homosexual clients whose presenting problems involve relationship or sexual issues, or clients who construct gender role presentations in ways radically unfamiliar to the therapist, which may require extra work on the part of most therapists to examine and contain countertransference responses.

Those of us, straight and gay, who are attempting to illuminate our conscious and preconscious biases about gayness in our work with lesbian and gay clients have special challenges. We have to look carefully at our own beliefs and values and how they influence our reactions to our patients. Do our patients challenge our own beliefs and experiences about maleness and femaleness, about the dangers of resisting dominant norms, about acceptable ranges of sexual expression, about what a healthy relationship looks like? What is our comfort or discomfort in accepting affectionate and sexual feelings from our clients and how does sexual orientation affect our receptiveness? If we codetermine the analyses we participate in, our own conscious and unconscious affects and cognitions about these issues are of central importance in our work.

I've been asked to present a case to illustrate some of the ways in which a lesbian analyst who foregrounds gender and sexual orientation as central organizing principles might conceptualize these ideas clinically. The following case illustrates some of the above ideas, of course embodied in the subjectivity of the client and myself, and the relationship we have created together. I don't believe there is any way to "objectively" describe the progress of this "treatment." I have highlighted areas in which I feel her transference, and mine, have been deeply affected by the ways in which we have each experienced gender, culture, sexuality, femaleness, and sexual orientation, among a myriad of other themes in her work.

I have seen Paula in ongoing therapy twice weekly for 6 years. She was referred to me by a colleague when Paula asked for a referral to an experienced lesbian therapist. Paula was in her mid-twenties when she first presented for treatment, was stably employed in the health care profession, and had been living with her woman lover for several years. Paula stated she felt she needed to be in therapy because she was tormented by the question of whether she should stay or leave her lover and had frequent extremely intense crushes on heterosexual women friends, which were beginning to feel obsessive and burdensome to her and to the recipients of her attentions. She had started to attend a 12-step support group for "sex and love addicts" and was disturbed by her identification with other participants' stories. She felt that "sharing" her story was not enough and that she needed "to get to the bottom" of her symptoms in psychotherapy. When asked what her previous experiences with psychotherapy had been, she replied that they had been good and bad. The good experiences had been with two couples therapists in conjoint treatment of her and her partner; the bad experience had been with a psychologist when she was a teenager. Paula did not want to discuss that earlier psychotherapy initially, and details about it emerged over time.

The initial period of the therapy involved my asking questions and Paula answering at some length about her life and history. She had a good deal of difficulty making eye contact but was highly alert to changes in my mood or health, asking frequently, are you tired? Are you mad at me? I found that the more I explored the reasons behind her questions, the more agitated and paranoid she would become, while if I self-reflected and responded truthfully (I am a little tired, but I feel capable of being here with you; I'm getting a cold, but I sound worse than I feel), she would appear soothed and capable of focusing on her own experience. She quickly entered into transferential work, using me for mirroring functions initially. She would demonstrate this by asking me for "feedback" at the end of each session, which we understood after some time to be her need to see that I had heard her and "digested" what she had to say, picking up themes and relating them to previous sessions. Paula was extremely impressed with my memory and asked me several times if I taped sessions covertly or had special training in memory. What emerged from our exploration of this question was her sense that no one else had listened to her as completely, that she wasn't capable of this kind of listening and understood it, not just as an occupational skill, but as a special gift. Other indications of her need to experience me as an idealizable selfobject became apparent when she would enter the therapy room, take off her shoes, and settle back with a deep sigh. She would often tell me how glad she was to be with me, that everything seemed safer with me near her.

Paula's presentation of past neglect and misattunement was profoundly influenced by her experience of having been uprooted from her first language, extended family, and country of origin at the age of 5. Her parents immigrated with Paula and an older sibling to the United States from a South American country due to a combination of economic and political unrest and the presence of relatives in the U.S. able to sponsor them. Her family had been solidly middle class in the country of her birth, living in a small town with many relatives close by. Upon immigration her parents were forced to work long hours in working class jobs to make it economically. They were cut off from social and cultural supports and their primary language and faced discrimination in the U.S. because of their accents. Paula had a very close relationship with her maternal grandparents, her grandfather in particular, and missed them terribly. Difficulties with the English language slowed down her school progress. She felt stupid and that she didn't fit in.

Much of what Paula remembered of her childhood in this period of the therapy were telescoped images of her mother's unavailability. Her mother had been dependent on her own parents and appeared to her children to be depressed for a long period after emigration. One image that occurred to Paula repeatedly was of herself as a child, between the ages of 6 and 8, waking up very thirsty. She walked out to the kitchen and saw her mother at the sink, staring out the window. She asked her mother for water and her mother appeared not to hear her and then, startled, snapped at Paula and told her to go back to bed, that it was too late to be drinking water. Paula stumbled back to bed and cried inconsolably. When she would be reminded of this memory, Paula would often feel thirsty in the moment, sometimes leaving the room for water. When I asked her to stay with the sensation if she could, she would often cry, rocking herself and whispering in Spanish, poor little one, pobrecita. We came to understand together that this memory, almost like a self-state dream, was a representation of a disavowed affect, the desire for responsiveness from a significant female figure. When I interpreted that this longing may have become sexualized, as a fragment of her original desire for selfobject responsiveness, and thus might explain the function of her "addictive" desires to be sexually engaged with women she felt a desire to be close to, Paula felt deeply understood.

After I was able to appreciate her idealized portrayal of life before emigration, with its sense of belonging, we moved on to understanding her sense of cultural and emotional dislocation. At this point more body-based and sexualized material emerged both in memory and the trans-ference. She described an intensification of desire for a woman in her 12-step group and began to describe sexualized feelings for me. By sexualized feelings, I mean both a preoccupation with sexual sensations and fantasies and a permeability between moments of emotional connection and sexual desire with me. For example, I might experience a moment of emotional connection with her after she would share a memory laden with deep feeling. She would look at my face, which I imagined was conveying appreciation for her emotional vulnerability, and she would ask me, "Do you find me attractive? If it weren't for the therapy rules [about sexual acting out within the therapy relationship which of course had been discussed a number of times], wouldn't you want to be with me? Really be with me?" When I explored what had precipitated this question, we would uncover that she experienced my attentive and interested looks as sexual desire for her. When I would examine this in my own self-reflection and consultation, I consistently found that I had no significant sexual feelings for Paula, but felt strongly maternal and protective feelings for her. My feeling, which was slightly puzzling, was that she wasn't psychologically ready for adult sexuality, much as one might feel for a sexually precocious adolescent displaying sexual readiness before being psychologically mature enough to self-regulate the intensity of sexual experience. Part of what may have allowed me to welcome Paula's sexual and intimate feelings may have been this disavowal of Paula's adult sexual attractiveness and, of course, my growing understanding of the desirability of working through these sexual issues in the transference as opposed to in destructive reenact-ments of both her mother's unavailability and of her own perception of herself as either sexual and unloved or asexual and full of longing.

My first major vacation since her beginning treatment was about a year into the therapy and was several weeks in duration. Upon my return I found multiple teary phone calls from her on my answering machine, which had literally used up the tape. Despite previous arrangements, she had been unable to use the therapist who was on call for me. She came back into therapy and did not bring up the phone calls but reported in a disengaged way about an escalation of her sexual acting out, including a casual sexual contact with a man and having two women ask her not to make any more contact with them after she was "supposedly too intense" (i.e., leaving multiple phone messages, calling frequently to talk or make dates, needing to "process" minor interactions in which Paula felt injured, etc.). When I wondered out loud whether the increase in her compulsive sexuality had to do with her missing me over vacation and that I was struck with the discrepancy between her flat tone now in session and the frantic affect present in her phone calls, she appeared taken aback. A pattern that was becoming clear to me was how, when interpersonal longing came up for her, this affect was intolerable and that her desire for connection fragmented into compulsive sexual activity or obsessive phone calls. The affect present in the phone calls, a desperate desire to be seen and understood, was "bound" by the obsessive and compulsive behaviors.

Shortly after our mutual understanding of the relationship of her longing for mirroring and sexual obsession, Paula brought in several looseleaf binders filled with a lengthy court transcript. "Here," she said. "I figure you need to know about this." When I asked her to explain, she relayed a good deal of historical material regarding a painful period in her adolescence, including her first psychotherapy experience, which she had been previously uninterested in discussing.

The previous therapy she had alluded to was with a male psychologist and was initiated by her mother at the age of 15 after a failed suicidal gesture. The gesture was related to a dawning awareness on Paula's part that she was a lesbian. Paula had been aware since childhood that she was attracted to other girls and wanted to be around them, to touch them, to protect them, and to cherish them. It was also clear to her that this longing was abnormal or wrong, although she couldn't say precisely how or when she learned that. "I just knew I had to hide it." However, few girls wanted to be her friend, seeing her as too tomboyish, not feminine, different, too intense. So she became frustrated socially and sexually. During this period Paula described her father as subjecting her to humiliation regarding her appearance, once dragging her in front of a mirror and yelling, "Look at yourself; you should be ashamed." Paula understood this to be in reference to her weight, which was too heavy according to him, although photographs she brought in of herself at latency age and adolescence show a well-muscled, athletic, normal weight youngster. Paula remembers him telling her she would never marry unless she learned how to act like a woman. He also told her brother that he was a *maricon* (homosexual) when he cried. Apparently influenced by rigid sex role stereotyping, consonant with his generation and cultural upbringing, her father was quite disturbed by the dress and behaviors of his children who were by now thoroughly assimilated into American culture. He was particularly outraged by Paula's refusal to dress in more feminine attire and would force her at family functions to wear lacy and frilly dresses that made her feel uncomfortable. Her mother would not protect her during these episodes and would come to her later begging Paula not to upset her father, to be a good girl.

Paula began to escape into activities that provided her with some version of the recognition she was hungry for. At the age of 11, a male neighbor a few years older than she took her into a basement and promised to be her boyfriend if she would fellate him. She complied. The next time he brought her over to his house, several other boys were there. She performed oral sex on all of them episodically for several years until they pressured her to have intercourse, which terrified her so much that she threatened to tell on them if they ever came near her again. Sexual contact gave her a sense of mastery but she also felt terribly lonely. She realized that she did not feel anything for these boys emotionally and felt hopeless about ever being able to be close to a girl in a sexual way. It was around this period that Paula saw a news story on gay liberation and decided she was a lesbian. This was deeply distressing for her because she saw no models of healthy homosexuals and knew her parents would be devastated by this revelation. She entered into a period of depression and decided to kill herself. She swallowed a bottle of aspirin, went to hide in the basement, and was discovered by her brother, who rushed her to the emergency room. Her stomach was pumped and she was returned home. When her mother asked her why she had tried to kill herself, Paula told her she was gay. Her mother asked her if she was sure; Paula said yes, and her mother left the room in tears. Nothing else was said about this conversation for years.

The hospital had given Paula's parents a referral to a psychologist and she began to attend weekly sessions. The psychologist told her he was sure she was not gay and could prove it to her. Then, according to Paula, the court transcripts, and the jury who convicted the psychologist of statutory rape, the psychologist initiated multiple sexual contacts with Paula during sessions. She described being both confused and pleased by their interaction, since she assumed that she was being cured of her homosexuality by this "treatment." About 7 months into their relationship, Paula asked a schoolmate if it was "right" for a psychologist to be having sex with her. The student told a teacher, who told the police, who asked Paula if she would be willing to go to a session "wired" with recording equipment in case he approached her sexually. She agreed. The wiretap produced sufficient evidence to indict the psychologist, and shortly thereafter the psychologist was arrested and released on bail, and a long trial ensued in which she was a major witness. The psychologist was convicted and his license suspended. Parenthetically a police department in another county recently contacted Paula in the process of investigating sexual complaints against the same psychologist.

Given this history of sexual exploitation, which had been conflated with attempts to socialize Paula to heterosexuality, I assumed that sexual themes would be remobilized in the transference relationship. These themes began to become more prevalent in our work together as Paula

ended several attachments to heterosexual women she had been roman-
tically obsessed with. I became aware of a sexual charge between us
through my own self-consciousness as I became aware of Paula looking
at me for extended periods, commenting upon my clothing, and
discussing her sexual fantasies and experiences with other women at
some length. She also began to bring me presents. Her choices were
very perceptive; she quickly discerned my favorite colors from the office
decorations and my clothes, my interests from my books, my gardening
abilities from flowers I would bring in, my interest in nature from the
rocks and shells in my office, my Jewishness from a Hebrew character
on an earring and my meditation practice from my ability to fold my legs
under me in my office chair. Her gifts reflected much attentiveness to
her perceptions of my specialness and indirectly commented upon her
valuing of my attentiveness to hers. She brought in several dreams about
me, in all of which one of us broke some frame boundary—I brought
other people into the office during her session, we met in a coffee house
or her bedroom for our sessions, or I touched her face tenderly when
she left the session.

After some time of increasing tension, I suggested she must both long
for me to be sexually close to her, which would make her feel loved and
lovable, and also must be hoping that she could explore these feelings in
the therapy without them being acted upon in any overtly sexual way.
She denied this in the moment but came back in the next session and
said her lover had told her that she was lucky to have me as a therapist.
When I asked why, she said, "because I get to talk about what I feel for
you without fucking or getting fucked." Exploration of these comments
revealed that she meant not only that she could talk about her sexual
and intimate feelings without me requiring sexual contact in order to
remain in relationship to her, but also that I was able to tolerate her
sexual feelings without becoming angry or retaliative with her, as many
other women (primarily heterosexual) had, usually after an initial period
in which Paula experienced them as being flattered or interested.

This series of insights precipitated a long period in the therapy in
which she was very interested in the phenomenon of transference,
particularly in how I would describe her needs of me as symbolically
enacted in the therapy—the gifts as a way of binding me to her in addition to her gratitude, her sexual desires as sexual but also as a somatic
way of concretizing her desire to be emotionally close, and her fantasies
of being breastfed by me as a form of her longing for the closeness with
her mother that had been ruptured. She also began to state that she
"wasn't ready" to be friends with women yet, given her powerful transferential needs of them, which were still incompletely understood.

My experience of Paula was that she was developing a stronger lesbian identity and, as a result, a more cohesive sense of self, through my toleration and mirroring of her sexual and emotional transferential love for me. Unlike the little girls in her childhood and adolescence or the heterosexual recipients of her adulthood crushes, I did not reject her. Unlike the boys in her neighborhood and the disastrous encounter with the psychologist, I did not exploit her desire for attention and recognition by requiring sexual favors. While at times the intensity of her longing and the sexual nature of her imagery was unnerving to me, the more I could interpret this sexualization as a fragmentation of her original desire to connect, the more she was able to channel her sexuality into her primary relationship and to begin to experience emotional intimacy in more symbolic, less concretely sexual ways. Because intimacy and sexual desire had become conflated for her early in her history, she felt shame about her desire for both, and as she felt more capacity to feel positively about her lesbian identity, she also felt more capable of feeling positively about her needs to be vulnerable.

This maturation of an archaic selfobject need took an interesting form in the next period of the psychotherapy, in which Paula began to write to me. Her enactments externally had substantially diminished, including hypersexualization, obsessive thinking about unavailable women, and heightened sensitivity to my perceived inattentiveness. Instead, she began to share with me an extensive journalling process in which she reviewed the origins of her sexual obsessions, remembered her childhood home in another country, and struggled with questions about her lesbian identity and difficulty making friends with women. The letters became increasingly longer, sometimes up to 20 pages, some handwritten, some typed. When I asked her what she wanted from me about the letters, she was able to say that she wanted to be completely known by me and that the time of the sessions was inadequate to that. They were becoming increasingly articulate and definitely showed a side of Paula that I rarely saw in person, a vulnerable, highly self-reflective, philosophical voice with a good deal of insight. At this point in the treatment I felt like a treasured aunt, similar to the "good uncle" transference Shelby (1994) describes in his experience as a gay man treating gay men when his patients begin to see him as an uncle figure who tells them, it's okay, you're just going to grow up gay. I felt that Paula was reconstructing a narrative of her history in which she was able to put much of her experience in the context of her having longed to be close to other girls and women and having felt like a sexual freak because of the inability of her surround to attune to her, not her inability to conform to her surround. The themes of displacement, assimilation, and homelessness appeared often, as did the redemptive power of love and the peace she experienced as she was able to identify and modulate previously puzzling affects, like anger and suspiciousness. These affects were now seen by her as signals of an experience of narcissistic injury and were also associated with the dysfunctional coping skills of her father, who dealt with feelings of humiliation and powerlessness by lashing out angrily and suspiciously at his family.

Paula and I had a crisis with the letters when I continued to insist that the content of the letters needed to be brought into the sessions in some form, whether that might be her reading them, me reading them, or her presenting me with the themes that were most important to her. I began to feel this was more crucial when she would refer to "the dream I told you about in the letter" or "that important thing I wrote you about" and would refuse to elaborate. The content of the sessions began to feel more and more dissociated from the content of the letters which were almost a parallel therapy. My own anxiety escalated as I began to feel like I wasn't "digesting" the volume of material in a thoughtful way and as I began to feel resentful about the extra time involved in reading the letters, which Paula couldn't reimburse me for. Paula experienced my comments about this and attempts to find a mutual solution as a rejection of her and an indication that I was overburdened by her, which made her both frightened and angry. She canceled a session for the first time and threatened to terminate the therapy. I decided to write her a brief letter which I read to her in a subsequent session, wherein I appreciated the vulnerability and openness she had shown me in allowing me to read her letters and that I needed certain conditions in order to use them productively in the therapy. Since the ocean was a powerful metaphor between us, I used the example of choosing not to ride each of a set of powerful waves, but to take the time to get in position and to enjoy the ride, coming safely into shore. I needed more time in sessions to deeply understand what she was trying to share with me, and I was becoming overwhelmed in a way that was diminishing my effectiveness as her therapist. She was quite responsive to this communication and we came to understand that, either unconsciously or as a consequence of our mutual vulnerabilities, I had experienced her intense desires for merger and mirroring yet again, but in a more symbolic form. My description of my needs and their intersection with hers initiated another period in the treatment, in which she became more genuinely interested in me as a person separate from her and was more tolerant of selfobject failures, assuming they might be unintended instead of the result of malevolence or incapacity.

This interest in mutuality took the form of a great hunger for information about relationships between women. She borrowed a number of books from my office, including the works of the Stone Center, and came back to sessions enlivened about the information she found there. "It's what I wanted with my mother," she said, "this kind of closeness, this mutual impact, this mutual recognition. It's what I have with you but there are limits because our relationship can't be really mutual; it's focused on me. I don't want to hear about your other clients or your partner but now I can imagine that you have them. I want you to have them; that's what allows you to be you, and to be here with me." This good intention was sorely tested when we ran into each other outside of the therapy room in a public park. I was carrying an infant. In the session following our contact, Paula had difficulty making eye contact and problems talking at all. When I wondered out loud what it had meant to her to see me with a baby, she eventually exploded with multiple fantasies, that the baby was mine by adoption or my partner's, that I was going to cut back my practice to spend more time with the baby and would need to see her less, that eventually I would leave clinical work entirely in order to devote myself to the baby. She wanted to be the baby, to suckle at my breast, to be held by me that closely. And she could tell the baby was a girl and very feminine and that's what I wanted, not a big old baby like her. In subsequent sessions she brought in dreams about penetrating me, impregnating me, about me impregnating her. We came to understand that her dawning ability to conceptualize our relationship as intersecting subjectivities, with her having experienced enough structure building to hold onto her self of herself in relationship, was too fragile to handle the loaded sight of me "mothering" someone else. This image recapitulated her experience of her mother wanting another girl, a more feminine girl. Our previous closeness had again become concretized and sexualized. If she couldn't be the baby, she would give me a baby. If she couldn't give me a baby, she'd have sex with someone else.

Eventually, this disruption was worked through. An interesting result was Paula's emerging interest in small children. Paula began to be able to imagine herself in a mothering role, and she and her partner started some dialogue about the possibility of having or adopting a child at some future date. This corresponded with Paula's increased separation from her own nuclear family, whom she continued to experience as misattuned to her, particularly to her lesbian self. Their religion considered homosexuality a sin, and rather than debate that issue as she may have previously, she minimized contact with them.

Burch (1993) discusses the potential space in lesbian relationships for gender role fluidity, or play. She argues that gender role identity is multiple, not fixed, and that lesbians have a high degree of freedom to reconceptualize maleness and femaleness in their identities and relationships. I have experienced this to different extents in different relationships, both personal and professional, but I experienced it particularly with Paula. As a young girl, she feared that she was a boy, not because she was confused about her sex, but because sexual desire for women was clearly the territory of men. As she grew older, in order to seek out lesbian relationships, she learned how to be sexually aggressive, typically seen as a male prerogative. Her lack of interest in conventionally feminine activities and appearance furthered this assumption on the part of others, as did her identification with her father and his more aggressive behavioral style. However, in her therapy, Paula was very preoccupied with "feminine" themes of relationship, vulnerability, and permeability of boundaries. Her most urgent hunger with me was to know me and to be known, to participate in mutual recognition, which is eloquently described by Benjamin (1988) to be assigned to women. In response to this need on her part, I felt a strong pull to be the "masterful mother" (Burch, 1993) Paula had had so little experience of. I felt more feminine, more receptive, more maternal, more enthusiastically mirroring than with others; I also experienced strong needs to individuate and to set boundaries, a more typically masculine task. Together, I experienced our relationship as consciously examining and expanding both our definitions of femaleness.

Paula and I continue in our work together. Her sexual acting out is no longer an active issue. She has taken up several sports and a spiritual practice which require her interested attentiveness to her physical and emotional experience. She has cautiously started some friendships with women, having consciously identified that she would be less likely to sexualize with lesbian women in stable relationships than with the heterosexual single women she had attempted to befriend previously. She and her partner, with whom she has now been involved for over a decade, continue to grow in intimacy and commitment. They discuss the possibility of adopting or having a child.

The process of asking Paula for permission to use some of her material for this presentation has been an interesting enactment of a number of the themes of our work. After working through some of my initial concerns about her history of exploitation, I decided to give her the choice to be presented or not. As had happened at several other points in our work, she initially said yes to a request of mine and then came back some time later with a strong no. When we explored this sequence, Paula described her initial need to preserve the relationship at any cost, including losing sight of her own preferences, then an increasing sense of unrest and self-alienation, culminating in strong feelings of entitlement to setting boundaries and saying no, even at the fantasized cost of the relationship. The act of saying no and my acceptance and appreciation of her capacity to self-assert then allowed her to get in touch with her curiousity about the purpose of the presentation. When I explained that its purpose, in my mind, was to show how important healing shame about lesbian identity can be for the psychological health of some lesbians, she was able to empathize with my goals and restate her consent. "If someone else can get a therapist who understands about that because of what you say about me, I'd feel pretty good." While there may be ways in which my request reactivated experiences of exploitation, fears of the consequences of saying no or saying yes, and conscious or unconscious perceptions of a dangerous specialness, I also believe this interaction has allowed us to achieve some mutual recognition. I honor her courage in allowing me to share my perceptions of her work and of her impact on me.

In closing, my work with Paula is one of a number of experiences I have had in my identity as a lesbian self psychologist, particularly in my work with lesbians, where I see my feminism, my lesbianism, and my intellectual understanding of intersubjective relational theory affecting the way I view the process of therapy. These aspects of my self-experience are critical to the transferences I evoke and that I bring to my work. While I don't (usually) believe that it is necessary to be lesbian or gay to work successfully with lesbian or gay clients, I do believe that in working with stigmatized aspects of self-experience, like femaleness, nonwhite racial identity, homosexual sexual orientation, and disability, that consciousness of the biases we bring and the stimulus value we hold through our own allegiances or resistances to dominant cultural norms is necessary. My own experiences, such as the one I described at the beginning of the chapter, have sensitized me to awareness of how difference is internalized. In addition my own explorations of gender role and sexuality have, I believe, allowed me to tolerate the vast range of expressions my patients bring to our work. While intellectual discussions of intersubjectivity and relationality have become much more tolerated in our professional discourse, our case presentations seldom reflect therapist identifications, the ways in which we bring our socialization as well as our psychology to the analytic encounter. As we explore the ways we individually construct our pictures of gender, gender role, and sexual orientation, we can begin to illuminate the ways in which our patients' self-experiences have been constructed in their particular nexus of culture, generation, and family, and the play back and forth between our woundedness and theirs, our healing and theirs. I can only hope that more of us will continue in the work of revising psychoanalytic thinking from within to more particulary reflect our experience and those of our clients.

REFERENCES

Bacal, H. (1985), Optimal responsiveness and the therapeutic process. In: *Progress in Self Psychology, Vol. 1,* ed. A. Goldberg. New York: Guilford.

Benjamin, J. (1988), *The Bonds of Love.* New York: Pantheon Books.

Boden, R., Hunt, P. & Kassoff, B. (1987), Shame and the psychology of women. Unpublished paper presented at the annual meeting of the Association of Women in Psychology, March, Denver, CO.

Burch, B. (1993), Gender identities, lesbianism, and potential space. *Psychoanal. Psychol.,* 10:359–375.

Corbett, K. (1993), The mystery of homosexuality. *Psychoanal. Psychol.,* 10:345–357.

De Monteflores, C. (1989), Strategies for managing difference. In: *Contemporary Perspectives on Psychotherapy with Lesbians and Gay Men,* ed. Stein and Cohen. New York: Plenum.

Frommer, M. (1994), Homosexuality and psychoanalysis: Technical considerations revisited. *Psychoanal. Dial.,* 4:215–234.

Gould, D. (1995), A critical examination of the notion of pathology in psychoanalysis. In: *Lesbians and Psychoanalysis,* ed. J. Glassgold & S. Iasenza. New York: The Free Press.

Isay, R. (1989), *Being Homosexual.* New York: Farrar, Straus & Giroux.

Jordan, J., Kaplan, A., Miller, J. B., Stiver, I. & Surrey, J. (1991), *Women's Growth in Connection.* New York: Guilford.

Kassoff, B. (1993), *Shame and Blame in Feminist Groups.* Unpublished paper presented at the Redefining the Givens of Feminist Psychology conference, Jan., Berkeley, CA.

—— Boden R., De Monteflores, C., Hunt, P. & Wahba, R. (1995), Coming out of the frame: Lesbians and psychoanalysis. In: *Lesbians and Psychoanalysis,* ed. J. Glassgold & S. Iasenza. New York: The Free Press.

Kohut, H. (1984), *How Does Analysis Cure?* ed. A. Goldberg & P. Stepansky. Chicago: University of Chicago Press.

Mitchell, S. (1981), The psychoanalytic treatment of homosexuality: Some technical considerations. *Internat. Rev. Psycho-Anal.,* 8:63–80.

—— (1988), *Relational Concepts in Psychoanalysis.* Cambridge, MA: Harvard University Press.

Ornstein, P., & Orstein, A. (1985), Clinical understanding and explaining: The empathic vantage point. In: *Progress in Self Psychology, Vol. 1,* ed. A. Goldberg. New York: Guilford.

Shelby, R. D. (1994), Homosexuality and the struggle for coherence. In: *Progress in Self Psychology, Vol. 10,* ed. A. Goldberg. Hillsdale, NJ: The Analytic Press.

Stolorow, R. & Atwood, G. (1992), *Contexts of Being.* Hillsdale, NJ: The Analytic Press.

—— Brandchaft, B. & Atwood, G. (1987), *Psychoanalytic Treatment.* Hillsdale, NJ: The Analytic Press.

Chapter 15

A Discussion of Lesbians and Psychoanalytic Culture and a Response to Kassoff's Treatment Of a Homosexual Woman

Sharone Abramowitz

This chapter serves two purposes. It comments on Kassoff's psycho-analytic psychotherapy of a lesbian patient, and it discusses the historical and cultural position of lesbians within psychoanalysis. We felt that offering only a discussion of Kassoff's case would be insufficient. Because this is self psychology's first real dialogue about female homo-sexuality, we felt that her case required placement within its wider psychosocial context. To discuss an analytic treatment of lesbians with-out this view would be like discussing the psychodynamics of gender without looking at the culture of sexism.

I will begin by offering a few comments on Kassoff's interesting work with her lesbian patient, Paula. First, her work is a rich example of how self psychology can be successfully blended with cutting edge analytic feminist theory and new perspectives on lesbian development. As I will discuss later, Kassoff's awareness of the psychodynamics of cultural

Adapted from a presentation for the 18th Annual Conference on the Psychology of the Self, San Francisco, October 1995.

positioning is grossly neglected within psychoanalysis, yet one cannot accurately discuss lesbianism without this perspective. Paula's story poignantly illustrates how the integration of a lesbian identity depends on the particular cultural milieu in which the patient sits. She was shamed for being tomboyish, seen as "unfeminine," "unmarriageable," and "too American." If Paula had become heterosexual, the humiliation for not fitting into a culturally prescribed gender role might have faded away. Instead, after Paula recognized herself as lesbian, her culture's, and in particular her religion's, even greater shaming of her "sinful" sexual orientation built upon this early shaming for gender role transgressions. I agree with Kassoff, one cannot discuss lesbian psychology without running right into the convergence of sexuality, gender role identity, and enculturation.

Second, I appreciated Kassoff's frank discussion of the sexualized aspects of Paula's transference to her. As it sounds like Kassoff did, it is especially important in analytic work with lesbian patients to emphasize both the symbolic and the embodied realities of their sexual feelings. Lichtenberg, Lachmann, and Fosshage (1992) brought concrete sexuality back into self psychology when they included within their five self-motivational systems, the sensual–sexual system. When self psychology rejected the sexual reductionism of classical psychoanalysis, it left behind (for a time) the very real motivation of our primal sex drive. To ignore the real, adult, and embodied nature of our lesbian patients' sexual desire colludes with shaming of women's sexuality in general, and erasure of lesbian sexuality in particular. Not surprisingly, work with gay men usually does not fall victim to this error. Gay men, as men, typically assert the concrete reality of their sexual desire. This is often not true for lesbians.

And here is one further comment about Kassoff's fine paper. She states that a central theme of work with lesbians is "the experience of difference as deficiency." And of course, this is so true. Psychotherapy with lesbians should strive to heal a narcissism that has been injured by cultural alienation and shaming. But in addition, the work is also about enhancing a hearty self-resiliency that I believe most identified homosexuals and bisexuals possess. Sitting side by side with the deficits are strengths. Within a culture that at a minimum ignores homosexuals and at worst will kill them for their orientation, it takes a great deal of strength to live a life that is true to one's nature, whether that nature feels inborn (a part of one's temperament) or is a choice (because life with another woman offers the possibility of greater gender role options). While the moment of recognition of oneself as lesbian is often traumatic, that moment also holds within it the possibility of liberation into self-authenticity, which is truly profound. Paula's resiliency rested not only on her experience of identifying herself as a lesbian, but also on her experience of immigration from Latin America, another "experience of different." And of course Paula's deep selfobject connection with Kassoff, her admired and beloved therapist, allowed her a twinship experience with Kassoff's self-resiliency as an "out" lesbian psychologist.

I want to thank Kassoff for such a rich chapter. I respect her refusal to shy away from telling us how her subjective position as a lesbian therapist intersected with that of her lesbian patient. I wish that more of our colleagues would tell us of their subjective position as heterosexual therapists when they describe their work with bisexuals and homosexuals.

Now I will move on to the other topic of this chapter, the position of lesbians within psychoanalytic culture. First, what do I mean by *psychoanalytic culture*? In fact, I am really speaking about a *subculture* that sits within a larger western, masculine, and bourgeois intellectual culture. It is a subculture with its own historical language, like "perversion," "masculinity complex," and "negative oedipal complex." It has its own rules of belonging and its own standards of normalcy. Because psychoanalysis emerged out of a modernist and positivist scientific tradition, it tends to ignore its own cultural relativism. It recognizes itself within its explicit theory, its clinical work, and its case presentations. It tends to ignore the spaces in between: what is said behind closed doors yet is left unsaid in public, but nevertheless is assumed; who gets invited to publish and present, and who doesn't; and the crevices where unchallenged bigotry is left to fester.

Let me position myself within psychoanalytic culture. A few years ago a senior self psychologist, whom I greatly admire, expressed surprise at my lack of formal analytic training. "What a shame," she said. "You're so bright." And while I was flattered, my heart got stuck in my throat. I did what we lesbians know only too well how to do. I quickly gathered myself and responded with a half-truth. I told her that our local institute was too anti–self-psychological and that there were no training analysts here with whom I would feel comfortable. I didn't also tell her that the same institute wouldn't, at that time, have allowed me in because of my sexual orientation. Even if they had, their biases against homosexuality would have been just as difficult for me as their biases against self psychology.

What I also didn't say and is especially pertinent to this discussion was that I was in the midst of a long-term psychotherapy with a lesbian psychologist. Because we lesbians, bisexuals, and gay men, until recently, have been shut out of American psychoanalytic institutes, and analysis with an "out" lesbian training analyst would have been an impossibility. Partially because of professional bias against us, I needed the twinship experience of working with an admired lesbian psychotherapist as I entered into my work.

I begin with this personal information because I will ask each of you to consider your own cultural position with regard to sexual orientation as I proceed with this discussion. The issue of lesbians and psychoanalysis is as much about culture as it is about theories of gender and sexuality. It is about how cultural bias disappears into theory, becomes institutionalized as the bias is being denied, and then reemerges within the space between psychoanalytic therapist and patient. As psychoanalysis creeks and groans out of its modernist biases, it has an opportunity to face its enculturation.

We self psychologists reject notions of "objectivity," of "blank screen neutrality," and of "experience-distant" interpretations. Instead, we embrace "empathy," "understanding before explaining," "experience-near" interpretations and "intersubjectivity." Kohut's (1984) recognition that the boundaries between therapist and patient are delimited by introspection and not the extrospection that connects the natural scientist to her specimen, revolutionized psychoanalysis. It shoved psychoanalysis into the emerging postmodern world.

While I respect Kohut's (1984) courageous vision of psychoanalysis as a relative space and his insistence that the domain of psychoanalysis is bounded by the intrapsychic, I believe that his vision fell slightly short. By insisting that psychoanalysis's terrain is not the "interpersonal," the culture that envelops the psychoanalytic process, the greater relativity that encompasses, shapes, and influences the particular relativities of analyst and analysand can become unseen. As I say this, I hear an argument. It goes something like this: "Of course, the patient's particular cultural influences enter into the analytic dialogue. They become incorporated into their unconscious organizing principles." Yes, but how these are greeted and intersected by the psychotherapist depends on the therapist's willingness to look long and hard at her or his own cultural boundaries, biases, and influences, and these include those of the psychoanalytic community in which she or he sits.

While some might dismiss this as merely a "political" issue, I argue that this is a clinical issue. As Kohut (1984) wrote, "Prejudicial tendencies deeply ingrained in us will often decisively influence what part of the potentially available data we perceive, which among the perceived items we consider important, and, ultimately, how we choose to explain the data that we selectively perceive" (p. 38). While most self psychologists accept Atwood's and Stolorow's (1984) idea that the space between psychotherapist and patient is an intersubjective one, a space where the therapist's and patient's unconscious organizing principles intersect, we have a harder time accepting what that means with regards to power and prejudice.

The power differential between therapist and patient widens if the therapist inhabits cultural spaces of privilege that the patient does not. And it widens further if the patient inhabits spaces that the culture especially maligns, such as is the case between a heterosexual analyst and a lesbian analysand. If the analyst does not examine this, then unconsciously she or he could, at best, impede the patient's growth toward accepting her whole self and, at worst, could subtly (or not so subtly) shame her regarding her identity as a lesbian.

At the 1990 national self psychology meeting, Trop and Stolorow presented Trop's case of a man who worked through his defensive use of anonymous sexual encounters with other men. The patient eventually entered into a stable heterosexual relationship, which Trop felt was an authentic outcome for this man. The case was later published in *Psychoanalytic Dialogues* (Trop and Stolorow, 1992). After the oral and published presentations, the authors faced a barrage of criticism. The criticism centered on how Trop during his presentation didn't discuss how his heterosexual identity might have unconsciously influenced the intersubjective mix between him and his analysand.

In a published response to the criticisms, Stolorow and Trop (1993) state that they make no judgments about heterosexuality versus homosexuality. If the man had heterosexual defensive enactments against his true homosexual nature, they would have presented that case as well. I accept that Trop and Stolorow have no overt biases against homosexuality. Trop and Stolorow did not discuss during their case presentation, however, the psychological impact of their culture, which privileges heterosexuality. Thus the unconscious impact that a heterosexual analyst might have over an analysand who is struggling against a desire for sexual contact with other men remained publicly unacknowledged. They did not predict the impact that their article would have on their gay and lesbian colleagues (Stolorow and Trop, 1993). Even when the analyst harbors no explicit prejudice against homosexual behavior, the background culture in which he, his analysand, and his colleagues sit, can deeply devalue such behavior, and this devaluation can unintentionally leak into both the consulting room's intersubjective milieu and the professional meeting ground.

Culture, as carried by the attitudes of others, rituals, institutions, the media, art, and language, serves as a wellspring of vital selfobject experience. Attendance at a heterosexual wedding can enliven the slightly dulled marriage of a straight couple. It can also isolate and alienate a lesbian guest. Thus, a wedding for a heterosexual couple could offer a *positive selfobject experience*, whereas for a lesbian it is likely to provide a *bad selfobject experience*. There is a controversy about whether we should reserve the term *selfobject* for self-sustaining functions (Wolf, 1988). However, like Bacal, Newman, and others, I believe that there is such an animal as the *bad selfobject* (Bacal, 1995). In particular, background culture is especially prone to providing bad selfobject experience. Certainly, we all look toward cultural expressions to provide us with good selfobject experience, to be an "exciting object," to quote Bacal quoting Fairbairn (Bacal, 1995, p. 355). We cherish movies that affirm our truths; we admire leaders who uphold our values. However, since culture is more distant and fixed than the fluid immediacy of interpersonal relationships, culture requires us to adapt to it, rather than the reverse. Thus when the individual deviates from cultural norms, cultural messages will then provide a bad selfobject experience, because the positioning of the person as "deviant" or "perverted" undermines the sense of self. This dynamic plays out frequently for homosexuals.

Certainly, this was true for Paula. For example, Paula learned from her parents and church that it was her duty and destiny to marry a man and mother children. When later, her church condemned her as a sinner for being lesbian, the religion's feminine "ideal" turned into a bad selfobject experience for Paula. As was once true within psychoanalytic culture (until Martha Kirkpatrick [1984] challenged this assumption), Paula's culture assumed that lesbians could not be mothers. Not until Paula saw her therapist carrying an infant in a park could something counteract that negating message. Yes, Paula competed with the infant for mothering from Kassoff. She now knew for sure that she was not Kassoff's only child. But more than that, she also experienced a profound twinship experience (one which her culture never provided) by seeing Kassoff, a lesbian, with a baby. Eventually, she could imagine herself as a mother. The good selfobject experience with Kassoff counteracted the bad selfobject experience of her background culture.

Psychoanalysis, as an institution, still struggles to the accept the issue of cultural relativism. Few of us kindhearted caretakers want to believe that our positions of cultural privilege impact our work with our patients. It is painful to recognize this. As we grow close to our patients through our care for them, we want to believe that we can escape the spaces of privilege that we have over them. When we work within an institution that disparages discussions of the cultural as "polemic" or "unscientific," yet naturally incorporates the biases of the culture in which it sits, it becomes difficult to own these real (yet unacknowledged) dimensions of the therapeutic space.

While a few self psychologists feel overt bigotry towards nonheterosexuals and most want their hearts to be free of such attitudes, many were trained within institutions that grossly pathologized lesbians. It is important to at least briefly review this troubled legacy, to look at what has been traditionally taught about lesbians and we still must struggle with.

Let me begin with Freud. While I reviewed most of Freud's work on lesbianism and female sexuality, it is his paper, "The Psychogenesis of a Case of Homosexuality in a Woman" (Freud, 1920), that most fascinated me. In fact, dare I say this? I enjoyed this paper. Like Adrienne Harris (1991), I enjoyed it for its confusion, biases, and contradictions. Freud's essay truly takes us into the center of the historical quagmire in which psychoanalysis sits with regard to lesbians.

Unlike most later psychoanalytic authors, Freud explicitly positions himself and his lesbian patient within their historical and cultural moment of meeting. He begins by reminding his reader that not only "the law" (that is, society), but also psychoanalysis, has ignored lesbianism (p. 123), a fact that is still true, as seen by the number of articles written about male homosexuals versus the paucity of ones about lesbians. Considering the historical analytic pathologizing of nonheterosexuals, this is both fortunate and unfortunate. Lesbian psychology was usually given direct translation from male homosexual experience. In general, psychoanalysis has ignored the intimate erotic and nonerotic relationships between women, despite the fact that, within the center of early psychoanalytic society, Anna Freud shared a "life partnership," one considered "chaste," with Dorothy Burlingham (Young-Bruehl, 1988, p. 138).

Here is how Freud's (1920) paper introduces his patient:

> A beautiful and clever girl of eighteen, belonging to a family of good standing, had aroused displeasure and concern in her parents by the devoted adoration with which she pursued a certain lady "in society" who was about ten years older than herself. . . . This lady was nothing but a *cocotte*. . . . She lived with a married woman . . . at the same time she carried on promiscuous affairs with a number of men. The girl did not contradict these evil reports, but neither did she allow them to interfere with her worship of the lady, although she herself was by no means lacking in a sense of decency and propriety [pp. 123–124].

As Harris (1991) points out, Freud's patient is never even given a pseudonym. This no-name "woman is relegated to object status"; Harris explains that she "is not positioned" (p. 198). And while I applaud Harris's attempt to rescue the subjectivity of Freud's lesbian patient, I disagree that her anonymous status does not position her. Invisibility or objectification are how lesbians often are positioned within mainstream culture. So the beloved of Freud's patient, a bisexual woman who lives beyond the confines of bourgeoise gender roles, is also left nameless. No name, no status other than "indecent" and "improper" are often given in traditional society when women cannot be defined primarily by their relationship to a man.

Freud's patient came to see him after she threw herself onto railroad tracks. After her father ran into his daughter in the company of her beloved, he shamed her with an "angry glance which boded no good" (p. 124). She became so humiliated that she attempted suicide. The suicidal behavior of Freud's and Kassoff's patients is common among homosexual youth. Developmentally, this time is a period of changing identities, and thus an especially vulnerable time for the self. The suicide attempt is not simply a response to the young person's recognition of herself as lesbian. Rather, at a time when mirroring is desperately needed to consolidate this new and culturally fragile identity, shaming by family can be especially catastrophic.

Freud sympathetically describes his patient's father "as an earnest, worthy man, at bottom very tenderhearted" (p. 137). The father's desperation over his daughter's homosexuality drove him to seek psychoanalysis for her. The daughter herself told Freud "that she could not conceive of any other way of being in love, but she added that for her parents' sake she would honestly help in the therapeutic endeavour, for it pained her very much to be the cause of so much grief to them" (p. 130). This young woman, like so many since, entered analysis caught between a rock and a hard place, squeezed between her true nature and the wish to escape parental and cultural disgust for that nature.

Freud took on the case knowing that there was little hope of a so-called "cure." In this paper, as he did 15 years earlier in the "Three Essays" (Freud, 1905), he struggles with what of sexual orientation is nature versus nurture. He even admits that his patient is not "ill" in the usual analytic sense, that is, suffering from a neurosis. He seemed to take on this case because he both identified with the father's distress and was trying to rescue this young woman from a difficult fate.

On the other hand, Freud joins in with the dominant cultural view that lesbianism is pathological, yet he implies that it is a part of the natural spectrum of human sexuality. As he treats his lesbian patient, Freud struggles between these two conflicting views. However, within a short time, he finds that she and he have arrived at an impasse. Freud wonders "how it is that such marked progress in analytic understanding can be unaccompanied by even the slightest change in the patient's compulsions and inhibitions" (p. 140). And here is where Freud ultimately takes a stand with regards to lesbianism.

He retreats to oedipal reductionism and transposition of male psychological themes onto female psychology to explain his patient's choice of a female love object and her relationship to restrictive gender roles. Although Freud offers no clinical evidence for his conclusions (again the patient disappears; he includes virtually none of her own utterances), he accuses her of a "masculinity complex," of reversing an unresolved oedipal conflict with her father, of wanting to be a man. He assumes that she wishes to assume "a masculine attitude towards the [female love] object" (p. 131). The notion that a woman can intimately relate to another woman in a space that might include, but can't be reduced to identification with the father, is left unacknowledged by Freud.

Freud understood the significance for his patient of her mother favoring boys over girls and the mother's view of her daughter as a competitor—common truths for women raised in rigid patriarchal spaces. Yet Freud strikes a stone of contempt when he says that his patient "was in fact a feminist; she felt it to be unjust that girls should not enjoy the same freedom as boys, and rebelled against the lot of women in general" (p. 146). He referred to her aversion to childbirth as "girlish narcissism" (p. 146). Just as with Kassoff's case, Freud's lesbian case propelled him into the concentric space where gender roles, enculturation, and sexual orientation meet.

As Freud sat in the midst of this muddle, he seems to have unconsciously used his cultural position as a privileged male to organize it. Some contemporary therapists might have interpreted this young woman's feminism as a healthy refusal to confine herself to a narrow range of gender roles. And, like Freud, they might have understood it as a compensation for the narcissistic injury of a mother who favors sons over daughters. However, Freud explained her feminist position as a defensive reaction to the latter. For Freud, his patient's feminism was regression, not progression.

Freud viewed his patient's beloved as a "mother substitute." However, his cultural position possibly kept him from also considering that this unconventional woman could have been, in self psychological terms, both an idealized and twinship selfobject. His young patient suffered genuine sexist assaults on her developing female identity. This made the image of a woman who chose to rebel against gender norms quite an idealizable figure. At the same time, as Freud's patient entered adolescence, she found herself sexually attracted to other women (a common experience in lesbian development). So the fact that her beloved was widely known to live a bisexual lifestyle affirmed, through a twinship selfobject connection, Freud's patient's right to do the same.

In the end, Freud refers his patient to be a woman analyst. He blames this outcome on the patient and not on himself. It was her bitterness against men, he asserts. As Harris (1991) picks up, he uses the sentence, "I broke it off." She suggests that this was Freud's own unconscious allusion to his feeling castrated by the daring of this young woman to inhabit a space that men claimed solely for themselves.

Harris (1991) ends up viewing this woman's overt homosexual object choice as a symbolic heterosexual object choice. She sees the young woman choosing to be a "fictive 'boy' [who] chooses a mother to idealize and save from an oedipal father" (p. 208). This conclusion doesn't include the very real contribution of the patient's genuine sexual attraction to other women. Is this sexualization or real sexual orientation?

This question seems to haunt most analytic discussions of homosexuality, while it rarely comes up in heterosexual cases. Maybe it is because that which is culturally deviant must be explained, while that which is considered normative seems to be self-evident. Even Harris doesn't escape entering into an analysis of the *why* of lesbianism. She tries to reconstruct why a woman has a visceral sexual attraction to another woman. She can't leave her analysis to the *how*, the way a particular woman uses her sexual orientation to resolve her intrapsychic dynamics—something analysis can explore.

This doesn't mean that the dichotomous categories of heterosexual versus homosexual (like feminine versus masculine) shouldn't be questioned. These are socially prescribed categories which contributes to maintaining heterosexuality's privileged position (Foucault, 1978; Cecco and Elia, 1993). But the raw fact that some of us are attracted to the opposite sex, some of us to the same sex, some of us to both sexes, and that some of us switch positions cannot be denied. On the symbolic level our desire, whether enacted with the same sex or the opposite, can still include fantasies of the opposite sex of the person we're actually sexual with (Harris, 1991; Suchet, 1995). A lesbian can image a man with a penis as her girlfriend enters her, and a heterosexual woman can image a woman's breast as she caresses her boyfriend's chest. And of course these symbolic fantasies are eminently analyzable.

However *why* one woman feels sexual desire for another woman, while another woman feels sexual desire for a man, can be analyzed, but not necessarily ultimately understood. While one might conclude that Kassoff's patient, Paula, became a lesbian because of her desire for responsiveness from a significant female figure, that could be a wrong conclusion. I can offer you a similar case from my practice of a woman who lost her mother to mental illness. Her desire for responsiveness from a significant female figure is also powerful. However, she is heterosexual and finds herself longing for noneroticized best female friends. As Freud (1905) reminds us in the conclusion of his essay on female homosexuality: "It is not for psychoanalysis to solve the problem of homosexuality" (p. 148).

While I agree with Harris (1991) that Freud's essay carries the potential for a radical model of sexuality, his "restrictive use of classical interpretation" carried the historical momentum (p. 197). As Deutsch (1995) points out, "[Freud's] descriptive accounts became prescriptive as he lost the fine distinctions between biological determinism and cultural determinism, inevitably conflating gender and sexuality" (p. 20) This led him to see "homosexuality and alternative gender arrangements . . . as aberrant developments, in need of psychoanalytic explanation" (p. 20).

Nevertheless, Freud was a revolutionary thinker, even as he was a man of his historical moment. He partially reached beyond the conventions to view homosexuality with a clearer eye than many of his contemporaries. In the "Three Essays" he recognized that homosexuals could be talented and successful people (Freud, 1905), and unlike his successors, he believed that being homosexual was not a reason to refuse someone analytic training (Deutsch, 1995). But instead of picking up on the progressive threads in his thinking about homosexuality, his successors picked up on his regressive threads. Why?

My belief is that, although Freud was a revolutionary, most of his followers were more conventional. As is true of most institutions, as psychoanalysis aged, a conservatism overtook it. Foreground analytic theory incorporated the background cultural pathologizing of nonheterosexuality. Thus, the few articles written about lesbians rigidly followed narrow reductionistic explanations. Initially, these explanations followed classical theory, and then as psychoanalysis expanded into ego psychology and object relations, lesbian pathologizing was fit into these theories (Deutsch, 1995).

For example, Adrienne Applegarth's 1984 American Psychoanalytic panel on homosexual women, used ego psychology to explain lesbianism. Applegarth viewed it (according to Wolfson, 1984), "as a complicated structure of gratification and defense" (p. 166). She felt that if the steps in the usual positive and negative oedipal phases or if a girl's wish for a baby arising out of penis envy become distorted, a range of outcomes, including homosexuality, could occur (Wolfson, 1984, p. 166).

Joyce McDougall, a frequently referenced analytic author on lesbianism, offers a pathologized pre-oedipal perspective. Referring to McDougall, Deutsch (1995) writes, "She believes that the analyst should not have a preconceived notion that his or her patients should become heterosexual. But this is based on a view of lesbianism not only as a form of loving, but as a dramatic effort at avoiding psychic disintegration" (p. 28). During an analytic panel on homosexual women, McDougall stated that her patients' lesbianism allows for an "intense dependence on their women lovers" and is a defense against separation, abandonment, feelings of depersonalization, and loss of body limits (Wolfson, 1984, p. 169). Here, McDougall seems to conflate lesbianism with severe character pathology.

I could go on with more examples of lesbian pathologizing by Helene Deutsch (1932), Marie Bonaparte (1953), Masud Khan (1979), and Elaine Siegel (1988). Suffice it to say that psychoanalysis has explained lesbianism as reactions to paranoia, borderline states, and narcissism. If lesbianism isn't a neurosis, as Freud argues, yet it isn't normal, this left only one alternative. It had to be deeply characterological.

This is why self psychology became so compelling to those of us who saw great promise in psychoanalysis, even while we bristled at the analytic prejudice against homosexuals and women. First, self psychology replaced oedipal reductionism and "resistance analysis" with an empathic focus on the vicissitudes of the patient's self. Thus, viewing lesbianism as the result of an oedipal process that went awry or as a characterological defense became less of an issue. Second, the focus on selfobject transferences allowed us a way to help our patients repair and feel whole after suffering the narcissistic assaults of homophobic culture. Instead of just reducing lesbianism to a character disorder, self psychology offered us a psychodynamic approach to healing the self disorder caused by cultural bigotry.

This doesn't mean that we self psychologists have escaped the influence of culture and prejudice in our treatment of lesbians. But selfobject and intersubjective theory offer us a way to work with these issues. Selfobject theory allows us to link the social experience of culture to its intrapsychic impact on the self. Intersubjective theory offers us a means to understand how cultural *good* and *bad* selfobject experience can be telescoped into the space between the therapist and the lesbian patient. Overcoming historical psychoanalytic prejudice against sexual minorities can be realized if we psychotherapists remain conscious and not disavow out of our own shame, how this background of prejudice can potentially hamper any of us.

REFERENCES

Atwood, G. & Stolorow, R. (1984), *Structures of Subjectivity*. Hillsdale, NJ: The Analytic Press.

Bacal, H. (1995), The essence of Kohut's work and the progress of self psychology. *Psychoanal. Dial.*, 5:353–366.

Bonaparte, M. (1953), *Female Sexuality*. New York: International Universities Press.

Cecco, J. & Elia, J. (1993), A critique and synthesis of biological essentialism and social constructionist views of sexuality and gender. *J. Homosexuality*, 20:1–26.

Deutsch, H. (1932), On female homosexuality. In: *The Psychoanalytic Reader*, ed. R. Fleiss. New York: International Universities Press, 1948, pp. 208–230.

Deutsch, L. (1995), Out of the closet and on to the couch: A psychoanalytic exploration of lesbian development. In: *Lesbians and Psychoanalysis*, ed. J. Glassgold & S. Iasenza. New York: The Free Press, pp. 19–37.

Foucault, M. (1978), *History of Sexuality*. New York: Vintage.

Freud, S. (1905), Three essays on the theory of sexuality. *Standard Edition*, 7:135–246. London: Hogarth Press, 1953.

—— (1920), The psychogenesis of a case of homosexuality in a woman. *Standard Edition*, 18:145–172. London: Hogarth Press, 1955.

Harris, A. (1991), Gender as contradiction. *Psychoanal. Dial.*, 1:197–224.

Khan, M. (1979), *Alienation in Perversions*. New York: International Universities Press.

Kirkpatrick, M. (1984), Some observations on lesbian women. Panel at American Psychoanalytic Association Annual Meeting, San Diego, CA, May 4.

Kohut, H. (1984), *How Does Analysis Cure?* ed. A. Goldberg & P. Stepansky. Chicago: The University of Chicago Press.

Lichtenberg, J., Lachmann, F. & Fosshage, J. (1992), *Self and Motivational Systems*. Hillsdale, NJ: The Analytic Press.

Siegel, E. (1988), *Female Homosexuality*. Hillsdale, NJ: The Analytic Press.

Stolorow, R. & Trop, J. (1993), Reply to Blechner, Lesser, and Schwartz. *Psychoanal. Dial.*, 3:653–656.

Suchet, M. (1995), "Having it both ways": Rethinking female sexuality. In: *Lesbians and Psychoanalysis*, ed. J. Glassgold & S. Iasenza. New York: The Free Press.

Trop, J. & Stolorow, R. (1992), Defense analysis in self psychology: A developmental view. *Psychoanal. Dial.*, 2:427–442.

Wolf, E. (1988), *Treating the Self*. New York: Guilford.

Wolfson, A. (1984), Toward the further understanding of homosexual women. *J. Amer. Psychoanal. Assn.*, 35:165–173.

Young-Bruehl, E. (1988), *Anna Freud*. New York: Summit Books.

Chapter 16

The Leather Princess: Sadomasochism as the Rescripting of Trauma Scenarios

Doris Brothers

While most of Heinz Kohut's contributions to psychoanalytic theory and technique have gained increasing recognition and acclaim since his untimely death in 1981, his insights about sadomasochism remain relatively unheralded. Kohut's prominence was secured, in large part, through his bold efforts to replace Freud's outdated drive-theory formulations with a psychology of self-experience far more congruent with contemporary thought. It is noteworthy, therefore, that his understanding of sadomasochistic fantasies and their behavioral enactment retraces Freud's earliest steps in theory building to a time when psychoanalysis was guided by a trauma paradigm (Cohen, 1980, 1981). Although a number of investigators (e.g., Menaker, 1953; Stoller, 1975, 1979; Schad-Somers, 1982) produced convincing evidence that Freud's first efforts to explain sadomasochism were on the right track, Kohut's discoveries about selfobject experience pointed the way toward a deeper, more experience-near, and clinically meaningful understanding of the relationship between sadomasochism and trauma.

In this chapter, I first briefly review several theories that link sado-masochism to trauma. I then discuss Kohut's contributions and their elaboration by such others as Ornstein (1974, 1991), Stolorow (1975), Stolorow and Lachmann (1980), and Ulman and Brothers (1988). Next,

I present a fresh understanding of certain sadomasochistic phenomena. Using a self-psychological framework, I have developed a theoretical perspective in which trust betrayal is viewed as fundamental to trauma. From this perspective, sadomasochistic fantasies and their enactment may be understood as the means by which some trauma survivors attempt to "rescript" their trauma scenarios. I conclude with a clinical example of a young woman involved in the "leather community" of sexual sadomasochism.

SADOMASOCHISM AND PSYCHIC TRAUMA

In a 1921 revision of "Beyond the Pleasure Principle," the paper in which Freud described his idea that trauma is compulsively repeated, he hinted that the function of recurrent traumatic nightmares relates to "the mysterious masochistic trends of the ego" (1920, p. 14n). In this and in subsequent writings, Freud explained the essence of masochistic phenomena in terms reminiscent of his explanation of the repetition compulsion in that both were manifestations of the death instinct (e.g., Freud, 1937). However, as Freud developed his understanding of masochism, he increasingly downplayed its roots in trauma and emphasized instead its relationship to the psychological development of women (Freud, 1919, 1924, 1925). We are all familiar with Freud's developmental scenario in which the little girl, in the phallic phase of development, recognizes the penis as a superior genital and is consumed by envy. Noticing that her mother does not possess a penis, the child assumes her mother deprived her of one. Consequently, she renounces her mother as primary love object and turns to her father. If development proceeds optimally, she gives up her wish for a penis and replaces it with a wish to have a child by her father. From this point on, the girl's personality develops a masochistic character. In subsequent writings, Freud (1919) made it clear that masochism is always "feminine" regardless of whether it occurs in men or in women.

Even in Freud's own time, such analysts as Adler (1927) and Horney (1924, 1926, 1933) took strong exception to his understanding of masochism. A number of contemporary analysts, recognizing the connection between sadomasochism and trauma, have emphasized its self-restitutive function. Menaker (1953), for example, suggested that masochistic self-hatred, self-devaluation, and feelings of worthlessness are the outcome of traumatic deprivation and serve self-preservation insofar as they are "a means of perpetutating whatever bond there is to the mother" (p. 224). Stoller (1975, 1979) viewed sadomasochism and other "perversions" as fantasies that revive traumatic childhood experiences of victimization in order that these humiliating experiences may be transformed into triumphant victories. Similarly, Bach and Schwartz (1972) interpreted the sadistic and masochistic fantasies of the Marquis de Sade as functioning to stave off narcissistic decompensation.

It is in the elucidation of this concept that Kohut's discoveries are indispensable. From Kohut's (1977) perspective, narcissistic decompensation as it relates to sadomasochism results from traumatic disappointment in those experienced as selfobjects and the consequent need for self-restitution. For example, in discussing the case of Mr. A, who suffered severe developmental traumas related to shattering disappointments in his parents as a providers of selfobject experiences, Kohut (1977) wrote:

> This patient's sadistic fantasies—the chaining of the self-object in order to rob it of its power—became understandable when examined within the framework of the relation of the self to the self-object. . . . The puzzling nature of sexual masochism, too, is broadly illuminated if examined in the light of the explanation that, after the child's healthy merger wishes with the idealized imago breaks into fragments, the merger needs are sexualized and directed toward these fragments. The masochist attempts to fill in the defect in the part of the self that should provide him with enriching ideals through a sexualized merger with the rejecting (punishing, demeaning, belittling) features of the omnipotent parental imago [p. 127].

Kohut's (1979) famous case study, "The Two Analyses of Mr. Z," which appears to have been based on his own life (Cocks, 1994), illustrates the dramatic differences between a traditional psychoanalytic understanding of sadomasochism and a self-psychological approach. Using a classical drive-theory understanding, Kohut viewed Mr. Z's masochistic fantasies as resulting from his presumed oedipal victory over his absent father. In other words, his masochism was blamed on intrapsychic processes involving a pathological fantasy of defeating the father.

When viewed from the vantage point of self-psychological theory, the same masochistic fantasies were understood in terms of traumas Mr. Z had incurred in his relationship with his mother. Kohut suggested that Mr. Z's fantasies of being forced to perform sexually by a strong, demanding, insatiable woman were reflections of his experience of psychological enslavement by his mother.

Concomitant with this shift in understanding of the meaning of Mr. Z's masochistic fantasies was a shift in understanding of their function. In keeping with classical theory, they would be seen as providing unconscious protection against castration. Using a self-psychological perspective, Kohut viewed their function, particularly insofar as they accompanied masturbation, as enabling Mr. Z to experience "the reassurance of being alive, of existing" (p. 425). In other words, they served self-restorative functions.

Implicit in Kohut's conceptualization of sadomasochism is the idea that it must be understood within a relational context. The meaning and function of Mr. Z's masochistic fantasies are comprehensible only within the intersubjective field created by him and his mother. As Stekel (1929) expressed it, "There is no sadism without masochism, and no masochism without sadism" (p. 138).

Anna Ornstein (1974, 1991), building on Kohut's approach, also suggested that sadomasochism, or what she prefers to call "self-defeating" behaviors, originates in childhood trauma. She viewed masochism as arising out of the child's experience of the emotional environment as indifferent, while she associated sadism with childhood experiences in which the emotional environment is unpredictable, volatile, and violent. Stolorow (1975) and Stolorow and Lachmann (1980) concerned themselves with what they termed the "narcissistic function" of masochism and sadism. They understood the masochistic search for acute pain by a person with a "diffuse or dissolving self-representation" in terms of his or her need for "a desperate exaggeration of experiences." Such exaggeration provides a sense of being alive and real, of existing as a "bounded entity" (1980, pp. 32–33).

Richard Ulman and I (Ulman and Brothers, 1988) extended these insights in our effort to understand women's rape fantasies. We concluded that they are best conceptualized as symbolic expressions of trauma, as well as faulty efforts at self-restitution. Rape fantasies from this perspective are associated with traumas that attend growing up in a society in which male power and female subordination are blatantly manifested. In other words, a woman's fantasies of herself in relation to others represented as providing mirroring, idealizing, or twin selfobject experiences may be shattered by situations involving the devaluation or disempowerment of women. Rape fantasies not only symbolically express these shattering experiences, but also, insofar as women who create the fantasies regain a sense of power and control in doing so, they often prove restorative. This formulation derives from a self-psychological theory of trauma in which self-experience is held to be organized by unconscious fantasies of self in relation to selfobjects.[1] Trauma, according to the "shattered fantasy" theory, is defined as "a real occurrence, the unconscious meaning of which so shatters central

---

[1] I subsequently discovered that the selfobject fantasies that organize self-experience consist not only in fantasies of oneself as the recipient of selfobject experience provided by others, but also in fantasies in which one is represented as providing selfobject experiences for others (Brothers, 1992, 1995a).

organizing [selfobject] fantasies that self-restitution is impossible" (p. 3). My subsequent study of trust and its betrayal has led me to propose a number of refinements of the shattered fantasy theory of trauma that bear on the relationship between trauma and sadomasochism.

TRAUMA AS THE BETRAYAL OF "SELF-TRUST"

In the belief that the importance of trust for the development, maintenance, and restoration of self-experience has been insufficiently recognized, I (Brothers, 1992, 1995a, b, c) have recently investigated the aspect of trust that most vitally pertains to selfobject experience and its traumatic disruption. I contend that in the absence of "self-trust," as I call this sort of trust, selfobject experience is impossible. Self-trust, defined as the hope or wishful expectation of receiving or providing for others, the selfobject experiences on which cohesive selfhood depends, comprises four dimensions: trust-in-others—the tendency to view others as trustworthy providers of selfobject experiences; trust-in-self—the tendency to view oneself as capable of eliciting selfobject experiences from others; self-as-trustworthy—the tendency to view oneself as a trustworthy provider of selfobject experiences for others; and others-as-self-trusting—the tendency to view others as trusting of their capacity to obtain and provide selfobject experiences.

As a result of my attempt to understand the nature of various disturbances in self-trust that I found among trauma survivors, I discovered that trauma not only shatters selfobject fantasies; it profoundly affects the survivor's perception of reality as well. In keeping with Noy's (1980) thesis that all areas of cognitive functioning, including thinking, perception, and communication, develop and operate simultaneously in two organizational modes—the self-centered mode that employs primary process and the reality-oriented mode that employs secondary process[2]— I propose that in tandem with the largely unconscious realm of selfobject fantasy is the realm of "subjective reality." In this realm, which operates according to the reality-oriented, secondary process organizational mode, self and others are consciously experienced as separate, independent centers of initiative.[3]

---

[2] In contrast to traditional Freudian analysts who believed primary process to be nothing more than a primitive discharge system, Noy (1980) viewed the two organizational modes as forming "two developmental lines whose courses of development are determined by the same intrinsic maturational factors" (p. 172). In other words, the primary process mode normally develops synchronously with the secondary process mode.

[3] The two organizational modes appear to be congruent with research on the lateralization of function in the cerebral hemispheres (Gardner, 1975; Gazzaniga, 1983; Geschwind, 1981; Sperry, 1984). The right hemisphere, associated with self-referential awareness and "felt-meaning," appears

Self-trust operates in the shadowy region that connects the world of selfobject fantasy and the world of subjective reality. This is, I believe, the same psychological locale in which Winnicott (1951, p. 2) located transitional phenomena, the "intermediate area of experiencing, to which inner reality and external life both contribute" and in which Kohut's (1971, 1977, 1984) bridging concept of transmuting internalization also belongs.

Self psychologists focus primarily on that which is observable via introspection and empathy, that is, on the realm of selfobject fantasy. Anything else, as Kohut (1959, 1981) cogently argued, belongs to the domain of the natural sciences and not to psychoanalysis. At the same time, Kohut has persuasively demonstrated that self-experience (and, therefore, the unconscious selfobject fantasies that organize it) is powerfully shaped by the ways in which children perceive the responsiveness of their caretakers according to the reality-oriented mode—for example, how empathically attuned they are—just as the restoration of self-experience depends on patients' perceptions of their therapists' responsiveness. Self-trust, like Kohut's concept of transmuting internalization, helps to explain how interactions between self and others affect self-organization. Insofar as self-trust is determined by our interactions with others but is accessible only via introspection and empathy, it may be thought of as a sort of psychological corpus callosum connecting subjective reality and selfobject fantasy. That is, we place trust in ourselves and others as participants in selfobject relationships on the basis of interpersonal interactions that are evaluated according to highly idiosyncratic criteria.[4] Only those who meet our self-trust criteria will be represented in selfobject fantasies. Consequently, the developmental transformation of self-experience, as well as its cohesiveness and vitality, depend on the trustworthiness of our selfobject connections with others. As long as we are convinced that we and others are trustworthy, our selfobject fantasies remain intact and we are likely to enjoy a sense of comfort, familiarity, safety, and general well-being in our lives.

I contend that it is the betrayal of self-trust that lies at the heart of trauma. In other words, the meanings that shatter selfobject fantasies are those involving betrayals of trust in oneself or in others as providers of selfobject experiences. Selfobject fantasies shattered by self-trust betrayals can be restored only when trust in selfobject relationships is reestablished. Because those experienced as betrayers will not be represented

---

to correspond to the self-centered mode, while the left hemisphere, associated with language as the core for all symbolic cognition, appears to correspond to the reality-oriented mode.

[4] These criteria tend to change over the course of development, becoming more realistic (less phantasmagorical and perfectionistic), abstract, complex and differentiated.

in selfobject fantasies, survivors must alter their experience of subjective reality so that self and/or others are experienced as trustworthy despite evidence to the contrary. While this alteration is necessary to quell mounting disintegration anxiety and the looming menace of psychological catastrophe, it has many psychological drawbacks. The experience of subjective reality loses its clarity and distinctness as the meanings of traumatizing betrayals are disavowed (Basch, 1983) and the maturation of thought processes on which this experience depends is arrested.

As Noy (1980) has pointed out, healthy self-experience depends on there being a sound balance between the self-centered (primary process) and the reality-oriented (secondary process) organizational modes and on both modes reaching optimal levels of development and maturation. The shattering of selfobject fantasies and attempts at their restoration not only interfere with the developmental transformation of these fantasies (Ulman and Brothers, 1988), but insofar as trauma profoundly affects the experience of subjective reality, it creates imbalances between the two organizational modes. These imbalances are primarily responsible for dissociative phenomena such as depersonalization, derealization, and disembodiment.

The dissociative alteration of subjective reality is reflected in changes that take place in the organization of the trauma survivor's self-trust as well as in a variety of psychological and behavioral measures taken to support or confirm these changes. There are two main ways in which the organization of the survivor's self-trust is affected by traumatizing betrayals: (1) trust in affected dimensions is either diminished or intensified, and (2) immature criteria used to evaluate trust in self and in others are retained or reinstated. That is to say, trauma survivors tend to base their trust in self and in others on phantasmagorical, perfectionistic criteria and such superficial qualities as physical size, beauty, or wealth rather than more enduring, psychological ones. Furthermore, they may fail to differentiate adequately between their own level and quality of trustworthiness and that of others.

EXPERIENTIAL "BLACK HOLES"

Extreme measures may be required to confirm the trustworthiness of a betrayer, particularly if he or she is a family member, as is true in incest trauma. For example, memories of traumatizing betrayals may be eliminated from consciousness creating "black holes" in the survivor's self-experience into which affects and meanings associated with the traumatic memories as well as "healthy, developmental relational needs" (Sands, 1994) may be swept (see Cohen and Kinston, 1984: Kinston and Cohen, 1986 for a similar conceptualization). Even when memories are recovered, other aspects of self-experience may remain dissociated. Moreover, these black holes often result from unsymbolized, preverbal experiences of trauma that occur very early in life and are never symbolically represented (Gales, 1995). Without access to that which has been dissociated, a sense of self-cohesion is impossible. Consequently, survivors attempt to "fill in" their experiential black holes by means of a wide range of posttrauma symptoms and psychological strategems, including attachments to others who embody the disavowed, hidden aspects of self-experience and therefore serve as alter-ego selfobjects (see Brothers, 1993, 1994). In cases in which severely traumatizing betrayals occur early in life and repeatedly, multiple personality disorder may result, whereby dissociated "selves" substitute for alter-ego selfobjects. In addition, as we shall see, trauma survivors sometimes experience those with whom they are involved in sadomasochistic enactments as alter-ego selfobjects.

RETRAUMATIZATION AND SADOMASOCHISM

This conceptualization of trauma and trust betrayal as fundamentally interrelated is incompatible with the notion of a repetition compulsion. The shattering of selfobject fantasies as a result of self-trust betrayal is accompanied by the most excruciating affective state imaginable—disintegration anxiety (Kohut, 1971). Without recourse to Freud's death instinct, there is no way to understand why anyone might seek to reexperience the terror of self-dissolution, yet the reexperiencing symptoms of posttraumatic stress disorder (PTSD) do contain symbolic representations of traumatic experience and many masochistic and sadistic enactments do closely mimic past traumas.

My solution to this apparent paradox serves as the basis for my understanding of the relationship between sadomasochism and trauma. It is my contention that trauma survivors are not driven to reexperience self-dissolution, nor do they unconsciously wish to. Although they may, through intrusive recollections in the form of nightmares and flashbacks, reexperience aspects of traumatic experience, traumatic events themselves are not compulsively repeated. Moreover, although trauma survivors are often retraumatized, their repeated traumatizations are usually inadvertent consequences of faulty efforts at self-restitution. As Ulman and I (1988) pointed out, the dissociative symptoms of PTSD give symbolic expression to both the shattering *and* efforts to restore selfobject fantasies. Even the feeblest effort at restoration changes the traumatic experience to some degreee. In other words, what appear to be efforts to recreate trauma as it originally occurred turns out, on closer examination, to be efforts to revise it or, as I now think of this, to rescript the original trauma scenario. In other words, in order to avoid reexperiencing actual betrayals of self-trust, trauma survivors may attempt to change the meaning of the old trauma through enactments in their present lives. These enactments, which are intended to confirm their altered versions of subjective reality, often contain sadomasochistic meanings.

THE SADOMASOCHISTIC RESCRIPTING OF TRAUMA SCENARIOS

The realm of sadomasochism covers a bewilderingly complex range of psychological experiences. Moreover, the terms *masochism* and *sadism* have been assigned many meanings by various theorists (see Ornstein, 1991; Stolorow and Lachmann, 1980). To explain the relationship between sadomasochism and trauma as I understand it, I (Brothers, 1995a) have found it necessary to limit the meaning of these terms by redefining them from the perspective of self-trust in the following way:

> *Masochism from this perspective refers to experiences of being betrayed or of being vulnerable to betrayal by those needed as providers of selfobject experience.* Broadly speaking, it refers to the experience of being a victim. Masochistic experience may be limited to fantasy or may be expressed in a wide variety of activities that derive from such fantasies.

> *Sadism refers to fantasies of betraying others who are dependent upon one for the provision of selfobject experiences or any activity that reflects such fantasies.* . . . Sadistic activities often entail revenge, a shift from betrayed to betrayer [pp. 83–84].

Trauma survivors often require confirmation of their dissociatively altered subjective realities, particularly when they are threatened with retraumatization. To confirm an altered reality, masochistic and/or sadistic enactments may be employed. Consider, for example, survivors who, in the wake of traumatizing betrayals, alter subjective reality by intensifying trust in others. These survivors may adopt the stance of vulnerability to betrayal in relation to others experienced as potential betrayers in the hope that this time things will come out differently; this time trust in someone who resembles the original betrayer will prove warranted. Such an outcome would rescript the original betrayal and, hence, justify the survivors' intensified trust in others. Similarly, survivors who alter subjective reality by intensifying trust in their ability to elicit selfobject experiences from others may adopt the stance of betrayers in relation to others dependent upon them for selfobject experiences. As the betrayers instead of the betrayed, powerful instead of helpless, hurtful instead of wounded, these survivors attempt to confirm trust in their ability to elicit selfobject experiences from others. Survivors who attempt the sado-masochistic rescripting of their trauma scenarios are apt to vary their enactments; at times they may adopt the stance of the betrayed and, at other times, the stance of the betrayer.

Sadomasochistic enactments undertaken in the hope of rescripting trauma are usually doomed to failure and lead to retraumatization for a number of reasons. First, the rescripting of trauma requires a situation that closely resembles the original trauma scenario, and those chosen by survivors for roles in their enactments often resemble the original betrayers in many respects. Second, the immature criteria used by survivors for placing trust in self and others often blind them to the possibility of additional betrayal. Thus, instead of achieving a new outcome, the survivor is likely to experience a repetition of the old trauma.

SADOMASOCHISM AND ALTER-EGO SELFOBJECTS

In previous volumes (Brothers, 1993, 1994) I have described the search for alter-ego selfobject experiences by trauma survivors. It is now possible to appreciate the importance of these selfobject experiences in terms of their use in "filling in" experiential black holes created by dissociative processes. That is, by relating to others who embody disavowed and hidden aspects of themselves, survivors regain a sense of cohesive self-hood. It is often the case that survivors who attempt to rescript their traumas through sadomasochistic enactments do so as a means of finding alter-ego selfobjects. For example, survivors who adopt a masochistic posture as a means of rescripting traumatic betrayals frequently repudiate their rage and wish for retaliation. Because their sadistic partners may give full expression to rage and aggression, they may be experienced as alter-ego selfobjects. Similarly, survivors who adopt a sadistic posture frequently disavow their vulnerability and fearfulness. They may experience their masochistic partners as alter-ego selfobjects who embody these qualities.

LINDA IN LEATHER

I now present the case of Linda, a 21-year-old college student, whom I have treated for over 2 years, twice weekly. My purpose in what follows is less to describe my approach to her treatment than to use her story to illustrate how sadomasochistic enactments may serve efforts to rescript trauma scenarios. Linda was referred to me by the therapist her parents had consulted for marital therapy. Having separated some months earlier, their reason for seeking treatment was to explore reconciliation.

My first session with Linda was among the most memorable of my clinical career; no other patient, much less one this young, has so completely dominated a session with the sheer impact of her presence. Although she is of only medium height and somewhat overweight, she seemed huge to me. Dressed in black from headband to boots, her long hair flowing to her waist, Linda strode forcefully into my office as if leading a march. After booming her greeting in a voice I thought might be heard a block away, she said confrontingly, "Look, I need to know if you think being gay is sick." I told her I did not. It was the last thing I remember saying until the end of the session when we discussed fee and appointment hours.

Linda filled the rest of the session with a presentation that might have passed for performance art. With great exuberance she displayed her biting wit, well-developed flair for drama, and disarming openness. Her use of language was dazzling and her knowledge of literature impressive. She recited lines of poetry including some she had written, sang a song she had composed, and quoted from the works of several of her favorite authors. Linda's virtuosity achieved what I took to be its aim: I was completely enchanted by her. At the same time, I remember feeling that she had a great deal at stake in enchanting me; securing my fascinated, unwavering attention seemed to be her most urgent priority. Linda's need to feel that she had me in thrall—that it was she who dominated the treatment—as well as her strenuous efforts to stay in my good graces, occupied much of the beginning phase of the therapeutic relationship.

Linda hinted broadly that, although the breakup of her parents' marriage had led her to seek psychotherapy, the pain and confusion she felt had much deeper roots. Her complaints, including depression, anxiety, difficulties with memory and concentration, an eating disorder, a tendency to feel emotionally numb and detached from her environment, and sleep disturbances caused largely by terrifying dreams and nightmares, were suggestive of posttraumatic stress disorder. However, she made no reference to trauma. Her immediate problems, she noted, concerned her parents. She feared that a confrontation with her father, a powerful businessman, was imminent. She described him as a tyrant and a bully who put his professional life before the needs of his family, yet who maintained absolute control over the household through outbursts of rage. She recalled that he once trembled with frustration at having been kept waiting by a salesperson. Although she had refused to have anything to do with him since their last battle some months earlier, she imagined that he would unexpectedly appear on campus to force her to relate to him. She worried that she might be provoked to physical violence if he tried to bar her way. She also felt concerned about having to leave school if he refused to pay her tuition unless she complied with his requests for contact.

In contrast to the somewhat shrill tones she used when speaking of her father, her voice grew quiet and solemn when describing her worries about her mother. Was she to blame, she wondered, for her mother's severe depression? After all, she had insistently urged her mother to end what had seemed to her an abusive and loveless marriage. Linda's description of her close and affectionate relationship with her mother rang with idealization. She mentioned her mother's many professional accomplishments, her gentleness, and her devotion to Linda, yet I was struck by the extent to which she appeared to view as commonplace and unremarkable what seemed to me an extreme role reversal. Her mother, she announced with considerable pride, confided her most intimate thoughts and feelings to Linda and often sought her advice, if not her approval, before making decisions.

Linda admitted feeling disturbed by her mother's anxious bid for reconciliation with her father. "She's not doing as well without him as I'd imagined she would," she said, sounding sad and disappointed. She noted that she would be forced to stop visiting her mother at home if her father returned. "*I* don't want a reconciliation with him," she said, adding after a dramatic pause—"ever!"

Linda opened the second session with the following dream:

> I'm in a house with someone who's asleep and will not wake up. People are trying to get into the house. First it's a UPS delivery man, then it's a Jehovah's witness knocking very persistently. Then I realize that a burglar has climbed up on the roof from the back porch and I think I'll have to throw him off. I keep trying to get rid of the intruders but it gets progressively harder. Then water comes in under the door and through cracks around the windows. I try to nail them shut but it does no good. I carry things upstairs to save them but I see that water is coming in from the upstairs windows too.

Linda believed that the dream reflected her situation with her parents. Her mother's depression, she confided, left her feeling alone to face her father's intrusions, which were becoming progressively more difficult for her to avoid. He had left dozens of telephone messages and had sent many notes and letters insisting that she meet with him. I wondered if the sleeper might also have been a self-representation and if her efforts in the dream to keep the deliveryman and the Jehovah's witness from entering might also have represented her efforts to keep herself from becoming aware of some unwanted knowledge or painful memories (in effect, a representation of dissociation). I also wondered if the images of intrusion and wetness were sexual in nature. Might they signify sexual abuse? Dream after dream in subsequent sessions repeated these themes. Each contained vivid images of warding off intrusion and of exteme measures taken to avoid receiving information, particularly by visual means. In one dream, for example, she is blind; in another, her mother removes the eyes of a cat whose black coat revealed it to be a symbol for the dreamer herself.

Some months later, as her mother emerged from her depression and her father abandoned his efforts to force a meeting with her, the content of our sessions turned from her concerns about her parents to her relationships with peers. Linda, it appeared, was enormously popular. Friends often accompanied her to sessions and waited for her outside my office. She introduced me to her boyfriend, Dean, a handsome young man who gazed at her adoringly.

At this point I remember feeling that Linda was testing my trustworthiness through a series of self-disclosures. In one dramatic session, for example, she announced that she was bisexual. She was attracted to her female roommate and feared that her feelings would not be reciprocated. In the next session, she mentioned feeling stifled in her relationship with Dean. "He's adorable and I love him, but he's so 'vanilla,'" she complained. Although he had accepted her bisexuality, he would not tolerate her wish to have other lovers. Monogamy would not be so bad, Linda explained, if sex with Dean were truly satisfying. In response to my questions, she disclosed her longing for sadomasochistic sex. "What I really love is being spanked," she said, "but Dean just can't bring himself to do anything remotely approaching S&M." Despite her growing sense of frustration and dissatisfaction, fears of hurting Dean kept her from ending their relationship for quite a while.

Her tearful break up with Dean followed her increasing involvement with members of what she called "the leather community," several of whom were fellow students. She found great satisfaction, she explained, in participating in "scenes" of BDSM (bondage, dominance, sadism, and masochism), as well as sexual play involving such forms of sexual sadomasochism as floggings and applications of hot wax to various parts of her body. Linda was jubilant as she announced her sense of belonging with the "leatherfolk." "I used to think I was a freak for liking this sort of play, but now I feel like a member of a big family," she said. It appears that Linda experienced other members of the BDSM community as providing twinship selfobject experiences. She also enjoyed seeing herself as a novice who could "learn the ropes" (i.e., etiquette and safety rules) from older and more experienced members of the group. "In scene," as she put it, while playing the role of "bottom" (the masochistic role), she derived enormous pleasure from experiencing the "tops" (those in sadistic roles) as skilled in their exertion of powerful dominance. Thus, her participation in BDSM appears to have provided her with idealizing selfobject experiences (see Benjamin, 1988).

At the same time the leather scene provided myriad opportunities for her to test her own trustworthiness and that of others. As a "bottom," the opportunities for trust betrayal abounded. Could she trust herself to select tops who would behave responsibly? Could she trust herself to control the scenes adequately so as to avoid injury, for example, by using a "safe word" to end an activity that became too painful? Could she trust others to remain in control of themselves and to abide by the safety rules?

Linda traced her interest in sadomasochistic play to childhood, confiding that her masturbation had always included such self-inflicted pain as that which she could obtain by pinching her nipples. She recalled that as early as 5 she had staged sadomasochistic "scenes" with a little girlfriend during which they inflicted pain on one another as part of their pretend games. As the more dominant and mature of the two, she wondered if she had taken advantage of her little friend. Were the games really mutually desired or had she forced their enactment?

Not surprisingly, Linda's worries about perceiving herself as hurtful toward others, which arose with respect to her mother, her boyfriend, and her childhood friend, were also evident in her relationship with me. For example, she went to great lengths to reassure me that an unavoidable lateness was not a sign of dissatisfaction with me. She apologized profusely after uttering an exasperated comment on my failure to understand a literary allusion. She seemed only slightly less fearful about having to perceive herself as the one hurt by others. For example, she admitted with considerable shame that her first sexual relationship in her early teens had been with an unusually charismatic young man who treated her cruelly. Linda confessed that, in the hope of keeping him, she agreed to participate in sexual scenarios involving humiliation and bondage. In contrast to her current participation in BDSM scenes, these had not felt safe or in her control.

With increasing fervor, Linda spoke of sadomasochism as a legitimate sexual orientation that should be freed of pathological connotations. She was proccupied with "coming out" as bisexual and as a member of the leather community. Many sessions were filled with agonized soliloquies on revealing the truth about her sexuality to her mother.

Linda's crestfallen expression at the beginning of one hour let me know, more than her words, that her mother's reaction to her revelations had been extremely disappointing. Like Dean, she seemed to have little difficulty accepting Linda's bisexuality, but she too was greatly upset about her daughter's sadomasochistic activities. Denouncing sado-masochism as perverse, she urged Linda to "work hard to get over it" in therapy. She let Linda know that she feared her own reputation would be harmed if Linda's sadomasochistic proclivities became public knowl-edge. Suddenly looking like an injured child, Linda cried, "All she cares about is herself. She doesn't see how wonderful it is for me to know who I am." Dramatically, she proclaimed her intention to be "out" as a member of the leather community even if it cost her relationship with her mother. Although Linda never completely severed her connection to her mother, she discontinued her daily phone calls and weekly visits home.

Gleeful about a surge of creativity she attributed to her emergence as a "leatherfolk," Linda showed me a short story she had written about a princess dressed in a medieval-style gown made of "finest" black leather. It ended with the following sentence: "And she mounted her horse, and she rode off to meet a friend, and neither of them was particularly in need of rescue."

Linda confided that she had always regretted her inability to play the role of "the sweet princess." Other girls got to feel like fragile creatures whose beauty would melt the hearts of all the princes of the land. But not she. "I was always better suited to leather than silk and brocade," Linda sighed and then added, defiantly, "Ah well, the leather princess gets to have more fun." As I attempted to explore her remarks in greater depth, Linda revealed that even imagining herself in the posture of the demure, sedate, ladylike "princess" filled her with dread. "Princesses always get menaced by dragons, or locked up by witches, or given away in marriage to evil kings," she said. "They never have any say about what happens to them. The most they can hope for is to be rescued by the prince. Being a princess means setting yourself up for mental torture."

When I commented on what appeared to be similarities between the submissive posture she often assumed in BDSM scenes and the way she portrayed "the sweet princess," Linda cried, "Oh, you don't get it! In scene, I'm totally in control. I feel powerful and strong—nothing like the soppy princess." Then she observed quietly. "Mom always plays princess with Dad. I can't stand it because he uses his power to hurt her and she puts up with it."

Gradually, Linda's defiant good spirits gave way to gloom and brooding. It became painfully evident that she missed the closeness she and her mother had shared for so long. She soon found many reasons to rationalize her mother's hostility toward BDSM. She observed, for example, that a woman of her mother's generation would naturally need time to accept her daughter's participation in what seemed to be a dangerous and alien world. Noting that her mother's voice in a recent phone message sounded depressed, she said, "I worry that I'm causing her as much pain as my father does." While Linda spoke vehemently of her disgust at discovering qualities in herself that resembled her father's, particularly his need for control over others, I was struck by the extent to which her relationship with her mother resembled his. Indeed, husband and daughter seemed to vie for exclusive domination over the woman's life.

It was not long before Linda resumed her position as her mother's confidante and advisor. She once again appeared to perceive her mother as well-intentioned and devoted, but misguided in her fears about her daughter's participation in BDSM. In one session during this period, Linda described a "strange" experience that occurred while she was having sex with a new boyfriend. She had suddenly felt overwhelmed by a terrifying sense of imminent catastrophe. Trembling uncontrollably, she became aware of a peculiar image—a pattern of light and dark stripes, disturbed by a large dark form. She wondered if it might be a "flashback," since several of her BDSM partners who were sexual abuse survivors had described them to her. The image reminded her of the shadows cast by the railing on the stairway in her childhood home when a light was turned on in her parents' bedroom. "I would love this to be about my father sexually abusing me," she said. "I would tell my Mom and she would never want to have anything to do with him." She was distressed to find that, despite intense effort, the only memories she could recover of her father as even mildly inappropriate sexually involved his barging absentmindedly into her bathroom when she was a child.

After having three similar experiences within a month, Linda decided to describe them to her mother. Her mother assured her that, with all his faults, her father was far too principled a person to have sexually abused her. Reacting with undisguised distress to Linda's plan to establish a campus support group for students interested in BDSM, she voiced dire fears of public humiliation. Reluctantly, Linda agreed to keep her participation in the group anonymous.

Soon Linda's involvement in the BDSM support group became the primary focus of her life. Although others ostensibly assumed leadership of the group, she worked tirelessly to recruit members and to establish its legitimacy on campus. As she wrestled with her longing to emerge from her self-imposed anonymity, it became clear that she now experienced herself as locked in a no-win struggle with her mother. If she revealed herself as a leader of the group, she would betray her mother's trust in her. However, she felt increasingly martyred and humiliated by her closeted position. Tending to her mother's needs meant self-betrayal.

Linda's participation in the leather scene now changed. She experimented with "topping" (i.e., assuming the role of the sadist) and found it rewarding. A dream she reported during this period echoed themes of those introduced earlier but shed greater light on Linda's situation:

> Mom is in bed, asleep. I come home from school and Dad stops me from entering her room. He tells me she has cancer, but doesn't seem upset. He says she is going blind. It will be slow and painful unless I gouge out her eyes. I do it with my thumbs and feel sick. Then I'm on the street. I realize that I don't know for sure if she has cancer and that I may have blinded her needlessly.

Associating to the dream, Linda recalled a time, early in her childhood, when her father had set aside more time in his hectic schedule to spend at home. He had actually been her favorite playmate. She remembered games he invented that depended on their mutual delight in whimsy and their shared pleasure in exuberant physical activity. Yet, as she now realized, their play, like every other aspect of their relationship, served her father's needs above her own. He often refused to play when she felt bored and lonely, yet he would interrupt her when she was engrossed in solitary play to insist that she join him. Moreover, he imposed his version of reality on all they shared and never inquired about her thoughts or feelings. For example, after some upsetting experience, he might say, "Oh you weren't scared at all. You knew it was just a joke." She learned it was far better to agree than to risk incurring his wrath and contempt.

Linda also remembered that their most exciting games took place in her mother's absence. As if in compliance with an unspoken pact with her father, she never told her mother about these games. Would her mother have felt hurt or angry that she was not part of their shared adventures, she wondered? "No, that wasn't it," she said quietly. Her expression darkened as she remembered that her father's games had sometimes seemed wild and driven and that she had wished her mother had been there to stop them. She wondered if he had been sexually aroused during the times they played with terrifying intensity.

Then in a strained and breaking voice, she said, "It wouldn't have mattered if Mom had been home. She couldn't control him at all. She was completely at his mercy." Linda recalled many instances in which her father's rages had reduced her mother to apologies and tears. "I didn't exist for her then," she said sadly. "All she cared about was appeasing him. But the minute he was gone she would become my strong, wise, wonderful Mom again and we would pretend these things never happened."

The dream, it appears, reflected Linda's growing awareness and fears concerning the sadomasochistic relations that pervaded her world. After several weeks in which Linda again distanced herself from her mother, this time more completely, her mother asked to see her, noting that she had something "important" to tell her. Amidst tears and self-recriminations, her mother confessed that sadomasochism had been a feature of her sexual behavior with her husband all during Linda's childhood. "I don't know why she feels so ashamed of it," Linda said coolly and added, "Our tastes are very much alike in many respects. It's no wonder that we share the same sexual preferences." In the hope that her mother would not only come to accept Linda's sadomasochistic sexuality, but also her own, she plied her mother with literature describing the joys of BDSM.

It soon became apparent that, despite her seeming nonchalance and air of sophisticated acceptance, Linda was greatly affected by her mother's disclosure. "I think I always knew they were into it," she said. "But it seems repulsive to think about. Maybe anything having to do with my father's sexuality is disgusting to me." Shortly after, in the midst of a BDSM scene, Linda had another recurrence of "the flashback." This time the visual image clearly represented her father at the top of the stairs. Reflecting further, Linda speculated that, as a child, she had witnessed some sadomasochistic sexual act between her mother and father. Images of her mother bound and blindfolded occurred to her. Dissolving in tears, Linda cried that she could not bear the thought of her mother in sexual bondage to her father. Such images would have confirmed the reality of her mother's subjugation to her father and her sacrificial abandonment of Linda. Also, as we later came to realize, they destroyed her illusion that she was the sole and, therefore, special object of her father's exciting and frightening games. In other words, the flashback recorded a scene of betrayal that shattered her selfobject fantasies in which her uniqueness was mirrored by her father.

Eventually her parents decided to divorce. Linda's jubilation quickly turned to anger and despair when, in the course of one of their "heart-to-heart" discussions, Linda's mother disclosed other hidden features of her marriage. She announced that she had begun an affair with Linda's father years before his first divorce, not after, as she had always claimed, and that he had numerous affairs during *their* marriage. She had secretly welcomed his extramarital involvements because, during these periods, she was spared sexual contact with him. She admitted to experiencing pleasure only in their sadomasochistic games.

Despite her realization that she had "always known" but had disavowed knowledge of these infidelities, Linda was devastated by her mother's disclosures. Not only did they destroy her cherished belief in her parents' "basic honesty and integrity" (her foremost criterion for trust-in-others), thereby crushing what remained of her idealizing self-object fantasies, but they all but severed what had been the strongest bond connecting Linda and her mother. Discovering that her mother had kept such important secrets from her contradicted her perception of herself as her mother's trusted confidante. The fantasies of herself as the indispensible and sole provider of her mother's selfobject needs that powerfully organized her self-experience were all but shattered. Working through the meaning and effects of this betrayal occupied the treatment for many months.

CASE DISCUSSION

Although the therapeutic relationship is still far from completion at this point, we have learned enough about the environment in which Linda grew up and the ways in which her self-trust was betrayed to begin to understand her sexual sadomasochism. Her father's exertion of tyrannical control, his terrifying rages, his extramarital affairs, and his exploitative play repeatedly betrayed Linda's trust in him as a strong, loving provider of selfobject experiences. Her mother's humiliating submissiveness, her blindness to Linda's intense and sexualized connection to her father, and her abandonment of her maternal role repeatedly betrayed Linda's trust in her as well. As a result of her parents' untrustworthiness in these vital areas, Linda also appears to have lost trust in her own ability to elicit the selfobject experiences she needed.

My preliminary efforts to reconstruct Linda's self-restitutive strategies in the aftermath of these traumatizing betrayals suggest that her hopes for psychological survival lay in a dissociative alteration of her subjective reality that resulted in the following changes in her self-experience: As a young child she appears to have greatly intensified her trust in her parents as providers of selfobject experiences. Anything that challenged the version of reality espoused by her parents, that is, that she was a treasured child of admirable, loving, and devoted parents, was dissociated, swept into experiential black holes along with the painful feelings associated with them. Included among these lost experiences was any awareness of her parents' infidelities and her memories of her parents' sadomasochistic sexual activities. These scenes were undoubtedly traumatizing insofar as they shattered fantasies of herself in relation to her parents as providers of idealizing and mirroring selfobject experiences. They not only revealed her father as victimizer and her mother as a blind and helpless victim who could offer her no protection, but they revealed that she was not the only participant in her father's abusive play. Hence, it was not merely her observations of the "primal scene" and their associated oedipal meanings that shattered her selfobject fantasies of herself in relation to her parents; it was the betrayal of her trust in herself and in them as providers of selfobject experiences that these scenes represented.

As Linda grew older and her father withdrew more and more from family life, her mother appears to have turned to her highly intelligent, competent, and charming little girl as her primary companion, parentifying her and using her to fulfill a variety of selfobject needs. Linda's self-experience became organized chiefly around fantasies of herself as providing selfobject experiences for her mother. Linda, it appears, strove to enact these fantasies through her efforts to replace her father in her mother's affection. Rather than relying on brutality and coercion as her father had, Linda appears to have attempted to dominate her mother by becoming indispensable to her as a psychological support as well as by fashioning herself into the endlessly fascinating woman she knew her mother would admire. This fantasy of domination can be viewed as an effort to rescript trauma scenarios involving her mother's sacrificial abandonment of her. Her hope was to prevent a dreaded recurrence of disintegration anxiety, the terror of ceasing to exist, which she undoubtedly experienced every time her mother abandoned her in order to appease her raging and controlling husband. Her efforts at the outset of treatment to captivate me with her brilliance and charm suggests that a similar fantasy served to ward off threats of retraumatizing betrayal within the therapeutic relationship.

Unlike most children, Linda could not delight in discovering her resemblances to her parents and thereby enjoy selfobject fantasies of twinship in relation to them. Aspects of her own self-experience that in any way resembled her parents' sadomasochistic relationship were disavowed and dissociated. Hence, she could not bear to think of herself as hurtful and controlling like her father. Nor could she even pretend to be "the sweet princess" because doing so too clearly brought to mind the submissiveness she loathed in her mother and in herself.

Linda's solution was to assume the persona of the leather princess, a strong, competent, adventurous woman who is never in need of rescue. Her sadomasochistic activities with her childhood friend and her adolescent crushes, as well as her involvement in the leather community of sexual sadomasochism, can now be seen as efforts both to fill in her experiential black holes and to rescript her trauma scenarios. To the extent that these experiences enabled her to adopt the posture of the betrayed or the betrayer, she was enabled to experience a sense of cohesive selfhood.

Let us consider some of the means by which her BDSM participation provided opportunities for rescripting her childhood traumas by adopting the masochistic role of the betrayed or the sadistic role of the betrayer. As a little girl, Linda had no alternative but to submit to her father's overpowering and exploitative games. In scenes of sexual bondage, her dominators are also endowed with great power. But "in scene" Linda is in control. The means by which pain is inflicted, the duration and the intensity are all determined by her. The crucial point of masochism for Linda was not "pleasure in pain," but, as Benjamin (1988) suggested, submission to an idealized other. Unlike her disappointing experiences with her father who lost control of himself and terrified her, her BDSM dominators do not. Moreover, in scene there is no denying it is she who is the object of domination. Thus, it may be that as the bottom, she is enabled to recapture her blissful selfobject fantasies of herself in relation to the powerful father of her childhood.

Linda also attempted to rescript her trauma scenarios by "topping." It is probably no coincidence that she first experimented with this BDSM role at a time when she felt disappointed in her mother and estranged from her. By rejecting Linda's involvement in BDSM as perverse, her mother made it painfully clear that she was not completely dominated by her. By enacting this role "in scene" Linda is able to switch from betrayed to betrayer and to rescript trauma scenarios in which she felt totally unable to trust in her capacity to elicit the selfobject experiences she needed from others. These enactments seem to be directed primarily to traumas involving selfobject failures by her mother. In scene she can play the role of brutal sadist, which she identifies with her father. In so doing she may feel a sense of selfobject connectedness with him. At the same time she is able to rescript trauma scenarios of abandonment and loss of control over her mother and others needed as selfobjects.

SUMMARY

The case of a young woman involved in BDSM within the "leather community" was presented in an effort to demonstrate that sadomasochistic enactments may be used to rescript trauma scenarios related to self-trust betrayal. In this case, enactments of sexual sadomasochism were employed in the hope of rescripting trauma scenarios that occurred in the patient's early life. By adopting the stance of the betrayed or the betrayer in BDSM scenes, she attempted to rescript trauma scenarios that occurred as she grew up in a sadomasochistic childhood environment in which her trust in herself and in her parents as providers of self-object experience was repeatedly betrayed. Her rescripting efforts were undertaken in order to confirm her dissociatively altered subjective reality in the hope of restoring her trust in self and in others.

REFERENCES

Adler, A. (1927), *Understanding Human Nature*. New York: Permabooks.

Bach, S. & Schwartz, L. (1972), A dream of Marquis deSade: Psychoanalytic reflections on narcissistic trauma, decompensation, and the reconstruction of a delusional self. *J. Amer. Psychoanal. Assn.*, 20:451–475.

Basch, M. F. (1983), The perception of reality and the disavowal of meaning. *Internat. J. Psycho-Anal.*, 11:125–153.

Benjamin, J. (1988), *The Bonds of Love*. New York: Pantheon.

Brothers, D. (1992), Trust disturbance and the sexual revictimization of incest survivors: A self-psychological perspective. In: *New Therapeutic Visions, Progress in Self Psychology, Vol. 8*, ed. A. Goldberg. Hillsdale, NJ: The Analytic Press, pp. 75–91.

—— (1993), The search for the hidden self: A fresh look at alter ego transferences. In: *The Widening Scope of Self Psychology, Progress in Self Psychology, Vol. 9*, ed. A. Goldberg. Hillsdale, NJ: The Analytic Press, pp. 191–207.

—— (1994), Dr. Kohut and Mr. Z: Is this a case of alter ego countertransference? In: *A Decade of Progress, Progress in Self Psychology, Vol. 10*, ed. A. Goldberg. Hillsdale, NJ: The Analytic Press, pp. 99–114.

—— (1995a), *Falling Backwards*. New York: Norton.

—— (1995b), Sadomasochism and the rescripting of trauma scenarios: Effects on treatment. Presented at the 4th European Conference on Traumatic Stress, Paris, May.

—— (1995c), Beyond the black holes: Understanding and treating dissociative disorders from a "self-trust" perspective. Presented at the 5th Annual Conference for the International Society for the Study of Dissociation, Amsterdam, May.

Cocks, G. (1994), *The Curve of Life*. Chicago: The University of Chicago Press

Cohen, J. (1980), Structural consequences of psychic trauma: A new look at "Beyond the Pleasure Principle." *Internat. J. Psycho-Anal.*, 61:421–432.

—— (1981), Theories of narcissism and trauma. *Amer. J. Psychother.*, 35:93–100.

—— & Kinston, W. (1984), Repression theory: A new look at the cornerstone. *Internat. J. Psycho-Anal.*, 65:411–422.

Freud, S. (1905), Three essays on the theory of sexuality. *Standard Edition*, 7:130–243. London: Hogarth Press, 1953.

—— (1919), A child is being beaten. *Standard Edition*, 17:175–204. London: Hogarth Press, 1955.

—— (1920), Beyond the pleasure principle. *Standard Edition*, 18:3–64. London: Hogarth Press, 1955.

—— (1924), The economic problem of masochism. *Standard Edition*, 19:154–170. London: Hogarth Press, 1961.

—— (1925), Some psychical consequences of the anatomical distinction between the sexes. *Standard Edition*, 19:248–258. London: Hogarth Press, 1961.

———— (1937), Analysis terminable and interminable. *Standard Edition*, 23:216–253. London: Hogarth Press, 1964.

Gales, M. E. (1995), Discussion of "The Leather Princess: Sadomasochism as the Rescripting of Trauma Scenarios" by Doris Brothers. 18th Annual Conference on the Psychology of the Self, San Francisco, October.

Gardner, H. (1975), *The Shattered Mind*. New York: Basic Books.

Gazzaniga, M. (1983), Right hemisphere language following brain bisection: A 20-year perspective. *Amer. Psychol.*, 38:525–537.

Geschwind, N. (1965), Disconnection syndromes in animals and man. *Brain*, 88:237–294, 585–644.

Horney, K. (1924), On the genesis of the castration complex in women. In: *Feminine Psychology*, ed. H. Kelman. New York: Norton, 1967, pp. 37–53.

———— (1926), The flight from womanhood: The masculinity-complex in women as viewed by men and women. In: *Feminine Psychology*, ed. H. Kelman. New York: Norton, 1967, pp. 54–70.

———— (1933), The problem of feminine masochism. In: *Feminine Psychology*, ed. H. Kelman. New York: Norton, 1967, pp. 214–233.

Kinston, W. & Cohen, J. (1986), Primal repression: Clinical and theoretical aspects. *Internat. J. Psycho-Anal.*, 67:337–356.

Kohut, H. (1959), Introspection, empathy, and psychoanalysis: An examination of the relationship between mode of observation and theory. In: *The Search for the Self, Vol. 1*, ed. P. H. Ornstein. New York: International Universities Press, 1978, pp. 205–232.

———— (1971), *The Analysis of the Self*. New York: International Universities Press.

———— (1977), *The Restoration of the Self*. New York: International Universities Press.

———— (1979), The two analyses of Mr. Z. In: *The Search for the Self, Vol. 4*, ed. P. H. Ornstein. New York: International Universities Press, 1991, pp. 395–446.

———— (1981), Introspection, empathy, and the semicircle of mental health. In: *The Search for the Self, Vol. 4*, ed. P. H. Ornstein. New York: International Universities Press, 1991, pp. 537–568.

———— (1984), *How Does Analysis Cure?* ed. A. Goldberg & P. Stepansky. Chicago: The University of Chicago Press.

Menaker, E. (1953), Masochism: A defence reaction of the ego. *Psychoanal. Quart.*, 22:205–220.

Noy, P. (1980), The psychoanalytic theory of cognitive development. *The Psychoanalytic Study of the Child*, 35:169–216. New York: International Universities Press.

Ornstein, A. (1974), The dread to repeat and the new beginning. *The Annual of Psychoanalysis*, 2:231–248. New York: International Universities Press.

———— (1991), The dread to repeat: Comments on the working-through process in psychoanalysis. *J. Amer. Psychoanal. Assn.*, 39:377–398.

Sands, S. (1994), What is dissociated? *Dissociation*, 7:145–152.

Schad-Somers, S. P. (1982), *Sadomasochism*. New York: Human Sciences.

Sperry, R. W. (1984), Consciousness, personal identity, and the divided brain. *Neuropsychologica*, 22:661–673.

Stekel, W. (1929), *Sadism and Masochism, Vol. 1*, trans. E. Cuthell. New York: Liveright, 1953.

Stoller, R. J. (1975), *Perversion*. New York: Pantheon.

—— (1979), *Sexual Excitement*. New York: Pantheon.

Stolorow, R. D. (1975), The narcissistic function of masochism (and sadism). *Internat. J. Psycho-Anal.*, 56:441–448.

—— & Lachmann, F. M. (1980), *Psychoanalysis of Developmental Arrests*. New York: International Universities Press.

Ulman, R. B. & Brothers, D. (1988), *The Shattered Self*. Hillsdale, NJ: The Analytic Press.

Winnicott, D. W. (1951), Transitional objects and transitional phenomena. In: *Through Paediatrics to Psycho-analysis*. New York: Basic, 1975, pp. 229–241.

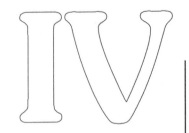

Therapy

Lonely as a Cloud: Finding Daffodils in The House of Terror. Transference and Countertransference In Drama Therapy With a Ten-Year-Old Boy

Rosalind Kindler

The treatment of Michael, a 10-year-old boy, illustrates a blend of drama therapy and psychoanalytic psychotherapy informed by self psychology. This chapter will focus on the first 6 months of Michael's treatment and describe how, through the expressive media of art and drama, Michael actively used me to articulate, illustrate, and illuminate his subjective world. As I describe the art work, play and dramatic enactments that Michael created, I want to add my own voice—not simply the objective experience-distant voice of the therapist describing the process of therapy, but a narrative of my subjective experience as I attempted to join Michael in his fantasy world of confusion, chaos, and fear. As I take you with me, much as Michael took me with him, I can highlight the clinical and technical points I wish to make. I will also discuss the theoretical concepts that shaped my thinking about him, focusing primarily on the issues of transference and countertransference.

I wish to thank my colleagues and friends who generously offered suggestions and criticisms, and particularly Alan Kindler for his invaluable help in preparing this manuscript.

271

Before I go on to describe Michael, it would be useful to compare and contrast the significance of enactment in drama therapy and psycho-analysis. Drama therapy is a treatment modality in which enactment is central. The notion of enactment in drama therapy comes from a tradition that has its roots in theater and drama. Enactments, according to this approach are not inadvertent, but a deliberate undertaking on the part of both the therapist and the patient as a necessary, healing part of the work (Dr. Shelley Doctors, personal communication). In this model enactment is the primary vehicle for the transference and a way of engaging unconscious meaning in the child or adult. This is in contrast to the traditional psychoanalytic model in which enactments in the therapeutic relationship were viewed as resistance and even now are often regarded as defensive "acting out." As such, enactments were, and by some still are, seen as impediments to the analytic process. (Indeed, transference, which now lies at the very center of the analytic process, was also initially considered to be a form of resistance.) Enactments on the part of the analyst were regarded as countertransferential acting out that would hinder the analytic work. Currently, there is an emerging appreciation of enactments as being *intrinsic* to the psychoanalytic process. They are more often understood as a valuable dimension of the transference, and analysts are beginning to be aware of the value and significance of the myriad interactions that occur outside of the verbal mode. This shift in perspective brings the positions of the psycho-dynamically oriented drama therapist and the psychoanalyst closer together. Using the ideas of Freud (1914) and Meares (1990), the dramas that are played out in the psychoanalytic "*Spielraum*" are enacted verbally and non-verbally both within and between the minds of the patient and the analyst in the intersubjective field (Stolorow, Brand-chaft, and Atwood, 1987) to which they both contribute.[1]

Drama therapy is the bridging of theater/drama techniques and psychotherapy. It exists, as do all the expressive therapies, to "communicate those things that otherwise cannot be expressed" (Jennings, 1992). Drama therapists draw from a range of related disciplines, from play and play therapy, through developmental psychology, psychoanalysis, sociology, and performance theory (Landy, 1986).

Drama therapy should be distinguished from its close cousin psychodrama in several important ways. Psychodrama requires the theatrical context and structure of a scene played out with certain carefully defined roles, a stage setting, and an audience. It relies on catharsis for its curative effect. Jacob Moreno, its originator, believed in

---

[1] The concept of Stolorow et al.'s (1987) intersubjective field is crucially important as an aid in understanding the dramatic enactments that take place in therapy with children and adults alike.

"encounter" rather than transference as a principle of cure (Fox, 1987). Drama therapy embraces a more broadly defined group of activities, which includes many of those used in psychodrama but is not restricted to them. Drama therapy is often conceived as the umbrella under which many other expressive techniques can flourish. As well as the world of theater/drama, which would include such activities as scene-setting, improvisation and role play, drama therapists routinely make use of storytelling, poetry, puppet play, masks, movement, music, and art.

Although drama therapy is widely used with adults, it is a natural medium for children, most of whom engage naturally in dramatic play; enactment, rather than verbalization, is most often the child's preferred way of communicating, and the child's primary mode of expression is in the symbolic and metaphoric realm. A play therapy or child psychotherapy session might often include dramatic process or techniques, like role play and role reversal, story-making or puppetry. Given these areas of overlap, what is it that distinguishes drama therapy from other child therapy models? One important distinguishing feature is that drama therapy training requires familiarity with dramatic structure, improvisation, role theory (Landy, 1993), and theater/drama processes. Another is the orientation towards eliciting expression through the active, often proactive, participation of the therapist. This active participation may consist of facilitation and elaboration of the child's themes in play, or it may take the form of a clearly directive approach. (Descriptions of both of these approaches follow later in this chapter.) For example, if a child has been having difficulty getting to sleep at night, fearing monsters and engaging in nightly battles with parents, the drama therapist might well suggest that they play out the night-time scene together in a variety of ways. The child can then be invited to take the roles of monster, parents, or themselves, trying them all in turn, with the therapist playing the other parts. Irwin (1985) states, "Drama therapists, like other mental health professionals, attempt to understand others by seeing the world through their eyes" and suggests that "one of the primary ways the patient communicates data from his world is through the portrayal of roles which are enacted in an improvised way" (p. 34).

Play therapy has its roots in the application of psychoanalysis to work with children. The writings of Axline (1947), Freud (1965), Klein (1932), Mahler, Pine, and Bergman (1975), and Winnicott (1971) have all contributed to our understanding of the function of play and its implications for child therapy, albeit from differing perspectives. It is beyond the scope of this chapter to discuss the various theoretical positions of these eminent theorists and clinicians. However, the demise of the blank screen abstinence of the classical analyst, the one-person psychology model, and with it, the sessile position of the child therapist, has opened the door to an increasingly active and interactive model of psychoanalytic work with children. Psychoanalytically oriented play therapists and child psychotherapists now subscribe more and more to the notion that the way to a deeper understanding of the child's conscious and unconscious world is through the active participation of the therapist. Drama therapy fits naturally into this model. It takes the notion of a two-person psychology one step further, transforming it and allowing it to flow freely into the realm of active interaction and enactment.

The slogan of the National Association for Drama Therapy is "Healing Through Action." Many drama therapists subscribe to the notion of drama *as* therapy (Dr. Eleanor Irwin, personal communication). They reject the value of insight gained through verbal interpretation and believe that the therapeutic value of the work is in staying with the patient within the dramatic metaphor, that the healing, growth, and mastery is contained within the creative act and achieved without the use of verbal intervention. Others feel that it is important to make interpretative comments and therefore carry the work outside of the metaphoric, symbolic realm. There is among expressive therapists a wide range of views on this subject, and it will have a familiar ring to those of us who struggle with the issue of the use of interpretation: when to speak and when to keep quiet?

I believe a broader, more inclusive conceptualization of these "either/or" questions would allow a transformation into "both/and" answers, thereby opening our experience and deepening our understanding. In my work, drama becomes a tool to be used *within* therapy, as are talking, play, music, movement or art. As a child therapist trained in both psychoanalytic and drama therapy principles, it has been my experience that these two therapy models can work powerfully together and have much to offer each other. On the one hand I believe that psychoanalysis can learn something from the "action" orientation of the drama therapist. On the other hand, drama therapists can very profitably reach into psychoanalytic and developmental theory to deepen their understanding of the therapeutic relationship. The word *drama* is derived from the Greek *drao* meaning "I do" or "I struggle." Surely the task common to us all is to facilitate the "doing" and "struggling" of our patients by containing, supporting, understanding, and explaining (Kohut 1971).

Michael was a 10-year-old boy who, in his mother's words, "wandered lonely as a cloud." A passive, isolated, and silent boy, Michael did indeed "wander" in a world full of terrifying and threatening voices and images. He struggled painfully to protect himself from both the external world into which he could not fit and his internal world: the domain of his inner terrors. Michael's fears were global and crippling:

The pictures of animals on his bedroom wall would surely, in the dark of night, leap out at him and devour him. Bedroom windows must be securely locked and curtains kept tightly closed to keep out the carnivorous bats that constantly lurked there, waiting their chance. Fish, if eaten, would "come alive" in his stomach and consume him from within. Incessant voices threatened to kill him and exhorted him to do things that were dangerous or self-destructive.

At 10 years of age Michael had no friends of any constancy. He liked best to play in his parents' bedroom, making forts out of their bedding. At bedtime he was unable to stay in his room alone. Michael was exquisitely sensitive to overstimulation of any kind, whether sensory or affective. Sounds, smells, loud noises, or the excitement of those around him could cause him to feel overwhelmed. Outings to the theater or movies could be threatening. The music or the action might be too loud or too sad or too happy. The audience might applaud too loudly. The movie may be too funny. People around him might laugh too raucously and send him into panic. Walking to and from school was an ordeal that evoked in Michael the certainty that someone would come up behind him and silently slip a dagger into his back. He kept his collars turned up or hoods pulled down over his face, revealing only his eyes, to prevent someone from seeing his entire face. A murderer might photograph him and come back in the night to kill him. In the face of these terrifying fantasies that constantly threatened to overwhelm him, Michael took refuge in obsessional rituals. Talismans of many kinds had to be used before he could sleep. A stuffed tiger was kept close by. Tiny pieces of paper were carefully placed around his bed with drawings and words appealing to the monsters to "Stay Away!" or "Leave Immediately!" His bedroom was organized as if it were a fort.

Michael was the youngest of four children. His two oldest siblings, half-sisters, were from a previous marriage of his mother. The older half-sister lived in another city and had virtually no contact with him. His other half-sister, Emma, seven years his senior, seemed to Michael to be only peripherally aware of his existence and showed little interest in him, but he adored and idealized her. Michael's full sibling was his tyrannical older brother, Julian, born a scant 18 months before him, who visited upon him a full repertoire of sadistic and aggressive behaviors. Michael spent a great deal of his time hiding in the bathroom, in retreat not only from the demons inside his head, but also from the violent attacks of this brother. Michael's relationship with his brother was a major source of conflict for him. Thus, his description of his relationships within the family sounded to me very much like "Goldilocks and the Three Bears." Sisters were "too busy," brother was "too rough," and Michael's benign but ebullient father was, like A. A. Milne's Tigger, "too bouncy." Only

Michael's mother, a gentle but somewhat distracted woman, was experienced by him as "just right."

Michael's parents, Barbara and Ted, were compassionate, but psychologically unsophisticated people. They displayed a kind of bemused puzzlement regarding their children's behavior. Michael's father, a vigorous and successful owner of a chain of fitness centers, stated that he made it a priority to spend time with all of his children. However, he found it difficult to engage Michael in the activities that the father liked and in which Michael's older brother so easily excelled. His mother, a busy law professor, had clearly forged a strong bond with her younger son. Her career was demanding however, and when at home, she was often absorbed in her work. She seemed to relate to all her children in a loving but slightly disengaged manner.

Michael's history, as described by his parents, included a very comfortable pregnancy during a most stable time in their lives, followed by an easy birth and the developmental history of a nearly perfect infancy and toddlerhood. Michael was described as an easy to calm, responsive baby, who was quiet and attentive, an alert infant who engaged happily in face-to-face play. However, if he was in distress he would cry weakly for only a few moments and then wait passively until someone came. He slept in his parents' bed for the first 6 months, and he liked to be carried around a lot. As a baby and toddler Michael would startle easily and was extremely sensitive to any physical and emotional stimulation. He was extremely fearful in the playground, preferring the swings to all the other play activities.

When Michael and I first met, I saw a gentle-looking boy with neatly cut blonde hair and clear blue eyes. He had a careful, decorous style about him which seemed to belong to another era, and a watchful, slightly apprehensive demeanor. There was a tender, almost feminine quality about him. He was clearly fearful about leaving his parents in my waiting room and seemed relieved to have them accompany him into the playroom. He was cooperative and polite but avoided eye contact. During this first session Michael hardly spoke. However, with 20 minutes left in the session, Michael unexpectedly turned his body to me, looked straight at me, and began to pour out a steady flow of confidences. Speaking in a monotone he confided his fears, his nightmares, his dreadful fantasies, scary movies (which ran the gamut from *Vampires* and *Jaws* to *Bugs Bunny*), his terror of being devoured by fish and his experiences of being beaten up by his older brother. He spoke of his memories of "jumping out of his crib with nightmares" as a small child. Although he spoke of things that clearly caused him great anguish, there was little range of affect either in his voice or his body. As he spoke, his parents remained very still and quiet. At the end of the session he had made two mask-like pieces constructed from paper and glue, one of which was described as "a naughty spirit" and the other "a spear and two pebbles," which he politely but firmly suggested I hang on my desk.

I was delighted to find myself drawn to Michael, and I felt moved by what he told me. Any concerns about parental fragility and intrusiveness were alleviated by the parents' behavior during this initial session. They listened quietly and gave him plenty of space to interact with me once he started to talk. A mutually respectful alliance seemed already to be underway. I was hopeful that we could all work well together.

Over the next few sessions, Michael continued to confide in me. He gradually began to speak more freely and his tone became more expressive. He routinely brought along a snack, a ritual that continued for the first twelve sessions and then stopped. There was a hungry, messy quality to his eating. He was like an infant, completely unaware of the sticky mess all over his mouth, as he would mindlessly drop copious amounts of muffin over himself, the table, and the floor. Michael also seemed oblivious to the perpetually runny nose he had at that time. I was reminded of his mother's comment that he was "unappealing," referring to her son's inability to keep himself clean. During this time Michael confided an enormous amount in terms of his troubles, wishes, fantasies, and fears. He talked about his father who, he said, "for some reason seems to like my brother better than me." At my request he drew a picture of his family. Julian was drawn first, in the center of the page, large, taking up a lot of space. Michael added a huge dagger dripping with blood sticking into the head of his brother. His oldest sister was entirely missing. Michael appeared close beside mother and was represented as tiny, with no face and no feet. This kind of self-representation, along with his psychotic-like terrors and affective dissociation raised concerns in my mind about the extent of his pathology. Although Michael was quite talkative, his speech was disorganized and he was often hard to track.

In describing the following clinical material, I have allowed myself the license of moving into the present tense. This is in the service of attempting to bring the play sessions to life and to present the counter-transference experience more fully.

SESSION 5

Today Michael draws his brother Julian and the numbers 1–10 saying he only likes his brother #2 on the scale. Michael continues to draw with increasing intensity, a figure that he says is 10 on a scale of 1–10 in scariness. He adds a huge knife. He is now drawing furiously. A series of mask-like faces emerge which all are rated in terms of their scariness. They are all identified as feelings: Happy, Sad, Mad, plus an "Evil" mask, which is rated 20. He continues to draw other "illness" faces and identifies these: Germs, Virus, Contagious, AIDS, Death, and Poison. He talks about how these faces all speak to him and tell him things he must do. He imitates the voices at my request, producing a high pitched, whispering, cajoling sound. "Climb up on the roof" or "Jump out the window." He tells me that sometimes they are all mixed up together in his head. He continues to draw more after I say that it is time for us to stop. He reminds me of a starving person determined to finish every scrap of food on his plate before leaving the table. A figure with many mouths and teeth appears on the page, which he says threatens to eat him. Before he leaves I ask, "Michael, do you believe that germs can really speak?" "Yes," he answers.

SESSION 6

Michael recounts a dream he had last night. It was a good dream, he says, and he never has good dreams. But last night he dreamed that a bad guy was trying to make off with a bag containing his collection of gemstones. These stones are prized possessions he has told me about, which have "good" voices and which keep him company. He draws this dream and depicts himself in a long robe holding aloft a short but quite thick stick, which can bring down hail and snow on his opponent. He is saying, "Go away!" The figure is drawn as solid and substantial; a powerful self-representation. He tells me that he wants to take this picture home to work on it some more. And he says that maybe he might continue to have this dream for the rest of his life.

I am enormously moved at hearing about this dream and at the knowledge that he is feeling stronger and more able to act effectively, to retaliate and defend himself. I feel a strong bond with Michael, and I'm glad that he is sharing his inner world so completely with me. I too feel strong now, effective, competent, and hopeful. Michael's improvement strengthens me.

In a meeting with Michael's parents at this time, they reported that Michael had shown dramatic improvement in all areas of his life. He was doing better in school, was more focused and able to work, was more assertive with his brother, and could now be seen playing with boys his own age in the school yard.

This dream was, in a sense, the nodal point in Michael's therapy. Both Michael and I were strengthened and transformed by the dream. This mutually regulating experience (Beebe, 1986) undoubtedly had an important effect on the treatment process. My sense of myself as competent and effective with this child had a subtle but clear impact on my work and allowed for a wider range of creative responses. The selfobject needs of the therapist and the implications for the process of therapy have been discussed by Bacal and Thomson (1996). For Michael it represented the first stirrings of a sense of himself as other than passive, fearful, and helpless—the mobilization of his assertive self and the beginning of a sense of hopefulness. The dream coincided with the recovery of many crucial aspects of Michael's functioning. I, in turn, felt transformed from my state of fretful anxiety to one of positive confidence. The dream represented the new-found strength that Michael derived from the selfobject tie as it appeared in this early phase of the transference and it heralded the subsequent phases. He could now take me with him into his terrifying world, because he was connected with me in a way that made it safe to enter there and explore. I want to take you with me through five subsequent phases of therapy, as I describe the dramatic enactments that constituted the working through of these transferences.

PHASE 1

The Captain and the Navigator

Michael is more active now, enacting regular dramas on which I try, without success, to impose some form. Initially, they are enactments that Michael creates with shadow-play using colored paper cut-outs, flashlight, and lamps which he projects onto the wall. The room is always made as dark as it can be, blinds closed, and all other lights out. Drawing on the psychoanalytic principle of "starting where the child is," I create a dramatic context for his play and suggest the idea of Space Travel. I put him in the role of ship's captain and I am the navigator. Michael accepts this scenario, and the action now centers around the galaxy and things we can see on our spaceship's "screen" (his light and color projections on the wall). His themes are good versus bad and life and death struggles with threatening aliens, but there is no form to these dramas, no story line. I struggle to stay with him as he singlemindedly refuses my attempts to introduce a structure. He does allow a beginning and an end to our dramas in the form of "count-down and take-off" and eventual landings back on earth, which I "navigate" but he politely ignores my questions and comments about the action that takes place in between. At the end of sessions he does, however, accept my suggestion to use the tape recorder for use as the Captain's Log to record our adventures. After his captain's report, he routinely signs himself off using his mother's name.

PHASE 2

The House of Terror

The following ten sessions are a dramatic distillation reconstructed from my process notes written at the end of each session. This distillation will perhaps convey the lack of form and the bizarre quality of the sessions. I take some license in presenting them in this more poetic form. If there is some confusion as to whose voice belongs to whom, it is because my intention is to convey both subjectivities, mine and Michael's, as he took control with his "demon" role and imposed his fearful experiences onto me as the "victim."

Michael does not wish to eat today. He draws. Asking me, "Can you guess what this is?" I can't. It looks very odd. He says it's a strange kind of house: The House of Terror. He tells me it is made up of endless tunnels, but they all spiral inwards. They begin to look like eyes. He continues to draw what he calls "endless steps" and the drawing looks more and more like a face. He adds "exclamation points" at each side and says they are earrings. The house might be female. I ask about how it feels to be inside this house of endless things. He answers breezily, "It's OK. You can have a happy life here; only THEY won't let you out again, once you go in." The house is a prison. He asks me if I want to explore this house with him. He turns out all the lights. And leads the way.

> The house has never-ending passageways that offer the choice of different doors.
> There are many possibilities here. You can open any of the doors.
> "But be careful!" he warns me. "You might easily make the wrong choice."
> If you open this one, you're inside a cage. And then there's no escape.
> If you choose that one, you're just faced with another door, and no way out either.
> Once you enter into this house, you will never return to the outside world.
> So—"Choose! And hurry up about it!"
> But this is terrifying. Any and all of these choices may be the wrong one.
> I'll take this door,
> Ah . . . there's a friend in here. It's comfortable and nice.
> But I'm not allowed to stay here.
> "Out and choose another door!" Michael commands, "And don't go in that door!
> Owl-Woo lives in there. He's always depressed. So will you be if you go in there."
> It's dark. I'm scared and confused. I hear a strange and horrible sound.
> Like a howling-screaming.

It's coming from behind that door.
I'm not going in there. But I can't stay out here in the corridor either.
It's too dangerous.
He's got a light, but I haven't. It's horrible here.
I hear the eerie sound of bells ringing.
Suddenly a creature jumps out at me, dressed in robes with no face.
Yes it has a face, but it's a terrible mask.
It shines the light in my face and orders me to go on through the passageways or die.
It tells me its name is Night.
Behind the next door is another robed figure.
Where her face should be there's just a blank, black mask!
She is evil and full of rage.
Now she's smiling.
"But be careful," Michael says. "She might decide to kill you or transform you.
She might even forgive you."
Inside this next room there's a helper, Michael tells me.
"She can help you get used to it here. Because you know you can never leave."
He is radiant as he waves his magic wand.
I am his prisoner.
Entrapped and transformed into a Wolverine. He cuts out my brain;
Takes away my ability to speak or communicate.
My very humanity.
He takes me into another world. Because the real world is full of danger.
It is clear that if you stay you risk being transformed, altered, or worse;
You might simply disappear forever.

Thus, Michael took me with him into his terrifying inner world.

During this phase I often felt a sense of foreboding in the pit of my stomach before Michael's sessions, knowing it would be hard for me. The content was always fragmented and structureless. I found it exhausting trying to stay with him. I was also exhausted trying to keep us in contact with the sane world, because he was at pains to have none of it, would hear none of my questions: the "why?" the "what happened to make it so?" Any of the who, what, why, when, and where of the contained drama session.

PHASE THREE

The Journeys: The Benign Leader

Over the next few weeks, we travel from one land to another. We now have with us on our journeys several fellow travelers, puppets, the most prominent being "Platy" the platypus, Michael's co-leader and self-representation in these dramas. I am the bearer of all the others. We are a small band, a community, a family. Michael is the intrepid leader. Good versus bad is the prevailing theme. But Michael now becomes extremely benign, caring for us all, feeding us, finding comfortable places for us to be. He equips me with the power of invisibility, a guard dog, and much else from the "store" of goods on the toy shelves. He hurries us along, for we must not stay long or we'll begin to age very, very quickly and die before we can escape and find immortality. He is God, a female God. His power is unchallengeable. He is an intrepid leader. He jumps into chasms, explores and reassures the group. I must be encouraged, sometimes with threats, to follow. "Jump into the volcano NOW or you will die!" he commands. The themes are immutable: The world of humans is a dangerous place. To be human is perilous. To be male is risky. Most of us on this journey are female or can change back and forth with ease. Freedom lies in fleeing that world, leaving behind parents who are dead. But there is to be no sadness. All sad, angry, or negative feelings must be excised. No comments; no questions; no clarification is permitted. To ensure my cooperation in this, he operates on my brain again.

At the end of each of these sessions, I feel terribly tired. I worry that I am not keeping enough structure in the sessions. I am rigorous at the end of each session as we tidy up to bring us back to the real world. My feelings of helplessness while immersed in his crazy world are very painful for me as I struggle to stay with him. He politely but firmly ignores my attempts to make any interpretive comments. When I try to introduce goals, problem solving, story line, and so forth, he operates on my brain to remove my resistance.

PHASE FOUR

The Champagne Bath—Sensual/Sexual Delights

As Michael assumes a more benign role, he moves from the House of Terror to a land of sensual delights. The Land of Chocolate, of Blueberries and Champagne. One land is a place of fabulous wealth and luxury, bright with gold, diamonds, and jewelry. He has named me "Entrancis." We splash in the Champagne Fountain of Youth. There is also an erotic flavor to these scenes as Michael feeds me copious amounts of chocolate and intoxicating drinks.

PHASE FIVE

Evolving Cohesion—Emergence of Self

Session 47

Michael draws a platypus and says that it is sad. He draws a tear in its eye and then adds a tiny red dot and says that it is also angry. He colors the body with streaks of gold for happy. We have just had a 5-week break and during that time, he has moved into a new house from the one he has known all his life. Also a close family friend has just died, and today he will attend the funeral. He accepts my comment that Platy has many different feelings and maybe he and Platy are not so very different. Platy, you will remember, has been an oft-used self-representation. He listens as I say how sad and left out he might feel when his parents are so distracted or sad and too busy to pay him much attention. The loss of a friend is a hard thing to experience. He agrees, nodding. He draws a beautiful woman in a long magnificent gown, which he then cuts up into little pieces and carefully places in his drawer.

In this session, some 6 months into therapy, Michael is able to express, through his art, an integration of his affective world. He is now able to let go of the ferocity with which he had earlier dominated the sessions, and there is a calm acceptance of my comments. It seems that my interpretation about himself and Platy has a liberating effect, and he can then allow the expression of some angry and retaliatory feelings to come to the fore. His rage has been kept severely walled off, and any of my interpretations around this aspect of his emotional life have always been rejected.

The woman he cuts up is not identified by either of us. I feel that it is best to stay quiet on this. However, the following week, Michael embarks on a series of scenarios in which parents are imprisoned, shut out and otherwise excluded from his life. I am reminded of the poem quoted by Bowlby (1979), written by an 11-year-old delinquent boy whose mother had died.

> Jumbo had a baby dressed in green,
>   wrapped it up in paper and sent it to the Queen.
> The Queen did not like it because it was too fat,
> She cut it up in pieces and gave it to the cat,
> The cat did not like it because it was too thin,
> She cut it up in pieces and gave it to the King.
> The King did not like it because he was too slow,
> Threw it out the window and gave it to the crow [p. 10].

DISCUSSION

Stolorow and Lachmann's (1984/1985) concept of the transference as having two dimensions of "figure" and "ground" was helpful in thinking about Michael. They suggest that the transference contains aspects of both repetitive and self object configurations (Stolorow and Lachmann, 1984/1985, 1987; Lachmann and Beebe, 1992). The repetitive or representational aspects of the transference, that is, the expectations stemming from past experience, or the selfobject needs for idealizing, mirroring, or twinship experience will appear to be either "figure" or "ground," depending on the analyst's view of the transferential picture. The developmental or selfobject dimension of the transference, the need for a safe environment in which to enact his experience of the world, provided Michael with the selfobject experiences of both idealizing and mirroring; that is I did not forget him, become distracted, or lose interest in him. The repetitive configurations were played out in his role-reversed dramatic enactments of the house of terror. For example, "I (you) are helpless, confused and terrified." In effect, Michael achieved the validation he needed by handing over his experience to me to taste. He did this by seizing the dominant influence in the role play we enacted together. Michael's need was for me to follow or "track" him as an interactive partner, allowing him to take the lead. Beebe (1986) might have stated this in terms of mutual influence between Michael and me in which Michael was the dominant partner. Also, his experience of me in role was that of new kind of dyad; someone who *did* have a face (I used no mask) and who *did not* fragment in the face of the terrors. The five phases reflected evolving transference configurations that were played out using art and dramatic enactments. When I first met Michael he was affectless, disorganized, fearful, and incompetent. In the early transference configurations Michael needed me to be strong, idealizable, and accepting. Then Michael had a dream whose strengthening effects were experienced mutually by both of us and which allowed him to move on.

Phase 1

Michael began to enact *space ship* dramas, initiated by me, in which I cast him in a role of leadership and authority. The suggestion of space travel with Michael as captain and myself as navigator was designed to offer Michael a new and alternative way of experiencing himself. Landy's (1993) theory on the meaning of role in drama therapy is congruent with the self-psychological approach to self-enhancement. He describes role as "an essential concept that provides coherence to the personality." By placing Michael in the role of leader, I communicated my confidence that he would take charge of our travels competently. The use of the "captain's log" was a device to encourage him to verbal- ize and synthesize the experience. This was effectively the last time I took the initiative in our sessions. After this, Michael took command. In effect I was providing him with a context in which I offer him the role of the dominant partner in our self- and mutual regulatory dyad (Beebe and Lachmann, 1988). It is as if I had offered the baby a chance to play by shaking the rattle a little in his direction. The baby is interested. I am gratified and happy to hand over the rattle to him when he reaches for it. From then on, *he* is in charge of the rattle. Michael took the rattle and tried it out in various ways over the next months, including rattling it in my face.

Phase 2: The House of Terror

The use of art and its unique relationship to drama therapy should be noted here. For the drama therapist, a drawing is the visual depiction of relationships, events, and fantasies that can then be taken, expanded into scenes with characters in role, and enacted. Michael began with a drawing of his house, and then he took me with him to explore inside. Had Michael not invited me to explore this house with him, it would have been my task to use my judgement as to whether to take the initiative to issue the invitation to us both. In short, which hat would have fit better in those circumstances? My psychoanalytic one or my "action"-oriented drama therapy one? Michael's invitation was a gift to both of us. By enacting the demons that terrorized his world, he acquired a sense of mastery and competence in place of the fearful aversive state in which he had become trapped. In these scenes he was firmly in the role of master, and I was the fearful victim. He dressed in robes, donned horrifying masks, turned out the lights, shone a flashlight in my face, and by dint of hiding, howling, wailing, or erupting suddenly out of nowhere, he generally took command of me. This is what I will coin the "I'm the monster, you be the kid" or "role-reversal" selfobject transference. I introduce this new term since role-reversal is so commonly used by children as a means of having the therapist understand their experience. Further, role-reversal could also be understood as a reversal of influence which then leads to the recovery of efficacy. For Michael the experience of being the partner who exerted the dominant influence was clearly an important and novel development.

Phase 3: The Journeys

Michael became the assertive, competent, and benign leader on a series of journeys. His need here was for my presence as an unquestioning, noninterpretive follower. Michael's role here shifted to one of caretaker and nurturer of what was in effect a large family, a theme that later reemerged and predominated for many months. The implications for Michael's developing and strengthening sense of self could also be seen in his use of the puppet Platy as a commanding and reliable alter-ego.

Phase 4: The Champagne Bath

This phase evolved into a riotous immersion in the realm of sensual delights. Here he immersed himself in the world of the sensual, enjoying with me the joyous intimacy and riotous fun reminiscent of the interactions between mother and infant at bath time. There was also an erotic tinge to these sessions. It seemed as if in these enactments, Michael was enjoying the mastery of all those things that had previously terrified him. He made lots of noise, whooped and hollered, jumped and rolled around, and ate and drank immoderately.

Phase 5

Michael demonstrated an *evolving self-cohesion,* which brought with it a new ability for reflection and a stronger sense of self.[2]

COUNTERTRANSFERENCE

The countertransference issues were complex. There were times when I found it terribly hard to stay with Michael; that is, I had difficulty at times allowing him to regulate me. It will already have been noted from the session in which Michael finally had to remove my brain in order to make me keep quiet, my own personality is organized very much around the need for order, not chaos. For my part, there were times when Michael was engaged in making art, that I found myself unbearably sleepy. I believe my sleepiness in these sessions was a manifestation of my aversive withdrawal in response to a variety of issues. For example, Michael's requirement was often for me *not* to take part in what he was doing. When that happened I suffered from the loss of initiative in my own fundamental need to be actively involved. I also suffered in the face of Michael's requirement that I *not* make sense of things and my sleepiness may have grown out of my need to withdraw in the face of his craziness. For the most part, I enjoyed Michael enormously. He had a wonderful wit, and I was frequently charmed by his intelligence, originality, and humor. I delighted in his creativity and his artistic skills, and I enjoyed sharing in the excitement of creative expression together.

---

[2] These phases should also be understood in terms of Lichtenberg's "motivational systems" (Lichtenberg, 1989). In the dramatic enactments that cradled the transferences, Michael worked through his needs for attachment affiliation, physiological regulation (his eating in the early weeks), for adversarial and antagonistic expression (the master/victim enactments), for assertive/exploratory excitement (following my casting him as the captain of our spaceship, he could later become the leader in our journeys), and he staked his claim in the domain of sensual and erotic pleasures (the champagne fountain of youth).

I have focused here on only a very small piece of the work with Michael. It is likely that Michael's "fit" within his complex family structure, along with his constitutional factors, predisposed him to his developmental disturbances. I was presented with a boy who had a predilection to terror; a child who suffered psychotic episodes and experienced the world as a noxious and apocalyptic place, where parents are dead or mothers forget about their babies, leaving them lost and abandoned; a child who was unable to adequately protect himself from the violent treatment meted out by his brother and whose play revealed some gender disturbance. We know that his mother was distracted and that his father found a better fit with Michael's brother. We also know that from infancy, Michael had a temperamental sensitivity to overstimulation across the spectrum of sensory modalities. It was also evident that there were attachment difficulties that had left him impaired, caused in part by his mother's distracted and distant style of parenting and partly because he could not adequately signal his needs. This had left him with a limited capacity for self-regulation in all of the motivational systems described by Lichtenberg (1989 and Lichtenberg, Lachmann, and Fosshage 1992). He was also a boy who was multitalented, highly intelligent, even brilliant at times, and possessed of a lovely sense of humor.

At the end of treatment, which lasted 3 years, Michael still at times moved back and forth in sessions between cohesion and coherence and others in which he could be scattered and difficult to track. At times he could be a witty and articulate raconteur, and at others the old familiar themes of chaos, annihilation, loss, and abandonment prevailed, although this was seen less and less. Just before the end of therapy Michael recounted and drew a profoundly meaningful dream that contained representations of himself and his family, which he interpreted by himself with some skill and insight. I have not discussed the working through of Michael's gender disorder, and although by the end of therapy his self-representations were predominantly male, I believe this issue will require more work in the future, as Michael moves fully into adolescence.

For the moment Michael's house of terror has given way to more complex and far less threatening domiciles, and the world of sensual and sensory pleasures can be explored with less anxiety and a greater degree of comfort.

REFERENCES

Axline, V. (1947), *Play Therapy*. New York. Ballantine Books.

Bacal, H. & Thomson, P. (1996), The psychoanalyst's selfobject needs and the effect of their frustration on the treatment: A new view of countertransference. In: *Basic*

Ideas Reconsidered, Progress in Self Psychology, Vol. 12, ed. A. Goldberg. Hillsdale, NJ: The Analytic Press, pp. 17–35.

Beebe, B. (1986), Mother–infant mutual influence and precursors of self-and-object representations. *Empir. Stud. Psychoanal. Theories,* 2:27–48.

—— & Lachmann, F. (1988), Mother–infant mutual influence-precursors of psychic structure. In: *Frontiers in Self Psychology, Progress in Self Psychology, Vol. 3,* ed. A. Goldberg. Hillsdale, NJ: The Analytic Press, pp. 3–25.

Bowlby, J. (1979), *The Making and Breaking of Affectional Bonds.* London: Tavistock, pp. 1–11

Fox, J., ed. (1987), *The Essential Moreno.* New York: Springer.

Freud, A. (1965), *Normality and Pathology in Childhood.* New York: International Universities Press.

Freud, S. (1914), Remembering, repeating and working through. *Standard Edition,* 12:147–156. London: Hogarth Press, 1958.

Irwin, E. (1985), Externalizing and improvising imagery through drama therapy: A psychoanalytic view. *J. Mental Imag.* 4:33–42.

Jennings, S. (1992), *Dramatherapy, Theory and Practice 2.* London: Tavistock/ Routledge.

Klein, M. (1932), *The Psychoanalysis of Children.* London: Hogarth Press.

Kohut, H. (1971), *The Analysis of the Self.* Madison, CT: International Universities Press.

Lachmann, F. & Beebe, B. (1992), Representational and selfobject transferences: A developmental perspective. In: *New Therapeutic Visions, Progress in Self Psychology, Vol. 8,* ed. A. Goldberg. Hillsdale, NJ: The Analytic Press, pp. 3–15.

Landy, R. (1986), *Drama Therapy, Concepts and Practices.* Springfield, IL: Thomas.

—— (1993), *Persona and Performance.* New York: Guilford.

Lichtenberg, J. (1989), *Psychoanalysis and Motivation.* Hillsdale, NJ: The Analytic Press.

—— Lachmann, F. & Fosshage, J. (1992), *Self and Motivational Systems.* Hillsdale, NJ: The Analytic Press.

Mahler, M., Pine, F. & Bergman, A. (1975), *The Psychological Birth of the Human Infant.* New York: Basic Books.

Meares, R. (1990), The fragile spielraum. In: *The Realities of Transference: Progress in Self Psychology, Vol. 6,* ed. A. Goldberg. Hillsdale, NJ: The Analytic Press.

Stolorow, R. & Lachmann, F. (1984/1985), Transference: The future of an illusion. In: *The Annual of Psychoanalysis,* 12/13. New York: International Universities Press, pp. 19–38.

—— Brandchaft, B. & Atwood, G., with F. Lachmann (1987), Transference— The organization of experience. In: *Psychoanalytic Treatment.* Hillsdale, NJ: The Analytic Press, pp. 28–46.

Winnicott, D. W. (1971), *Playing and Reality.* London: Tavistock.

Wordsworth, W. I wandered lonely as a cloud. In: *Master Poems of the English Language,* ed. O. Williams. New York: Washington Square Press, 1968, p. 427.

Chapter 18

An Intersubjective Approach to Conjoint Family Therapy

David Shaddock

In the Epilogue to *The Restoration of the Self*, Heinz Kohut (1977), seeking to understand the increase in the number of self disorders he observed, turned his attention to the changing nature of family process: "The environment which used to be experienced as threateningly close, is now experienced more and more as threateningly distant; where children were formerly *over* stimulated by the emotional (including the erotic) life of their parents, they are now often under stimulated" (p. 271). These speculations, which shift the focus of the study of intra-psychic life from universal psychological structures to those that arise in the context of a relational field, foreshadow the paradigm shift that Stolorow (1994) calls the "most important development in psycho-analysis over the past decade ... the growing recognition that intra-psychic phenomenon must be understood in the context of the larger interaction systems in which they take form" (p. 3).

Families constitute one of the prime examples of such a "larger inter-actional system." The concept of the "intersubjective field—a system formed by the reciprocal interplay between two (or more) subjective worlds" (Stolorow and Atwood, 1992, p. 4) usefully lends itself to an examination of family process. In this chapter I will offer some theoreti-cal considerations in extending the intersubjective perspective to the study of family process and then discuss a case where the intersubjective approach facilitated a successful treatment of a 16-year-old boy.

Delivered at the 18th Conference on the Psychology of the Self, October 19, 1995, San Francisco, CA.

Several authors, including Lansky (1981), Scharf and Scharf (1987), and Slipp (1984) have lamented the schism between psychoanalysis and family systems theory. The unfortunate result of this schism is that, until recently, family systems theorists focused exclusively on the environmental causes of behavior, believing that intrapsychic life was a "black box" (Slipp, 1984).

The past 15 years have seen a significant body of literature that has attempted to bridge this gulf (Stierlin, 1977; Lansky, 1981). Drawing largely from theories of group process derived from the British School of object relations theorists, the Scharffs (1987) and Samuel Slipp (1984, 1988) have created a theory of object relations based family process. Lansky (1981) and Solomon (1989) have extended self-psychological concepts, especially the regulation of narcissism, to the study of couples.

So far, much of intersubjectivity's focus has been on the "developmental system" (Stolorow, 1994) and on the intersubjective field of the analyst/patient relationship. Recently, Trop (1994) and Ringstrom (1994) have extended the intersubjective approach to conjoint couples therapy. This chapter attempts to extend those pioneering applications to the treatment of families.

CONCEPTUAL DIFFICULTIES IN MOVING BEYOND THE TWO-BODY MODEL

The advent of the new paradigm in psychoanalysis has successfully moved the scope of analytic inquiry beyond the one-body model of endogenously derived conflict into a consideration of the psychological system formed between two differently organized subjectivities. In moving to a consideration of the couples therapy situation, both Trop and Ringstrom emphasize that the therapist is now part of a three-person system. According to Trop (1994): "The area of investigation of the therapist is the interaction between the subjective worlds of the two partners, as well as the meanings that occur at the interface of the interacting subjectivities of the therapist and each member of the couple" (p. 149). An investigation of family process involves looking at systems with three or more members, each of whom is simultaneously organizing their experience of relating to the others. In addition, each member is responding to the family system as a whole. Statements like "my family never supported my career" acknowledge that individuals yearn for the family to meet their selfobject needs. Statements such as "my family needs me to be strong" acknowledge that individual family members simultaneously experience the family as requiring selfobject functions *from* them.

In responding to the analogous dilemma of conceptualizing group process, Weinstein (1991) describes the "group self" in which the group is experienced as "an organism with its own boundaries, and its own self-cohesion-fragmentation spectrum" (p. 221). Solomon (1989) posits the existence of a "*mutual self* or *joint personality* that emerges from the marital interaction" (p. 27). In this spirit I propose to speak of a *family self*.

The reciprocal interactions of the different subjectivities in a family create a family self that is bigger than the sum of its parts. This family self is organized by each individual member into his or her subjective experience of being in the family. Simultaneously, the family self organizes family life and provides collective meanings to family experience. In understanding family process, the therapist is faced with the daunting task of examining the subjective experience of each family member's relationship to the others, the transferences each member has to the family self, the way the family self collectively organizes the family experience, and the requirements it makes on its members. Fortunately, I have found that even partial understanding of these different areas can be extremely illuminating.

THE SELFOBJECT DIMENSION OF FAMILY EXPERIENCE

Ringstrom (1994) uses Stolorow, Brandchaft, and Atwood's (1987) bipolar classification of the transference into the selfobject and repetitive dimensions to illuminate the subjective experience of couples, in which the partners "deeply hope their sense of self will finally be accepted, affirmed and encouraged while they also deeply fear that it will not be" (p. 159). Family experience is likewise marked by this combination of yearnings and fears.

Individual members look to the family to provide selfobject experiences such as being the small part of a larger, protective whole, and to register and respond to their affects. The alter-ego experiences of belonging and identity are perhaps the most important family function. Traditionally, to be cut off from one's family is to be a drifter, one who barely belongs to the human race. Other selfobject dimensions of the family include the following:

Thematically Organizing Individual Experience

The family provides underlying meanings for affective experience. For example, in a family that is organized around a theme of sacrifice, the underlying belief is that family members must subordinate their self-delineation to the greater needs of the family. Individual frustrations or disappointments, such as a mother's putting her career on hold, become organized by the family as worthwhile, even noble, accomplishments. I am here stressing the positive function of such thematizing as an amelioration of the disappointment. Of course, as I will discuss shortly, this process can also feel distorting and invasive.

The underlying organizing principles in families that contribute to the thematizing of experience are analogous to what Minuchin and Fishman (1981) call family myths. In the case where the myths support the family's problems, these theorists see the primary therapeutic task as "reframing" them in order to "move the family toward a more differentiated and competent dealing with their dysfunctional reality" (p. 74). These myths often derive from "invariant and relentless principles of organization that remain beyond the accommodative influence of reflective self-awareness or subsequent experience" (Brandchaft and Stolorow, 1990, p. 108). As the case I will discuss shortly demonstrates, a reframing of such an organizing principle is best achieved by a "stance of empathic inquiry" that "will lead to an awareness, deepening investigation, and gradual illumination of existing unconscious organizing principles and their continuing contribution to the repetitive course that life takes" (Brandchaft, 1994, p. 75). This is in sharp contrast to the stance that Minuchin and Fishman (1981) advise, in which the authoritarian therapist "challenges the family's accepted reality with an orientation toward growth" (p. 67).

Regulating Affect

Homeostasis (Jackson and Weakland, 1968) is a central tenet of systems theory. Families have a set-point for how much affect they can tolerate and have developed fixed ways to return the family to equilibrium when that set-point is exceeded. When powerful affects, especially shame and anger, threaten to destabilize the system, they are homeostatically modified. For example, a child may become increasingly symptomatic in response to increased tension in the couple relationship. The mechanistic metaphor of homeostasis belies the complex nature of the response, which is the result of simultaneous organizing of the affects by the individuals, followed by cueing and initiating the regulatory behavior. The more prone to fragmentation the family self is, the greater the burden on these homeostatic mechanisms. As Lansky (1981) points out, "A chaotic family homeostasis is maintained by collusive defenses, humiliation proneness, and terror of separations" (p. 9).

Boundary Formation

Stolorow et al. (1987) have described the derailment of self-differentiation that takes place when the boundary between the caregiver's needs and the child's emerging affect states is blurred. Such boundary issues are also important at the family systems level. A strong but flexible boundary between parents and children allows the children valuable access (both cognitive and affectual) to the adult world, while at the same time protecting them from intrusion. Conversely, enmeshed families tend to share affect states, preventing the child from experiencing the "differentiating responsiveness to [his] affect states [which] constitutes a central selfobject function of the caregiving surround, in establishing the earliest rudiments of self definition and self boundary formation" (Stolorow et al., 1987, p. 70).

Naming and Repairing Selfobject Injuries[1]

According to Stolorow and Atwood (1992), when a child has suffered a disappointment or rebuff to his selfobject needs, he will experience a "secondary selfobject longing for an attuned response that would modulate, contain and ameliorate his painful reactive affect state" (p. 53). Families potentially offer a number of avenues to such selfobject repair: the other parent, grandparents, siblings, and so forth. Even if an offending parent is too narcissistically vulnerable to acknowledge the child's feelings, another family member can confirm the validity of the child's experience, providing a vital self-delineating experience.

Kohut's (1984) assertion of the persistence of selfobject needs throughout the life span is central to my understanding of the way the yearning for these selfobject experiences colors family life. For the parents, providing children with selfobject experiences is the central task, but this provision does not replace, and in some cases actually exacerbates, the parents' yearning for the family to meet their own needs. The therapist's attuned response to these yearnings in all the family members can help the family lower its defenses. The family members can begin to feel a renewed sense of shared purpose, which can then be mobilized in the therapeutic task.

THE REPETITIVE POLE OF FAMILY EXPERIENCE

Of course, families can also violate or disrupt self-experience. Yearned for mirroring can be conditional, requiring the conforming to family

---

[1] This family selfobject function was suggested by Jeffrey Trop, M.D.

norms at the price of individuality. The sense of the family as admirable and protective can be traumatically disrupted, as when the myth of the happy family is shattered by the revelation of an affair. Conflicts in the family can lead to expulsion or voluntary cutoff from the family system, traumatically ending the family's being a source of alter-ego experiences. The meanings that the family gives to individual experience may be distorted or reductive, as when a family that is organized around a fear of abandonment exaggerates a child's problem in order to keep him dependent. The set-point for affect tolerance may be so high in chaotic families that the members are chronically overstimulated. Boundaries may be so diffuse or so frequently violated that self-delineation within the family becomes almost impossible. The family's defenses may be so pervasive as to preclude the acknowledgment or repair of an individual's injury. In an alcoholic family, for instance, the family might unite in defensive denial of the problem at the expense of a child who is a victim of the alcoholic's abuse.

When adults form their own families, negative or traumatic experiences in their family of origin color their expectations. These fears can become enshrined in the family organization. The family self then functions defensively, and all family members are limited by these defenses. The developmental stages that children progress through can trigger these defensive reactions. A 2-year-old's intense self-delineation can flood the family system with feelings of being frustrated or held back. An adolescent's relentless criticism can challenge the organizing principles of the family. The adolescent's budding sexuality challenges the family system to accept these expansive feelings .

CONCRETIZATION

When fears of traumatic repetition predominate, the family self is fragile and characterized by defensive organization. In such families children are called upon to concretize the family's subjective experience, to the detriment of their own development. Concretization is defined by Atwood and Stolorow (1984) as "the encapsulation of structures of experience by concrete, sensorimotor symbols" (p. 85). Stolorow and Atwood (1992) state that concretization's "most general, supraordinate function is to dramatize, reify, and thereby maintain the organization of the subjective world" (p. 44). Families concretize their experience in various ways, including the assigning of fixed identities (one child is the smart one, another is "cute" but ineffectual) and the enactment (Atwood and Stolorow, 1984) of fixed or ritualized behavior patterns.

Understanding the process of concretization and enactment allows the therapist to rapidly connect disparate parts of the family process to the underlying organizing principles and disavowed affects that support them.

I will now turn to a case that demonstrates the advantages of the intersubjective approach applied to conjoint family therapy. This treatment took place once a week over a period of 18 months, with decreasing frequency toward the end of that time.

CASE EXAMPLE

The B family was referred to me by the mother's analyst, who felt that the 16-year-old son's acting out was undermining his mother's analytic progress. The family consisted of Theresa, the mother, an attractive 44-year-old woman of Latin-American descent who worked as an executive in the food industry; Gerald, her 16-year-old son who dressed entirely in black and communicated almost exclusively with sarcasm or cryptic phrases such as "We'll see about that"; and the boy's stepfather, Don, a 45-year-old scientist who worked as an executive in a disaster relief organization. In making the referral, the analyst stressed that, although she was doing better recently, the mother was still extremely fragile, having been hospitalized twice in the last 6 years for depression, once following a suicide attempt. She was diagnosed as borderline in the hospital.

Don had been in the family since Gerald was two. Gerald saw Ken, his father, about once a month. Gerald behaved well and received excellent grades in school until he was 11, when things began to deteriorate. Gerald began doing poorly in school. Where before Don had actively participated in helping him with his homework, now Gerald began to refuse Don's help. By the time he entered treatment, Gerald was flunking nearly all of his classes. He spent a great deal of time in his room, and his only friends were two older neighbor boys of Chinese-American descent, with whom he shared a passion for kung fu style gangster movies.

I initially interviewed the family in different combinations, seeing the entire family, the parents conjointly, and Gerald alone. The family sessions revolved around the parents' desperate attempts to get Gerald to communicate. Gerald would thwart all such attempts, remaining silent or starting absurd arguments, such as a discussion of what it means to talk ("See, I'm talking to you. My mouth is moving. Talk, talk, talk."). Theresa would grow increasingly solicitous and desperate. In one session Don got very angry and confrontational (which was highly unlike him) and Gerald registered some hurt and anger and then pulled himself up. Soon after this, Gerald refused to participate in any more family sessions.

This was more or less the way it went in my individual sessions with Gerald. In one of these sessions he reached into his pocket and tossed me a disposable cigarette lighter. "What's that thing I just threw you?" he asked. Then, following my puzzled silence, he answered his own question: "It's a cigarette lighter. Sometimes things are just what they seem, not what some psychologist tries to make them into." After some thought I replied, "I think you're telling me to leave you alone, not to probe inside you. I guess you can't stand that right now." Gerald nodded in agreement. Soon after, he began refusing to come, either to individual or family sessions. The parents offered to try and force him, but I told them that I felt that this would be counterproductive.

I decided to work with the couple around parenting issues. Early on, I noticed that Theresa would stiffen when I made a parenting suggestion. I decided as much as possible to refrain from suggestions, and, instead, tried to remain empathically attuned to the parents' experience and to let the underlying meanings of that experience emerge. This stance was not achieved without anxiety on my part, because I had to let go of my own need to provide immediate solutions for these likable and struggling parents and help for this obviously troubled boy.

Many times Theresa presented in a highly fragmented state or became fragmented during the session. In the latter case it was usually in response to something I had said that made her feel criticized or slighted. In one instance she became anxious and withdrawn after a remark that I made concerning the discrepancy in income between Don and Ken, who was a factory worker. (I wondered if it wasn't confusing for Gerald to have a stepfather who could buy him things that his father couldn't.) Exploration of Theresa's reaction to my remark revealed that she felt that I was ignoring her contribution to the family income. This, in turn, revealed some significant parts of Theresa's family history. The oldest daughter of a large family, she was the only child who graduated high school and had risen far higher economically than anyone else in her family. She felt that her family didn't appreciate her success and was jealous of her. She also had considerable guilt about doing so much better than her parents.

When I asked about who in her family had appreciated her as a child, Theresa told me about her troubled relationship with her father, who had been very inappropriate sexually. As an adolescent she had been his favorite, and he used to enjoy showing her off. He even got her a job dancing as a go-go dancer in a cage in a nightclub he liked to frequent. When I asked what that was like for her, she replied that she remembered liking all the attention and then looked at me to see if I disapproved. I felt that one disapproving look from me would have sent her into a fragmented state, flooded with shame. She also remembered several instances when her father had tried to fondle her breasts. She had begun to recover memories of these incidents about 5 years ago, about the time that Gerald had entered puberty. She had begun to wonder if she had repressed memories of incest, and has been pursuing this issue in her own analysis.

Don's family history also emerged at this time. The oldest son of a working class family, he had been relentlessly pressured to succeed. As he put it, "Fortunately I fell in love with science, so my dad's pressure wasn't so bad." I came to believe that this statement reflected both the fact that the family pressure hadn't completely derailed his self-delineation and the fact that he had repressed his own desire to live a life free of others' expectations. Don had been married once before, to a stewardess who had become "crazily dependent on him." I wondered at the pattern of being a rescuer, and he acknowledged that there was something to it, that he was probably repeating his role in his own family. We both laughed when I remarked that in his job with the disaster relief organization he had made a career of it. Don repeatedly provided vital selfobject functions for Theresa, remaining very calm and empathic while she entered deeply fragmented states.

Don was puzzled and a little bitter that Gerald had so violently withdrawn from the family. He initially continued to try to be friendly and helpful to Gerald, but his disappointment came through with outbursts of anger. Lately he reported that he felt withdrawn and distant from Gerald. This feeling was not reflected in the early family sessions, in which Don actively tried to get Gerald to communicate.

About 4 months into treatment, Theresa came in saying that, though she didn't really understand why, she had something she needed to tell me. She then proceeded to reveal a secret that, until now, only Don and Ken knew: Gerald was conceived in a brief affair with a man she barely knew. She had not even revealed this to her analyst. (Later, on my urging, she was able to bring it up.) I was tempted to explore the way this secret functioned in the family system, but instead I focused on the meanings that this event had for her.

At times she showed compassion for herself: "I married Ken to get away from my father, and I had the affair to get away from Ken." At other times she would be overcome with shame and would repeat over and over that she was bad. She would lament that she had damaged Gerald terribly. Or she would worry that she had not done enough to keep him from being sexually molested. An exploration of this belief revealed a pervasive fear that Gerald might be molested at any time and that it was up to her to try and stop it. Clearly, at such moments the boundary between her and her son was blurred. I began to see that at such times Gerald became a concretization of Theresa's belief in her inherent badness and of the belief that her loving, expansive feelings were destructive. "I was so happy when Gerald was born, but look how it has turned out. I've really damaged him." Underlying this sense of badness were the powerful affects of shame that her father's misuse of her emerging sexuality had engendered.

Theresa was very afraid how I would handle this secret: "If you tell me I've got to tell Gerald, I'll leave and never come back." I reassured her that I would leave that decision up to her. My response to this material lowered the anxiety level in the family and created an important bond between the parents and myself.

This bond was severely tested a few months later when Gerald left home during a fight with his parents over sitting down to dinner with the family. He was not seen or heard from for the next 10 days. During this time I met with the family four times and was in daily phone contact. I shared with them their intense worry and also their anger at Gerald for doing this to them. Gerald reappeared, but would not say a word about what had happened to him or where he had been.

At this point I became increasingly concerned about Gerald. The parents were considering placing him in a locked residential treatment school. I made a referral to a colleague for Gerald to be tested, and Theresa assured me that she would get Gerald to the appointments.

The results of the testing were very illuminating. Though Gerald had been highly resistant, my colleague felt that he had been able to engage Gerald enough to get a valid profile. Gerald had a combined IQ of 122. He showed no learning disabilities that would have accounted for his poor school performance. Indeed, his math achievement scores showed that he had learned algebra, even while getting D's and F's in his math classes. His projective tests showed deep isolation, somewhat regressed object relations, and narcissistic defenses. On the other hand, the psychologist felt that he had a fairly intact sense of self. The psychologist used the phrase that he believed Gerald could be "socialized by his peers" if the negative relationship between him and his parents could be interrupted.

This testing was very helpful in organizing my own subjective experience of the family. I felt reassured by it that Gerald did not have some crippling pathology and was not actively sociopathic. Of equal importance was the way I was able to assimilate the information as coming from an idealizable expert. In turn, I was able to function in the family as an idealizable selfobject, directing changes in the family interactions. I now felt I understood the family system and had enough trust from the family to begin to intervene.

INTERVENTIONS

The underlying assumption that guided my attempts to intervene in the family process was a belief that, if the all-encompassing enactment could be interrupted, Gerald's longing for selfobject experiences with his peers could be mobilized and his developmental arrest reversed. To this end I made the following suggestions to the parents:

(1) They should stop endlessly questioning, arguing, complaining, and cajoling Gerald. I explained to the parents that this aspect of the family process was keeping Gerald stuck and, though he might try very hard to engage them in it, that they should try and resist as best they could.

(2) In the place of these endless go-rounds, they should use a strategy I called "touch and go," in which they gave Gerald short bits of feedback about the effect of his behavior on them, such as "I really dislike your sarcastic answers," or "you really worried us last night when you came in late." If Gerald responded to these by trying to argue, they were urged to break the argument off as soon as possible. In addition to interrupting the enactment, I felt that this suggestion would interrupt the faulty mirroring (i.e., the hovering, the fascination) that supported Gerald's grandiosity and replace it with more accurate responses that might foster his self-delineation.

(3) They should remove all academic pressure from Gerald and tell him that, from now on, his decisions were his own. All of their attempts to get Gerald to study—including grounding him for long periods of time—had failed and in many ways had been counterproductive. Grounding him had only isolated him further from any development-enhancing contact with his peers. Pressure to perform only heightened the anxiety that Gerald's oppositional imperviousness was trying to mask.

(4) They should try and facilitate his moving out into the world. Gerald was about to turn 17 and did not have a driver's license—a significant developmental delay for a young California boy. The parents told Gerald that they expected him to get a license and begin to provide his own transportation, and that if he would get a job for the summer, they would help him buy a car and pay for his insurance.

I framed these interventions around the interpretation that, based on the psychological testing, I now felt that Gerald was basically all right, but that he needed to stop being so embroiled in the family and get on with his life. I interpreted Gerald's attempts to recreate the family imbroglio as an attempt to hold onto something safe in the face of the daunting task of moving into the world.

The results were very encouraging. The parents were able to bring their confusion and struggles about these suggestions to the sessions and to ask for my help, which let me know that they were not reacting defensively to them. During this time I urged them to try and rely on each other for clarification and support, which they were able to do. The parents reported that Gerald's behavior began to change. Although he still frequently tried to engage them in absurd arguments, he also began to be more open and pleasant. He began having dinner with the family again and occasionally wore colors other than black. He took his family up on the offer to get a car. He got a summer job at a company that manufactured stereo speakers. He asked Don to teach him how to drive. He failed his driving test twice, yet persevered and passed it on the third time. Given the pervasiveness of his grandiose defenses, the fact that he was able to endure the failures and persevere was a most hopeful sign.

Several months after I made my suggestions, Don was called out of town to run his agency's relief efforts at a major natural disaster. Theresa was quite labile at first, but with the help of nightly phone consultations with Don, she was able to maintain the implementation of the interventions on her own. During this time I met with the parents whenever Don was in town, about twice a month on the average. Theresa gained great self-confidence in her parenting ability, and this confidence enhanced other areas of her life. She applied for and received a promotion to a more creative part of her company. As of this writing she is about to matriculate at a prestigious women's college to finish her degree. Gerald has developed a much wider social life, including many friends his own age. He has begun dating and is even bringing his girlfriends home. In a telling detail, Theresa reported that one of Gerald's girlfriends had looked askance at him when he went into one of his sarcastic tirades and that he had stopped himself and began to act more politely. It appears from this story that his desire for an approving selfobject response was stronger than his need to maintain his grandiose defenses within the family. Gerald's school performance has improved somewhat, but still remains an area of concern for the family. He is presently planning to attend a local junior college after high school.

DISCUSSION

From the time that Theresa married Don until the time that Gerald entered puberty, the family organization was relatively stable. Don's idealizable presence provided much of that stability. When Gerald entered puberty, Theresa began recovering memories of sexual abuse from her own adolescence—memories that were accompanied by terrible feelings of shame. This shame, concretized around the circumstances of Gerald's conception, threatened the family self's cohesiveness. Theresa would often lapse into fragmented self states that even Don's "goodness" wasn't enough to ameliorate. In fact, as Gerald began rebelling against the academic pressure that came with Don's parenting, Don came into contact with his own suppressed wishes to rebel. The family self was flooded with potentially destabilizing affects, which defensively became organized in the family as the belief that there was something bad or even destructive at its core that they must work very hard to fix. Gerald's behavior—acting mysteriously, being rude, failing in school—and the parents' response to Gerald—hovering solicitously, vigilantly monitoring his every action—were an enactment that concretized this belief. The enactment allowed the parents to try to control this badness and to attempt to keep the family self from further fragmenting. This family self was created by a confluence of the subjective organizations of the individual family members.

Gerald's mysterious and oppositional behavior, along with his kung fu gangster fantasies, were part of a defensive grandiosity (Stolorow, personal communication; Morrison and Stolorow, in press) against the underlying belief that he was bad or unlovable. According to Morrison and Stolorow, this "conscious, noisy grandiosity" is not a derivative of unmediated archaic grandiosity, still longing for an approving mirroring response, as Kohut (1971) thought, but a defense against the overwhelming experience of having that archaic grandiosity traumatically crushed: "The imperiousness ('I don't need you') keeps the longing for such mirroring repressed." We can speculate that Theresa nonverbally communicated to Gerald her shame at his being the product of an affair, perhaps by responding warily to his expansive moods or attempts at self-delineation. The family remembers Gerald as a very good little boy—evidence of his attempts to compliantly dispel any underlying worries about his badness. When he entered adolescence, Gerald's budding sexual interest and renewed attempts at self-delineation were crushed by the twin traumas of his mother's fragmented withdrawal (which would be followed by periods of overzealous parenting) and Don's rejection (which was also masked by periods of solicitous behavior).

Identifying the defensive nature of Gerald's grandiosity allowed me to see his behavior not as a disguised communication of his selfobject needs, as, for example, a cry for attention or an attempt to mobilize his parents, but rather as a strategy that was keeping him isolated both from his own selfobject longings and from any chance of a development-enhancing selfobject experience. The maintenance of this defense required his refusal to live in the real world, since doing anything on the material plane (taking a test, expressing a feeling) threatened to defeat the defense and expose the underlying affects of shame and rejection.

Don's self-organization was similar to Gerald's, if less all-encompassing in its defenses. His attempts to remain constantly idealizable in the family were a kind of defensive grandiosity. They functioned to ward off his needs for an attuned response to his own states of sadness or depletion, as well as his longing for mirroring approval for his attempts at self-delineation—selfobject experiences denied him by his family's requirement that he be their hero and savior. Gerald's adolescent rebellion concretized Don's disavowed longings for self-delineation. As the treatment progressed, Don begin to voice his own dissatisfactions with family life. When Gerald ran away, Don was able to say that he felt completely defeated and depleted: "This is just not the way I dreamed the family would turn out. I go back and forth between being worried sick about Gerald and being sick of the whole thing." When he would say things like this, Don would often look to Theresa to see if she disapproved. Theresa, to his surprise, would often express great relief, saying that his expressions of negativity helped her to accept her own negative feelings.

Theresa's self-organization reflected Stolorow et al.'s (1987) conceptualization of the borderline as a "precarious, vulnerable self in a failing archaic selfobject bond," but also showed impressive resilience in the presence of a restorative selfobject experience. Her relationship with Don included experiences of both types. As I mentioned earlier, Don often provided her with an idealizable, calm selfobject experience that brought her back from severe states of fragmentation. But there were other times when these same qualities were provocative. At these times she would grow agitated with Don and tell him to leave her alone. It was especially agitating to Theresa when Don would try and talk her out of her belief that she was a bad mother.

These two disparate experiences of Don reflected Theresa's disparate experiences with her father. As a young child she had felt consolidated by her relationship to this strong man who adored her. This idealizing tie was traumatically ruptured by his sexual misuse of her. Theresa's mother refused to acknowledge that anything abnormal was going on, thus depriving her of any self-delineating confirmation of her confused and ashamed feelings. In the earlier part of their relationship, Theresa had recreated an idealizable selfobject tie with Don. When she began to experience the shameful affects of the sexual abuse, Don's positivity felt unempathic and, indeed, sometimes had the effect of furthering her childhood belief that she was making all of the problems up. Conversely,

Don's expression of his own sadness and anger provided a self-delineating confirmation of Theresa's own family experience.

When we look at Gerald's situation systemically, we see that he is in a double bind, for he is being called upon to simultaneously concretize Don's grandiosity by succeeding and also to concretize Theresa's shame by acting as an extension of her badness. Many of my interventions were directed at freeing him from this bind.

CONCLUSION

Gerald's dramatic improvement demonstrates the power of family therapy as a treatment modality for children and adolescents. It offers the potential to change the intersubective field between the child and his caregivers, interrupting injurious patterns and replacing them with more development-enhancing ones. This shift was facilitated by a change in the way the parents organized their experience of Gerald. Prior to treatment, both parents habitually replaced their spontaneous feeling response to Gerald's obnoxious behavior, such as anger and disapproval, with one that was organized around their own sense of inadequacy. This organizing activity had the effect of reifying Gerald's "badness" and forcing him into his defensive grandiosity. The main achievement of treatment was that this "existing structure" could be "disarticulated and its power curtailed, so that alternative ways of organizing experience and new implementing structure may develop" (Brandchaft, 1994, p. 75). In a therapeutic atmosphere of sustained empathic inquiry, Don and Theresa began to believe that they could be adequate parents and that Gerald, though he had many fears, could successfully move into the world. The family self became reorganized into one that allowed greater self-delineation—Gerald's increased social life, Theresa's return to school, Don's career-enhancing relocation—while still providing connection.

Conjoint therapy is unique in that treatment simultaneously facilitates development-enhancing relationships among the family members and provides a new intersubjective relationship between the therapist and the individual members. The nature of family therapy, with its emphasis on symptom resolution, precluded a working through of these individual relationships. Nonetheless, I believe the successful outcome indicates that the interventions functioned as development-enhancing interpretations, in which past relationship experiences are disconfirmed, and "alternative principles for organizing experience gradually come into being" (Stolorow, 1993, p. 35). Several messages underlie the interventions: (1) you are basically intact, (2) your spontaneous feelings are valid,

(3) your longing to enact negative relationship patterns is regressive and should be renounced, because (4) your natural expansiveness can lead you to get your needs met by the world outside your family of origin. Because of her profound identification with Gerald, Theresa unconsciously heard the interventions as directed at her as well. The therapeutic relationship in general and the interventions in particular helped her to disarticulate two pathogenic organizing principles: that she was inexorably damaged by past trauma and that her expansiveness would damage others. The unfinished piece of business with Theresa remains the secret of Gerald's paternity. Of course, my willingness to accept this secret does not amount to a resolution. I believe the family therapy only removed this secret from its supraordinate place in the family organization.

For Don, the interventions challenged the notion that enmeshment in a system that doesn't meet your needs is the price you have to pay to maintain a relationship tie. The messages conveyed by the interventions: to keep interactions short and emotionally honest, not to get embroiled, and to "go get a driver's license" also conveyed to Don my approval of his own yearnings for self-delineation and expansion within a supportive relational matrix.

The intersubjective relationship between myself and Gerald was, of course, the most elusive. Had I been able to find a way to keep Gerald in treatment, the therapy might have looked quite different. As it was, I was able to convey to Gerald, in our brief encounter and through the interventions, two important relational messages: (1) that I would respect his boundaries and understood the need for his grandiose defenses, and (2) that I also understood that the maintenance of those defenses was keeping him from having the expansive and self-affirming experiences I knew he was longing for. It is worthwhile noting that, toward the end of the treatment, the parents reported that Gerald began expressing curiosity about the sessions and would offer his own critique with comments like "I could have told you that."

The shift in the family system does not amount to a complete cure for Gerald. Interrupting the family enactment merely allowed him respite from his need to maintain his grandiose defenses at all costs. This, in turn, allowed him to express some of the genuine expansiveness and self-delineation that is an intrinsic part of adolescence. The long-term effects of Gerald's missing these critical opportunities for self-development would have been very deleterious. It is probable that Gerald will need treatment at a later date, but there is a good chance that he will arrive at such a point with enough self-cohesion to readily avail himself of it.

I want to close by discussing the unique advantages that the intersubjective approach offered to this treatment. It is true that the same interventions could have been made by a therapist informed by other theories. An object relations oriented therapist would have looked at the good/bad splits in the family system, seen Gerald's behavior as a product of projective identification, and intervened to block the delegation of badness to Gerald. (The author at one point discussed this case with an object relations oriented family therapist, who recommended a residential placement for Gerald.) However, intersubjectivity, which does not reify intrapsychic structure, allows for the possibility of a much more fluid shift in the meanings and organizations of family experience, facilitated by the therapist's empathic attunement.

In addition, the intersubjective approach offers the following advantages:

(1) Intersubjectivity doesn't pathologize or blame. The family therapy movement, which originated as a reaction to the tendency to blame the individual for his pathology, has too often blamed the family for the child's pathology (Lansky, 1981). This often leads an authoritarian family therapist, redirecting the families communication patterns, to inadvertently recreate the traumatic intersubjective experiences that created the family's defenses in the first place.

(2) An atmosphere of sustained empathic inquiry allows the disavowed selfobject yearnings in the family to emerge. The repetitive dimension of Theresa's family experience led her to believe that revealing the secret of Gerald's conception would lead to discounting or further shaming. As a result of my staying empathically attuned to her experience, a myriad of selfobject dimensions emerged: the family became a place where the parents fostered a belief in each other's competency, family life became thematized by the possibility of change, and so on. A crucial component of this atmosphere was my willingness to work with the family without the participation of the identified patient. By remaining attuned to the meaning of Gerald's refusal to participate, I refrained from conveying a sense of blame either to him or to the family.

(3) Closely related to this was a commitment to investigate the intersubjective field created by my entrance into the family. The correct timing of my interventions was not the product of omniscience. I made numerous interventions prior to the ones that proved effective. However, these precipitated disjunctions. By exploring the meanings that my earlier suggestions had for the family, I was able to repair the disjunction and, most important, develop the empathic bond that allowed my later interventions to be effective.

REFERENCES

Atwood, G. & Stolorow, R. (1984), *Structures of Subjectivity.* Hillsdale, NJ: The Analytic Press.

Brandchaft, B. (1994), To free the spirit from its cell. In: *The Intersubjective Perspective,* ed. R. Stolorow, G. Atwood & B. Brandchaft. Northvale, NJ: Aronson.

—— & Stolorow, R. (1990), Varieties of therapeutic alliance. *The Annual of Psychoanalysis,* 18:99–114. Hillsdale, NJ: The Analytic Press.

Jackson, D. & Weakland, J. (1968), Conjoint family therapy. Some considerations of theory, technique and results. In: *Therapy Communication and Change,* ed. D. Jackson. Palo Alto, CA: Science and Behavior Books.

Kohut, H. (1971), *The Analysis of the Self.* New York: International Universities Press.

—— (1977), *The Restoration of the Self.* New York: International Universities Press.

—— (1984), *How Does Analysis Cure?* ed. A. Goldberg & P. Stepansky. Chicago: The University of Chicago Press.

Lansky, M. (1981), Major psychopathology and family therapy. In: *Family Therapy and Major Psychopathology,* ed. M. Lansky. New York: Grune & Stratton.

Minuchin, S. & Fishman, H. (1981), *Structural Family Therapy.* Cambridge, MA: Harvard University Press.

Morrison, A. & Stolorow, R. (in press), Shame narcissism and intersubjectivity. In: *New Perspectives on Shame,* ed. M. Lansky & A. Morrison. Hillsdale, NJ: The Analytic Press.

Ringstrom, P. (1994). An intersubjective approach to conjoint therapy. In: *A Decade of Progress, Progress in Self Psychology, Vol. 10,* ed. A. Goldberg. Hillsdale, NJ: The Analytic Press, pp. 159–182.

Scharf D. & Scharf, J. (1987), *Object Relations Family Therapy.* Northvale, NJ: Aronson.

Slipp, S. (1984), *Object Relations.* Northvale, NJ: Aronson.

—— (1988), *Object Relations Family Therapy.* Northvale, NJ: Aronson.

Solomon, M. (1989), *Narcissism and Intimacy.* New York: Norton.

Stierlin, H. (1977), *Psychoanalysis and Family Therapy.* New York: Aronson.

Stolorow, R. (1993). Thoughts on the nature and therapeutic action of psychoanalytic interpretation. In: *The Widening Scope of Self Psychology, Progress in Self Psychology, Vol. 9,* ed. A. Goldberg. Hillsdale, NJ: The Analytic Press, pp. 31–94.

—— (1994), The intersubjective context of intrapsychic experience. In: *The Intersubjective Perspective,* ed. R. Stolorow, G. Atwood & B. Brandchaft. Northvale, NJ: Aronson.

—— & Atwood, G. (1992), *Contexts of Being.* Hillsdale, NJ: The Analytic Press.

—— Brandchaft, B. & Atwood, G. (1987), *Psychoanalytic Treatment.* Hillsdale, NJ: The Analytic Press

Trop, J. (1994), Conjoint therapy: An intersubjective approach. In: *A Decade of Progress, Progress in Self Psychology, Vol. 10,* ed. A. Goldberg. Hillsdale, NJ: The Analytic Press, pp. 147–158.

Weinstein, D. (1991), Exhibitionism in group psychotherapy. In: *The Evolution of Self Psychology, Progress in Self Psychology, Vol. 7,* ed. A. Goldberg. Hillsdale, NJ: The Analytic Press, pp. 219–234.

Chapter 19

Restoring Complexity To the Subjective Worlds of Profound Abuse Survivors

Lisa Hirschman

When persons are profoundly abused, aspects of their inner ability to experience and develop become hidden. Sometimes these abilities are irretrievably lost, and no amount of therapy can recover them. Other times fragments remain, protected from further abuse. This chapter outlines a therapeutic method that searches for and recovers these hidden abilities, thus reclaiming aspects of relatedness and growth for those who have been profoundly abused.

Central to the therapeutic method developed here is the concept of *detailing*. Detailing in this chapter is a description of an aspect of therapist activity suggested by Stolorow and Atwood's (1992) self-delineating selfobject function, by Kohut's (1971) mirroring selfobject function, and by Stern's (1985) infant research. Detailing is a form of therapeutic attunement that helps to "lift the patient's affective experience to higher levels of organization by facilitating its articulation in verbal symbols—an example of what we have termed the self-delineating self object function" (Stolorow and Atwood, 1992, p. 49). The purpose of detailing is to increase the patient's "sense of the real primarily . . . through the validating attunement of the caregiving surround, an attunement provided across a whole spectrum of affectively intense, positive and negative experiences" (Stolorow and Atwood, 1992, p. 27). An attempt is made to exemplify what attunement might sound like where patients have been traumatically silenced. Detailing builds on concepts from

Kohut, Stolorow, and Stern. As a therapeutic approach, detailing's major qualities include description, invention, and creativity. Its effective use in the clinical situation serves to restore the patient's capacity for relatedness and thus the patient's ability to experience. Stern's (1985) theories of infant development are useful here. Stern asserts "that the acquisition of language is potent in the service of union and togetherness. In fact, every word learned is a by-product of uniting two mentalities in a common symbol system, *a forging of shared meaning*" (p. 172, italics added). The bulk of this chapter will focus on the appropriate use of detailing and a discussion of its particular relevance for the traumatized patient. It is my contention that detailing deserves to be talked about as a specific and discrete therapeutic approach because its application enriches the therapy hour and expands the tools that the therapist can use. Although conceptually it may be subsumed under larger concepts such as mirroring and self-delineating selfobject functions, it expands the repertoire of therapy by deconstructing and explicating these concepts and by pointing out effective and specific therapeutic methods.

For the profoundly abused patient to build a sense of complexity and vital functioning, she may require cognitive access to the therapist's imagination, creativity, knowledge, and activity. This detailing behavior expresses the therapist's attunement to the patient's selfobject experience and is often the crucial element of repair for those who have been profoundly abused. Detailing expands the description of what this creative imagination might sound like and seeks to identify what appropriate moments exist in therapy that highlight, describe, and bring to light the patient's existing as yet hidden, capacity for experience.

In the past 20 years, the issues of physical and sexual abuse have been named, witnessed and brought out of the dark (Herman and Hirschman, 1977; Finkelhor, 1984; Russell, 1986; Courtois, 1988; Herman, 1992). Although recognition and statement of the problem are important, some treatment problems have developed. These patients have been misunderstood and their condition wrongly diagnosed. They have alternatively been called borderline personalities, hysterics, and even masochists, labels that carry a condemnatory tone (Herman, 1992). Another problem is the emergence of treatment methods that inadvertently encourage overidentification with the victim role. This chapter seeks to examine a way out of these problems by focusing on the therapist–patient intersubjective field (Stolorow, Brandchaft, and Atwood, 1987) and by acknowledging the creativity that the interplay of these two subjective worlds can have on patient development.

HISTORY OF PSYCHOTHERAPY TREATMENT FOR IDENTIFIED VICTIM POPULATION GROUPS

The self-help movement has created a new technique for treating patients. As resources for psychotherapy have become scarce, particularly for those of lesser economic means, self-help and problem-defined, therapist-led groups have often supplanted long-term treatment. Members of problem-defined groups are often offered a structured, predetermined, short-term treatment.

These groups often focus on the healing power of the group and on self-disclosure. Victims of abuse, such as adults who have been molested as children, have found such groups helpful, where appropriate attention has been given to their selfobject needs. Often, however, group treatment is not enough. Patients tend to consolidate a sense of themselves as sexually injured persons first. Thus, the patient is seen as ill, and in this illness the victim feels supported by others who also define themselves as ill. However, this notion of an unhealed, undifferentiated person still exists, primarily defined by the patient's sexual trauma. Rather than having a comprehensive definition of herself—that includes the capacity for relatedness and new experience—the patient's primary definition continues to rely on a static definition of sexual victimization. This therapeutic result is imprisoning.

Although it is important for the patients to understand that they have been victimized, the ultimate search in therapy must be to find positive, dynamic definitions of themselves. These well thought out, rich, and complex understandings of who the patient is must include both concepts of possibility for growth and relatedness. In these understandings, the patient incorporates the truth about the abuse but is not defined by it. For purposes of discussion, I shall call this the search for complexity and the capacity to experience.

PSYCHOTHERAPY WITH A PURPOSE: THE USES OF DIFFERENT MODELS TO PROMOTE EXPERIENCE AND DEVELOPMENT

By identifying aspects of group treatment (Herman and Schatzow, 1984) that can also inform individual therapy, perhaps therapists can develop a descriptive and integrated conceptual model that begins to describe what constitutes successful individual and group treatment for patients who are victims.

Self psychology (Kohut, 1971; Basch, 1988; Goldberg, 1988; Wolf, 1988; Stolorow and Atwood, 1992) sustains an interactive therapeutic attitude that is more congruent than the traditional "tabula rasa" psychoanalytic stance, with the needs of the traumatically abused patients. The emphasis is on empathy, vicarious introspection, and the sustaining qualities of a therapy sensitive to the patient's selfobject experiences. Lichtenberg (1991) clarifies and explicates the term *selfobject experience*. "Selfobject experience designates an affective state of vitality and invigoration, of needs being met and of intactness of self" (p. 478). Certainly, groups provide the twinship or alter-ego selfobject experiences (Kohut, 1984) as the patient feels that sense of commonalty and identification with other group members. Although these selfobject experiences may be necessary components of a therapeutic cure, in cases of profound abuse, more may be needed.

Patients with a history of abuse come into psychotherapy with different views of their experience. Some have never talked to anyone about the abuse. Others, not uncommonly, have talked about it with some friends and are quite knowledgeable and well read in the field. Each patient has an understanding—however distorted—of the abuse. No matter what the source of understanding is—personal or derived from others—it is the patient's insight into the patient's past.

This understanding, however, has not enabled these patients to rise out of a sense of "fragmentation." Wolf (1988) uses a literary description from Sartre's novel *Nausea* to illustrate fragmentation:

> Aloneness for Sartre does not mean being without people around him, but being without selfobject experiences even in the presence of people. Sartre's description of the experience of inner disorganization that comes with such utter aloneness is unsurpassed: . . . "in order to exist (people) also must consort with others" (6). Otherwise they will experience a sudden estrangement from themselves in a somato-physiologic manner: . . . the Nausea. The sudden loss of inner cohesion is experienced as a sudden senselessness of the world, a change and disconcerting absurdity [p. 41].

Despair is a common feeling associated with fragmentation. The loneliness that comes from the patient's inability to sustain a sense of cohesion leads to an intolerable emptiness.

THE BEGINNING OF TREATMENT: PITFALLS THAT INTERFERE WITH THE EMERGENCE OF THE PATIENT'S NEED FOR DETAILING

The first moments of therapy are crucial to the development of trust. The patient's initial query, "Can you really help me?" reflects the concern about trust. It is a moment when patients, in a desperate attempt to overcome their feelings of fragmentation, ask the therapist to soothe them, thus enabling them to initiate selfobject experiences of idealization and merger with a knowledgeable and calm therapist.

The therapist may also experience fragmentation in the face of the extreme inhumanity of the patient's history. The unconscious desire is to be rid of this patient. In order to restructure his/her own experience, the therapist distances him/herself emotionally from the experience of the patient and, in so doing, removes the possibility of cure.

Alternatively, rather than acknowledge fear, the therapist defends against it, generalizing to the patient what we know about sexual abuse survivors and articulating stages of cure. Sometimes institutionally driven economic policies that promote referring these patients to group therapy mesh with the therapist's feelings of helplessness and disruption. The therapist makes the patient an unseen person, a part of a diagnostic, therapeutic, labeled group, and thus repeats the earlier injury of parental abandonment experienced by the patient. The abuser did not see the patient as a person or individual to be treasured, but rather as a representative of a population, a person to be sexually used, a person to be molested. Now once again, the patient is being relegated to an unseen and categorized group, this time by the therapist. The details of the patient's life and feelings are all but ignored. By referring the patient to a group, the therapist may fail to acknowledge that at least part of the search that this patient wishes to engage in is a *search for complex experience and relatedness outside the victim identification.*

In this critical moment of therapy, the therapist must not be in a similarly fragmented state caused either by institutional requirements that the patient be "processed" quickly into a group or by an inability to handle the patient's history. The intersubjective field defined as "a system of reciprocal mutual influence" (Stolorow and Atwood, 1992, p. 3) that reflects the therapist's and patient's fragmentation can quickly deny the patient a possibility of cure. The Kohutian concept of prolonged empathic immersion has particular immediacy for this therapeutic moment (Kohut, 1971). It is only by truly listening to the patient's story, creating a "holding environment" (Winnicott, 1965) and attending to the specific details and emotions of the patient's life that a cure can be effected.

The therapeutic environment must have at its base an unhurried, calm quality. The entire milieu must communicate that the problem that is so fragmenting to the patient has found a place of respite. A zone of consideration is established that allows the idealizing selfobject experience to emerge and begin the necessary restitutional process of soothing and relieving tension.

The overwhelming task for the therapist is to sustain both this soothing environment and allow the emergence of the patient's history. Part of the holding environment is the ability of the therapist to tolerate feelings of anger, disgust, hostility, and all the other emotions that emerge as the patient's story is told. The patient's understanding of the therapist's *interest* in the unfolding story is as important as the sense of the therapist's permanence and acceptance.

INCORPORATING THE USE OF INTEREST AND DETAIL AS ASPECTS OF THERAPIST ATTUNEMENT

The Definition of Interest

Interest is a manifestation of the positive countertransference bond that each therapist must develop in order to be willing to listen to the tales of inhumanity told by victims of abuse. Parents' intense involvement with each gurgle of their new offspring is a manifestation of *interest*. Such minute interest in detail is a necessity for development; it represents the mirror through which each child begins to be able to positively experience and grow from its interaction with the surround. We do not live if we are not touched and reflected in others. Interest is the cognitive and linguistic expression of what Bacal calls the patient's "entitlement to this special relationship that we have together" (Bacal, 1994, p. 28).

Most traumatized patients come to therapy untouched. No one gurgled or cooed. They had no mirror. Their details were not etched out for them to perceive, and so they come with false and incomplete notions of their possibility for growth and relatedness. Therapist and patient must jointly peel away these notions so as to help the patient restore experience and growth. Primarily, the job of therapy is to co-create with patients a life that becomes vitalized through the images, descriptions, and understandings that therapists extract when listening to fleeting questions, quiet moments, and fearful venturings of their patients.

The Use of Detail

Kohut emphasizes the aggrandizing quality of the mirroring selfobject function. For him the essence of mirroring rests in the qualities of recognition, admiration, and praise (Wolf, 1988, p. 125). I wish to emphasize a somewhat different quality, which I think is as important as praise for the development of a cohesive and enhanced subjective world. In essence, detailing is a descriptive function. It refers to the child's need for a detailed, intricate description of the child's environment that is linguistically more complex than the child would be capable of articulating at that stage of development. At the simplest level, when a child smiles the first time, the attuned parent will coo, smile back, and probably exclaim, "Ooh, a big smile!" Thus begins the kinesthetic and linguistic feedback that forms the basis for a healthy parent–child dyad. In normal environments, this simple influence grows along with the child's cognitive abilities. The parent is always somewhat ahead, linguistically expanding on the child's world while continously attuned to the child's need. When the child says "ball," the parent says, "Yes, a big red ball" thus expanding and detailing a world and providing cognitive explanation of that world, which the child as yet only incompletely understands. The attuned parent constantly brings together affect and cognition. This consorting with the "other" in a coherent cognitive and affective sphere protects the child from isolation and fragmentation. The excitement of the ball is understood and fed back by the parent along with the cognitive expansion of the big red ball. Masur (1989) states that maternal expansion of one-word utterances of children seems to encourage more advanced patterns of speech, with more novel vocalizations and words. These expansions are equally important to a child's emotional development.

Unquestionably, such detailed looking and observing of the child's world requires that the caregiver be both passionately involved with that child and carefully observant of the child's world. In her novella *The Age of Grief*, Smiley (1991) speaks of the involvement needed and of the risk such involvement entails:

> When you are in the habit of staring at your children . . . of talking about them, analyzing them, touching them, bathing them, putting them to bed, when you have witnessed their births and followed, with anxious eyes, the rush of the doctor and nurses out of the delivery room to some unknown machine room where some unknown procedure will relieve some unknown condition. When you have inspected their stools against yours, there is no turning away. Their images are imprinted too variously and plentifully on your brain, and they are with you always. When I agreed . . . that I wanted to be "an involved father." I foresaw the commitment of time. I didn't foresee the commitment of risk, the commitment of the heart. I didn't foresee how a number on a thermometer would present me with, paralyze me with every evil possibility [pp. 168–169].

With victims of profound abuse, the passionate, involved parent is lacking. The caregiver, for whatever reason, has no images imprinted and consequently no images are imparted to the child. Thus, the developmental need of the patient is for someone who experiences passion (defined as intense interest and curiosity), observes, and explains. The therapist may need to initiate these elements of interest, observation, and explanation in response to minute and unclear indications for their need from the patient. Through the relationship with the therapist and through the exercise of appropriate therapeutic detailing interventions, the patient can consider and ultimately internalize the therapist's creativity and inventiveness as part of the patient's subjective world.

Cognitive and affective distortions of their world are common in victims of profound abuse. For example, a sexually abused woman may place sexuality at the forefront of her description of herself; it becomes the dominating and defining characteristic of her being.

What must be recuperated in therapy are the unseen, nonexperienced details that are not necessarily sexual that fill out and complete the flat image that the patient has of herself. Again, this cannot be done if the patient is defined according to her sexual problem, and in this lies the difficulty of treatment. Therapists must carefully travel the road between the patient's perception of her reality as primarily sexual, and detailing, which seeks to understand, empathize, and cognitively expand her view of herself.

CASE EXAMPLES: INCORPORATING DETAIL
AND INTEREST INTO TREATMENT

The journey from a fragmented, sexually defined image to one that encompasses the whole person in relation to others is perilous. On the therapist's side, it requires a period where the therapist absorbs, understands, hears, and records the patient's view of life. It also requires that the therapist record what the patient does not see. Thus, the therapist details by cognitively expanding and reflecting back to the patient heretofore unnoticed aspects of the life of the patient. Therapeutic interventions that reflect this expansion often start with the phrase, "another way to see this might be." A particularly useful variant I have found in my own practice is to elicit memories and the parental reactions that existed toward the child in those memories. Such memories—not necessarily, but not exclusive of, traumatic ones—tend to show the paucity of parental reactivity to the child's everyday life. The therapist can then focus on how the parent might have responded if the child's appropriate developmental needs had been considered. It is often the first time that patients begin to understand and explain, through the therapeutic dialogue, how inappropriate all their parenting has been. They become aware that their childhood was devoid of the attunement necessary for healthy development. They focus on the entire spectrum of parental reactivity, not just on the sexual or physical abuse. The following are three case examples in which the patient experiences a need for detailing and growth emerges from the satisfaction of that need.

Case 1: The Use of Description

Mary was an extremely bright, accomplished scientist. She lived, however, a desolate internal life, compulsively attached to a rejecting, abusive, and sexually sadistic boyfriend. She had no female friendships. She had been raped by her father when she was 8 years old and had been sexually abused regularly by him until she was about 17 years old. Her mother was a cruel and narcissistic woman, unable to give care to her daughter in even the simplest ways. At age 35, Mary ignored her own needs and continued to serve her mother, in various ways. Often Mary would spend hours finding the right gift or token for her mother or boyfriend. Initially, Mary worked on the memory of the sexual abuse and on her stylized adult relationship with her father. She attempted to confront him in letters and on the telephone about the sexual abuse, a confrontation he greeted with silence, denial, and counteraccusations. Finally she broke completely with her father, which though relieving, also emphasized her utter aloneness.

Mary was technically accomplished. She could fix any car, was an expert rock climber, and had wilderness survival skills. To all outsiders she seemed extraordinarily physically courageous and resourceful. She could even tame wild birds. Nature had provided Mary with selfobject experiences unavailable to her elsewhere. From Nature she gained solace unavailable to her from her parents. She felt terrified, however, of the most normal female tasks such as getting a haircut or buying a brassiere or hose. Mary's mother had never bothered to take her shopping or instruct her in the basics of female dress. Though Mary yearned to be "more feminine," she felt she never would be. Mary felt that the female world was largely unavailable to her, and she felt that in this she had no choice. As Mary began to discuss these seemingly simple issues of self-care, the need for "detailing" emerged. She wanted more than confirmation and appreciation of her femininity (a "mirror" transference); she wanted to engage in a careful and detailed discussion of how to shop. She wanted to talk about how others did it.

Initially, she discussed her hair. She shared that her mother had never taken her to any hairdresser besides a barber. She wondered why her long, very thick hair could not be tamed. I took this question very seriously and encouraged Mary to understand how other women managed this problem. We discussed hair layering and other methods quite extensively. Although I worried that perhaps too much attention was being given to what seemed like minute concerns, the intense affect and excitement of these discussions and the spark that they generated in Mary convinced me to continue in this investigation. Clearly, what was emerging was Mary's tremendous need to talk and examine her femininity and to experience me as knowledgeable and helpful in this area. It seemed important in these sessions that I pay a great deal of attention to Mary's hair, that I describe it. Elements of an idealizing, mirroring, and self-delineating selfobject transferences were present. The most important aspect of the work clearly resided in my interest and in my ability to *accurately* describe and expand on Mary's version of her appearance. This had profound meaning for her. She was, at last, being taken seriously, as were her concerns about her self-care.

This moment in therapy unleashed a whole new set of behaviors for Mary. She became excited about shopping, something she had never done. Shopping was so precious and yet so frightening that at first she had to get on a plane and shop in a different city. This way she maintained anonymity and autonomy. She wasn't afraid of running into anyone she knew and she could come back to therapy and in the safety of that room examine to her heart's content why she had unexpectedly picked out a dress full of flowers and lace. I willingly responded to Mary's concern about patterns and hemlines, different fashions, and the minutiae of different brassiere construction and dress styles. This was not a derailing and defensive move in which Mary was talking about unimportant items. It was an attempt to recuperate that developmental moment of obsession in a girl's early adolescence when she learns (then decides whether to accept or reject) a cultural norm of dress. During these discussions my only comment about shopping in a different city reflected my respect for Mary's need to preserve in privacy what was clearly an area of importance to her. Like her beloved tamed birds she would hide herself to be sure not to lose it to those who were abusive or neglectful. The more we discussed these details of her life and the more I reflected back, described, and respected them, the braver Mary became. She came to see herself as being controlled by her boyfriend when he summarily rejected her treasured new haircut and dress. She understood that he had often acted sadistically toward her. She was able to acknowledge his behavior toward her when he refused to respect that which she had been so excited about. For the first time in their relationship, she was able to resist his insistence that she stay with him. She began to work intensively on her relationship with her mother and finally insisted that her mother come to town and help Mary buy an outfit for an important dinner and first date. In reviewing her therapy, near the end of treatment, Mary revealed how important it had been that I had noticed, respected, and not made fun of her intensity. In returning some years later to show me her daughter, she again referred to those sessions and how therapy had allowed her to be not only a scientist, but a complex, multifaceted woman.

In this case the most important element of detailing was the ability of the therapist to accurately describe and expand on concerns that existed for the patient. Intensity of affect was a clue to important new areas of investigation. An irreplaceable need for—a thirst for—cognitive input provided by the therapist in dialogue with the patient stimulates the therapist to create the ground for cognitive explanations that the patient needs for her own growth and development.

Case 2: The Use of Metaphor

Carol was 49 years old when she began therapy. She was neat but sad. She was often tearful and complained of a haunting problem, one that had afflicted her her entire adult life. She felt that she could not remember anything; often, she could not remember events from the previous hour or what she had meant to say. The results of many psychological and neurological tests indicated that she had a better than average ability to remember. She and I both felt stumped. I thought I had encountered a remarkable example of denial, but I could not see the road in—and yet she returned each week. She had a history of extreme physical abuse. Her father would often question her mercilessly until she would come up with some answer he considered wrong. Then he would beat her and her brother both. Thankfully, when she was 12 years old, he left the home, never to return. After he left, a succession of boyfriends, each more embarrassing than the next, noisily made love to her alcoholic mother in the next room. Carol remembers trying to disappear and silence herself so that they would not know she was there. That way, she would not be ashamed, and she would not embarrass anyone. Finally, after a poor performance in school and a desire to flee home, she became a hospice nurse, retreating into a spiritual life that gave her some relief from all the daily decisions that she would otherwise have to confront totally on her own. Her depression, however, followed her.

Dissatisfied with her professional life, she finally left it and married a minister. Their daughter, who was 9 years old when Carol first entered therapy, seemed to be Carol's great love. She admired, in particular, her daughter's ability to dress up, to be demanding, to sing with impunity, to speak her mind. Carol could describe in detail her daughter's life. Carol could hear her own daughter, but she seemed incapable of doing the same for herself. Carol never forgot a detail about her daughter; it was only about herself that she could not remember anything. This became convincing evidence that what we had was not a neurological problem but something else and how we defined it became very important in our work.

Consistent with a self-psychological approach, I attempted not to treat as denial that which was not experienced as denial. It was not as if Carol had forgotten things, it was as if nothing had ever happened to her except the abuse. From Carol's point of view this was actually true. Her life was empty. It had nothing to remember, nothing to recall. In defining her problem this way the need for attunement and specifically detailing emerged. Our job together was to begin to notice what other things existed in her life. We started with a little creamer she had seen in a discount store. The creamer itself was small but pretty, off-white with a blue flower. She had liked it when she saw it; more importantly, she had remembered it. Our work focused on whether she could feel comfortable responding to her attraction to it. Could she buy it? She asked me if I thought she should. I answered that it seemed important to her and that perhaps she should. This precipitated a vitriolic expression of self-hatred. Why couldn't she make these decisions on her own? What a waste to spend time in therapy on a stupid pitcher. Here she was almost 50 years old and unable to make the most simple decisions. A discussion ensued about whether her mother or father ever helped her to come to decisions in her life. Had they ever even known that she had had decision points where she could have used some help? Naturally, the answers to these questions were negative, Carol's life and growing up had been totally isolated. Then we returned to the pitcher. I tried as much as possible to describe to Carol why I thought she might like that pitcher: What was it that I, her therapist, knew about her, her love of simplicity, her love of flowers, attributes in her that made her respond to the little pitcher. I was attempting to very carefully detail to Carol what I knew about her so that she herself could begin to describe and experience herself more fully. The pitcher became a symbol for Carol of herself. She placed it in the sun, in a special place where it could be seen, and periodically as the therapy progressed, I would check up on the progress of the pitcher.

One of the hallmarks of when to use detailing is that as this particular striving for growth and experience emerges, it is almost hidden and, often, hard to capture. The desire for complex experience, definition, and growth is precious, and if it is under threat, it will, if at all possible, remain hidden. As this striving emerges, then, the therapist becomes detective, inventor, caretaker, and educator. In Carol's case, her unleashed self-hatred provided a clue that the exploration was important. Detailing unleashes the patient's selfobject experiences precisely in those areas that the patient at first denigrates and dismisses as unimportant. The therapist must invent meaning for this as yet unacknowledged part of the patient's subjective world and simultaneously must respect the patient's desire to hide a most precious and unrevealed part. As this process occurs, the therapist and patient together create a new language that has its own meaning. Often, it is metaphor that hastens the process. In this case, the pitcher was a metaphoric expression for the subjective world of the patient. As the pitcher was treasured, so was the patient's emerging experiences. I continued to ask about the pitcher as Carol understood that I was actually asking about Carol in her more complex manifestations.

Case 3: The Use of Imagination

The following case illustrates the necessity for the therapist to initially become immersed in the world of the patient and then try to expand what has been discovered and observed.

Andrea was referred to me by a college counseling center. She had been in counseling for a year to no avail. She was only becoming more depressed. She often would come to sessions and not speak for the entire hour. Andrea, the youngest of seven, had witnessed severe beatings of her sister and her mother by an alcoholic father. She had never been hit herself. As the referring therapist put it, "I think she's just hiding out from life, but I don't know how to reach her. In my center they just won't give me more time to try." When Andrea arrived in my office, she could not look at me. Most of the first sessions were spent trying to elicit, fairly unsuccessfully, some information in order to develop a treatment plan. One thing I had learned was that Andrea liked to draw. More out of despair than any other motive, I brought in a large pad and pencils and asked Andrea whether, since it was so difficult for her to speak, she might prefer to draw. Andrea's yes and her eye contact were the first connections I felt with this very withdrawn young woman.

Through pictures, most of which were desolate drawings of cemeteries, crying people, or broken inanimate objects, we began to describe Andrea's world. At first, I asked Andrea what she saw in those drawings. She did not know. She wanted to know what I saw. At first, I was hesitant to overinterpret or incorrectly interpret the pictures, concerned that if I were not empathically attuned to the patient, Andrea might withdraw once again. Andrea noticed the hesitancy and uncharacteristically insisted that I describe what I saw. Again, the hallmark of the patient's need for detailing was emerging: a heightened excitement and affect, an insistence, however subtle, for contact derived from description. I, somewhat gingerly, began the process of description and expansion. Surprisingly, Andrea responded, looking, judging the descriptions, correcting me, waiting for the response. She posed question after question. What did I think of families? How should children be treated? Why did Catholics think the way they did? Did I think adolescents ever had a right to sue their parents? Did I believe in evil? Were there evil people in the world? If I attempted to interpret these questions in light of her history, she became angry. It was not what she wanted. She wanted to know what I thought. She needed to know that I had opinions that I had considered these issues, that I had opinions and knowledge. In my description of her I began not only to address the content of these questions as Andrea wanted me to, but also to describe to her own mind how I thought she had come to these questions. It was as if this intelligent young woman had never had a place to talk and consider many philosophical issues that had plagued her.

The essence of what was important in the description of Andrea's mind had to do with her own interest in philosophy and how this intersected with the religious beliefs that she had been brought up with. As we attempted to describe her mind, I felt that she was sharing that place for the first time. This was the hidden aspect of Andrea's self-experience. She would describe how, as a child, she would go to the attic or bathroom and work on these problems, while she heard the screaming around her. She valued her mind immensely but had not wished to reveal it before. As we attempted to describe what it meant to her, she began, very occasionally, to smile. This process was agonizingly slow. Once she asked me, "Well what can I do with all this?" She was concerned about a career of some sort. Again groping for description of what she might be able to do, I said, "Well you are so interested in philosophy and religion, have you ever thought of becoming a minister? You seem to have so many ideas." This produced a laugh—certainly a rare occurrence—and her only comment towards the end of the session was, "Well at least you're imaginative."

The next week she bounced into the session and said, "The difference between you and my parents is that you have imagination and they are just dull!" She then proceeded to inform me that she really did not want to be a minister. In fact, she had spent entirely too much time in her thoughts, and she was going to sign up for a carpentry class and teach sports to small children. Although I had been quite wrong about Andrea's future profession, what had been important was that I had struggled, applied my imagination to help her dream. Once she experienced the flawed attempt at description, energy was released to help her begin to describe herself. Here, the effort at understanding was experienced as empathic attunement. The content of my interventions mattered less. The release of energy was caused by the mutual effort to understand Andrea's reality. As therapy progressed, she would often refer to my idea about the ministry with a kind of affectionate irony, and this interaction symbolically came to represent her acknowledgment of my interest in her.

In this case, it was not the accuracy of description that became important but the attempt by the therapist to take seriously what had remained hidden. The description was flawed, but the access to the therapist's imagination was experienced as honorable, caring interest. This example makes more obvious what is meant by the *interest* component of detailing.

CONCLUSION

Each of these cases elucidates aspects of detailing, a subconcept of mirroring and self-delineating selfobject functions. Therapeutic interventions should be used because the patient experiences them as useful and restores growth. As with many other aspects of our work, heightened affect often signals the appropriate use of detailing. Detail, accurate description of the therapist's reality, imagination, and metaphor are all important components of the technique. Because some of the desires expressed by the patients, such as with Mary the discussion of hair styles, with Carol the discussion of a pitcher, with Andrea the concrete discussion of her questions, may seem trivial to the therapist, error may occur. Classically trained therapists may interpret these moments as resistance and ignore important aspects of the patient's longings. Here the patient longs for the therapist to linguistically illuminate and cognitively expand her world.

Stern alludes to this kind of interaction when he writes, "Mother's meanings reflect not only what she observes but also her fantasies about who the infant is and is to become" (Stern, 1985, p. 134). Patients have often never had someone interested enough in them to dream about them, to fantasize, to describe. The therapist must be acutely aware of even the most minor clues that will lead to discovery of the patient's hidden need to experience the therapist's interest and imaginative mind. It is clear that with profoundly abused patients, *the therapist must be quite active.* Detailing provides a conceptual framework for that activity. Importantly, the basis for that activity must always be the patient's affect. In this sense, the patient offers the clue either verbally or through heightened expression of affect that then defines and determines the therapist's activity. There is no prescriptive way of being for the therapist; rather, the therapist responds through empathic immersion, paying special attention to the patient's language and affective tone. The patient slowly begins to be able to have an image of himself/herself that begins to accurately describe who they are in relation to themselves and others. This description must be carefully constructed as an artist would paint a portrait. Great portraits see through the face, project the inside of the person, and, at times, even predict how the face will change. Each brushstroke is a painstaking rendering of the person from within. Certain kinds of well-intentioned labeling, such as incest victim, incest survivor, codependent, adult child of an alcoholic, might militate against what is truly complexity-producing therapy. If patients are seen as only a part of a victim group, then they risk becoming less expansive, and their uniqueness and complexity remain hidden. The most important element that will help patients recover is to restore a belief in their ability to reauthor their own lives. This they do by enlisting the therapist to dream with them and by reflecting on what the therapist knows and has actively shared with them. Through this process they discover the idea that living is an interactive, dynamic, creative process and that they have as much right to an individual life as anybody who has not been profoundly abused.

Often, profoundly troubled and traumatized patients are the ones who teach the most about normal human needs. Their quest for healing and their courage causes therapists to also search and invent meaning where often, initially, only horror is seen and felt. The concepts that emerge during these therapies can subsequently be applied in many other therapeutic situations.

ACKNOWLEDGMENTS

This chapter could not have been written without the help and encouragement of Celia Falicov, Ph.D. and Antonia Meltzoff, Ph.D. Additionally, I received numerous helpful comments from Lindsay Alper, Ph.D., Bill Barron, M.D., Constance Breunig, Ph.D., Stephanie Covington, Ph.D., Peter Gourevitch, Ph.D., Barbara Manalis, M.S.W., Patricia Rose, Ph.D., and Sanford Shapiro, M.D.

REFERENCES

Bacal, H. A. (1994), The selfobject relationship in psychoanalytic treatment. In: *A Decade of Progress, Progress in Self Psychology, Vol. 10,* ed. A. Goldberg. Hillsdale, NJ: The Analytic Press, pp. 21–30.
Basch, M. (1988), *Understanding Psychotherapy.* New York: Basic Books.

Courtois, C. (1988), *Healing the Incest Wound*. New York: Norton.

Finkelhor, D. (1984), *Child Sexual Abuse*. New York: The Free Press.

Goldberg, A. (1988), *A Fresh Look at Psychoanalysis*. Hillsdale, NJ: The Analytic Press.

Herman, J. L. (1992), *Trauma and Recovery*. New York: Basic Books.

—— & Hirschman, L. (1977), Father–daughter incest. *Signs: J. Women in Culture & Society*, 2:735–756.

—— & Schatzow, E. (1984), Time-limited group therapy for women with a history of incest. *Internat. J. Group Psychother.*, 34:605–616.

Kohut, H. (1971), *The Analysis of the Self*. New York: International Universities Press.

—— (1984), *How Does Analysis Cure?* ed. A. Goldberg & P. Stepansky. Chicago: University of Chicago Press.

Lichtenberg, J. D. (1991), What is a self-object? *Psychoanal. Dial.*, 1:455–481.

Masur, E. F. (1989), Individual and dyadic patterns of imitation: Cognitive and social aspects., In: *The Many Faces of Imitation in Language Learning*, ed. G. E. Speidel & K. E. Nelson. New York: Springer-Verlag, pp. 53–71.

Russell, D. E. H. (1986), *The Secret Trauma*. New York: Basic Books.

Smiley, J. (1991), *The Age of Grief*. New York: Ballantine Books.

Stern, D. (1985), *The Interpersonal World of the Infant*. New York: Basic Books.

Stolorow, R. D. & Atwood, G.E. (1992), *Contexts of Being*. Hillsdale, NJ: The Analytic Press.

—— Brandchaft, B. & Atwood, G. E. (1987), *Psychoanalytic Treatment*. Hillsdale, NJ: The Analytic Press.

Winnicott, D. (1965), *The Maturational Processes and the Facilitating Environment*. New York: International Universities Press.

Wolf, E. (1988), *Treating the Self*. New York: Guilford.

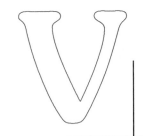

Applied

Chapter 20

The Evil Self of
the Serial Killer

Annette Lachmann
Frank M. Lachmann

Serial killings have been reported at least since the time of Gilles de Rais, a French nobleman who served under Joan of Arc, and the English serial killer, Jack the Ripper, in the 1880s. Accounts of serial killers have been a source of fascination to the readers of newspapers and fiction. Serial killers have been reported in Duesseldorf, Germany, in the 1930s, in Stalinist Russia, and in the United States. The increasing number of serial killers apprehended during the last two decades is a consequence of both increased cooperation among law enforcement agencies and increases in the actual number of serial killers (Norris, 1988). What kind of a person is capable of such heinous acts?

Serial murders are sharply distinguished from ordinary murders. Motivations for ordinary murders are extremes of humanly understandable motivations, such as greed, jealousy, revenge, gain in status, power, or prestige, rage, or self-defense. To want to act murderously is within the range of our fantasy or wishes. However, a serial killer deliberately kills strangers, for no apparent motive, except fulfillment of a private fantasy (Lachmann and Lachmann, 1994). Previously, we discussed the motivation for the serial killings in terms of specific fantasies of total control over another person, "to redress . . . painful early experience by reversing roles, temporarily revitalizing deadened feelings, and momentarily restoring a traumatically depleted sense of self" (p. 22). When the intended victim of the serial killer behaves so as to shatter the fantasy, the serial killer loses his resolve and the victim might then escape. To Fromm (1973), for whom evil consisted of the total domination and subjugation of another person, we added an absence of "humanly understandable" motives and a specific rigidly organized fantasy as attributes that make the serial killer the personification of evil.

Ironically, the inhumanity of the serial killer protects him. It is the absence of a human motivation, the absence of a personal connection between the serial killer and his victims, that has accounted for the difficulty in their apprehension. Until recently, only by chance or slipup, when a serial killer betrayed himself, would he be tracked down. It is mainly each killer's fantasy that forms a pattern that links his killings together. The fantasy provides a "content" of the serial killer's mental life. It defines the features of the victim to be sought and the script to be followed in the act of killing.

Serial killers are men who have killed three or more persons. Very few female serial killers have been documented. One woman, Aileen Wuomos, a prostitute who killed a number of her customers, has been considered by some as one of the rare female serial killers. However, based on her relationship to her victims and stealing their money, describing her as a serial killer is debatable. More typical was Elizabeth Bathory, a sixteenth-century serial killer, who imagined that by bathing in the blood of the young virgins she killed, she would retain her youth.

To illustrate the development and organization of the evil self as a source for the serial killings, the stories of two serial killers, Arthur Shawcross and Jeffrey Dahmer, follow. These summaries are based on reports and filmed interviews conducted by journalists, forensic psychologists, and law enforcement officials. Other sources of information were relatives of the victims, as well as the serial killers. A survey of serial killers would attest to the range of socioeconomic backgrounds, educational levels, and social skills that characterize this group.

Shawcross and Dahmer share certain similarities. Unlike many other serial killers, neither were subjected to physical brutality or abuse by their families in childhood. Both grew up in middle socioeconomic surroundings, attained at least a high school education, and were loners and "odd." Through different paths each became fascinated with stalking, catching, torturing, and killing animals.

CASE ILLUSTRATIONS

Arthur Shawcross

In his book, *The Misbegotten Son*, Olson (1993) gathered reports of interviews with the members of Arthur Shawcross's family, his teachers, neighbors, and Arthur Shawcross himself. This book, from which the following summary is drawn, provides a comprehensive background of Shawcross's life.

Shawcross was the oldest child in a two-parent home where the mother was the dominant figure. She spoke in the "short vocal style of an Adirondack lumber boss" (Olsen, 1993, p. 45) and was a meticulous housekeeper who ruled her home with an iron hand. His quiet and passive father was a county road worker. Arthur was intimidated by his mother and confused as to how to please her. He often put his father down for allowing his mother to take command. When he was 9, his mother discovered that her husband was a bigamist and had a wife and child in Australia. Thereafter, the mother became more bullying toward her husband and son.

The Shawcross family enjoyed a modest level of prosperity and lived in an almost idyllic country setting. The entire family, Arthur, his two younger sisters and younger brother, cousins, aunts, and uncles, attended church together and were involved in stockcar races, boat races, and other outings. However, Arthur tended to keep to himself. Early photos of Arthur show him to have a blank, affectless look. He is recalled as a clinging child who craved attention and wanted a great deal of physical comfort and love. His cousins believed that he was increasingly rejected by his mother after the other children came. As a result Arthur spent time with his maternal grandmother who loved him, and he did chores for her that he would not do at home.

By the age of 5 or 6 Arthur Shawcross already suffered from frequent nightmares and was a bed wetter. In the first and second grade in school he scored A's and B's. But later, on IQ tests he scored below normal. Behavior patterns began in first and second grades that subsequently become more and more pronounced. He resented younger children and seemed to enjoy making them cry through sadistic bullying. Provoking other children to feel pain, rage, fear, and humiliation may also reflect his own increasing emotional deadness. At the same time he retreated to a private fantasy world. By the age of 7, he imagined living with a boy his own age and a younger blond-haired girl. Speaking of this time in his adult years, he recalled how much he loved his little sister and imagined having sex with her.

In his family, punishment was meted out by the mother. When, as a young boy, Shawcross was spanked and sent to his room, he would try to make up to his mother by showering her with gifts. Being disciplined left him confused. He never felt it was justified, and he came away from it angry and retreated to fantasies in which he was a "boss" and in charge, accorded respect and dignity. By the age of 10 or 12 he would run away from home and, on one occasion, hid under his house to watch neighbors search for him.

By the time he entered third grade, Shawcross's grades went down and his aberrant behavior in school increased. Nightmares and bedwetting continued. His parents were contacted, but the school authorities found them to be indifferent to Arthur's deterioration. Instead, they blamed the school for their son's problems. Their indifference to their son's school problems may have reflected their general indifference toward his problems.

The imaginary friends Shawcross created and with whom he conversed gave the impression that he was talking to himself. Called "Oddy" by classmates, he was the butt of daily jokes and cruelties. When bigger boys abused him in school, he screamed, went home, and tormented his sisters and baby brother. Unsuccessfully, he tried to make friends in school by doing favors or distributing candy or coins, items that had been stolen from his mother or teacher.

Beginning at the age of 9 or 10, the magnitude of Arthur Shawcross's thefts increased. He stole from shops and grocery stores and bragged about his thefts. He teased and bullied other children relentlessly. The school nurse observed that he once boarded the school bus with an iron bar and menaced other children. At times, he carried a .22 rifle and threatened to shoot trespassers. More and more, Shawcross retreated to the woods near his home, gave up having friends, and withdrew into daydreams. He went home only to eat and sleep.

In his early adolescence and mid-teens, Shawcross was still a bedwetter, had nightmares, and made weird noises. At 12 a neighbor girl observed that he took everything literally, flew into a rage easily, and brooded over insults. When another girl said to him, "Don't act stupid," he took a baseball bat, waited for this girl to pass by, and hit her across the shins. He then grabbed an axe and threatened to chop off her head. Fortunately, her boyfriend rescued her. Instead of being alarmed by this kind of behavior, Shawcross's parents condoned his violence.

At about this time Shawcross started to torment and kill animals. His behavior was noticed by the townspeople, who speculated that perhaps Shawcross's mother had crossed the line into child abuse, that she had helped to create a tormentor.

Over the years, Shawcross had suffered numerous head injuries owed to accidents, such as falling from a 40-foot ladder and at another time being hit by a discus throw. There was some further speculation as to whether these injuries could have produced brain damage that would contribute to, if not account for, his aberrant behavior. Nevertheless, by age 16, Shawcross appeared to be well coordinated in sports and good at wrestling, yet, in this setting too, he was seen as a sore loser who could not control his rage.

At 17 Shawcross dropped out of school and held a series of odd jobs. His main interests, according to the neighborhood kids who recalled him, were stealing, setting fires, looking into neighboring windows, and watching his sisters undress.

At 19 Shawcross was married but never consummated the marriage. During this time he held one job longer than any other as an apprentice butcher at a meat market. He was fascinated with killing animals. In his twenties Shawcross married a second time, a woman with a 4-year-old son and a 2-year-old daughter. His second wife found him to be a good listener, who was fascinated by her children and played with them enthusiastically, almost as if he were a kid himself. She referred to him as a neat-freak, who demanded a freshly ironed white shirt every morning, even though he worked at the city dump. She remembered him as a quite live-in companion, who neither drank nor used drugs, was undemanding about sex, slow to reach a climax, and seemed to prefer to lie in her arms and be comforted. But to her dismay, he often disappeared after dinner and stayed out long after midnight.

Increasingly, Shawcross was drawn to children, invited them to go fishing, rough-housed with them, and ended up abusing them. He grabbed one 6-year-old, stuffed handfuls of dirt and grass into his shirt, and spanked him. He dumped another small child into a burning barrel of trash. A 10-year-old boy whom he befriended and took fishing became his first murder victim. A little girl became his second victim. He was caught, convicted of the rape and murder of both children, and went to prison.

Released after 15 years, Shawcross began a pattern of serial killing of prostitutes, dumping the bodies in the river. While he carried on this perverse secret life, Shawcross had another life in which he was married to his third wife and had a girlfriend, unbeknownst to his wife. However, he was also a familiar figure in the red-light district, and prostitutes willingly got into his car.

After several prostitutes had been found dead and mutilated, one prostitute, Joanne Van Nostrand, was alerted by Shawcross's manner. She had been informed that a serial killer was in the vicinity, and she told Shawcross that she was nervous, had a knife, and knew how to use it. Later, when she identified Shawcross as the man she had seen with one of the murdered prostitutes, she told the police that he was having erectile difficulties. He said to her, "Just play dead, bitch, and we'll get this over with in a few minutes."

Jeffrey Dahmer

Jeffrey Dahmer murdered 17 young men. Each murder was premeditated. Typically, before going out for the evening, Dahmer would pulverize some sleeping tablets and leave the drug handy on his kitchen countertop. Once he arrived at a bar, he would drink by himself and single out the man he found most attractive. At closing time he would approach his target to invite the man to his home for sex, drinks, to be photographed, or all three. If necessary, he would add the inducement of money (Lane and Gregg, 1994).

Some of the bodies were cannibalized. Dahmer explained to the police: "My consuming lust was to experience their bodies. I viewed them as objects, as strangers. . . . It's hard for me to believe that a human being could have done what I've done" (Lane and Gregg, 1994, p. 129).

According to Lionel Dahmer (1994) in his autobiography, A Father's Story, Jeffrey appeared to be a normal and responsive infant. Mystified, his father searched for early signs of Jeffrey's pathology and evil. He remembered that when Jeffrey was 4, he played with the skeletal remains of dead animals that had been found beneath the house and compared them to "fiddle sticks." At the same age, he pointed to his belly button and asked what would happen if someone cut it out. At about this time, Jeffrey also had a double hernia operation. When he awoke, he was in so much pain that he asked his mother if the doctor had cut off his penis. After this traumatic event, Lionel Dahmer noticed an emotional flattening in his son, which became permanent.

What at first seemed to be normal fantasies in young children now appeared sinister to Jeffrey's father in retrospect. He recalled that Jeffrey enjoyed nonconfrontational games full of repetitious actions, particularly those that were generally based on themes of stalking and concealment, such as "hide and seek." When seen crouching behind a tree or hiding behind bushes, Jeffrey was totally absorbed. These behaviors persisted and, as with Arthur Shawcross, included a fascination with dead animals. When Jeffrey was in grade school, he took home road kills of animals and kept the body parts in jars (Norris, 1988, p. 58).

Dahmer's loneliness and isolation were compounded by his mother's second pregnancy with his younger brother, whom he later grew to resent. According to the school nurse, he was feeling totally abandoned. His first-grade teacher made a notation on the report card that 6-year-old Jeffrey seemed to feel "neglected." He handled his sense of abandonment by withdrawal and by aggression toward helpless creatures. He switched from being a passive collector of road kills to an aggressive stalker of animals during his early adolescence. There were reports of missing dogs circulating throughout the area. A neighbor remembered seeing a dog's skull turned into a kind of totem pole a few hundred yards behind the Dahmer house.

Alcohol was the facilitator of Dahmer's violent acts. School friends already observed that he drank regularly in seventh grade. His violence was expressed toward animals and he increasingly withdrew, yet, according to schoolmates and school counselors, there appeared, briefly, another side. In his first year of high school, he became a strong tennis player and involved himself with the freshman band and the school newspaper. He also waited on tables in a local restaurant and worked out in his home. Counselors found him "a polite quiet kid." However, he could not keep his evil in check. Strangely, he would trace bodies on the floor in chalk, a foreshadowing of what the police would do in his apartment in Milwaukee years later (Norris, 1988, p. 75). When interviewed after his conviction, Dahmer stated that it was during these years, ages 14 to 15, that he became obsessed with thoughts of violence intermingled with sex.

At the time of his high school graduation, Dahmer's parents were involved in a bitter divorce. He was hardly ever in class during his senior year. When he did show up, he was usually drunk. After the divorce, he was left alone a great deal by his mother, who had custody of both children. His father and the father's new wife arrived at the house and found a young man with a "terrible vacancy in his eyes . . . who seemed shell shocked by the divorce" (Dahmer, 1994, p. 63). They saw very little food in the house and and the refrigerator was broken. On a round wooden coffee table in the family room, a pentagram had been drawn in chalk. Lionel Dahmer wrote that he was bewildered, but later learned that Jeffrey had conducted a seance to try to contact the dead.

A year later, when he was 18, Jeffrey Dahmer killed his first human being. He picked up a hitchhiker, took him home, drank beer with him, and engaged in sex. When the young man wanted to leave, he struck him with a barbell and killed him. The pattern of picking up his victims in bars and eventually killing them took shape. His method of killing reflected a need to have absolute control over another person, and his cannibalism further showed that he could not bear to be parted from his victims. He believed that by eating them they became a part of him. After his first murder, Dahmer moved to his grandmother's house, where he struggled against his compulsion to go hunting for a victim. He stole a mannequin out of a store window and took it home. He attempted to use the mannequin for sexual gratification, but it didn't work.

Dahmer's last victim, Tracy Edwards, got away because he didn't match Dahmer's fantasy of what the victim would be like and how the scenario would proceed. He was more alert and not as complacent as the others had been. Dahmer met Tracy Edwards and his friends in a bar. Chameleon-like, Dahmer feigned interest and friendliness. He claimed to be a photographer scouting for good-looking models whom he paid for their services. He asked if any of them wanted to pose for nude pictures. He told the group that they could have a party at his place and talk over his proposal. On the way to his apartment, the group stopped at a liquor store where Dahmer could buy rum and cigarettes. Outside the store, Edwards and his friends decided that only Edwards would accompany Dahmer and the others would go to Dahmer's apartment later. Dahmer gave them a false address and he and Edwards took a cab to his apartment. Dahmer made Edwards feel so comfortable that Edwards was curious, rather then suspicious, about a number of peculiar details. He didn't become concerned when the cab stopped about a block away from Dahmer's apartment, and the two men had to walk the final block through some back alleys. In addition, Edwards was not concerned when he saw five police locks on the door and a burglar alarm system. Dahmer explained that these precautions were necessary because the neighborhood was dangerous. The apartment looked decent but Edwards noticed a foul odor. Dahmer explained that the odor was due to faulty sewer pipes. Edwards also asked about the boxes in the living room in which Dahmer kept the body parts of his last victims. Dahmer calmly explained that they contained acid to clean bricks.

Dahmer prepared a drugged alcoholic beverage in advance, but Edwards barely sipped it and remained alert. However, Dahmer steadily drank his beer. Because his friends had not appeared yet, Edwards became nervous. Suddenly, Dahmer snapped a handcuff on his wrist, held a knife to his ribs, and forced him into the bedroom. Edwards instinctively knew that he had to calm Dahmer down. He reassured him that he would not try to escape and kept up a semblance of conversation. They watched a tape of *Exorcist III*, and Edwards noticed that Dahmer alternately became excited or calmer in accordance with the action in the film. As the evening wore on, Dahmer shifted from looking vacant to looking belligerent, as stimulated by certain scenes in the film. Edwards succeeded in drawing Dahmer out to talk about his feelings. This helped him control Dahmer's mood swings. By addressing Dahmer's difficulty in affect regulation and by attempting to calm him, Edwards may have succeeded in becoming a *specific*, calming person. He no longer matched Dahmer's fantasy and provided Dahmer with a momentary selfobject experience. Soon Edwards persuaded Dahmer to be allowed to go to the bathroom. Dahmer took off the handcuff. Edwards now attained more control. He got Dahmer to let him out of the bedroom and they went to the kitchen for a beer. At that point, it seemed to Edwards that Dahmer lost complete interest in his prey. In Edwards's words, "He started going out of himself again. He was like paying me no attention, like he wasn't there" (Norris, 1992, p. 27).

SOME SPECULATIONS

We based our previous study of the motivations of the serial killer (Lachmann and Lachmann, 1994) on self-reports, newspaper articles, books by journalists (for example, Newton, 1992; Rule, 1987, 1989; Moes, 1991) and law enforcement officials (for example, Norris, 1988; Ressler, Burgess, and Douglas, 1988). Using mainly secondary sources, numerous authors (for example, Abrahamson, 1992; Bollas, 1995; Miller, 1990; Shengold, 1989) have speculated about the dynamics of serial killers. In their formulations, these analysts propose motivations and dynamics also noted in psychopathology that does not approach the level of violence, evil, and inhumanity characteristic of serial killers. Familiar dynamic formulations, for example, turning a passively endured trauma into an aggressive act, place the serial killer on a dynamic continuum with other and lesser pathologies. The horror, perversity, and inhumanity of the serial killer seem lost when he is placed on a continuum with character disorders and "borderline" conditions. At one extreme, dynamic formulations either depict the serial murder as a variant of a pathological preoedipal or oedipal solution and at the other extreme, as the acts of a viciously abused child. We argued that the five motivational systems proposed by Lichtenberg (1989; Lichtenberg, Lachmann, and Fosshage, 1992) offer a more comprehensive perspective. These systems include needs for assertion and exploration, attachment and affiliation, physiological regulation, sensual pleasure and sexual excitement, and the need to react aversively with aggression or withdrawal.

In our previous account of three serial killers (Lachmann and Lachmann, 1994), Henry Lucas, Randall Woodfield, and Ted Bundy, we illustrated aversive motivations as reactions to narcissistic injuries and frustrations. In the histories of serial killers, aversive motivations were reactions to abuse, sexual assaults, or malignantly deceptive family relationships. We generalized that, early in the lives of serial killers, to react aversively, through rage and withdrawal, became the dominant response, overshadowing other motivations and replacing them. That is, exploration, assertion, sensuality, sexuality, and attachment were expressed through various forms of destruction and aggression. In addition, due to their early, massive, and pervasive arousal, aversive reactions such as withdrawal and rage can take on the quality of a proactive "need." Reactive aggression then turns into "unprovoked" rage. Sexuality is turned into necrophilia. Assertion is turned into absolute domination and control over another person. Exploration and attachment gain expression through cannibalism. Viewing these motivations as perversions of aversiveness provides a more complex model that fits the bizarre murders committed by the serial killers.

We have utilize four of the five motivational systems: attachment, assertion and exploration, sexuality, and aversive reactions. We now consider the fifth system, the need for physiological regulation. A crucial problem for the serial killer is his inability to regulate physiological requirements, which translates into the regulation of bodily experiences such as affects, arousal, tension states, and alone states. Self-regulation of states of tension and mood can then become a major challenge, requiring literal withdrawal from, or domination of, others or a script that takes killer and victim from a social world of tension and frustration to a private world of release through total domination of a subdued other. For any one serial killer, this script hardly varies and provides a source of regularity, repetition, and fundamental predictability to interactions.

Young Arthur Shawcross's blank, affectless look may have been symptomatic of a disturbance in self-regulation of affect and arousal. He developed a never-satisfied craving for comfort and love. From early childhood to his second wife's description of him as wanting to be held and comforted rather than sexually desirous, this craving persisted. Furthermore, his long history of nightmares and bedwetting also suggest uncontrollable tension states and an inability to regulate physiological requirements. Attempts to self-calm led to periods of social withdrawal. He was unable either to connect with others or tolerate being alone. Neither the invention of imaginary friends nor stealing, bribing, bullying, and threatening others provided social contact or personal satisfaction. As his capacity for affective connections withered, these behaviors increased. Shawcross's withdrawal, tormenting of animals, and violent attacks on other children seemed to be driven by attempts to regulate and restrain affects and arousal. His attacks on children may have lifted his sense of deadness while withdrawal may have offered some respite and sense of self-control. Voyeurism served as a highly unstable compromise between the two extremes, participating vicariously in social–sexual relations while remaining concealed and withdrawn. The instability of this solution is noted in the rapid, next step to pedophilia. Presumably, his sense of deadness required more drastic arousal, which led to the rape and murder of two children and ultimately to the serial murders.

Jeffrey Dahmer's fascination with the dead can be traced to age 4. The double hernia operation and his anxiety about castration were, according to his father, a turning point in his development. Afterwards, Jeffrey began to look emotionally flat and sought games of repetitive actions, possibly because their predictability provided a source of stability for him.

By age 5, Jeffrey's profound reaction of abandonment to his mother's pregnancy suggests increasing difficulty in regulating affect and arousal when alone. A short time later he began to collect road kills. A facile connection could be made between his interest in dead animals and the birth of his baby brother. But ascribing this activity to death wishes toward his brother may obscure a larger issue. The serious self-regulatory problem may have left Dahmer vulnerable to profound feelings of deadness. When he attributed his collection of road kills to "childhood curiosity," the question for which he sought an answer may have been "What are these feelings inside me?" rather than a more "relational" question, such as "What is inside my mother?" or "Where did my brother come from?"

Dahmer's next step was to stalk, torture, and kill animals, to drink, and to withdraw socially. These activities can be seen as a gross attempt to enliven feelings of deadness and to deaden overstimulating excitement. Withdrawal to a world of fantasy and of the dead increased. By 18 he committed his first act of murder. The inclusion of attachment, assertion, and exploratory motivation in his killings is noted in his insistence on total control, mutilation, and cannibalism and in his storing and preserving the bodies of his victims and their various organs.

A three-level model proposed by Goldberg (1995) that addresses the problem of sexual perversion can be restated as providing a detailed view of the fundamental problem of regulating affect and arousal, tension states and alone states. The inability to regulate these states may leave the person either overaroused or deadened, with frantic activity to counter these states. Goldberg postulates three levels at which the pathology of sexual perversion is organized. We extend this framework to the serial killer and add to the perversion of sexuality, perversions of assertion, exploration, and attachment. The serial killer well illustrates the extention of sexual perversion into the realms of violence and evil.

Following Kohut (1971), Goldberg posits a structural failure of the self. Development at this first level is ordinarily organized through the rhythms and regularity of mother–infant interactions. Structural failure at this level can result in chaotic inner experience, such as states of tension and emotional deadness. Noncontingent reactions from the environment increase the sense of aloneness, frustration, and deprivation. In turn, there are drastic efforts made to redress this sense of disorganization and unpredictability. In some instances, a threat of disintegration leads to sexualization in an attempt to secure stability. This is one of the preconditions for sexual perversion.

For the serial killer, sexualization alone does not seem to be sufficient to bring about a feeling of vitality and stability. Sexualization must be buttressed with repetitive violence to provide stability, counteract deadness, and regulate tensions. According to Goldberg (1995) and Kohut (1971) at this level of organization, the sources of structural stability are interchangeable and are free of psychological content or meaning. Dahmer may have sensed this when, after his first murder, he attempted to use a mannequin for sexual gratification. It did not work. We may speculate that sexual satisfaction was not enough. He needed to dominate, kill, and dismember his victims to achieve the needed effect.

At a second level of organization of the self, rather than developing stable selfobject ties, a split in the self-structure is necessary. The split enables the child to maintain vital ties to the parents but at the expense of living in two worlds or, put differently, disavowing an aspect of reality. In the histories of Shawcross and Dahmer, the parents, rather than offering a path toward unification of the self, support a split. They reinforced an experience of living in two disconnected, even antithetical worlds. For Shawcross, one world was a world of consequences. He could not control the humiliation he felt at the hands of his classmates and he could behave in conformance with social expectations. Ostensibly, as an adult he seemed to want to spare his girlfriend Clara from being implicated in his crime spree. The other world was one in which his violent acts had been tolerated by his family and there were no consequences for them.

For Dahmer, parental "blindness" to his increasing preoccupation with dead animals and killing animals was interpreted as "childhood games." He felt accountable to no one. When Dahmer as an adult explains his preoccupation with road kills as beginning childhood curiosity, he may well have been echoing the atmosphere of denial and pretense in which he lived.

Lionel Dahmer's tendency to "deny" his son's activities was illustrated during a visit to his son's apartment. Lionel Dahmer became suspicious of the contents of a locked box. However, he did not pursue his suspicions but permitted his son to keep secret the contents of the box: mummified heads and genitals. If we keep in mind Kohut's (1971) suggestion that a traumatic deidealization of the parents can be precipitated by their failure to catch their child in a lie, Lionel Dahmer's failure to catch Jeffrey in a lie in his adult years may reflect a long-standing pattern. Lionel Dahmer revealed his inability to deal with Jeffrey's dangerous behavior, and Jeffrey may well have felt that either his behavior was condoned or that it had no consequences, contributing to a failure to establish guiding ideals. Both Shawcross and Dahmer developed split worlds, a private amoral world and a public pretense of conventionality.

Previously, we focused on the third level of organization, the dynamics and history, the specific themes, conflicts, fantasies, and motivations that converge in the act of killing. We now add the role of structural failure and splits in the self as underpinnings to the dynamics and motivations of the serial killer. This added framework recognizes the interchangeability of the killer's sources of stability. It is specifically the lack of uniqueness of his victims, their anonymity, that makes them suitable for shoring up the stability of the self-structure. By analogy, we might have little difficulty eating a steak that came from an anonymous steer, but we might find it far more difficult to eat a steak that was once the flank of a pet calf. When Joanna Van Nostrand threatened Arthur Shawcross by announcing she had a knife, she differentiated herself from the docile woman Shawcross needed her to be. She was then no longer anonymous and she succeeded in escaping. When Tracy Edwards succeeded both in defining himself as different from the manner in which Dahmer needed his victims to behave and in providing some affect regulation and calming for Dahmer, Dahmer's impulse to kill subsided.

Using dead animals and later dead people as a source of enlivenment began early in the lives of Arthur Shawcross and Jeffrey Dahmer. Proposed motives having to do with killing siblings and turning passively endured trauma into active mastery address only the level of the dynamics of the behavior. Based on the bizarreness of the acts, a felt deadness derived from a structural failure captures the irrelevance of meaning or content and peremptory need to stave off disorganization that eventuates in the inhumanity of the serial killings.

Shawcross's and Dahmer's early fascination with dead animals and the progression from this fascination to the acts of serial killing suggest early signals by both children that something was dreadfully wrong. In both instances the signals were ignored and the behavior was condoned and even supported. Similar signals are noted in the histories of other serial killers. Perhaps such powerful signs of distress are more often than not picked up by parents or the police. In those instances, having the signal responded to may be crucial. The response may serve to put a brake on an escalating pattern of destructiveness or it may be felt as a sign of recognition. In either case there are deterring implications. To what extent an unresponsive environment, parental denial, or law enforcement officials' indifference contribute to the construction of the evil self of the serial killer is in need of further study.

Our construction of the organization of the serial killer's evil self can remain only on the level of speculations. Material from the lives of two serial killers can illustrate an approach that utilizes the three levels of self-organization in conjunction with the five motivational systems to understand extremes of bizarre perverse behavior. In presenting our ideas through essentially unverifiable propositions, we hope that other hypotheses can be generated that will be open to more direct exploration, verification, or refutation in clinical practice.

REFERENCES

Abrahamson, D. (1992), *Murder and Madness*. New York: Donald I. Fine.
Bollas, C. (1995), *Cracking Up*. New York: Hill & Wang.
Dahmer, L. (1994), *A Father's Story*. New York: Avon.
Fromm, E. (1973), *The Anatomy of Human Destructiveness*. New York: Holt.
Goldberg, A. (1995), *The Problem of Perversion*. New Haven, CT: Yale University Press.
Kohut, H. (1971), *The Analysis of the Self*. New York: International Universities Press.
Lachmann, A. & Lachmann, F. M. (1994), The personification of evil: Motivations and fantasies of the serial killer. *Internat. Forum Psychoanal.*, 4:17–23.
Lane, B. & Gregg, W. (1994), *The Encyclopedia of Serial Killers*. New York: Diamond Books.
Lichtenberg, J. (1989), *Psychoanalysis and Motivation*. Hillsdale, NJ: The Analytic Press.
—— Lachmann, F. M. & Fosshage, J. (1992), *Self and Motivational Systems*. Hillsdale, NJ: The Analytic Press.
Miller, A. (1990), *For Your Own Good*. New York: Noonday Press.
Moes, E. (1991), Ted Bundy: A case of schizoid necrophilia. *Melanie Klein and Object Relations*, 9:54–72.
Newton, M. (1992), *Hunting Humans, Vol. 1*. New York: Avon.
Norris, J. (1988), *Serial Killers*. New York: Dolphin.
—— (1992), *Jeffrey Dahmer*. New York: Pinnacle Books.
Olsen, J. (1993), *The Misbegotten Son*. New York: Dell.
Ressler, R., Burgess, A. & Douglas, J. (1988), *Sexual Homicide*. New York: Lexington.
Rule, A. (1987), *The I-5 Killer*. New York: Signet.
—— (1989), *The Stranger Beside Me*. New York: Signet.
Shengold, L. (1989), *Soul Murder*. New Haven, CT: Yale University Press.

Chapter 21

Sándor Ferenczi and The Evolution of a Self Psychology Framework in Psychoanalysis

Arnold Wm. Rachman

THE FERENCZI RENAISSANCE

Although it is generally difficult to pinpoint the exact date of interest in returning Sándor Ferenczi's work to the mainstream of psychoanalysis, the publication of his *Clinical Diary*, first in French in 1985 (Ferenczi, 1932a) and then in English in 1988 (Ferenczi, 1932b), was a milestone in this process. The *Clinical Diary* was heralded as a major contribution to the analytic literature (Grosskurth, 1988; Hoffer, 1990; Roazen, 1990; Wolstein, 1990) and educated contemporary analysts to a lost legacy of clinical innovation and daring, not often present, since the pioneering times of psychoanalysis. What is more, the *Clinical Diary* was seen as a historical link in the development of one of the alternate frameworks within mainstream psychoanalysis (Wolstein, 1989).

The most recent impetus to fuel the Ferenczi Renaissance is the much awaited publication of the Freud/Ferenczi Correspondence, of which two volumes of the three-volume series have just been published (Brabant, Falzeder, and Giampieri-Deutsch, 1993, 1996). Both the extensive content and the large number of the correspondence (1,500

Presented at the 18th Annual Conference on the Psychology of the Self. Crosscurrents in Self Psychology, October 21, 1995, San Francisco, CA.

I am grateful to Charles B. Strozier, Ph.D., for a thoughtful and scholarly review of this manuscript.

letters) help the present generation of psychoanalysts to realize the influence of Ferenczi's life and work for Freud as well as in the evolution of
psychoanalysis.

Elsewhere I have chronicled the series of events during the 1970s
and 1980s, which laid the foundation for the present Renaissance
(Rachman, 1997). In the late 1970s when I began to research Ferenczi's
life and work, there was almost no interest shown, either in the field of
psychoanalysis or psychotherapy, in one of the most significant and
influential analytic figures and, I believe, a precursor to analytic self
psychology.

With the growth of self psychology in the last 25 years, concepts such
as empathy, trauma, and the reevaluation of transference and resistance
have encouraged interest in Ferenczi's contribution to these issues, since
his work is not only a historical antecedent to Kohut, but his ideas and
methods have relevance for contemporary analytic thought and clinical
practice.

The major aim of the present discussion is to outline the pioneering
clinical and theoretical work of Sándor Ferenczi and demonstrate its
relevance as a precursor to self psychology. There are several authors,
both within and outside the self psychology movements, who have
pointed out that psychoanalysts and psychotherapists who preceded
Kohut laid the foundations for self psychology (Stolorow, 1976; Cohler,
1980; Basch, 1984; Chessick, 1985; Kahn, 1985; Bollas, 1986). In an
earlier discussion, I introduced the notion that Ferenczi was the originator of the empathic method in psychoanalysis (Rachman, 1988). It is
necessary at this juncture to expand this perspective to add Ferenczi to
the list of psychoanalytic thinkers who pioneered an alternate form of
psychoanalysis that anticipated many aspects of the self psychology
framework. In this regard, there are several basic concepts that bear
comparison between Ferenczi and Kohut:

(1) The role of empathy in psychoanalysis
(2) The selfobject transference
(3) Reintroduction of the trauma theory
(4) Revision of the resistance model

1. THE ROLE OF EMPATHY

Ferenczi's approach to psychoanalysis was a function of his personality
as well as his intellect and clinical capacity. His predominant personal
qualities were enthusiasm, warmth, tenderness, giving, optimism, and
compassion. It was the full array of these qualities, plus their intensity,

that encouraged in others the feelings of trust, openness, understanding, and empathy.

It was a special blend of Ferenczi's family background, his warm and vibrant personality, his interpersonal skills and his active, searching intellect that moved him toward an empathic method of psychoanalysis. Ferenczi's family background has been chronicled (Balint, 1949; Barande, 1972; Bergmann and Hartman, 1976; Sabourin, 1985; Rachman, 1997). He identified with the revolutionary spirit of his father, whom he idolized, and had an intensely ambivalent relationship with his mother: Ferenczi wrote to Freud on October 13, 1912, that he was the "son of an 'otherwise harsh mother'" (Simitis-Grubrich, 1986, p. 274). Therefore, he was an individual who experienced empathic failures as a child. He turned the emotional awareness of his own "traumatic" childhood into a gift to his analysands by developing his personal empathy into clinical empathy, thereby empathizing with their sense of deprivation and trauma.

Ferenczi's interest in empathy began with his technical recommendations for changing the emotional atmosphere of an analytic session. His keen powers of clinical observation allowed him to become the first analyst to employ nonverbal cues to interpret unconscious processes (Ferenczi, 1919a, b, 1920, 1924, 1925). He began to observe and concern himself with the nature of resistances to the analyst's interventions:

> I recall, for instance, an uneducated, apparently quite simple patient who brought forward objections to an interpretation of mine, which it was my immediate impulse to reject; but on reflection, *not I, but the patient, turned out to be right,* and the result of his intervention was a much better general understanding of the matter we were dealing with [Ferenczi, 1928, p. 941].

This is clearly the beginnings of a departure from the Freudian tradition of the analysis of resistance. What is more, it is also a focus on experience between analyst and analysand to inform the process and technique. From empathic interchanges like the one just illustrated, Ferenczi reached the following conclusion, which ushered the use of tact, or empathy, into psychoanalytic practice:

> I have come to the conclusion that it is above all a question of psychological tact whether one should tell the patient some particular thing. But what is "tact?" *It is the capacity for empathy* [Italics added]. One gradually becomes aware how immensely complicated the mental work demanded from the analyst is . . . One might say that his mind swings continuously between empathy, self-observation and making judgements [Ferenczi, 1928, pp. 89, 96].

Ferenczi's observations lead to the clinical recommendations that, in order to reduce resistances, the analyst should present any interpretation in an empathic manner. Ferenczi was recommending that "a rule of empathy" be added to the convention of interpretation, so that analytic interventions be characterized by an empathic awareness by the analyst as well as an empathic response. What is more, the more difficult the analysand, the more need for empathy. Ferenczi developed a worldwide reputation as "the analyst of difficult cases." This reputation was well deserved since patients came to see him in Budapest from as far away as the United States. For example, Clara Thompson (one of the founders of Interpersonal Psychoanalysis) went every summer to Budapest, from 1926 to 1933 (when Ferenczi died) to be analyzed, having been recommended to Ferenczi by Harry Stack Sullivan who thought Ferenczi was the only European analyst worth seeing. Thompson was a difficult analysand, in that she had a failed analysis before Ferenczi, was the survivor of childhood trauma, and had a tendency to act out. Ferenczi used his empathic method with Thompson to both analyze her childhood trauma of emotional and sexual abuse and to deal therapeutically with her acting out (Ferenczi, 1932b; Rachman, 1997).

When Ferenczi first introduced the empathic method into psychoanalysis Freud's reaction was positive and congratulatory:

Dear Friend

Your accompanying production ["The elasticity of psychoanalytic technique," Ferenczi, 1928] displays that judicious maturity you have acquired of late years, in respect of which now one approaches you. The title is excellent and deserves a wider provenance. . . . The only criticism I have of your paper is that it is not three times larger. . . . There is no doubt that you have much more to say on similar lines and it would be very beneficial to have it [Jones, 1953, p. 241].

This praise did not last. As Ferenczi extended his empathic method to more and more difficult cases, ones we would now consider narcissistic, borderline, or psychotic, he experimented with the empathic response beyond the established boundaries of psychoanalysis. When, for example, Thompson bragged that she could have physical contact with Ferenczi, this activity reached Freud's ears. This time Freud sent Ferenczi another letter, the so-called "Kissing Letter," which was very critical of Ferenczi's relaxation measures, such as therapeutic touching. Freud warned Ferenczi, that allowing a patient to touch you, such as Thompson kissing Ferenczi would lead to analysts having sex with their analysands (Jones, 1957, p. 197).

Freud, unfortunately, could not distinguish between the analyst's capacity to push the empathic method beyond interpretation and verbal interaction to affectionate, nonseductive touching. Ferenczi allowed Clara Thompson to touch him (he, by the way, did not initiate this activity with her) because he wanted to be a "corrective selfobject" (Bacal, 1990). Specifically, he wanted to provide her with an experience of optimal responsiveness (Bacal, 1985), where she could correct the abusive experience with her father, by accepting her need for affection and *not sexualize the contact* (Ferenczi, 1932b, 1933). I believe this exposition of Ferenczi's far-reaching clinical application of his relaxation therapy indicates how contemporary his pioneering work was and how close it is connected to the advances in self psychology.

Ferenczi's elaboration of his empathic method involved changes in the process of an analytic session (Ferenczi, 1930), development of an empathic communication with an analysand (Ferenczi, 1931), focus on the analyst's contribution to empathic failures (Ferenczi, 1928, 1932b, 1933), and the development of psychopathology based on empathic defects in childhood (Ferenczi, 1932b, 1933).

His thinking and technical experiments can be viewed as opening up the vista of empathy within the psychoanalytic framework. But he realized he had only begun the process and that the generations of analysts to follow would need to continue his pioneering efforts (Ferenczi, 1928, p. 100). The concept of empathy did receive some attention in the years to follow, but it was not until Kohut's work evolved that empathy was to receive the same significant attention as an essential variable in the analytic process that it had been originally by Ferenczi.

Kohut, it can be said, reasserted the central place of empathy in psychoanalysis, expanding on the contributions of Ferenczi and others. He did show some awareness that the concept had a history, although he did not refer to Ferenczi's significant contributions: "Although self psychology must not claim that it has provided psychoanalysis with a new kind of empathy, it can claim that it has supplied analysis with new theories which broaden and deepen the field of empathic perception" (Kohut, 1984, p. 175).

Kohut outlined the far-reaching conceptualization of empathy to expand its boundaries in four basic ways: (1) as the principal mode of observation in psychoanalysis (Kohut, 1959, 1971, 1977, 1978, 1984); (2) as the significant emotional experience in the psychoanalytic situation (Kohut, 1975, 1984); (3) as the significant ingredient that bonds human beings (Kohut, 1975, 1977); (4) and as a force for good in the interaction of groups, whether colloquial, political, or national (Kohut, 1971,

1975, 1978). The implication of Kohut's thinking, which was close to Ferenczi's idea, is that empathy is curative, in and of itself.

2. THE SELFOBJECT TRANSFERENCE

Many consider Kohut's discovery of the selfobject transference to be his single most important contribution to psychoanalysis (Gedo, 1986b, p. 114). These transferences, which are mirror transference, the twinship transference, and the idealizing transference, emerge naturally in a self psychology analysis of patients with narcissistic personality disorders. Inherent in this idea is the "spontaneous emergence" of selfobject transference and the "proper conduct" of their analyses (Ornstein, 1978). These transferences are not defensively regressive in nature, as has been characteristic of the object-instinctual conflicts of traditional psychoanalysis. The differences that exist between Kohut's view of selfobject transference and traditional view of object-instinctual transference are based on the differences in the notion of development of pathology.

The selfobject transference provides the opportunity for healing. The analyst is internalized through "transmuting internalizations." Bit by bit, the individual acquires psychic structure, when the clinician empathizes with the developmental strivings, which were not acknowledged in childhood by parental figures. Through the positive experience of the analytic selfobject acquired through continued empathic interaction, the various fragmented self-images coalesce around the stable introject of the analyst. Healing comes about through empathy, but an analytic cure can only occur through interpretation.

By virtue of the splitting that occurred during childhood, the selfobject transference allows cohesion of the split-off fragments of the self. Splitting (or more specifically, lack of integration) is overcome, not by its interpretation as a defense, but because the self is strengthened by the empathy and understanding of the analyst. In the self psychology model one interprets what the patient needs to maintain rather than what he is defensively warding off (Stolorow and Lachmann, 1980). This is in contrast to the traditional approach in which interpretation is a means of uncovering the defense that wards off sexual and aggressive wishes. Empathy and interpretation link the disavowed parts of the self.

Ferenczi believed that the analyst needed to function as a responsive tender parent (which is the precursor to the notion of a "corrective selfobject") whereas Kohut believed in interpreting this need. But in the humanistic method that Ferenczi pioneered, he assumed the role of the empathic parent, as well as interpreting the need for one. When he felt it was necessary, when a traumatized individual needed demonstration of caring, he "gratified" the mirroring selfobject need in the here-and-now of the analytic situation. In an interaction where Ferenczi was attempting to understand the childhood failures in empathic parenting, he role-played a responsive parent (Ferenczi, 1931, p. 129). In fulfilling the role of the empathic parental figure, Ferenczi attempted to correct the emotional deficits caused by the narcissistic wounds of childhood. The use of the analyst as a corrective selfobject was put to its most flexible application in Ferenczi's "Grand Experiment" (Balint, 1968) and his last clinical cases as reported in his clinical diary (Ferenczi, 1932b).

The apparent difference between the self psychology and humanistic analytic approaches is that Kohut espoused the interpretation of the selfobject need. An empathic explanation is offered of how the need is necessary for the patient's self-esteem, yet, in his last work, Kohut (1984) began to talk about the corrective emotional component in the selfobject transference.

3. TRAUMA THEORY

Ferenczi's clinical innovations, especially his later work, were the first dissident alternatives to classical psychoanalysis (Ferenczi, 1928, 1930, 1931, 1932b, 1933). Among these works was his last clinical presentation, entitled "The Confusion of Tongues Between Children and Adults: The Language of Tenderness and Passion" (Ferenczi, 1933).

The "Confusion of Tongues" paper raised enormous issues of a professional, personal, and social nature for psychoanalysis, Ferenczi, and the psychoanalytic community. It solidified the new method of humanistic psychoanalysis, reintroduced the seduction hypothesis, encouraged professional acceptance of sexual abuse of children by parents and parental surrogates, and introduced the concept of retraumatization within the analytic interaction. Unfortunately, it also brought the Freud/ Ferenczi relationship to the brink of disruption (Rachman, in press).

There are those who consider Kohut's work as encompassing a similar significant event in the history of psychoanalysis:

> We now have enough compelling "analytic" clinical data that necessitate a revision of the classical paradigm to incorporate Kohut's findings into what might well turn to be a contribution toward a unified theory of the psychoanalytic treatment process. Freud changed the paradigm of the psychoanalytic treatment process with his *The Ego and the Id* (1923). Kohut's *The Analysis of the Self* (1971) might turn out to be a landmark of no lesser significance [Ornstein, 1974, pp. 127–128].

Ferenczi's introduction of the seduction hypothesis was based upon his clinical work with narcissistic, borderline, and psychotic conditions, where he observed a high incidence of childhood sexual seduction and emotional trauma. At the time, Ferenczi wished these ideas to be integrated into Freudian psychoanalysis (Gedo, 1976, 1986a). He was always ambivalent about his deviations from Freud and never seemed to realize how far afield he had deviated or how much he was founding an alternative view (Thompson, 1944; Rachman, 1997).

Ferenczi challenged the traditional notion, found both in Freudian psychoanalysis and in the culture at that time, that the report of sexual abuse is the fantasy of the child and therefore is unreliable (a notion that is still held by many). Ferenczi's empathic plea for the reality of child abuse and its pathological effect on personality development can be outlined in the following way:

1. The child is traumatized by the adult (parent or parental surrogate) when the adult seduces the child sexually.
2. The child wanted "tenderness," not "sexual passion."
3. The adult is not really showing love or tenderness to the child but is aggressing against the child, intruding adult sexual needs onto the innocent longings of a child for love and parental tenderness.
4. The child is "tongue-tied," confusing sexuality for love, but cannot speak of the confusion.
5. The child cannot refuse the sexual advances of the adult because he or she feels helpless and paralyzed by fear and needs "tenderness."
6. The child brings to bear, instead, a "pathogenic defense mechanism," identification with the aggressor (Ferenczi, 1933, p. 162), which Ferenczi was the first to name (Masson, 1984, p. 148).
7. Besides identification with the aggressor, a host of pathological defenses can develop to cope with the seduction experience, for example, dissociation, depression, schizoid withdrawal, blunted affect, and splitting.
8. "These children feel physically and morally helpless, their personalities are not sufficiently consolidated in order to be able to protest, even if only in thought, for the overpowering force and authority of the adult makes them dumb and can rob them of their senses" (Ferenczi, 1933, p. 162).
9. "The same anxiety, however, if it reaches a certain maximum, compels them to subordinate themselves like *automata* to the will of the aggressor, to define each one of his desires" (Ferenczi, 1933, p. 162).
10. The guilt of the parental abuser is denied: "The most important change produced in the mind of the child by the anxiety-fear-ridden identification with the adult partner, is *the introjection*

of the guilt feelings of the adult which makes hitherto harmless play appear as a punishable offence" (Ferenczi, 1933, p. 162).

11. The parental abuser, in denial, threatens the child with physical harm if she/he reveals the evil secret. An emotional connection between sex and violence is then solidified. The child's view of sexuality and love is altered.

12. The childhood pathology lays the groundwork for adult perversions, disturbed object relations, lack of trust, special need of empathy, and the establishment of a narcissistic or borderline adaptation. Ferenczi was suggesting that sexual abuse in childhood plays a significant role in the development of severe narcissistic, borderline, or psychotic conditions.

4. EMPATHIC FAILURE AS TRAUMA

Perhaps no analyst has ever spoken so empathically on behalf of abused children and their adult traumatized selves than Ferenczi. It would be comforting to dismiss these conclusions about sexual seduction of children as a function of a different era, where puritanical values forced covert sexual activity within families. But the evidence mounts regarding the incidence of sexual abuse of children in contemporary society (Burgess et al., 1978: Groth and Birnbaum, 1979; Rush, 1980; James and Nasjleti, 1983).

Using the Confusion of Tongues metaphor, Ferenczi was the first analyst to identify the traumatic aspects of the psychoanalytic situation (Rachman, 1989a, 1994a, 1997). It was a remarkable observation because it meant the complete willingness to examine his own responsiveness, or lack of it, without concern for a loss of status in the relationship. In addition, he pioneered an emotional openness to severe criticisms by the analysand; risked navigating transference reactions with difficult patients, which places an enormous emotional strain on the analyst; and was willing to respond in novel and uncharted ways to provide an empathic milieu.

Ferenczi identified a "confusion of tongues in patients" caused by what he called the "professional hypocrisy" of the analyst. The unstated and unexplored negative feelings and thoughts by the analyst towards the patient create an emotional atmosphere of insecurity and nongenuine contact, which leaves the patient confused, feeling badly about herself, and eventually traumatized by the neurotic interaction with the analyst:

Something had been left unsaid in the relation between physician and patient, something insincere and its frank discussion freed, so to speak, the tongue-tied patient; the admission of the analyst's error produced confidence in his patient. It would almost seem to be of advantage to commit blunders in order to admit afterwards the fault to the patient [Ferenczi, 1933, p. 159].

According to Ferenczi, the Freudian analytic situation recreated the original trauma for an analysand who had suffered childhood abuse. The deliberate "restrained coolness," "professional hypocrisy," the focus on the patient's criticisms of the analyst as resistance, and the clinical façade behind which an analyst hides from a genuine interpersonal encounter all contribute to producing a nongenuine and therapeutically limited experience. Ferenczi alienated the entire analytic community by contending that the traditional analytic stance was akin to "reproducing the original childhood trauma."

Kohut is clear that emotional disturbance is related to trauma, for example, "disturbances in the relationship with the idealized object":

1. Very early disturbances in the relationship with the idealized object appear to lead to a general structural weakness . . . a personality thus afflicted suffers from a diffuse narcissistic vulnerability.
2. Later, yet still preoedipal traumatic disturbances in the relationship with the idealized object (or, again, especially, a traumatic disappointment in it) may interfere with the (preoedipal) establishment of the drive-controlling, drive-channeling and drive-neutralizing basic fabric of the psychic apparatus [Kohut, 1971, p. 47].

It is the trauma of interpersonal relations with parents to which Kohut is referring even in the most intense pathology:

As I have stressed repeatedly, in the vast majority of even the most severe narcissistic personality disturbances, it is the child's reaction to the parent rather than to gross traumatic events in the early biography which accounts for the narcissistic fixations [Kohut, 1971, p. 82].

Kohut (1971) also talks about the "susceptibility" to the trauma: "The susceptibility to the trauma is, in turn, due to the interaction of congenital structural weaknesses with experiences which antedate the specific pathogenic trauma" (p. 52). The "essential genetic trauma" is also "grounded in the parent's psychopathology, in particular in the parent's own narcissistic fixations" (Kohut, 1971, p. 79).

Kohut demonstrated his continued adherence to a trauma theory when, during the latter part of his career, analysts began to label self psychology a supportive therapy. In a surprising response to what is usually "the kiss of death" criticism in psychoanalysis, to wit, labeling a method "a corrective emotional experience," Kohut (1984) defended his method as follows:

> If an ill-disposed critic now gleefully told me that I have finally shown my true colors and . . . demonstrated that I both believe in the curative effect of the "corrective emotional experience" and equate such an experience with analysis, I could only reply: so be it. To my mind, the concept of a "corrective emotional experience" is valuable as long as, in referring to it, we point to but a single aspect of the multifaceted body of the psychoanalytic cure [p. 78].

Kohut (1984) was also clear that both the analyst's interpretations in the form of empathic responses and his selfobject function in the analytic relationship inherently correct the traumatic childhood experience:

> The more accurately your theories correspond to the psychic realities that underlie our patient's disturbances, the closer our interpretations will come to providing for the patient, in an adult setting and in an adult form, the optimal frustrations that were not forthcoming from the imperfect selfobject responses of early life. Should an ill-disposed critic again claim gleefully that he has caught me red handed, that once more I have openly admitted that "horrible dictu"—we are indeed providing "corrective emotional experiences" for our patients, I could only reply once more with "so be it!" [p. 153].

Psychoanalytic self psychology, as described by Kohut, is also concerned about the retraumatization of the analysand in the psychoanalytic situation. Kohut, like Ferenczi, struggled with his own clinical functioning in arriving at this theoretical understanding. In one vignette he described the crucial moments of interaction in dealing with a borderline condition, when continued empathic resonance prevented retraumatization. This individual developed self-fragmentation symptoms as a response to Kohut's transference interpretations:

> He had indeed felt overwhelmed by the traumatizations to which he was now exposed by virtue of his expanding activities, and he continued to react with prolonged intense suffering as a result of remaining broadly engaged with the world. What I had not seen, however, was that the patient had felt additionally traumatized by feeling that all these explanations on my part came only from the outside: that I did not fully feel what he felt, that I gave him words but not real understanding, and that I thereby repeated the essential trauma of his early life [Kohut, 1984, p. 182].

Kohut's struggle emerges from between the lines and parallels the more explicit emotional encounter Ferenczi described in his *Clinical Diary* (Ferenczi, 1932b):

> To hammer away at the analysand's transference distortions brings no result; it only confirms the analysand's conviction that the analyst is as dogmatic, as utterly sure of himself, as walled off in the self-righteousness of a distorted view as the pathogenic parents (or other selfobject) had been [Kohut, 1984, p. 182].

Kohut, like Ferenczi, realized that the key to the treatment process was the analyst's willingness and capacity for countertransference analysis, the analyst's avenue for personal and professional growth:

> The task that the analyst faces . . .—is largely one of self scrutiny. . . . Only the analyst's continuing sincere acceptance of the patient's reproaches as (psychologically) realistic, followed by a prolonged (and ultimately successful) attempt to look into himself and remove the inner barriers that stand in the way of his empathic grasp of the patient, ultimately have a chance to turn the tide [Kohut, 1984, p. 182].

5. REVISION OF THE "RESISTANCE MODEL"

Ferenczi pioneered the reformulation of the resistance model in psychoanalytic therapy in an attempt to understand the expressions of intense negative affect, verbal attacks, continual exclamations of dissatisfaction, resentment, and the protestations of rejection and hurt that were part of the clinical work with difficult cases.

When he became "the analyst of difficult cases," the need to deal with resistance in an empathic way became even more evident and Ferenczi was prepared to meet the challenge. He was unfailing in a belief in himself, the growth potential of the individual and the curative power of psychoanalysis: "I have refused to accept such verdicts as that a patient's resistance was unconquerable, or that his narcissism prevented our penetrating any further, or the sheer fatalistic acquiescence in the so-called drying up of a case" (Ferenczi, 1931, pp. 128–129).

Ferenczi's willingness to view the analytic situation as a two-person experience, as well as a genuine sense of personal humility, moved him to examine his own functioning when there was a resistant interaction: "Is it always the patient's resistance that is the case of the failure? Is it not rather our own convenience, which disdains to adapt itself, even in technique, to the idiosyncrasies of the individual?" (Ferenczi, 1931, pp. 128–129).

In the analysis of Miss F, Kohut observed the manifestation of resistance that needed to be understood from a new framework (Kohut, 1968, 1971, pp. 283–293). He described how the patient would become violently angry and accusatory if he went a single step beyond what she had verbalized. The moment of insight was described as follows:

> the crucial recognition that the patient demanded a specific response to her communications and she completely rejected any other . . . after a prolonged period of ignorance and misunderstanding during which . . . was inclined to argue with the patient about the correctness of . . . interpretations and to suspect the presence of stubborn, hidden resistances [Kohut, 1968].

Ornstein described the "creative leap" that Kohut was able to take when he could examine his own "inner resistance" (and not the patients'), enabling him to develop an alternate attitude and response, for example, the capacity to empathize with the childhood reality that drove the individual to reenact them in the analytic session (Ornstein, 1978, pp. 53–54).

The analysis of Miss F was a pivotal experience for redefining the concept of resistance in psychoanalysis. Kohut viewed the anger, whining and complaining in the transference, not as a regressive defense against instinctual wishes, but as an expression of a developmental need. He was able to view Miss F as reactivating a frightened child state that needs reassurance. Lacking the internal resources to provide it for herself, she was asking the analyst to do so. When Kohut responded in a more empathic way, by clarifying what she needed and empathizing with the distress she experienced in not getting it, she improved.

There are some who feel Kohut's greatest contribution to psychoanalysis was his reformation of the resistance model: "Among these lasting accomplishments, I would rank highest Kohut's challenge to psychoanalysis not to seek alibis—above all, never to blame patients!— when analytic efforts fail as a consequence of the contemporary limitations of knowledge" (Gedo, 1986b, p. 127).

Thus, one of the most salient expressions of both Ferenczi's and Kohut's empathic focus was their behavior, in all of its subtleties, effecting the self-experience of the analysand. Consequently, they were able to appreciate the analysand's subjective restless, motivating resistance and more empathically convey these understandings to them.

6. FERENCZI'S INFLUENCE ON KOHUT

Although Kohut did not officially designate Ferenczi as a direct influence on his thinking and clinical method (Rachman, 1989b), it is clear that self-psychological concepts and methods owe a great debt to analytic and non-analytic pioneers (Stolorow, 1976; Kahn, 1985; Bollas, 1986; Detrick and Detrick, 1989; Rachman, 1997). Kohut's reluctance to acknowledge his analytic predecessors appeared to be a general method of functioning (Gedo, 1987, personal communication).

There are three possible sources of influence of Ferenczi on Kohut, even if unacknowledged. Kohut's training as an analyst took place at the Chicago Institute, where Franz Alexander was the Director. Alexander was clearly influenced by Ferenczi (Alexander, 1933; Alexander et al., 1946). It would be inconceivable that Alexander's flexible, experimental and active approach to psychoanalysis was not part of the emotional and interpersonal climate at the Chicago Institute.

In a recent course I was teaching on Ferenczi for the Training and Research Institute for Self Psychology (TRISP) (Rachman and Menaker, 1996), the historian of psychoanalysis and biographer of Kohut, Charles Strozier, was an auditor interested in Ferenczi's ideas and work in the history of psychoanalysis and its possible connection to self psychology. We had an interchange about this issue, with my suggesting that there were very meaningful parallels between their work. In addition, I noted that John Gedo (Gedo, 1976, 1986a, in press), was a member of Kohut's original seminar on self psychology at the Chicago Institute. Strozier clarified the history of the original Kohut seminar and Gedo's relationship to it. The seminar came together in 1969 around Kohut as he was writing *The Analysis of the Self*. It consisted of close colleagues and supervisees and included, among others, John Gedo, Paul Ornstein, Arnold Goldberg, and Ernest Wolf. Gedo was the senior member of the group and, in general, the most prominent psychoanalyst in Chicago at the time to recognize the real significance of Kohut's emerging ideas. The Saturday meetings of the seminar consisted of Kohut reading sections of his manuscript and asking for comments. When *Analysis* was published, the seminar disbanded for a time, came back into being in 1974 in expanded form to produce the casebook (which is when Gedo broke from it), and later developed into the regular monthly self psychology meetings (Strozier, 1996, personal communication).

I wondered out loud if Gedo had not discussed Ferenczi's work with Kohut, since at the time of the original self psychology seminar, Gedo had reread all of Ferenczi's publications in order to write an introduction to the German editions of Ferenczi's work (Gedo, 1968). It would be inconceivable that Gedo did not discuss Ferenczi's work at a time when he was preoccupied with its meaning.

As a result of our discussion, Strozier decided to contact Gedo about Kohut's knowledge of Ferenczi. It is now clear that Kohut knew of

Ferenczi's work and admired it, witness Gedo's statement in a recent letter he sent to Strozier:

> I received the commission for my 1967 Ferenczi article for *Psyche* through Heinz. He was my first reader and commented *specifically* about how odd he found it that candidates at that time no longer studied Ferenczi in detail. He was clearly *thoroughly* familiar with SF's contributions and esteemed them very highly. (He wrote me that Abraham was Ferenczi's only equal among Freud's early adherents.) I certainly did not have to carry *Those* Coals to New Castle [Gedo, 1996].

What is still open to question is what influence Ferenczi's ideas had on Kohut's thinking.

One additional source is a potential link between Kohut and the emphasis on empathy found in the humanistic work of Carl Rogers. While I was a graduate student at the University of Chicago, Rogers was in the Clinical Psychology Department and Kohut was in the Psychiatry Department in the medical school. The only contact between them, of which I was aware, was a rumor that Kohut's wife had attended some lectures of Rogers. If true, Betty Kohut could have discussed Roger's work with her husband. Whether any discussion was useful in Kohut's formulations is still open to exploration.

7. DIFFERENCES IN FERENCZI'S AND KOHUT'S CLINICAL THERAPEUTICS

Although Ferenczi's formulation of such issues as empathy, transference trauma and resistance liberated the first dissident force in psychoanalysis, creating a pathway for Kohut's later dissidence (Gedo, 1986a), there were very important differences in their formulations and clinical practice. What I would call a Ferenczian or humanistic analytic approach is based upon an attempt to link Ferenczi's theory of the Confusion of Tongues (Ferenczi, 1933) with his clinical experimentation. The Confusion of Tongues (COT) Theory is the closest that Ferenczi comes to developing an alternative voice to Freud where he spells out the fundamental psychodynamics of actual sexual seduction as well as emotional trauma and their effects on personality development (Rachman, 1989a, 1993, 1994a, 1995b, 1997, in press). Expansion of the COT Theory beyond considerations of sexual seduction to emotional trauma, over-stimulation, or deprivation in dyadic relationships has proven fruitful (Rachman, 1992, 1997, Rachman and Mattick, 1994).

With Ferenczi's departure from the Oedipal Theory as essential to psychoanalytic thinking, departures in clinical method also occurred, particularly when attempting to successfully negotiate the analysis of the incest trauma (Rachman, 1994b).

8. CLINICAL THERAPEUTICS

One of the areas of greatest divergence in Ferenczi's and Kohut's frameworks is the clinical application of theory. Although they both share a fundamental view of childhood trauma as central to the development of psychopathology, Ferenczi both specifies the trauma in real experiences of sexual seduction (Ferenczi, 1932b, 1933) and extends it to empathic failures (Ferenczi, 1928, 1930, 1931, 1932b, 1933). With a focus on real traumas of sexual seduction and empathic failure, Ferenczi developed an active emotional and interpersonal engaged technique which created an ambivalence of therapeutic regression in the psychoanalytic situation. His departures from Freudian method, which constitutes his most original contributions, all focus on the analyst extending the empathic method to the furthest reaches of active and humanistic functioning (Ferenczi, 1930, 1932b). Interpretation and verbal interaction were but one aspect of the empathic experience, which also incorporated relaxation measures (Ferenczi, 1930; Rachman, 1994b, 1995a, 1997). These measures covered a host of nontraditional interventions, ranging from verbal activity such as prohibitions, commands, encouragement of affect release, and self-disclosure to physical intervention such as therapeutic touch, role playing, extended sessions, making house calls, and reversing roles (Ferenczi, 1930, 1931, 1932b, 1933; Thompson, 1942, 1964; Rachman, 1997). Ferenczi's nontraditional interventions must be understood as a function of a special blend of his vibrant personality, clinical capacity for extraordinary empathy, and the development of a dissident viewpoint regarding the structure and function of psychoanalytic cure. This unique combination of personal, professional, and intellectual qualities were present from the onset of his analytic career, witness this poignant early episode:

> I recall . . . the very first case I treated. The patient was a young fellow-physician whom I met in the street. Extremely pale and obviously struggling desperately for breath, he grasped my arm and implored me to help him. He was suffering, as he told me in gasps, from nervous asthma. He had tried every possible remedy, but without success. I took a hasty decision, led him to my consulting-room, got him to give me his reactions to an association-test, and plunged into the analysis of his earlier life, with the help of this rapidly sown and harvested crop of associations. Sure enough, his memory pictures soon grouped themselves round a trauma in his early childhood. The episode was an operation for hydrocele ["an accumulation of serious fluid in a sacculated cavity (as the scrotum)"—

Webster's Seventh New Collegiate Dictionary, Springfield MA: G&C. Merriam Co., 1963, p. 407]. He saw and felt with objective vividness how he was seized by the hospital attendants, how the chloroform-mask was put over his face, and how he tried with all his might to escape from the anesthetic. He repeated the straining of the muscles, the sweats of anxiety, and the interrupted breathing which he must have experienced on this traumatic occasion. Then he opened his eyes, as though awaking from a dream, looked about him in wonder, embraced me triumphantly, and, said he felt perfectly free from the attack [Ferenczi, 1930, p. 112].

Kohut's use of therapeutic touch appears to be a more shadowy experience not linked to his clinical therapeutics, but as a rare and exceptional humanistic gesture. Kohut's humanistic deviation from traditional therapeutic seems akin to Freud's use of noninterpretative behavior. Without specifying such measures as standard procedure, there are many instances where Freud would go beyond interpretation in order to respond to the needs of an analysand (Roazen, 1975; Rachman, 1997). There are two such instances of Kohut's touching an analysand, of which I am aware. One was reported by Kohut in his last video tape, where he described taking the finger of a female analysand, when he experienced her as needing physical affirmation as a selfobject need (Kohut, 1978). Recently, a portion of a personal analysis was reported in an open forum (Bacal, 1995). During a period when the analysis centered on paternal deprivation, the analysand intensely experienced the need for a demonstration of fatherly love. Apparently, Kohut intuitively sensed the need for a "corrective selfobject" (Bacal, 1990) at that moment and gave the analysand a "fatherly hug."

Although the use of touch became a part of Ferenczi's Clinical Therapeutics, it was used sparingly. In cases of severe and multiple childhood trauma, therapeutic touch was allowed as a pioneering form of a corrective selfobject experience (Rachman, 1993, 1994b, 1997). The experience that occurred during the latter part of the development of Ferenczi's relaxation therapy with Clara Thompson is an excellent illustration of the use of therapeutic touch to aid the working through of the effects of childhood sexual trauma. As reported in Ferenczi's *Clinical Diary* (Ferenczi, 1932b), Clara Thompson, identified as Dm, initiated a series of experiences where she wished to physically touch her analyst Ferenczi (Ferenczi, 1932b). Dm wanted to hug, kiss, and sit in her analyst's lap, in other words, "regress" to a childhood stage of need. Ferenczi *allowed* Dm to interact on a physical level, because he wished to create a fully empathic ambience in the psychoanalytic situation, where the analyst is a "tender mother" (Ferenczi, 1930) corrective selfobject in contemporary self psychology terminology (Bacal, 1990). The relaxation of the traditional clinical atmosphere of interpretation, detached observation, and abstinence was exchanged for the active, responsive, and empathic functioning of the analyst. This change was predicated on contributing to the curative function of the analytic process for severe childhood trauma, such as emotional, physical, and sexual abuse (Ferenczi, 1933). When Ferenczi felt the relaxation measures were no longer necessary or were, themselves, producing a new form of resistance, he urged their termination (Ferenczi, 1932b; Rachman, 1994b, 1995a, 1996b).

The theoretical rational for such elasticizing of the analytic boundaries (Ferenczi, 1928) was to allow for "therapeutic regression," "down to rock bottom" (a geological metaphor that was not lost on his famous student and literary executor, Michael Balint when he coined the phrase *the basic fault,* referring to the core split in the personality, which results from severe childhood trauma [Balint, 1968]). Any relaxation measure was also intended to be curative of the basic fault by allowing for a new experience with the analyst, which repaired the damage of childhood trauma (Ferenczi, 1932b, 1933).

Kohut's system is based upon the elaboration of a theory of the self and is clearly a more refined and comprehension framework (Kohut, 1971, 1977, 1978, 1984). In this system, verbal interaction and interpretative behavior are almost exclusively used. There is no focus on enactments, regression and providing new experiences. In this sense, Kohut's therapeutics are closer to classical psychoanalysis. They differ in that interpretations pay much greater recognition to the selfobject needs of the analysand, as well as to how the analysand needs the analyst's responses for self-definition and cohesion.

Kohut's system relies on the steady, ever-present willingness of the analyst to provide empathic acceptance in the form of verbal interventions. Nonverbal, physical activity, or relaxation measures are not encouraged or seen as an integral part of the clinical procedure. At first, Kohut was concerned about the issue of the manipulation of the transference by the psychoanalyst and not having self psychology be designated as a "corrective emotional experience" à la Alexander's Technique (Alexander and French, 1946). Alexander's legacy had been significant at the Chicago Psychoanalytic Institute, where he was its first director. Kohut was a critic of Alexander and did not wish self psychology to be identified with Alexander's time-limited analysis or his biological emphasis (Strozier, 1996, personal communication). The issue of a corrective emotional experience, however, did haunt Kohut, as critics of self psychology in the 1980s did characterize this orientation as "not psychoanalysis." Kohut struggled with these criticisms and, in his last publication, seemed to indicate he had come to terms with the idea that self psychology had actually deviated from the classical approach. He was, by the 1980s, willing to accept that the continued accepting presence that an emphatic analyst provides may be considered providing a new experience, which does correct the unempathic parental experience that produced the childhood trauma (Kohut, 1984). In a somewhat defensive statement, suggesting that the criticisms of self psychology by classical analysts had an emotional impact on him, Kohut responds with what has by now become a famous statement:

> The task that the analyst faces at such moments—the crucial moment in which a "borderline" condition either will or will not become an analyzable narcissistic personality disorder—is largely one of self scrutiny. To hammer away at the analysand's transference distortions brings no results; it only confirms the analysand's conviction that the analyst is dogmatic, as utterly sure of himself, as walled off in the self-righteousness of a distorted view as the pathogenic parents (or other selfobjects) had been. Only the analyst's continuing sincere acceptance of the patient's reproaches as (psychologically) realistic followed by a prolonged (and ultimately successful) attempt to look into himself and remove the inner barriers that stand in the way of his empathic group of the patient, ultimately have a chance to turn the tide. And if some of my colleagues will say at this juncture that this is not analysis—so be it. My inclination is to respond with the old adage that they should get out of the kitchen if they cannot stand the heat [Kohut, 1984, pp. 182–183].

9. WORKING IN THE COUNTERTRANSFERENCE

It is the area of working in the countertransference that there are also significant differences between Ferenczi and Kohut. Ferenczi's humanistic analysis is actually predicated on the clinical analysis of the countertransference reactions (DeForest, 1954; Rachman, 1997). Countertransference analysis became a central part of Ferenczi's method for two important reasons. Ferenczi expanded his empathic method by being willing to examine his own functioning in a fearless and daring way (DeForest, 1954; Rachman, 1997), as well as to develop a theory that was informed by the response to the expressed needs of traumatized individuals (Dupont, 1988; Rachman, 1997). Ferenczi's later clinical work can be viewed as focusing on the analysis of incest survivors (Rachman, 1993, 1997). Individuals suffering from severe multiple traumas of childhood (sexual, physical, and emotional) pushed Ferenczi to respond to their needs in an actual, rather than symbolic, way. What prompted Ferenczi to leave the terrain of classical psychoanalysis and fulfill needs, rather than interpret their genetic origins or the need for responsiveness based on childhood empathic failures, is a question that has prompted much debate, by Ferenczi's critics as well as his admirers. His critics, which have been legions, range from his teacher, analyst, and closest analytic friend, Freud (1933), to his analysand and later political assassin, Jones (1957, 1958) to such critics as Glover (1924, 1955), Grünberger (1980), and Nemes (1988). All these critics have emphasized, in one way or another, Ferenczi's psychological disturbance as the most salient reason he developed his dissident viewpoint and technical innovations. Even a Ferenczi scholar has recently joined the chorus of criticism (Gedo, 1995).

The history of psychoanalytic politics has often been determined by Freud's reaction to individuals. Sigmund Freud's approval or disapproval determined the fate of an analytic pioneer. When the founder of psychoanalysis died, his daughter Anna assumed the mantle of approval. The disapproval of Ferenczi's last dissident activities was given "the silent treatment." The silent treatment is one form of disapproval, which has evolved in the history of psychoanalysis to remove an analyst from the mainstream. By ignoring the analyst's contributions and his/her significance in the history of psychoanalysis, the theory and technique became invisible and impotent. Ferenczi's fate in the history of psychoanalysis was seriously injured by the silent treatment. In the 1930s, in the European capital of psychoanalysis, Vienna, Ferenczi's fate had already been settled for generations to come. As an eyewitness has noted, the announcement of Ferenczi's death in a class at the Vienna Psychoanalytic Institute, in 1933, was met with studied silence so that none, teacher or student alike, could speak about the man, his life, clinical work, or significance to psychoanalysis (Menaker, 1986, personal communication). A recent study has verified that deliberately ignoring Ferenczi's work produced a 50-year silence that negatively affected his reputation as a significant figure in the history of psychoanalysis as well as dramatically reducing the relevance of Ferenczi's work for contemporary clinical thinking and the evolution of psychoanalytic technique (Rachman, 1997). Although Ferenczi's clinical ideas and techniques are certainly not above criticism, the silent treatment, as well as the mean-spirited criticisms led by Jones (1957, 1958), have prejudiced serious examination of Ferenczi's humanistic ideas and methods.

Ferenczi's working in the countertransference is an area of his clinical therapeutics, which is very different from Kohut's framework and functioning. There are two clinical cases in Ferenczi's clinical practice, one conducted in the United States during his year-long stay, in 1926–27 (Mrs. F.H., 1952, 1954), the other conducted in Budapest, from 1926 until his death in 1933 (Ferenczi, 1932b), that detail the daring and controversial clinical work with the analyst's self and the elasticizing of the boundaries of analytic behavior (Ferenczi and Rank, 1925; Ferenczi, 1928), which Ferenczi called relaxation therapy and relaxation measures (Ferenczi, 1930, 1931, 1932b, 1933).

The case of R.N. was the case Michael Balint described as "The Grand Experiment" (Balint, 1968, pp. 112–113). Many of Ferenczi's pioneering methods of working in the countertransference were developed in his clinical work with R.N. as he struggled to be a corrective selfobject with this severely traumatized individual (Ferenczi, 1932b; Fortune, 1993; Galdi, 1996; Rachman, 1997).

Kohut's self psychology does not embrace either the conceptualization or clinical practice of countertransference analysis. Whereas a Ferenczian analysis is predicated on a countertransference analysis (DeForest, 1954; Rachman, 1997), in Kohut's system countertransference reactions are not conceptualized as separate experiences in the analytic process, but as part of the matrix of empathic failures. The reparative work is not a move toward greater clinical transparity activity and need satisfaction; rather, the disappointment, deprivation, or trauma is interpreted. The interpretation of the need for empathic selfobjects, although primary, also is augmented by the empathic ambience created in the psychoanalytic situation. Such an ambience does function to "sooth" and hold the analysand, creating a new form of selfobject experience to the privations of childhood (Kohut, 1984).

CONCLUSION

Kohut's emphasis on the empathic bond, selfobject transference, a two-person psychology, and the curative elements in the relationship has returned psychoanalysis, or at least provided an alternative, to those of us who wish to continue the humanistic tradition that Ferenczi pioneered. Psychoanalysis has taught us how identification with lost object of our past histories continues to enrich our personalities and influences our current motivations and actions. I believe this is also true in regard to former theoretical contributions and the subtle and silent ways they are woven into our current psychoanalytic theories, continuing to enrich and further them. In demonstrating the relationship between the theories of Ferenczi and Kohut I have tried to show the manner in which Ferenczi's seminal contributions to clinical work and, especially, the critical importance of empathic functioning began the tradition of humanistic analysis continued in Kohut's work.

REFERENCES

Alexander, F. (1933), On Ferenczi's Relaxation Principle. *Internat. J. Psycho-Anal.*, 14:183–192.
———— & French, T. M. (1946), *Psychoanalytic Therapy*. New York: Ronald Press.
Bacal, H. A. (1985), Optimal responsiveness and the therapeutic process. In: *Progress in Self Psychology, Vol. 1*, ed. A. Goldberg. New York: Guilford, pp. 202–227.

—— (1990), The elements of a corrective selfobject experience. *Psychoanal. Inq.*, 10:347–372.

—— (1995), Listening Perspectives and the Quest for a Facilitating Responsiveness Discussion. 18th Annual Conference on the Psychology of the Self, San Francisco, CA, October 22.

Balint, M., ed. (1949), Sándor Ferenczi. *Internat. J. Psycho-Anal.*, 30:entire no. 4.

—— (1968), *The Basic Fault*. London: Tavistock.

Barande, I. (1972), *Sándor Ferenczi*. Paris: Payot.

Basch, M. F. (1984), The Selfobject Theory of Motivation and the History of Psychoanalysis. In: *Kohut's Legacy*, ed. P. E. Stepansky & A. Goldberg. Hillsdale, NJ: The Analytic Press, pp. 3–17.

Bergmann, M. S. & Hartman, F. R., eds. (1976), *The Evolution of Psychoanalytic Technique*. New York: Basic Books.

Bollas, C. (1986), Who does self psychology cure? *Psychoanal. Inq.*, 6:429–435.

Brabant, E., Falzeder, E. & Giampieri-Deutsch, P., eds. (1993), *The Correspondence of Sigmund Freud and Sándor Ferenczi, Vol. 1*. Cambridge, MA: The Belknap Press of Harvard University.

—— (1996), *The Correspondence of Sigmund Freud and Sándor Ferenczi, Vol. 2*. Cambridge, MA: The Belknap Press of Harvard University.

Burgess, A. W., Groth, N. A., Holmstrom, L. L. & Sgyoi, S. S. (1978), *Sexual Assault of Children and Adolescents*. Lexington, MA: Heath.

Chessick, R. D. (1985), *Psychology of the Self and the Treatment of Narcissism*. New York: Aronson.

Cohler, B. J. (1980), Development perspectives on the psychology of the self in early childhood. In: *Advances in Self Psychology*, ed. A Goldberg. New York: International Universities Press, pp. 69–115.

DeForest, I. (1954), *The Leaven of Love*. New York: Harper & Row.

Detrick, D. W. & Detrick, S. P., eds., (1989), *Self Psychology*. Hillsdale, NJ: The Analytic Press.

Dupont, J. (1988), Ferenczi's "madness." *Contemp. Psychoanal.*, 24:250–261.

Ferenczi, S. (1919a), Technical difficulties in the analysis of a case of hysteria: Including observations on larval forms of onanism and onanistic equivalents. In: *Further Contributions to the Theory and Technique of Psychoanalysis, Vol. 2*, ed. J. Rickman. London: Hogarth Press, 1950, pp. 189–197.

—— (1919b), On influencing of the patient in psycho-analysis. In: *Further Contributions to the Theory and Technique of Psychoanalysis, Vol. 2*, ed. J. Rickman. London: Hogarth Press, 1950, pp. 235–237.

—— (1920), The further development of the active therapy in psychoanalysis. In: *Further Contributions to the Theory and Technique of Psychoanalysis, Vol. 2*, ed. J. Rickman. London: Hogarth Press, 1950, pp. 198–217.

—— (1924), On forced phantasies: Activity in the association technique. In: *Further Contributions to the Theory and Technique of Psychoanalysis, Vol. 2*, ed. J. Rickman. London: Hogarth Press, 1950, pp. 68–77.

—— (1925), Psycho-analysis of sexual habits. In: *Further Contributions to the Theory and Technique of Psychoanalysis, Vol. 2*, ed. J. Rickman. London: Hogarth Press, 1950, pp. 259–297.

—— (1928), The elasticity of psychoanalytic technique. In: *Final Contributions to the Problems and Methods of Psychoanalysis, Vol. 3*, ed. M. Balint. New York: Basic Books, 1955, pp. 87–102.

—— (1930), The principle of relaxation and neo-catharsis. In: *Final Contributions to the Problems and Methods of Psychoanalysis, Vol. 3*, ed. M. Balint. New York: Basic Books, 1955, pp. 108–125.

—— (1931), Child analysis in the analysis of adults. In: *Final Contributions to the Problems and Methods of Psychoanalysis, Vol. 3*, ed. M. Balint. New York: Basic Books, 1955, pp. 126–142.

—— (1932a), *Journal Clinique: Janvier-Octobre 1932*, ed. J. Dupont. Le Groupe du Coq-Héron. Paris: Payot, 1985.

—— (1932b), *The Clinical Diary of Sándor Ferenczi*, ed. J. Dupont (trans. M. Balint & N. Z. Jackson). Cambridge, MA: Harvard University Press, 1988.

—— (1933), The confusion of tongues between adults and children: The language of tenderness and of passion. In: *Final Contributions to the Problems and Methods of Psychoanalysis, Vol. 3*, ed. M. Balint. New York: Basic Books, 1955, pp. 156–167.

—— & Rank, O. (1925), *Development of Psychoanalysis*. New York: Nervous and Mental Disease Publishing.

Mrs. F. H. (1952), Recovery from a long neurosis. *Psychiatry*, 15:161–177.

—— (1954), Ferenczi. *Psychiatric Quart. Supple.*, 28:10–14.

Fortune, C. (1993), The case of R.N.: Sándor Ferenczi's radical experiment in psychoanalysis. In: *The Legacy of Sándor Ferenczi*, ed. L. Aron & A. Harris. Hillsdale, NJ: The Analytic Press, pp. 101–120.

Freud, S. (1923), The ego and the id. *Standard Edition*, 19:12–66. London: Hogarth Press, 1961.

—— (1933), Sándor Ferenczi: Obit. *Standard Edition*, 22:227–229. London: Hograth Press, 1964.

Galdi, G. (1996), *The Terrorism of Suffering*. Karen Horney Psychoanalytic Institute, New York City, April 11.

Gedo, J. E. (1968), Noch einmal der Gelehrte Säugling (The wise baby reconsidered). *Psyche*, 22:301–319.

—— (1976), The wise baby reconsidered. In: *Freud*, ed. J. E. Gedo & H. H. Pollock. New York: International Universities Press, pp. 357–378.

—— (1986a), Ferenczi: Psychoanalysis' first dissident. In: *Conceptual Issues in Psychoanalysis*. Hillsdale, NJ: The Analytic Press, pp. 36–50.

—— (1986b), Hero of our time: The dissidence of Heinz Kohut (Chapter 7). Barred from the promised land: Heinz Kohut in the wilderness (Chapter 8). In: *Conceptual Issues in Psychoanalysis*. Hillsdale, NJ: The Analytic Press, pp. 99–115, 116–131.

—— (1995), *The Tradition of Ferenczi and the Treatment of Archaic Transference*. First Ferenczi Congress of Latin America. Sao Paulo, Brazil, August 25.

—— (1996), J. E. Gedo. Letter to Charles Strozier, March 15.

—— (in press), Ferenczi as the orthodox vizier. *Psychoanal. Inq.*, 17(4) (1997).

Glover, E. (1924), "Active therapy" and psychoanalysis: A critical review. *Internat. J. Psycho-Anal.*, 5:269–311.

—— (1955), Active technique. In: *The Technique of Psychoanalysis*. New York: International Universities Press, pp. 165–185.

Grosskurth, P. (1988), The lovable analyst. *The Clinical Diary of Sándor Ferenczi. The New York Review of Books*, 35:45–47.

Groth, N. A. & Birnbaum, J. H. (1979), *Men Who Rape*. New York: Plenum Press.

Grünberger, B. (1980), From the "active technique" to the "confusion of tongues": On Ferenczi's deviation. In: *Psycho-Analysis in France*, ed. S. Lebovici & D. Wedlocher. New York: International Universities Press, pp. 127–152.

Hoffer, A. (1990), *The Clinical Diary of Sándor Ferenczi*. Book Review. *Internat. J. Psycho-Anal.*, 71:723–727.

James, R. & Nasjleti, M. (1983), *Treating Sexually Abused Children and Their Families*. Palo Alto, CA: Consulting Psychologists Press.

Jones, E. (1953), *The Life and Work of Sigmund Freud, Vol. 1*. New York: Basic Books.

—— (1957), *The Life and Work of Sigmund Freud, Vol. 3*. New York: Basic Books.

—— (1958), Letter to the editor. Dr. Ernest Jones comments. *Internat. J. Psycho-Anal.*, 39:68.

Kahn, E. (1985), Heinz Kohut & Carl Rogers: A timely comparison. *Amer. Psychol.*, 40:893–904.

Kohut, H. (1959), Introspection, empathy and psychoanalysis: An examination of the relationship between mode of observation and theory. In: *The Search for the Self, Vol. 1,* ed. P. Ornstein. New York: International Universities Press, 1978, pp. 205–232.

—— (1968), The psychoanalytic treatment of narcissistic personality disorders: Outline of a systematic approach. In: *The Psychoanalytic Study of the Child*, 23:86–113. New York: International Universities Press.

—— (1971), *The Analysis of the Self*. New York: International Universities Press.

—— (1975), The psychoanalyst in the community of scholars. In: *The Search for the Self*, ed. P. Ornstein. New York: International Universities Press, 1978, pp. 685–724.

—— (1977), *The Restoration of the Self*. New York: International Universities Press.

—— (1978), *The Search for the Self, Vol. 1*, ed. P. Ornstein. New York: International Universities Press.

—— (1984), *How Does Analysis Cure?* ed. A. Goldberg & P. E. Stepansky. Chicago: The University of Chicago Press.

Masson, J. M. (1984), *The Assault on Truth*. New York: Farrar, Straus & Giroux.

Nemes, L. (1988), Freud and Ferenczi: A possible interpretation of their relationship. *Contemp. Psychoanal.*, 24:240–249.

Ornstein, P. H. (1974), On narcissism: Beyond the introduction of highlights of Heinz Kohut's contributions to the psychoanalytic treatment of narcissistic personality disorders. *The Annual of Psychoanalysis*, 2:107–129. New York: International Universities Press.

—— (1978), The evolution of Heinz Kohut's psychoanalytic psychology of the self. In: *The Search for the Self*, ed. P. H. Ornstein. New York: International Universities Press, pp. 1–06.

Rachman, A. W. (1988), The rule of empathy: Sándor Ferenczi's pioneering contributions to the empathic method in psychoanalysis. *J. Amer. Acad. Psycho-Anal.*, 16:1–27.

—— (1989a), Confusion of tongues: The Ferenczian metaphor for childhood seduction and emotional trauma. *J. Amer. Acad. Psycho-Anal.*, 17:182–205.

—— (1989b), Ferenczi's contributions to the evolution of a self psychology framework in psychoanalysis. In: *Self Psychology*, ed. D. W. Detrick & S. P. Detrick. Hillsdale, NJ: The Analytic Press, pp. 81–100.

—— (1992), The confusion of tongues between Hedda Nussbasum and Joel Stein-
berg: Dynamics of an abusive relationship. Presented at International Conference of
the Psycho-History Society, John Jay College, New York City, June.
——- (1993), Ferenczi and Sexuality. In: *The Theoretical and Clinical Contributions
of Sándor Ferenczi*, ed. L. Aron & A. Harris. Hillsdale, NJ: The Analytic Press, pp.
81–100.
—— (1994a), The confusion of tongues theory: Ferenczi's legacy to psychoanalysis.
In: *100 Years of Psychoanalysis*, ed. A. Haynal & E. Falzeder. London: Karnac,
pp. 235–255.
—— (1994b), Non-interpretative behavior by the psychoanalyst on the psychoanalytic
situation. Presented at the IX Forum-International Federation of Psychoanalytic Soci-
eties, Florence, Italy, May 14.
—— (1995a), Ferenczi's relaxation-principle (Nachgiebigkeit) as an antecedent to the
concept of optimal responsiveness. Unpublished manuscript.
—— (1995b), Theoretical issues in the treatment of childhood sexual trauma in spinal
cord injured patients: The confusion of tongues theory of childhood seduction. *SCI
Psychosoc. Proc.*, 8:20–25.
—— (1996), The confusion of tongues between Sigmund and Anna Freud: Theoretical
and clinical issues of Seduction. Presented at 8th Biennial Conference, The Psycho-
Analytic Society of the NYU Postdoctoral Program, February 3.
—— (1997), *Sándor Ferenczi: The Psychotherapist of Tenderness and Passion.*
Northvale, NJ: Aronson.
—— (in press), The suppression and censorship of Ferenczi's confusion of tongues
paper. *Psychoanal. Inq.*, 17(4) (1997).
—— & Mattick, P. (1994), The confusion of tongues between Freud and Dora: A
matter of tenderness not sexuality. Unpublished manuscript.
—— & Menaker, E. (1996), Ferenczi and Rank. Senior Course, Training and
Research Institute for Self Psychology, spring semester, New York City.
Roazen, P. (1975), *Freud and His Followers*. New York: Knopf.
—— (1990), *The Clinical Diary of Sándor Ferenczi*, Book Review. *Amer. J.
Psychoanal.*, 50:367–371.
Rush, F. (1980), *The Best Kept Secret*. New York: McGraw-Hill.
Sabourin, P. (1985), *Ferenczi*. Paris: Editions Universitaires.
Simitis-Grubrich, I. (1986), Six letters of Sigmund Freud and Sándor Ferenczi on the
interrelationship of psychoanalytic theory and technique. *Internat. Rev. Psycho-
Anal.*, 13:259–277.
Stolorow, R. (1976), Psychoanalytic reflections on client-centered therapy in the light of
modern conceptions of narcissism. *Psychother. Theoret. Res. & Prac.*, 13:26–29.
—— & Lachmann, F. (1980), *Psychoanalysis of Development Arrests*. New York:
International Universities Press.
Thompson, C. (1942), The therapeutic technique of Sándor Ferenczi. *Internat. J.
Psycho-Anal.*, 16:64–66.
—— (1944), Ferenczi's contribution to psychoanalysis. *Psychiatry*, 7:245–252.
—— (1964), Ferenczi's relaxation method. In: *Interpersonal Psychoanalysis*, ed. M.
R. Green. New York: Basic Books, pp. 67–71.
Wolstein, B. (1989), Ferenczi, Freud, and the origins of American interpersonal rela-
tions. *Contemp. Psychoanal.*, 25:672–685.
—— (1990), The therapeutic experience of psychoanalytic inquiry. *Psychoanal.
Psychol.*, 7:565–580.

Chapter 22

The Prostitute
in the Film *Klute*:
A Self-Psychological
Analysis

Gordon A. Schulz

One of the beauties of art is its potential to portray life realistically and to offer insight into human experience. This is arguably the finest merit of the 1971 film *Klute*, a psychological thriller produced and directed by Alan J. Pakula, written by Andy and Dave Lewis, and starring Jane Fonda and Donald Sutherland. On the surface, *Klute* is a rather conventional Hollywood detective story about a small-town private investigator, John Klute, who comes to the aid of a high-class call girl, Bree Daniels, who is being stalked by a sadistic killer in New York City. On a deeper level, the mistitled film is a sophisticated character study of Bree, an aspiring but unsuccessful actress and model, who struggles, with the help of Klute and a psychiatrist, to give up her life of prostitution. Played by Jane Fonda in an intelligent and fascinating performance that won her an Academy Award, Bree is a compelling and dynamic portrait of a deeply troubled and psychologically complex woman involved in the difficult process of personal change. Initially a tough, cynical, and manipulative character who prefers the emotional detachment of "the life," Bree eventually comes to appreciate the emotional intimacy of a mutual love relationship with Klute.

The story opens with Klute taking on the case of his missing friend, Tom Gruneman. Klute's only clue to his friend's sudden disappearance is an obscene and threatening typewritten letter to Bree found in

Special thanks to Ronald R. Lee, Ph.D., and Mary E. Connors, Ph.D., for reading earlier drafts of this paper.

Gruneman's desk. Although Bree has received similar letters and anonymous "breather" phone calls, she initially refuses to help Klute with his investigation. However, she reluctantly complies after Klute blackmails her with incriminating tape recordings of her making dates with her "johns"—and after her stalker appears on her apartment rooftop. In the course of their investigation, Klute and Bree delve into the prostitution underworld and develop a conflictive love relationship. While Klute and Bree believe that her stalker is Gruneman, the viewer learns that it is really Gruneman's employer, Peter Cable, who became psychotically obsessed with Bree after a sexual encounter 2 years before. Cable murders one of Bree's associates, a fellow prostitute, and trashes Bree's apartment, leading her to turn to her former pimp for protection. When a jealous Klute assaults the pimp, Bree impulsively, but unsuccessfully, tries to stab Klute. Subsequently, in the climax of the film, Cable captures Bree and reveals that he murdered Gruneman after Gruneman discovered that he had sadistically killed a prostitute, another of Bree's associates. Klute heroically arrives on the scene to rescue Bree from Cable, who throws himself through a window to his death. In the film's ambiguous resolution, Bree and Klute reconcile and then possibly go their separate ways, with Bree tentatively leaving the city and, with it, her life as a prostitute.

Throughout the film, the character Bree Daniels strikingly illustrates psychological themes and issues identified and conceptualized by self psychology. This attests both to the ability of self psychology to understand and explain human experience, including the experience of prostitutes, and to the apparent authenticity of Jane Fonda's portrayal of that experience. Fonda reportedly greatly developed the role of Bree by persuading the director to expand the part and by improvising in crucial scenes, including Bree's therapy sessions, which directly reveal her innermost thoughts and feelings (Davidson, 1990). Fonda's characterization also benefitted from her interviewing and socializing with Manhattan prostitutes in preparation for the role and from the advice of a call girl that the director hired as a technical consultant for the film. Although the portrayal of Bree is limited by the lack of any information about her past, it will be assumed that Fonda's characterization realistically represents common experiences of women in the life. However, it would probably be excessive and therefore unwarranted to generalize this fictional character's particular psychodynamics and problems to prostitutes as a group.

A review of the relevant social scientific literature suggests that the psychology and motivations of prostitutes are diverse or are at least a subject of debate among investigators. Psychoanalytic researchers, drawing on clinical data and theory, have attributed women's pursuit of prostitution as an occupation to, variously, oedipal hostility toward fathers and consequent frigidity (Abraham, 1953; Choisy, 1961), atonement for guilt induced by incestuous fantasies (Winick and Kinsie, 1971), preoedipal maternal deprivation (Greenwald, 1970), rivalry with mothers during the daughters' adolescence (Deutsch, 1945), and a denial of latent homosexuality (Greenwald, 1970; Hollender, 1961). Other, more empirically based researchers have found, as partial motivating factors for women's entry into prostitution, the economic benefits of the work (especially for uneducated, unskilled lower-class women), a desire for independence, the excitement and adventure of the prostitution lifestyle, family conflict, parental neglect and/or abuse, and early sexual experience, including early sexual trauma (Diana, 1985; James, 1976). The only studies that compared prostitutes to demographically matched nonprostitute controls found that most of the prostitutes exhibit no more detectable signs or symptoms of psychopathology than their controls (Exner et al., 1977; Gray, 1973; Polonsky, 1984; Potterat et al., 1985). However, Diana (1985) observed that prostitutes often manifest a certain constellation of personality traits, including gullibility, emotional lability, impulsivity, low self-esteem, self-centeredness, supersensitivity to slights, resentment toward authority, and cynicism regarding intimacy.

It is noteworthy that the fictional character of Bree Daniels fits the psychological profile of the sample of high-class Manhattan call girls whom Greenwald (1970) studied. Greenwald characterized these women as having a confused self-image, an inability to establish warm interpersonal relations, limited emotional controls, and feelings of isolation, loneliness, and worthlessness. Most of these characteristics are common to the antisocial personality, which is prototypically defined by impulsive behavior, irresponsible interpersonal conduct, deviant thinking, an autonomous self-image, debased images of others, a callous mood, acting out and projection of hostile feelings, and an inner emptiness and deficiency in internal controls (Millon, 1996). As she manifests these traits to one degree or another, Bree may exemplify a particular real-life, antisocial subtype of call girls. In any case, the purpose of this analysis is simply to demonstrate the potential of self psychology to explicate behavior like Bree's that otherwise might remain foreign or mysterious, not to offer a comprehensive understanding of the psychology of prostitutes.

BREE'S FLATTERY AS FALSE MIRRORING

As a prostitute, Bree sells herself, mainly her body, to her wealthy male customers, her johns. Primarily, she provides sexual stimulation and gratification to them. Additionally, she *mirrors* them "by providing the experience of acceptance and confirmation of the self in its grandness, goodness, and wholeness" (Wolf, 1988, p. 184). According to self psychology, mirroring satisfies a basic psychological need that begins in infancy and lasts through adulthood. However, Bree's mirroring of her johns exemplifies "false mirroring," in which a person gives unwarranted or unearned praise and flattery (Lee and Martin, 1991, p. 135). Bree flatters her johns excessively by suggesting to them that their sexual potency and attractiveness are greater than they really are. Prostitutes typically engage in such false flattery to bring their customers back and build their clientele (Symanski, 1981). The johns come back not because the mirroring is false or manipulative, but because such unusually high praise is narcissistically gratifying because it bolsters self-esteem. The risk of false mirroring—as will be shown in extreme form by Peter Cable— is that it potentially raises false hopes, expands grandiosity, and thereby makes its subject more susceptible to narcissistic injury and fragmentation.

The first john portrayed whom Bree falsely mirrors is a Chicago businessman. When he shyly whispers his sexual request in her ear, she exclaims, "Wow, that sounds fantastic! Oh, that's so exciting!" and caresses his cheek. "Hmm, I like your mind," she beams in admiration. After she strips naked in front of him, she embraces him, looks him in the eye with a gleam in her eye, and says, "Oh, you're so nice!" In the next scene, Bree is lying underneath this customer's thrusting body, apparently lost in the throes of sexual ecstasy and moaning, "Oh, my angel! Oh, my angel!" However, the viewer learns that this seemingly passionate outcry is nothing but an act, a mere part of the job, when, in between moans, she sneaks a glance at her wristwatch.

The second customer whom Bree falsely mirrors is a garment industrialist, one of her regular johns, a 70-year-old widower, the benevolent Mr. Goldfarb. Unlike the typical customer, Mr. Goldfarb does not actually have sex with Bree but merely has her slowly disrobe for him as she recounts a romantic interlude that she supposedly experienced with an older man during a visit to France. While Bree's disrobing is, of course, sexually graphic, her story is not. The power of her narration lies not so much in its ability to sexually arouse Mr. Goldfarb as in its ability to mirror his aspired potency that he enjoys through vicarious identification with the romantic lover in her story. When she recollects her first meeting with the lover, she describes him, "Not young, he wasn't young. He had gray sideburns. Actually, he looked rather like you." Inflating Mr. Goldfarb's grandiosity, Bree wonders, "Was he an exiled prince or mercenary?" She continues in an affected, self-disclosing tone, "You know, I've never liked young men. . . . And I knew that he had awakened something in me that no young man had ever awakened." Just as she is concluding her story, Bree lets her dress drop and mirrors Mr. Goldfarb vicariously, "He was so wise, and he taught me so many things with his hands and his mind. I felt so beautiful."

Perhaps the best example of Bree falsely mirroring her customers can be found in the tape recording of her voice that Peter Cable compulsively plays to himself throughout the film. Cable had made the recording during their sexual encounter, which ended with Cable beating up and trying to kill Bree. Presumably, the sexual intimacy and mirroring that Cable experienced with Bree expanded his grandiosity and thereby precipitated the psychotic fragmentation and sadistic aggression to which he is predisposed. On the tape, Bree flatters Cable excessively: "You're not a man who would have to pay for a woman. You could have any woman you wanted." She promises almost total sexual compliance: "I like pleasing. As long as you don't hurt me more than I like to be hurt, I will do anything you ask." She encourages him to abandon restraint: "Oh, inhibitions are always nice because they're so nice to overcome." She gives him unconditional acceptance and invokes moral relativism: "I'm sure that as you're sitting at your great desk, you have all kinds of strange things going through your mind. You should never be ashamed of things like that. Nothing is wrong." She espouses a libertarian philosophy: "I think the only way that any of us can ever be happy is to let it all hang out, you know, do it all, and fuck it." She indicates that her sexual availability and permissiveness are unlimited: "The only responsibility you have to me is to enjoy yourself. You know that I will do anything you ask, since you know that there are no limits to my imagination, and I place no moral judgments on anything."

THE COSTS OF PROSTITUTION

Prostitution exacts great costs from Bree. Her work requires that she cater to the sexual fantasies, perversions, and narcissistic needs of her customers, whom she must pretend to enjoy and admire. Prostitutes have reported that the strain of such pretending can be overwhelming (Symanski, 1981). Focused on servicing—and manipulating—strangers to whom she is not even necessarily sexually attracted, Bree does not experience physical pleasure during sex. She is able to submit to the sexual demands of her johns time after time presumably by employing the defense of *disavowal* (Basch, 1983), in which she recognizes the occurrence of the experience but not the significance of its emotional impact. Consequently, she does not feel the disgust and resentment that, minimally, would normally be aroused in the course of servicing sexually undesired partners. Instead, she tells her psychiatrist, she feels "numb."

Bree expresses her ultimate aversion to these encounters in a wish that she discloses in therapy: "What I'd really like to do is be faceless and bodiless and be left alone." However, Bree's social withdrawal and related failure to receive adequate compensatory social support in other areas of her life only exacerbates her experience of simply being an object for the sexual and narcissistic gratification of others. The cynical, *counterdependent* stance that she adopts toward her psychiatrist manifests a corresponding disavowal of her needs for emotional support so typical of the antisocial personality: "Oh, I don't know why I'm here. It's just so silly to think that somebody else could help anybody."

Indeed, for Bree, a woman in the life, close, caring relationships are rare. Hers is a world peopled with pimps who "just take your money," "freaks" who beat the women who service them, jealous "in-laws" who set up fellow prostitutes with "freaks," and other "girls" who are "sort of" friends at best. Thus, Bree's tough, hardened, and detached exterior partly represents a defensive adaptation to a lifestyle defined by extreme individualism, competition, exploitation, aggression, anonymity, loneliness, and superficial, transitory encounters. It also reflects the autonomous self-image, contempt for sentimentality and tenderness, and projection of hostile, mistrustful feelings onto others that is characteristic of the antisocial personality (Millon, 1996). The paucity of real friends in Bree's life is indicated after she attacks Klute, when the only person other than her psychiatrist whom she thinks to call when she desperately needs to talk to someone is one of her johns, Mr. Goldfarb. However, apparently unaccustomed to Bree turning to him for social support, Mr. Goldfarb misinterprets her request to talk and leaves money for her instead, just as he always does, since their relationship presumably and expectedly has never developed beyond the bounds of an amicable business deal. The image of a disappointed Bree finding the cash that Mr. Goldfarb left her, juxtaposed with the image of a nude female mannequin without a head or limbs, symbolizes the utter barrenness and one-dimensionality of the interpersonal relations of a professional sex object who has no true friends.

Of course, far more destructive than the sexual objectification and loneliness of the life is the threat of physical violence from sadistic men like Cable who terrorize, beat, and even kill the prostitutes who service them. The first sign that Cable gives Bree of his aggressive potential appears on the tape recording of their sexual encounter when Bree tells him that she will figure him out, and he replies ominously, "I hope you do, and in a way I hope you don't." Tragically, through her naive, reckless and manipulative misuse of mirroring and her permissive encouragement to "let it all hang out," Bree inadvertently expanded Cable's grandiosity and precipitated his psychotic fragmentation and sadistic aggression against her.

Cable's fragmentation and aggression are most dramatically expressed when he trashes Bree's apartment, cuts up her clothes, ejaculates into her underwear, and then phones her and plays her a recording of her own voice excerpted from their sexual encounter: "I can be a very bad girl, you know. I sometimes need a spanking." Having merged with Bree and behaved like a bad boy himself, Cable appropriates her voice to speak for—and mirror—his exhibitionistic display of aggression against her.

Just before he attempts to murder her, at the climax of the film, Cable angrily confronts Bree for falsely mirroring him:

> You make a man think that he's accepted. It's all just a big game to you. You're all obviously too lazy and too warped to do anything meaningful with your lives, so you prey upon the sexual fantasies of others. I'm sure it comes as no great surprise to you when I say that there are little corners in everyone which were better off left alone—sicknesses, weaknesses, which should never be exposed. But that's your stock and trade, isn't it—a man's weakness? And I was really never fully aware of mine until you brought them out.

In order to blame Bree for his aggressive behavior, Cable grossly exaggerates the predatory nature of prostitutes, who essentially provide a service to their customers for a fee. However, Cable's words reveal genuine insight into the antisocial tendency of Bree, who, partly for the sake of personal profit, deceives her johns and plays with their minds, without any regard for the possible harmful effects of her actions. When Cable makes his angry self-disclosure to her, Bree surely regrets her falsely mirroring the anonymous and potentially disturbed and dangerous men who solicit her for sex. The consequences of her antisocial, ultralibertarian philosophy of a world with no moral limits and no moral responsibilities to self or others have become horrifyingly self-evident. Although earlier in the film the dangers of her profession had not yet reached their logical extreme, they were nonetheless present, and Bree recognized them and disclosed that understanding to her psychiatrist. In spite of such awareness, however, Bree struggles with much difficulty to completely quit prostitution, and in true antisocial fashion she continues to subject herself to its dangers. Although the lucrativeness of her profession surely provides her with a strong material incentive to sell her body, she seems primarily psychologically compelled to remain in the life. She angrily asks her psychiatrist for the reason why: "Well, I mean, I've been coming here all of this time, and I've been paying you all of this money, and why do I still want to trick? Why do I still walk by a phone and want to pick up the phone and call?"

BREE'S TRICKING AS A PERVERSION

The main reason Bree struggles to give up the life is that she suffers from a narcissistic behavior disorder (Kohut and Wolf, 1978), in which she shores up her self-esteem through sexually perverse behavior. Goldberg (1995) defined *perversion* as sexual behavior that is based on a particular combination of underlying psychological components— namely, sexualization, splitting, and disturbed psychodynamics—that cause the person pain or discomfort or make optimal functioning diffi- cult. Sexualization is the assertion and intrusion of the sexual impulse into nonsexual activity or onto a nonsexual object. Splitting is the *vertical split*, a defense that results in "the side-by-side existence of cohesive personality attitudes in depth, i.e., the side-by-side existence of cohesive personality attitudes with different goal structures, different pleasure aims, different moral and aesthetic values" (Kohut, 1971, p. 183). Disturbed psychodynamics are the person's early childhood experience of faulty relations with the idealized object, that is, the parental figure who is responsible for the smooth regulation and handling of tension in the everyday life of the child. These faulty relations with the idealized object predispose the person to fragmenta- tion and depletion, or empty depression. Thus, with a perversion, this predisposition to fragmentation and depletion motivates the person to develop a vertical split so that part of the person, the split-off perverse part, can seek sexual stimulation through a nonsexual activity or with a nonsexual object in order to shore up and vitalize the self.

All three of these psychological elements can be assumed to underlie Bree's compulsive tricking. Bree participates in sexualization by seeking sexual contact with men to whom she is not necessarily sexually attracted and with whom she does not experience sexual pleasure. Her vertical split is manifested by the existence of both this part of her that pursues tricks and that part of her that seeks professional help. Although the film does not provide any information about Bree's background, her psychodynamics can be inferred, based on a consideration of the empirical research on prostitutes. Such research has found that the childhood home lives of many prostitutes were characterized by fear, tension, conflict, inconsistency, chaos, the lack of warm and close relationships with parents, and sexual abuse (Diana, 1985; James, 1976). These findings suggest that many future prostitutes were unable to merge with an adequately calm, strong, and protective idealized object. Indeed, some prostitutes have reported that the first time they ever felt powerful was the first time they turned a trick (Alexander, 1987). In therapy, Bree reveals that she enjoys a grandiose fantasy of power and control over her johns, to whom she feels emotionally invulnerable:

> Because when you're a call girl, you control it, that's why. . . . They're usually nervous, which is fine because I'm not. I know what I'm doing. . . . Oh, because it's an act. That's what's nice about it. You don't have to feel anything. You don't have to care about anything. You don't have to like anybody. You just lead them by the ring in their nose in the direction that they think they want to go in. And you get a lot of money out of them in as short a period of time as possible. And you control it. And you call the shots. And I always feel just great afterwards. . . . It made me feel like I wasn't alone. It made me feel that I had some control over myself, that I had some control over my life, that I could determine things for myself.

Bree's grandiose fantasy of control compensates for an underlying tendency toward fragmentation and depletion. Her comment that she feels "just great afterwards" suggests that she is able to shore up and vitalize herself through tricking. Her statement that her johns make her feel that she is not alone reveals that her sexual encounters satisfy some need for social connection. However, this particular, discrete social connection does not conflict with her overall disavowal of her needs for social support but, on the contrary, reinforces it. As Bree notes, tricking does not require her "to feel anything" or "to care about anything" or "to like anybody." She is thereby able to maintain her tough, hardened, detached, and defensive exterior. She is also able to bolster her self-esteem by derogating and being contemptuous of others, in the fashion of the antisocial personality (Bursten, 1972; Millon, 1996).

Tricking also meets Bree's needs for mirroring. After all, her occupation essentially entails that she disrobe and exhibit her body to her customers, whose visual and tactile pleasure attests to her physical desirability and thereby enhances her self-esteem. Bree explains to her psychiatrist, "Because someone wants you—not *me*—I mean, there are some johns I have regularly that want *me*, and that's terrific. But they want a woman. And I know I'm good." Bree indicates that tricking provides her with a sense of professional pride and partly satisfies her frustrated ambition to be a great actress: "For an hour, I'm the best actress in the world and the best fuck in the world." Even Bree's aspiration to become a successful actress and model, in which she would exhibit herself for the admiring gaze of the audience and the prospective consumer, respectively, reflects her strong needs for mirroring.

OTHER PSYCHOLOGICAL FUNCTIONS OF THE LIFE

In addition to the sense of control, confirmation, and vitalization that Bree derives from selling her body, the people and norms of the prostitution subculture serve other psychological functions for her. Accustomed to viewing sex as a means to an end, Bree uses her sexuality to assert control over others who threaten or anger her. For example, when Klute blackmails her with incriminating tape recordings of her phone conversations with her johns, she offers sex in exchange for the tapes. When she learns that Klute spied on her encounter with Mr. Goldfarb, she angrily confronts the straitlaced detective for his presumed self-righteous disapproval of her exhibiting her body for money to a lonely old widower who does not even touch her. "What harm is there in that?" she asks rhetorically. In this moment, Klute becomes for her a representative of "straight" society, whose members condemn the victimless sale of sex as immoral, criminalize its participants, and then secretly partake in its pleasures themselves. "Goddamn hypocrite squares!" she blasts them. Bree then begins to strip in an unsuccessful attempt to seduce Klute and thereby regain control. Later, when she feels herself becoming frighteningly dependent on Klute for his support and protection, she again attempts to seduce him, this time successfully, in order to regain control and thereby maintain her self-cohesion.

Prostitution also offers Bree a sense of pride in belonging to a profession that inspires both fear and fascination in straight society. This pride is revealed by Bree's attempt to elicit a mirroring response from Klute at an early point in their relationship. "Tell me, Klute," she taunts him, "did we get you a little, huh, just a little bit—us city folk—the sin, the glitter, the wickedness, huh?" Having met a call girl and a pimp and having witnessed a trick, the small-town detective can reasonably be expected to have been impressed, if only negatively, by the sheer deviance of Bree's illegal urban subculture. Instead, Klute is disgusted by her hostile solicitation of recognition and replies coldly, "Oh, that's so pathetic." Wishing and expecting to hear an admission of fearful acknowledgement of the power of her deviant world, Bree is narcissistically injured by Klute's contemptuous response. Overwhelmed by rage, she is unable to maintain a mature, controlled, dignified, and articulate stance. She responds in the only way that she is able to respond when she is wounded, by impulsively lashing out. She tells him, "Fuck off!" and withdraws by walking away.

Bree also turns to others in the prostitution subculture to shore herself up. After witnessing the depressing and anxiety-provoking condition of a drug addict, a fellow prostitute that "could have been me," Bree fragments somewhat. She impulsively jumps out of a moving car and runs into a disco frequented by her associates in the life. Sweaty and feverish, she unsuccessfully attempts to buoy herself by forcing a smile and dancing in tune to the music. Overwhelmed and disoriented, she trips and falls into the company of some sexually interested young men. She fleetingly soothes herself by throwing herself onto the lap of one of them and necks with him passionately but briefly. When this sexual stimulation fails to calm her, Bree abruptly, callously abandons the now aroused young man and attempts to find solace in the warm embrace of a girlfriend, probably a fellow prostitute. Ultimately, Bree can find temporary comfort, relief, and soothing only at the side of her former pimp, who, after grabbing her roughly by the back of the hair, strokes her cheek and allows her to snuggle up against his shoulder. Later, Bree turns to her ex-pimp again for protection after her stalker trashes her apartment. Although devoid of truly healthy relationships, the life offers Bree a measure of continuing, if unreliable, social support that helps to sustain her. The social appeal of the prostitution subculture for her is captured most explicitly in the warm invitation that the madam extends to her at the high-class brothel: "Bree, if you ever get lonely or you haven't got any other place to go, you come here. You'll always have a home here."

KLUTE AS A SELFOBJECT

While powerful forces keep Bree in the life, Klute exerts a countervailing force of attraction that pulls her in a different direction. Whereas prostitution offers her a sense of control, confirmation, pride, and belonging without the risks of intimacy, Klute offers her a sense of protection, acceptance, and connection with the pleasures of intimacy. Although their relationship is initially fraught with antagonism, it takes a turn toward eventual love after Klute praises Bree's performance in an acting audition that he watched in genuine admiration. Klute both mirrors her and offers himself as an idealizable figure, who protects her from her stalker and takes care of her when she gets sick. Thus, Klute functions as a stable *selfobject* for Bree, as he facilitates her "maintenance, restoration, and transformation of self experience" (Stolorow, 1986, p. 274). However, the very qualities that attract Bree to him also repel her. Suffering from a narcissistic behavior disorder, lacking a cohesive sense of self, and possessing an antisocial personality, she fears merger and the loss of herself in an intimate bond with the strong and nurturing Klute. This simultaneous attraction to and fear of Klute constitutes Bree's ambivalence toward him and the dynamic tension in their relationship.

This intersubjective dynamic is dramatically portrayed in the scene in which Bree successfully seduces Klute. One night, after hearing Cable prowling around on her apartment rooftop, a scared Bree turns to Klute for comfort. Much like a young child who, frightened by a nightmare, regressively retreats to the parental bedroom, Bree shows up at his door and tells him that she does not want to be alone. Klute more than honors her request by inviting her to sleep over, in a separate bed. Klute's support prevents Bree from fragmenting but inadvertently stimulates her fear of merger with him. She copes with this fear in the usual way, by using her sexuality to regain control. She slips into bed with Klute and makes sexual advances. After they have sexual intercourse and he climaxes, Bree lies in bed, hands folded behind her head, with a complacent "cat-that-got-the-canary" smirk on her face. Klute, however, looks troubled. "Are you upset because you didn't make me come?" she asks contemptuously. "I never come with a john." Having finally successfully seduced Klute and demonstrated her emotional invulnerability to him, Bree regains control and temporarily forestalls her feared merger with her protector. As she triumphantly strolls out of his apartment, she gloats over her victory, "Don't feel bad about losing your virtue. I sort of knew you would. Everybody always does."

In spite of this temporary maintenance of self-cohesion, the stress of the investigation, of being stalked, and of being exposed to the seamier side of the life finally takes its toll on Bree. She begins to fragment somatically as her immune system is overtaxed. She becomes very ill and is troubled by turbulent nightmares. However, Klute, functioning as a stable and consistent selfobject, is there to soothe her and take care of her until she gets well. Debilitated by her sickness, Bree is defenseless and completely vulnerable to Klute's gentle paternal nurturance and holding. Consequently, she becomes increasingly attached and dependent on him and thereby increasingly afraid of him.

In her following sessions with her psychiatrist, Bree insightfully reflects on the meaning of her recent reimmersion into the prostitution subculture and her relationship with Klute. She bluntly identifies her dilemma: "I was trying to get away from a world that I had known because I don't think it was very good for me, and I found myself looking up its ass." She is obviously disturbed and depressed by the sad example of the very troubled lives lived by former associates who, unlike her, remain in the life full-time. Her depression also reflects the chronic sense of emptiness and meaninglessness characteristic of the antisocial personality (Millon, 1996)—an experience poignantly expressed in her statement, "Well, I guess I just realized that I don't really give a damn." She then explores her ambivalence about Klute taking care of her. When her psychiatrist asks her if she feels threatened by Klute, she replies, "Well, I don't know, when you're used to being lonely and somebody comes in and moves that around, it's sort of scary, I guess." When her psychiatrist prompts her to explore these feelings further, Bree discloses that she feels angry at Klute for scaring her and that, in turn, she wants to manipulate him: "I mean, it's easy to manipulate men, right?"

PERSONAL GROWTH AND SELFOBJECT FAILURE

By the time of her next portrayed therapy session, Bree has become more emotionally involved with Klute. Having partially relinquished her defense of disavowal and allowed herself to become emotionally intimate with a man, Bree discloses to her psychiatrist that she experiences pleasure during sex for the first time in her life, with Klute. "I feel physically, that's what's different," she explains. "I feel, my body feels, I enjoy, uh, making love with him." Thus, the relationship between Klute and Bree can be likened to the therapist–client relationship, insofar as Klute, functioning as a stable selfobject, helps Bree to increase her tolerance of disavowed feelings and thereby open herself up to new emotional experiences. Bree insightfully identifies the conflict between intimacy and control that her emotional involvement with Klute poses for her:

> I just wish that I could let things happen and enjoy it, you know, for what it is and while it lasts and relax about it. But all the time, all the time, I keep feeling the need to destroy it, to break it off, to go back to the comfort of being numb again. I keep hoping in a way that it's going to end. Because, I mean, I had more control before when I was with tricks. At least I knew what I was doing, and I was setting everything up.

Bree continues her self-exploration by elaborating on her newly discovered capacity to authentically give of herself sexually in a relationship, in which she is receiving mirroring acceptance from Klute, who remains interested in her, whatever her outward appearance:

> It's a new thing, and it's so strange—the sensation that something that is flowing from me naturally to somebody else without its being prettied up or—I mean, he's seen me horrible! He's seen me ugly. He's seen me mean. He's seen me whorey. And it doesn't seem to matter. And he seems to accept me. And I guess having sex with somebody and feeling those sort of feelings toward them is very new to me, and I wish that I didn't keep wanting to destroy it.

The two opposing poles of Bree's ambivalence toward Klute are portrayed in two scenes that follow. In the first one, Bree lies down next to Klute in bed, and projecting her fear of her own attachment on to him, she asks him, "You're not going to get hung up on me, are you?" In the second scene, in the open-air market, her full-fledged idealization of Klute is vividly depicted. Klute notices Bree steal a piece of fruit, and in a firm but calm tone he asks her, "What have you got in your bag?" Bree looks down in shame like a child who has been caught by her parent. She gazes at him admiringly and shakes her head in seeming disbelief that he could be so good. Then she grabs the back of his jacket and trails behind him. The apparently extreme degree of Bree's idealization of Klute can be attributed to her inferred experience of not having received adequate calming and protection from the idealized object in early childhood, combined with her current experience of being protected by Klute in the context of extraordinary danger.

However, Bree becomes disillusioned with Klute in the next phase of their relationship, after they return to her apartment and, much to Bree's terror, find that it has been broken into and trashed. Bree is further horrified when she subsequently discovers a deposit of semen in her underwear and receives a harrowing phone call from Cable, who plays her the tape recording of her own voice excerpted from their sexual encounter. This traumatic experience emotionally overstimulates Bree and shatters her fantasy that Klute is powerful enough to protect her absolutely from her stalker. Thus, she experiences a *selfobject failure*, that is, the subjective experience of the selfobject as failing to maintain, restore, and transform the self (Stolorow, Brandchaft, and Atwood, 1987). Initially, Bree reacts to this selfobject failure by simply withdrawing from Klute. When he calls her name when they are lying in bed together, she pretends that she is asleep. Then she actively seeks out a substitute for Klute, a new protector, in the form of her ex-pimp.

When Klute realizes that Bree is reattaching herself to the pimp, he physically assaults his rival in a jealous rage. Klute's assault precipitates Bree feeling overwhelmed with the suppressed rage that she harbors for his failure to protect her absolutely, as well as with the fresh rage generated by the present threat that he poses to her new protector. Additionally, the narcissistic rage that she feels in this moment partly flows from her experience of having been hurt and objectified as a prostitute. In a fit of angry panic, she temporarily fragments and impulsively, violently lashes out by attempting to stab Klute with a pair of scissors. This fragmentation and consequent inability to contain her rage reflect her narcissistic vulnerability originating with her disturbed childhood relations with the idealized object. Although Bree misses Klute, ripping only his jacket, he is obviously narcissistically wounded by this near fatal attack by the woman he loves. Stunned and hurt, he withdraws quietly and immediately from the scene of the crime. Bree is left standing alone, scissors in hand, immediately overcome by remorse.

REPARATION AND TRANSMUTING INTERNALIZATION

The final phase of Bree and Klute's relationship is concerned with its reparation. Initially, Bree searches for Klute to apologize for her attack on him, but she cannot find him. Feeling guilty and distraught by her own behavior, she goes to her psychiatrist's office in hopes of receiving support and help in integrating her experience of aggression. When she learns that her therapist has left for the day, she arranges to meet with Mr. Goldfarb to talk. Cable then captures her at Mr. Goldfarb's garment factory and forces her to listen to a tape recording of his murdering one of her associates. Ultimately, Klute redeems his image as Bree's idealized protector in the film's climax, when he heroically appears, in conventional Hollywood style, to rescue her from Cable.

In the ambiguous resolution of the film, Bree and Klute are depicted in the midst of a reconciliation, followed by a possible breakup and separation. Bree's disclosure to her psychiatrist indicates that she does not plan to stay with Klute, but the final scene of the film, in which she leaves her empty apartment accompanied by Klute, suggests the opposite. In any case, Bree replaces her former idealization and subsequent devaluation of Klute with a more mature and realistic view. She explains to her psychiatrist that she and Klute are too different to pursue a life together. "I mean, I know enough about myself to know that whatever lies in store for me it's not going to be setting up housekeeping with somebody . . . and darning socks and doing all that," she reflects. "I mean, that's just—I'd go out of my mind."

Although Bree tentatively rejects the prospect of such a traditional lifestyle with Klute, she has been changed irrevocably through her experience with him. She enjoyed the first emotionally intimate relationship with a man with him. Because of his acceptance, caring, and protection, Bree felt safe enough to risk being vulnerable and intimate with him, at least to a certain degree. She admits, albeit reluctantly and with much struggle, that she will miss him—a sure sign of her attachment. However, she can tolerate their possible separation because a part of him will remain with her permanently. Through her relationship with the empathic Klute, through his selfobject failure, and through the reparation of their relationship, Bree hypothetically experienced a *transmuting internalization,* that is, an "acquisition of permanent psychological structures which continue, endopsychically, the functions which the idealized self-object had previously fulfilled" (Kohut, 1971, p. 4). Such hypothesized structuralization, coupled with her experience of her near-fatal encounter with Cable, can be inferred to contribute to Bree's decisive ability to finally forsake her life of prostitution. At least she rejects the last phone call from a prospective john that she receives before she moves out of town.

The prospects of Bree permanently refraining from prostitution are unclear. Certainly, her leaving New York City, the site of the entrenched prostitution subculture to which she belongs, is positive in this regard. However, the absence of any definite, alternative source of meaningful work and social support that can provide her with adequate selfobject experiences is discouraging. Particularly, her separation from her psychiatrist and her possible separation from Klute, with whom she may or may not be breaking up, can be expected to impair her ability to remain out of the life permanently. "I have no idea what's going to happen," Bree freely admits to her psychiatrist. "I just can't stay in the city, you know."

Then, realizing and accepting the extent of her dependence on her psychiatrist—and the difficulty of change—she adds, "Maybe I'll come back. You'll probably see me next week." Bree's final disclosure to her psychiatrist is a testament to her continuing need for social support and connection—a need that she disavowed in herself as a prostitute, a need that she eventually allowed herself to feel with Klute. It is a legitimate need that self psychology recognizes as basic to healthy human nature.

REFERENCES

Abraham, K. (1953), *Selected Papers on Psychoanalysis.* New York: Basic Books.

Alexander, P. (1987), Prostitution: A difficult issue for feminists. In: *Sex Work,* ed. F. Delacoste & P. Alexander. Pittsburgh: Cleis Press, pp. 184–214.

Basch, M. F. (1983), The perception of reality and the disavowal of meaning. *The Annual of Psychoanalysis,* 11:125–154. New York: International Universities Press.

Bursten, B. (1972), The manipulative personality. *Arch. Gen. Psychiat.,* 26:318–321.

Choisy, M. (1961), *Psychoanalysis of the Prostitute.* New York: Philosophical Library.

Davidson, B. (1990), *Jane Fonda.* New York: Dutton.

Deutsch, H. (1945), *The Psychology of Women, Vol. 1.* New York: Grune & Stratton.

Diana, L. (1985), *The Prostitute and Her Clients.* Springfield, IL: Charles C. Thomas.

Exner, J. E., Wylies, J., Leura, A. & Parrill, T. (1977), Some psychological characteristics of prostitutes. *J. Personal. Assess.,* 41:474–485.

Goldberg, A. (1995), *The Problem of Perversion.* New Haven, CT: Yale University Press.

Gray, D. (1973), Turning-out: A study of teenage prostitution. *Urban Life & Cult.,* 1:401–425.

Greenwald, H. (1970), *The Elegant Prostitute.* New York: Ballantine Books.

Hollender, M. H. (1961), Prostitution, the body, and human relatedness. *Internat. J. Psycho-Anal.*, 42:404–413.

James, J. (1976), Motivations for entrance into prostitution. In: *The Female Offender,* ed. L. Crites. Lexington, MA: Lexington Books, pp. 177–198.

Kohut, H. (1971), *The Analysis of the Self.* New York: International Universities Press.

—— & Wolf, E. S. (1978), The disorders of the self and their treatment. *Internat. J. Psycho-Anal.*, 59:414–425.

Lee, R. R. & Martin, J. C. (1991), *Psychotherapy after Kohut.* Hillsdale, NJ: The Analytic Press.

Millon, T., with Davis, R. D. (1996), *Disorders of Personality,* 2nd ed. New York: Wiley.

Polonsky, M. (1984), *The Not-So-Happy Hooker.* Knoxville, TN: University of Tennessee Press.

Potterat, J. J., Phillips, L., Rothenber, R. B. & Darrow, W. W. (1985), On becoming a prostitute: An exploratory case-comparison study. *J. Sex Res.,* 21:329–335.

Stolorow, R. (1986), On experiencing an object: A multidimensional perspective. In: *Progress in Self Psychology, Vol. 2,* ed. A. Goldberg. New York: Guilford, pp. 273–279.

—— Brandchaft, B. & Atwood, G. (1987), *Psychoanalytic Treatment.* Hillsdale, NJ: The Analytic Press.

Symanski, R. (1981), *The Immoral Landscape.* Toronto: Nutterworths.

Winick, C. & Kinsie, P. M. (1971), *The Lively Commerce.* Chicago: Quadrangle.

Wolf, E. S. (1988), *Treating the Self.* New York: Guilford Press.

Author Index

385

Subject Index